Grace after Genocide

Grace after Genocide

Cambodians in the United States

Carol A. Mortland

berghahn
NEW YORK · OXFORD
www.berghahnbooks.com

First published by

Berghahn Books

www.berghahnbooks.com

© 2017, 2019 Carol A. Mortland
First paperback edition published in 2019

Library of Congress Cataloging-in-Publication Data
Names: Mortland, Carol A. (Carol Anne), 1945-author. Title: Grace after
genocide : Cambodians in the United States / Carol A. Mortland. Description:
New York : Berghahn Books, 2017. | Includes bibliographical references and
index. Identifiers: LCCN 2016054880 (print) | LCCN 2016056907 (ebook) |
ISBN 9781785334702 (hardback : alk. paper) | ISBN 9781785334719 (eBook)
Subjects: LCSH: Khmers--United States. | Refugees--Cambodia. | Refugees-
-United States--Social conditions. | Cambodian Americans--Cultural
assimilation.
Classification: LCC E184.K45 M67 2017 (print) | LCC E184.K45 (ebook)
| DDC 305.8959/32073--dc23 LC record available at https://lccn.loc.
gov/2016054880

British Library Cataloguing in Publication Data
A catalogue record for this book is available from the British Library

ISBN 978-1-78533-470-2 hardback
ISBN 978-1-78920-497-1 paperback
ISBN 978-1-78533-471-9 ebook

For survivors and victims of the Cambodian holocaust, particularly
Cambodian refugees and their descendants in the United States

Contents

Preface and Acknowledgments

Grace after Genocide: Cambodians in the United States describes the experiences of Cambodian refugees as they struggled to transition from agrarian life in Cambodia to survival in postindustrial America. Based on research conducted across the country for over thirty years, this ethnography explores the similarities and differences in the lives of those resettled in the late 1970s and early 1980s with their children, many of whom are native-born Americans. While first-generation Cambodians have focused on maintaining their identities as Cambodians by re-establishing their traditions, values, and relationships, their children have dealt with being second-generation descendants of holocaust survivors and striven to become Americans in a society that has defined them as different.

America's history in Southeast Asia and the subsequent resettlement of Cambodian refugees in America may have faded from public awareness, but the fortieth anniversary of the end of the Vietnam War can remind Americans of the consequences of their country's actions overseas and at home. Some of the heaviest war consequences fell on Cambodian refugees and their children and, to a much less extent, the Americans with whom they interacted. By describing Cambodians' experiences before becoming refugees, the cultural values and customs they brought with them, and the reception and situations they faced after arrival, this book illuminates the strengths and weaknesses of American refugee programs and the ways Americans can better react to future waves of refugees.

In addition to providing information for Cambodian Americans about their heritage and the experiences of their elders, *Grace after Genocide: Cambodians in the United States* also increases our awareness of the experiences of our ancestors over the centuries. It is of crucial importance in today's world for Americans to know more about our individual and collective histories and other cultures.

A few editing notes here. First-generation Cambodians speak English as their second, and sometimes third or fourth language, thus their grammar and word choice often differ from those of Americans who speak English as their first language. I have not edited their comments, but left them intact, and will not add [*sic*] to indicate grammatical or spelling mistakes.

Cambodian names are written in the traditional Khmer way, with the family name first and the given name second.

Acknowledgments

My gratitude first to the Cambodians who have shared their lives with me, including the Oum and Pong families, Hin Sithan, the Venerable Ouch Chanmony, Korath Norin, and the late Narith Kong and Thom Thach. Thanks also to John M. Marston and other colleagues who have increased my knowledge and insight about Cambodians and the refugee experience.

I am very grateful to Dr Judy Ledgerwood and to my family for inspiration and help throughout the years of research, and to my brother James Mortland, sister Annette Gililland, and Dolores Maggiore for editorial assistance. Thanks also to Jo and Rene.

I am grateful also to the editors at Berghahn who devoted their time to bringing this work to fruition.

Introduction

From Cambodians to Refugees

Cambodians are in America because Americans were in Cambodia. America's gradual entry into the Vietnam War eventually involved over 2.7 million American military personnel, left 58,000 Americans dead and tens of thousands wounded, brought societal conflict, and all at a cost of $738 billion (Daggett 2010). Vietnam also suffered devastating consequences, as did neighboring Cambodia. After just a few years of war, Cambodia was in shambles, thousands were dead, and millions were without homes. After Americans fled the region in 1975, Cambodians experienced displacement, depravation, and death, followed for some by flight from Cambodia and resettlement in America. Few could have predicted that refugees from a small, agricultural, and predominately Khmer and Buddhist nation would be resettled in a large, industrialized, and diverse country. Never had so many Cambodians fled their home to resettle in over nineteen countries across the globe, including China, New Zealand, Denmark, Argentina, and the United States.

From the first spread of prehistoric man across the globe to later population movements, seldom have migrations involved so many people and destinations in such a short period of time as the modern movement of refugees, including Cambodians. Before the 1975 communist takeover in Cambodia, few Cambodians had traveled outside their homeland, and only a couple hundred Khmer students, diplomats, and soldiers lived in America. By the early 1980s, however, after hundreds of thousands of Cambodians had fled Cambodia, there were large concentrations of Cambodians not only in Cambodia but in several Thai refugee camps and in Long Beach, California. Most were without resources, English, or familiarity with American ways.

Research with Cambodians

This ethnography provides a glimpse into the lives of Cambodian refugees in America and their Cambodian American children. The descriptions are written in the ethnographic present, and are based on data-gathering techniques including formal and informal interviews, tens of thousands of hours of conversation, and observation and participation in multiple settings. Before the 1950s, French scholars such as Adhémard Leclère (1914), George Coedès (1968), Louis Finot (1916), and Eveline Porée-Maspero (1962–1969) contributed most writings on Cambodia. After 1950, Americans contributed publications on history (Briggs 1951), language (Huffman 1970), and anthropology (Ebihara 1971).

The refugee crisis that followed Cambodia's turmoil in the 1970s was the catalyst for an extensive body of research by Americans on Southeast Asian refugees in Thailand's refugee camps and resettlement in America. Most of the work focused on refugees' physical and mental health, and much of what renowned historian Chandler calls "the revival, or more properly the birth, of twentieth-century Cambodian cultural studies" (1994: xi) was done in researchers' neighborhoods. Smith-Hefner conducted extensive research in the Boston area (1999), F Smith (1989) and Hopkins (1996) worked in the Midwest, and Needham and Quintiliani have written over the years about their research in Long Beach (2007).

Over the past three and a half decades, I have conducted research with Cambodians in their homes, schools, workplaces, and temples, spending thousands of hours listening and observing as Cambodians described, practiced, and explained their traditions and rituals. After receiving a doctorate in anthropology in 1981, I worked the next nine years in refugee resettlement offices at the local, state, and national level, serving with Khmer job developers, counselors, clerks, interpreters, translators, and volunteers to aid refugees with their immediate and long-term needs. I served as president of a county refugee resettlement forum, as a member of a state refugee advisory board, and as a consultant at the Philippines processing center in 1982. I was advocate, fictive kin, student, teacher, foster parent, board member, coauthor, business advisor, and temple consultant for Cambodians, who were warm and generous, offering food or drink on every occasion.

I shared with colleagues conducting research among refugees and immigrants who resided in their community a perspective different from that of traditional anthropologists who had transitioned from dependent students in the field to specialists back home with no one to contradict them. Such a transition was not possible for researchers working with Khmer refugees who lived nearby and increasingly spoke for themselves in English. We were able to take a longer look at one another. As Cambodians became aware of how they were being perceived or described by Americans, they responded. They corrected me constantly, if not immediately. In addition, their stories were riveting, which led to another conflict with traditional academia: detached writing. Other scholars also found that research with non-refugees did not leave them untouched. Chandler wrote that he was "unready as a scholar to confront the enormity of recent Cambodian history," finding the anguish of refugees in Thailand "very moving" (2010).

Assisting refugees also placed difficulties in following another traditional research aim: to affect those with whom the research is being conducted as little as possible. A number of researchers were employed by service agencies or worked as volunteers providing assistance to refugees. By definition, their goal was to help refugees change: learn English, gain American job skills, or become familiar with public transport. In this case, the change being instigated was considered advantageous by all those involved, including those receiving it. Initially seeing little difficulty in helping refugees with doing research because I was neither social worker nor applied anthropologist and was assisting refugees with anthropological awareness in doing what they wished, I soon realized that Americans' and refugees' visions of desired change often differed. In addition, I was pressed by refugees to take sides in their conflicts. When I refused, I was accused of doing so anyway, sometimes by several groups simultaneously. When I listened to one leader, I was seen as belonging to his group by both Cambodians and Americans, despite the number of other leaders I consulted. Increasingly, my simplistic view of "helping" refugees shifted as I realized how limited and powerless I was to effect change on their behalf. My goal remained the same throughout my years of employment with refugee agencies.

Americans were often unable to understand the experiences Cambodians had had, either in Southeast Asia or as refugees in America (also Beydoun 2004). Some Americans suggested it was time for Cambodians to forget the past, be grateful for resettlement, and move on with the future, but Cambodians said often that they could not forget what they had endured. Their experiences were inscribed on their minds and on their bodies; Sann pointed to his forehead every time he spoke of being struck on the head with an axe, and Prak grabbed his knee when he described being hit by Khmer Rouge soldiers. Cambodians occasionally said they disliked being questioned by Americans about their past and often resisted their questions or concealed information from them.

Americans who worried about being "used" by Cambodians often did not acknowledge the extent to which they themselves were using Cambodians for research, jobs, or spiritual or personal gratification through "helping" refugees or friendship with them. Cambodians viewed relationships through a different lens than did Americans; for example, definitions of "friend" differ between people who value equality and those who value hierarchy. I call the members of one family I met when director of a refugee program "friend," while they call me "sister" or "auntie." Their terms are more accurate, reflecting a relationship that has endured through time—valuable, usually satisfying, but occasionally tense and for them hierarchical.

Being employed in refugee services does not preclude doing ethical research with refugees, but it does necessitate looking squarely at issues and viewing refugees as rational, complicated, ambitious, and inquisitive human beings. Ethical research requires researchers to struggle against viewing Americans as able to give assistance and refugees in need of it; researchers need to explain their work as best they can and recognize refugee hierarchical distinctions and relationship constraints. Researchers must also protect the identities of those about whom they write without distorting data, a difficult task because meaning comes in great part from context. In describing conflict situations, it is especially important to conceal participants' identities. I have maintained confidentiality while providing context by using pseudonyms for people both living and dead, moving them to different jobs and communities, and expanding the usual village of a traditional ethnography to the entire United States.

Communication was often difficult. Cambodians struggled to learn English, particularly those with little education in Cambodia and no experience with being students. Americans, in turn, were often impatient and intolerant of Cambodians' poor English and often discounted Cambodians' ability to learn. A woman who in 1984 said her husband wanted money for an operation "to make the fat on your stomach shrink" explained twenty-five years later that although she had never learned the name of that procedure, she became increasingly fluent in English, but that many of the Americans with whom she worked continued to talk with her "like I am stupid or cannot hear them." Misunderstandings between Americans and Cambodians were common. Americans often spoke too rapidly and directly, and Cambodians often prefaced even negative responses with an affirmation—"Yes, I do not want to go to the store"—or agreed to arrangements to avoid offending others and then neglected to keep them.

Speaking slowly and softly and enunciating clearly helped communication, as did maintaining physical distance and avoiding prolonged eye contact. Using language appropriate for new English speakers and repeating statements or questions were helpful, as were writing down instructions or arrangements and indicating one's lack of comprehension when it occurred. Although uncomfortable for speaker and listener, asking speakers to repeat themselves indicated interest and aided comprehension. Although it was sometimes uncomfortable to comply with Khmer expectations, such as not assisting with food preparation or eating with men while women served the food, Cambodians said they appreciated Americans respecting their customs.

Cambodians and I were informants to one another. I provided information about America, both while working and during evenings and weekends, and they told me about their lives and experiences. When Cambodians learned I wanted to know more about their traditions and lives, they facilitated data collection, talking at length and introducing me to informants who knew about particular events or topics. When they learned I wanted to know about Buddhism, I was taken to interview monks; about mushroom picking, to talk with mushroom pickers. When I asked about music, I was introduced to a man who made traditional musical instruments, and when I asked about fortune-telling, I was taken to have my fortune told. In these settings, Cambodians expected me to ask prepared questions and record the answers.

I tape-recorded informants or wrote down the information, and if I was unprepared, Cambodians often grabbed pencil and paper, demanding that I make a record, asking questions on my behalf or telling me what to ask, often taking notes for me. Over the years, as we watched one another struggle to understand the other's world, Cambodians "put a hook in my heart" in a traditional "weapon of the weak" to increase attention, services, and resources (Scott 1985). Attempting to bind me to them with endearing words, Cambodians told me how much they missed me even after a few days and how important I was in their lives. I responded in full measure, alternately overwhelmed, confused, sad, or comforted in reaction to the intentional and unintentional wounds that haunt human relationships.

Brief History of Cambodia

Cambodian refugees fled a country they said had been an empire, a republic, and a revolutionary communist regime before becoming a Vietnamese puppet state. Cambodia was then a United Nations client before becoming a constitutional monarchy. Cambodia is small in area and population. Comparable in size to Washington State, the country is bordered south and west by Thailand and the Gulf of Thailand, north by Laos, and east by Vietnam. In the early 1970s about 80 percent of the Cambodian population of seven million was rural. Most Cambodians lived in villages of about two hundred inhabitants near streams on the central plain. Most were rice cultivators; many also had gardens, raised pigs, fished, and traded (Whitaker et al. 1973). Six cities contained less than 15 percent of the population, although they were expanding rapidly with refugees fleeing areas within Cambodia affected by the war.

Population density in Cambodia in the early 1970s was less than one hundred people per square mile. Today, some Cambodians refer to Cambodians who live in the central plain as "central Khmer" (*khmer kandal*). They are distinguished from Khmer Krom in southern Vietnam, Khmer Surin in northwest Cambodia and Thailand, and Khmer Lao in northern Cambodia. Cambodia is also home to Chinese Cambodians, Cham Cambodians, Vietnamese, tribal groups, and Europeans. Most Cambodians are Khmer Buddhists; the remaining 15 percent are Mahayana Buddhists, Cham Muslims, and Christians.

Cambodia's history extends back many centuries. Archaeological evidence from 10,000 to 12,000 BP indicates the presence in the region of wanderers gathering, hunting, and fishing for sustenance (Higham 1989). By 4,000 BP, early people also cultivated rice, made pottery, and lived in permanent villages near lakes and rivers. Several hundred years later, residents made iron and bronze and operated a regional network of trade. An archaeological site in central Cambodia reveals similarities between prehistoric and modern Khmer physiology and lives, such as residing in stilt houses and eating a diet based on rice and fish.

Khmer legend traces the country's origin to the union of a foreigner from India and a local dragon princess whose father ruled *Gok Dhlak*, a waterlogged island in southern Cambodia (Chandler 1983). In one version, a Brahman priest named Kaundinya shot an arrow from a magical bow at the princess, frightening her into marrying him. Drinking the water from the land, the princess's father enlarged the region ruled by his son-in-law, called it "Kambuja," and built a capital. By 2,000 BP, southern Cambodia's early Funan polity had an extensive canal system, high population density and productivity, and complex trade. From India came concepts of governance, architecture, dance, music, literature, Hinduism and Buddhism, and a writing system. Society had become increasingly hierarchical, with a majority of farmers; a middle stratum of administrators, priests, soldiers, and craftsmen with more resources; and a few at the top who controlled the labor of the many.

By the ninth century, the center of power in the region had shifted north to the area of Siem Reap. Early in the century, King Jayavarman II united numerous small polities, took the title "god king," and was the first Angkor ruler to combine divine status with temporal rule.

For the next six hundred years, Angkor dominated Southeast Asia. Complex canal networks utilized topography to divert water from rivers into manmade reservoirs, and overflow channels collected water during monsoons so it could be dispersed when needed. The irrigation and transportation provided by the system facilitated an expansion in agriculture and population, whose size and power were evidenced by over a thousand temple ruins, including Angkor Wat and Angkor Thom.

Angkor Thom was the largest preindustrial city in the world (Fletcher et al. 2006). It consisted of an urban sprawl of at least one thousand square kilometers, with temples at its core, and was home to as many as 750,000 residents. Angkor's control of water deteriorated over the years, however, and the polity was left vulnerable to floods and drought. Temple building projects and costly wars may also have drained the empire of resources and people (Buckley et al. 2010). With Angkor weakened, Thailand sacked Angkor in 1431 and killed many of the elite. Vietnam then invaded the region and imposed their own culture and language on the inhabitants of present-day Cambodia.

For centuries, Khmer rulers struggled against invasion and exploitation by Vietnam and Thailand, generally yielding land or power to one or the other and often using one neighbor to avoid the advances of the other (Chandler 1983). A respite from persistent attacks occurred during the time of King Ang Chan (1516–66) when the new capital, Lovek, became a major trading center, and Spanish from the Philippines, Portuguese from Macao, and Chinese, Arabs, Japanese, and Malay introduced new ideas and practices to the region. Invasions from neighboring regions again occurred; Lovek was captured by the Thai, and by the 1770s, Vietnamese settlers had moved into Cambodia's Mekong Delta, an occupation that angers Cambodians to the present.

By the mid-1800s, Cambodia was shrinking in size and influence. The country's freedom from ongoing depredations by its neighbors came from a country six thousand miles away that few Cambodians even knew existed. France was interested in Southeast Asian trade and resources and, fearing British competition, made Cambodia a protectorate in 1863. France left Cambodia's ceremonial powers to the king, encouraged Chinese Cambodian involvement in business, used Vietnamese as administrators, and generally restricted the economic activity of ethnic Cambodians to food production, fishing, and crafts. Europeans tended to see Cambodia as a tranquil backwater populated by smiling, gentle people; one English anthropologist was harsher, describing Cambodians as "ugly, dull-looking people, diseased and under-nourished, cowed and frightened, drably dressed in dingy black; with Buddha as their god, and opium as the way to Him" (Gorer 1936: 155).

Many French colonists were similarly dismissive, but whatever their reactions to Cambodians, French academics recorded the country's history and restored numerous temples. During their colonial rule of Cambodia, however, the French exploited Cambodia's resources, levied exorbitant taxes on the people, looted some antiquities, and provided education for only a few elite children. By 1954, a mere 144 Cambodians had graduated high school (Kiernan 1996). Cambodians benefited little, and traditional divisions between urban and rural and between the elite and the peasantry intensified. At the death of the Khmer king in 1941, the French appointed his nineteen-year-old great-nephew, Norodom Sihanouk, as his successor, assuming they could easily manipulate him to do their bidding. By 1950, however, King Sihanouk was advocating for independence, and with global pressures mounting against colonialism and anxious to maintain its holdings, France agreed to give up Cambodia as a colony.

After independence in 1953, Sihanouk became the dominant figure in Khmer political life, yielding his throne to operate as a politician but continuing to act and be viewed as a semi-divine royal exhibiting a concern for "his" children that contrasted sharply with French paternalism. Although modernization, educational opportunities, the middle class, and business expanded, Cambodians became increasingly unhappy with Sihanouk's arrogant and autocratic ways, government corruption, and the concentration of wealth among the king's family and cronies. Despite the country's problems, refugees later said they had appreciated living in peace during the years Sihanouk was in control.

The years of calm were threatened when civil war between South Vietnam and its communist opponents spread into Cambodia, and American military action expanded throughout Southeast Asia in support of the anticommunists. Worried about the consequences of war on Cambodia, Sihanouk cited a proverb, "When the elephants fight, the grass is trampled." He tried to appease both communists and anticommunists, allowing Vietnamese communists to establish bases inside Cambodia but not objecting to South Vietnam pursing them. Disturbed by America's deepening involvement, Sihanouk cut off economic and military aid from the United States in 1963 and broke off diplomatic relations in 1964. Nonetheless, he was unable to halt foreign intrusions or the transport of weapons and ammunition across Cambodia into Vietnam. Cambodian disillusionment over the state of the country led to a coup against Sihanouk in 1970, but his successor, Prime Minister Lon Nol, was unable to deal with the country's problems, and Cambodians' dismay continued.

Trusting that his "friendship" with President Nixon would render Cambodia invincible, Lon Nol reversed Cambodia's stance toward the United States and allowed America to turn Cambodia into a military staging area in its support of anticommunist South Vietnam. In 1971 alone, American military aid to Cambodia grew from $20 million to $180 million, and the bombing of invading Vietnamese communists within Cambodia increased. Between 1965 and 1973, the United States used almost a third more bombs than the Allies dropped in World War II, most concentrated on less than 25 percent of Cambodia, without the knowledge of Khmer leaders and the American Congress (Shawcross 1979).

Although American war rules decreed that targets such as religious buildings and ruins were not to be hit, the rules were often violated, for example, when pilots learned enemy soldiers were hiding in temples (Wood 2002). Cambodians painted "pagoda" on their roofs to prevent destruction, but often to no avail. An American pilot involved in the bombing said years later that Cambodians "had different feelings about pagodas than we did." Khmer refugees disagreed, saying Khmer pilots and troops who benefited financially were content with the American presence, but the vast majority of Cambodians were not. One man said homes, villages, schools, and temples were wiped out by bombs and chemicals dropped by B-52s (large United States Air Force bombers), and skin, health, land, and forests were affected. He added, "We're talking about people whose land had been passed from generation to generation."

Despite America's infusion of funds, military supplies, and advisors, the stability of Cambodia grew ever more precarious. The quantities of American economic and military aid actually overwhelmed Cambodia's absorption capacity, resulting in corruption and chaos. Some officers purchased their rank, and thus many lacked talent or training to perform their duties. Supplies were often stolen, and soldiers were fed poorly and paid late or not at all; consequently, many deserted. Officers turned in lists of "ghost" soldiers who had died or deserted to collect their wages, turning the army into a literal "paper army." With an ineffectual army in the field and massive bombing occurring in parts of the countryside, 35 percent of the population had fled to the cities by 1975. Phnom Penh swelled from half a million to three times that. Believing that faith would expel nonbelievers from the country, Lon Nol ordered Vietnamese communists to leave within forty-eight hours; in the hysteria, almost half were expelled, murdered, or detained. Weakened by incompetent and erratic leaders, Cambodia and Vietnam fell to the communists in April 1975. The American ambassador and a handful of diplomats and Khmer associates were airlifted by helicopter out of Cambodia, and on the seventeenth, on the Khmer New Year (*chol chnam thmey*), Cambodian communists took control of the country and began a new reign; two weeks later, Vietnamese communists took over Vietnam. The war toll was considerable: hundreds of thousands dead, many more wounded, property destroyed, and millions of refugees. For millennia, the lives of Cambodians' ancestors had often been tumultuous and violent as they focused on survival. Their lives were to become so again, for the suffering caused by Cambodian leaders' incompetence and America's misguided military actions were surpassed only by the suffering inflicted by the new communist regime.

Before 1970, Cambodian communists, named Khmer Rouge (*khmer krahom*, or "red Cambodians" in French) by Sihanouk, were a marginal force influenced by Vietnamese communists or by Marxists and Leninists while studying in France (Hin Sithan 1992). Their leader, Pol Pot, described them as fewer than five thousand scattered and poorly armed guerrillas (Owen and Kiernan 2006), and observers said they had no hope of attaining power in Cambodia. By 1973, however, they had grown to number 68,000 cadre (referring to both individual and collective Khmer Rouge) (Becker 1986). Although the Khmer Rouge gradually took over Cambodia from the late 1960s and retained control of some areas until 1996, their rule over the whole country began with the 17 April 1975 takeover of Phnom Penh and endured until the Vietnamese invasion in December 1978. The Khmer Rouge consisted of a small elite led by Pol Pot, 120,000 soldiers, and 20,000 civilian cadres. Their goal was to restore Cambodia to what the Khmer Rouge saw as its former greatness by establishing an egalitarian social order, maximizing agricultural production, and replacing the family household with work teams.

The Khmer Rouge regime ended abruptly, when intrusions by the Khmer Rouge into Vietnam and long-standing enmity between the two countries led to Vietnam's invasion of Cambodia at the end of 1978. The 150,000 Vietnamese troops and several hundred Khmer escapees fighting with them met little resistance. The Vietnamese set up a government in Phnom Penh administered primarily by former Khmer Rouge, and the new People's Republic of Kampuchea focused on the restoration of order. Although Cambodians were again free to resume their lives, many fled their homeland. Cambodians took with them memories of what had occurred in Cambodia and talked among themselves about those experiences. As soon as they began learning English, they started telling Americans about their lives under the Khmer Rouge and flight from Cambodia. First, however, they waited in Thailand's refugee camps to hear about possible resettlement.

America's Migration History

If accepted for resettlement, Khmer refugees would join a nation of migrants whose mythology is that America has always welcomed oppressed people. Americans point to the words adorning the Statue of Liberty pedestal: "Give me your tired, your poor, / Your huddled masses yearning to breathe free." American leaders boast of immigrant ancestors, and Americans often note that the ancestors of all Americans were immigrants or refugees. In Tyrity's words, the refugee is "no oddity, caught in strange and impossible situations," but a "universal citizen" writing a story that could apply to any American (1981).

Both Puritans in the 1600s and presidents in the modern era have called America "a city upon a hill"; in President Reagan's 1989 words, a "God-blessed" place with doors that "were open to anyone with the will and the heart to get here." Yet America's immigrant mythology ignores the restrictive legislation that has shaped immigration (Johnson 2003) and disregards unwilling participants, such as slaves from Africa, conscripts from Asia, and Native Americans considered problems to be solved through displacement, education, or elimination. America's migrant reception has shifted between generous hospitality and indifference or rejection. Americans have long worried about immigrants being different and not learning American ways. Native-born residents of North American have always been cautious with newcomers, and often with reason.

The arrival of explorers, adventurers, and settlers into the New World after the fifteenth century brought violence and disease to the original immigrants who had migrated from Asia millennia before. Surviving Native Americans were then displaced by white Europeans, most from the English-speaking British Isles. These new immigrants established a world based on Protestant values of individual accomplishment, values that immigrants in the centuries since have been pressured to emulate. The bigotry Americans have displayed to immigrants has stemmed not only from immigrants' differentness, but from American assumptions about the superiority of their own values and their attempts to protect what they have considered their own resources and privileges (Steinberg 1989).

The largest migrant influx to America occurred from the mid-1800s to the 1930s, when millions of Europeans migrated, attracted by work and inexpensive steamship fares (Grognet 1981). America's industrial development resulted in the largest economic expansion the world had yet seen, and by 1920, one-third of the country's workforce consisted of foreign-born workers. However, the new arrivals made many Americans uncomfortable. Controlling Native Americans and African Americans with restrictions and segregation, majority Americans were leery of newcomers who did not fit existing categories and instead spoke little English and observed unfamiliar customs and religions. An official commission concluded that immigration from southern and Eastern Europe should be strictly restricted because of its threat to American society (Dillingham Commission 1911).

Americans were also suspicious of migration from China and Japan. Although welcome when their labor was necessary, Asian immigrants were subjected to considerable discrimination when Americans saw them as competition rather than essential, particularly during the economic depression of the 1870s. In 1882, the United States banned Chinese altogether, and those already in the country were prohibited from applying for citizenship. In certain places and times, Asian migrants were prohibited from marrying or testifying against whites, attending public schools, forming corporations, owning real property, or hunting and fishing. Not until 1965 were Chinese allowed to migrate to the United States under immigration regulations applicable to other migrants. Through the centuries, Americans continued to prefer fair-skinned, European migrants with similar language, habits, and values.

Processing Khmer Refugees

The restrictions America placed on immigrants has applied also to refugees. The first influx of refugees to America, and also the first to be allotted resettlement funds by Congress, were twenty thousand Haitian plantation owners in the 1790s, escaping the slaves who had revolted against them (Grognet 1981). A century and a half later, the inhospitality America showed Jews seeking to flee Europe in the 1930s was reversed, and the 1940s and 1950s became known as the "age of the refugee." Refugees included concentration camp survivors, people fleeing communism, and escapees from Castro's Cuba (Paludan 1974). Another major movement of refugees occurred in the 1970s as Southeast Asians fled the communist takeover of Vietnam, Cambodia, and Laos. Public awareness of the fleeing refugees, international pressure, and extensive lobbying pressured the American government to increase the number of Southeast Asians accepted for resettlement. Unanticipated and unprecedented in America's history, America sponsored over two million Southeast Asian refugees between 1975 and 1990.

Few Cambodians were living in America when the Khmer Rouge took control of Cambodia. In addition to a small number of diplomats in Washington, DC, and New York and military personnel training at various installations (Coleman 1987), there were several hundred students, a number at California State University in Long Beach, Fresno State College, and the University of California at Berkeley. Most Cambodians were relieved to be out of Cambodia when the Khmer Rouge took over, but a small group of pilots wished to return home. After discussions with the American government and the United Nations, 114 pilots and a few others were returned to their homeland (Coleman 1987). A Cambodian resettled in 1975 said he met the group in Camp Chaffee, Arkansas, where his father tried to talk them out of returning, but the group was determined to leave. Several of their names later appeared on Khmer Rouge execution lists, and none was heard from again.

With Cambodia closed to all but a few during the Khmer Rouge years, Cambodians in the United States worried for years about the fate of their countrymen. In 1979, however, thousands of sick and starving refugees straggled into Thailand with stories, most too extreme to be believed. As the stories multiplied and evidence of Khmer Rouge atrocities mounted, Cambodians in America reacted with shock, grief, and guilt. A graduate student at Cornell University said he found it almost impossible to continue his studies when he learned what had occurred in Cambodia, and if his professors had not delayed his studies, he could not have completed his degree. As Cambodians received pleas for assistance and sponsorship from relatives and friends in the camps, they described their relief at being able to help.

To be accepted for resettlement in the United States in the twentieth century, a person first had to be defined as a refugee. "Refugee" is a legal term in America and much of the world, with a status different from "citizen" or "immigrant." The United Nations and the United States define a refugee as a person who, "owing to a well-founded fear of being persecuted for reasons of race, religion, nationality, membership of a particular social group or political opinion, is outside the country of his nationality, and is unable to, or owing to such fear, is unwilling to avail himself of the protection of that country" (UNHCR 2014). Political factors are usual in the creation of refugees, as when struggles for power result in war or persecution against a particular group. Defining an individual as a refugee places that person in an international arena in which the needs and rights of national groups carry more importance than individuals, and decisions about refugees by countries with conflicting interests make refugee processing complicated and confusing. For example, the United States is more likely to define refugees as people fleeing countries considered its enemies than those fleeing nations friendly to America.

After arrival in the United States, refugees have the rights of citizens, with the exception of voting and journeying to other countries without travel documents. Rights include eligibility for social services, public education, and employment, and refugees are able to adjust their status after one year to permanent residency and, after four years, can apply for citizenship. Resettlement is permanent, and Khmer refugees were unable to shift resettlement to another country. The American president determines the number of refugees admitted to the country following procedures laid out by the Refugee Act of 1980.

The process for becoming legally defined as refugees began for Cambodians when they learned about resettlement interview procedures, usually in a Thai refugee camp. The first step was an interview with an officer of the Immigration and Naturalization Service (renamed in 2003 the United States Citizenship and Immigration Service, or ICE). Assisted by nongovernmental agency personnel, the officer determined eligibility. Acceptance for resettlement in the United States was enhanced if Cambodians had ties to Americans, service as a government soldier before 1975, or close family members already resettled in America. At each step in the eligibility-determination process, Cambodians had to convince skeptical officials their lives were in danger if they returned to Cambodia, give consistent answers, and appear truthful. Resettled Cambodians said they had considered the interview a life-or-death event, and they feared repatriation to Cambodia or retention in a Thai camp if they failed to obtain acceptance.

Refugees said the interview process and relationships between American officials and international agency personnel were confusing. One refugee asked a Swedish child-care worker for assistance in gaining American resettlement. Years later, the resettled refugee laughed, saying he had not realized that was out of her purview. Cambodians said they grew increasingly anxious as they awaited appointments. They prayed, scraped together money to make offerings to Buddha and the spirits, sought advice from those who had been interviewed, conferred endlessly about what to say, and practiced answering questions consistently. Cambodians often described their terror during interviews.

In 1982, I witnessed an immigration officer at the Philippine Refugee Processing Center reinterviewing two Khmer men after learning from the American Embassy in Thailand they had misrepresented their relationship, describing themselves as brothers (Mortland 1987). Trembling, the men stood before him trying to explain that while they did not have the same parents, they were brothers because of the suffering they shared. One man said in barely audible Khmer, "He saved my life. I saved his life. He is my brother." The officer said brusquely he would take away their refugee status or keep them at the processing center; "That will teach you not to lie." At lunch, the officer told me he saw his primary job as catching refugees in their lies, "and they all lie." Hours later, the two were still shaking from their experience.

Khmer refugees said acceptance for resettlement brought them joy, more prayers, and new anxieties. Would they pass the physical examinations? Would someone discover information that nullified their acceptance? How long would they have to stay in the Phanat Nikhom Transit Center, Thailand's final processing center? Would other refugees bribe officials to take their seats on the bus to the airport or on the airplane? Several told me they were not certain they were actually going until the plane began to move away from the gate. Somath said his relief was brief; even airborne, he began worrying that the airplane might return to Thailand and he would be removed for one reason or another. Others said they were relieved when they exited the plane after a long flight and saw signs they could not read. "But," said one man soon after arrival, "I wasn't certain the signs were in English because I couldn't read them!"

It did not take long for American personnel to decide that Cambodians needed to be prepared for resettlement before going to America. Strikingly similar to early twentieth-century American assumptions that immigrant problems resulted from their dissimilarities to Americans, 1970s Americans concluded that reducing refugee difference would hasten their becoming Americans: in the classroom, refugees could learn to shed their subservience, dependency, and inherited ideas of hierarchy and become rational, democratic, hardworking, and self-sufficient. The emphasis of early twentieth-century educators remained: to teach refugees to be on time and self-sufficient. Early social activists considered learning English the major goal of Americanization and saw a failure to learn English as un-American, because immigrants could not then become "real" Americans. Americans thought English would bring migrants into the workplace, acquaint them with American cultural mores and laws, help free them from traditional values, and lessen their impact on Americans.

After the first Southeast Asians were accepted for resettlement in 1975, they were sent directly to four sites in the United States considered adequate for processing tens of thousands of refugees, including Camp Pendleton in California, Fort Chaffee in Arkansas, Fort Indiantown Gap in Pennsylvania, and Eglin Air Force Base in Florida. During processing, cultural orientation was offered to the refugees, and at Fort Chaffee, the local college set up English-language classes (Maher 2010). American interest in preparing refugees for life in the United States intensified as the resettlement of refugees expanded dramatically after 1979. Some Americans argued that dislocation and the stresses of resettlement required that refugees receive preparatory education and assistance; others said refugees needed the preparation before entry into the United States or they would overtax state and local resources. The Refugee Act of 1980 addressed these issues by establishing centers on Bataan Peninsula in the Philippines, Galang Island in Indonesia, and Phanat Nikhom in Thailand where refugees spent an average of six months completing bureaucratic processing and receive English training and cultural and employment orientation (Consortium 1982).

A plethora of materials was prepared for training purposes. The Center for Applied Linguistics (CAL) developed survival-language phrase books and teaching English as a second language materials for adults and children; pre-employment training curricula, instructional and testing materials; and a series of twelve videotapes called *Working in America* (Cultural Orientation Resource Center 2012). In 1983, CAL staff in Washington, DC, shipped over two hundred pounds of teaching material to Southeast Asia each week, and by 1985, staff in Manila maintained a library of over 3,000 slides, 150 videos, and 3,650 books. Staff also offered a quarterly newsletter, a magazine called *Passage: A Journal of Refugee Education,* a national hotline, on-site workshops, employer guides, and information in Khmer on finding employment and family assistance.

In the processing centers, refugees were taught to change their living patterns, social structures, and values and replace ties to their culture and community with aspirations to individual independence and wealth (Tollefson 1989). They were told to "pick up English" in America after getting a full-time job, although little research suggests that having a job is more effective in learning English as a second language than is attending classes. Lacking fluent English does not always preclude employment; for centuries, migrants adjusted to America without learning English, and many jobs do not require workers with much English. In addition, migrants gain most of their adjustment information from fellow countrymen. Tollefson suggests that American policymakers wanted refugees to be taught to be satisfied with minimum-wage jobs, aspire to prosper through hard work, and stay off welfare; they would be perceived as less competitive with middle-class Americans. Claiming to teach democracy and independence, processing centers taught refugees to listen and obey. Many refugees said they resented camp restrictions on boundaries, class and work hours, and activities and the resettlement delay, but most complied with training and work requirements. By the late 1980s, over two hundred thousand Southeast Asian refugees had completed the program.

Before being flown to the United States, refugees were shown how to change money, navigate an airport, and get through customs, although most had no money and could not speak English. They viewed films on how to sit in an airplane seat, use the toilet, and ask a flight attendant for assistance, but despite the efforts of Cambodians and teachers, most refugees were unprepared for the journey. Cambodians said later the journey was difficult. An older man said he did not eat for several days before the flight so he would not need the bathroom, and several said they did not use the toilet because they feared falling "down the hole." One man said he thought the swooshing sound meant the toilet was trying to grab him. An airline attendant said refugees often did not lock bathroom doors, and attendants kept trying to get them to do so until they realized that refugees were then getting locked inside. Several Khmer said they thought they would go crazy before the flight attendant got the door opened. Airline personnel posted instructions in the bathrooms on toilet, towel, paper, and soap use, but many Cambodians were illiterate or too anxious to read them.

Many Cambodians said they ate nothing on the flight, worried that the food would make them sick, disgusted at their first sight of non-Khmer food, or because, as one woman said, "I didn't think it looked like food." Some refugees smuggled food onto the airplane, worried that Americans would forget to feed them. Some spoke of their unease around people who looked different, one man saying, "I don't think the black stewardess liked me because she wouldn't help me." When I suggested she did not understand what he was saying, he repeated, "Yes, I don't think she liked me." Even compassionate flight attendants and passengers frightened the refugees. One Cambodian said, "I started to shake every time someone turned to talk with me because I didn't know what they were saying, and I was worried that I wouldn't do what they wanted me to do or I would offend them. Mostly, I tried to avoid looking at anyone." Cambodians breast-fed their babies, tried not to throw up, and prayed. Whatever their uncertainty, however, Cambodians said they were glad to be leaving camp life. Young Veata said no one in her family ate breakfast when they had a stopover in Japan, but she ate everything on her plate because she was "so glad to be going to America."

Refugee transportation was arranged by the Intergovernmental Committee for Migration, an organization that has administered loans to refugees for their transportation to resettlement countries since its founding after World War II. Refugees sign a promissory note stating they will repay the money, and the committee uses the loan repayments to make new loans. Both refugees and advocates expressed outrage that with virtually no resources, refugees were expected to repay transportation costs. One Khmer shook his head muttering, "I don't understand this country. People so generous, and then they take it back." When another Cambodian responded, "But you signed the paper to pay it back," he replied, "Everybody sign the paper. Who wouldn't sign to get out of there?" An American said heatedly, "We spend billions to destroy their country, then millions to bring them to America, but refugees must pay for the airplane seat? Seems pitiful to me." Confusion about how the travel loans worked was considerable, and most Cambodians and Americans were unaware that the loans were being made by a nongovernmental organization and not the government.

Transportation costs were only one of the concerns Khmer refugees had in their new country.

Chapter One

Being in America

The arrival of hundreds of thousands of refugees in the United States was unprecedented. Although America had received refugees before, they had never done so on the scale that occurred in the late 1970s and early 1980s, following the end of the Vietnam War. The challenge was to place and resettle the refugees and assist them in achieving economic independence.

Voluntary Agencies and Sponsorship

The federal government entrusts refugee resettlement to nongovernmental organizations called voluntary agencies (volags) that include the United States Catholic Conference, Church World Service, and International Rescue Committee. Volags competed for sponsors, refugees, and public and private funding; cooperated in screening and allocating refugees; and provided local services to Southeast Asian refugees. They allocated refugees to their affiliated offices throughout the country, who then recruited local sponsors. The United States Catholic Conference resettled refugees through one of its 185 resettlement offices, and the Church World Service through its fifteen denominations.

Rather than place refugees in hostels or refugee centers for months of language and orientation training, as occurred in Europe (Campbell 1983), many American volag offices gave responsibility for refugees to sponsors, providing advice, interpretation, emergency assistance, and a portion of a $525 federal per capita grant given the volags. Congregations, organizations, schools, and individuals served as sponsors with temporary ethical responsibility for refugees. The initial placement of refugees depended primarily on the location of Cambodians in the United States, the availability of American sponsors, and employment and housing realities. Students and alumni of schools in Long Beach, Massachusetts, and Washington, DC, responded (Chan 2004), and as the numbers of refugees and needs increased in additional locations, Cambodians turned to American friends and set up self-help groups to provide refugee services (Mortland 1993).

When refugees were settled in locations where Cambodians already lived, sponsoring was easier because procedures were in place and local Cambodians, the sponsoring community, and service providers were familiar with resettlement processes. American sponsors willing to follow the suggestions of Khmer sponsors, businessmen, and leaders found their work easier, but others ignored them. One sponsor told me in 1981, "I know there are other Cambodians around, but they don't know as much about living in America as I do." When I suggested that Cambodians knew more about adjusting to American society than Americans did, she replied, "Oh, I can't believe that. I've lived in this town for forty-three years. I know all the streets and all the offices." She ended up having to redo a number of resettlement appointments because she did not follow the procedures set up for Southeast Asians in the region, and she missed registering the family's children for school because she was unfamiliar with the system. The family she sponsored said years later they were grateful for her assistance, but they had not seen her for years because she became angry at them for not following her advice.

Sponsor duties included meeting refugees at the airport, providing housing and supplies for a month or until refugees were self-sufficient, referring refugees to services, and enrolling children in school. Volags typically expected sponsors to visit sponsored refugees at least every two weeks during their first three months after arrival, maintain contact with the sponsoring agency, complete a ninety-day follow-up questionnaire, and provide emergency and backup services when needed. Most of the first refugees joined kinfolk or countrymen, but as arrivals increased, volags sought American sponsors, who eventually sponsored most Khmer refugees.

Other volags retained the per capita grants to pay overhead for staff to provide direct services to refugees (North, Lewin, and Wagner 1982). The United States Catholic Conference and Church World Service utilized the first model, usually with congregation and individual sponsors, while the International Rescue Committee relied on the second model. Volags offered a range of services to refugees and sponsors, and volag staff members were often the liaison between refugees and agencies providing financial assistance, medical care, interpretation and translation, and employment advice. Sponsoring information was initially scarce. In the mid-1970s, the United States Catholic Conference produced a four-page pamphlet called *Cultural and Historical Notes on the Cambodians*. Volags described lists of cultural differences between Americans and "Indochinese" refugees, listing American characteristics on one side and

Asians on the other: "Easterners revere interdependence / The Westerners value independence" (Chareundi 1992: 25). Some pamphlets provided shopping lists that included rice, fish, and soy sauce (United States Catholic Conference 1975). In the early 1980s, the federal Department of Health and Human Services published a four-page paper entitled *An Overall Approach to Providing Therapy to Khmer Families*, offering tips to social workers.

Local organizations provided information on health, food, housing, furnishings, clothing, transportation, health, education, legal require-ments, and cultural information. Tacoma agencies created a handbook in 1981 that included illustrations of gestures offensive to Asians, as well as addresses for public and service offices and Asian markets. The Refugee Assistance Program of Ithaca produced a handbook for sponsors that pro-vided over fifty pages of information, including telephone numbers for doctors and dentists. Volunteers and sponsors collected the information, which was typed up by refugee assistance staff and revised frequently. One sponsor said she "made a copy to keep in my car because I use it so much."

Most voluntary agencies are religiously affiliated, and many Khmer refugees were sponsored by churches. Americans often quoted scripture to explain their sponsoring commitment: "For I was hungered, and ye gave me meat: I was thirsty, and ye gave me drink: I was a stranger, and ye took me in" (Matthew 25:35), and "Inasmuch as ye have done it unto one of the least of these my brethren, ye have done it unto me" (Matthew 25:40). California Mennonites said they assisted Cambodians not only "in the name of Jesus Christ" but because they were inspired by their own memories of suffering (Froese 2006). Other sponsors spoke of being able to demonstrate a volunteer spirit and perpetuate "a pioneer tradition" in which frontier neighbors "built each other's cabins" (Carter 1992: 245).

Some Americans saw sponsorship as a patriotic or moral duty or described feeling pride in helping others. A few Americans said their con-cern for refugees came from their recognition that efforts on behalf of Jews before World War II had been inadequate. Some Americans acknowl-edged that they benefited from the presence of Khmer refugees. Some said they benefited religiously, that by helping the poor they were "laying up riches in heaven" (Matthew 6:20). Others recognized that they gained socially from contact with Cambodians as contributors and volunteers. In addition, refugees' actual and perceived deficiencies brought funding for services and provided Americans with employment in social work, health care, mental health, and education.

American individuals and agencies provided hundreds of millions of volunteer hours and dollars in financial assistance to Khmer refugees. By

1981, eight hundred thousand Americans had directly assisted Southeast Asian refugees; billions of government dollars and millions of public and private funds had been expended on their behalf, a good portion of it for Cambodians (Perkins 1981). Volags were proud of their work. The Church World Service described serving as "trustworthy referrals" for various services and playing "a key role in ensuring quality resettlement" for refugees while working "closely with denominational offices as well as local churches and sponsors" (Church World Service 2001). Catholic parishes and Protestant churches with an interest in social action, including Presbyterian, Methodist, and Episcopal congregations, were especially active in refugee sponsorship, although a number of conservative, evangelical, and Pentecostal churches also made significant contributions. Many Americans said relationships established between congregations and refugees were some of the most intimate Americans and Khmer refugees experienced (Fein 1987).

First Encounters between Cambodian Refugees and Americans

The arrival of Khmer refugees was dramatic for both Cambodians and Americans. Cambodian refugees and Americans knew virtually nothing about one another. Excepting American diplomats, intelligence agency personnel, and missionaries, only a few Americans were familiar with Cambodians (Coleman 1987), and most Cambodians knew only about Americans from what they had learned in the refugee camps. American sponsors said they found pamphlets, handbooks, and advice helpful, but far from sufficient for understanding Khmer culture or experiences. First encounters often occurred at the airport, where exhausted, stunned, and frequently ill refugees stumbled off an airplane to be met by excited Khmer relatives, countrymen, and Americans. Like most refugees, Cambodians had fled with little planning and few resources. They had just experienced their first baffling air trip, were often speechless from fear and lack of English, and knew their lives were forever changed. Nonetheless, relieved to find refuge, their grace and composure on arrival were striking.

In northern sites, refugees often walked off the airplane shivering in their thin clothes, sometimes wearing donated coats similar in stripe, color, and style to those of refugees across the country. Some families arrived with a plastic string-wrapped bag or box on which camp staff had written their names and new addresses in large English letters. Luggage contained donated clothing, a gift or two made in the refugee camps for sponsors, maybe a battered language workbook, and whatever snapshots or amulets refugees managed to salvage from Cambodia. A member of each family carried a large, square, white plastic bag emblazoned with "ICM CIM," the English and French acronyms denoting Intergovernmental Committee for Migration, the organization that arranged refugee transport. The bag held the family's official papers, including an entrance form with a black-and-white, 1¾ by 2½ inch mug shot of each individual attached. Refugees had been told the bag was the most important item they carried. A few refugees worried about losing it, one woman saying, "They told us if we lost it, they wouldn't let us stay in America." Refugees sometimes refused to let the bag out of their hands until they were "home," wherever that now was.

Cambodians later described indistinct memories of their arrival. They remember being startled at the presence of so many Americans and delighted by the presence of their countrymen. They said they had already realized they did not know how to live in the new environment; without help, most were unable to find the bathroom, get a drink of water, light a cigarette, throw away trash, or find an acceptable place to change a diaper. Despite their uneasiness, they greeted their greeters warmly, smiled throughout the bustle of leaving the airport, and listened as well as they could to instructions on how to operate in their new surroundings.

Sponsors' first priority was to settle refugees into homes and routines as quickly as possible. Refugees joining family sponsors usually stayed with them from a few days to years, moving into their own housing when they had the necessary resources. Cambodians who joined non-kin sponsors were usually placed in their own apartments. A few American sponsors living in areas without many Cambodians housed refugees in their own homes so the newcomers could become familiar with their new environment, but both Americans and Cambodians found living together stressful. Some Cambodians remembered fondly and humorously their initial days using unfamiliar faucets, switches, and handles. Others said they enjoyed the experience because they felt safe and were learning about America. Achariya said she was grateful she could "eat in front of Americans and not have them laugh at me." Others were unhappy in their sponsors' homes, saying they felt childlike, powerless, and out of place. One woman said, "I couldn't wait to get out of there. They treated us like heathens, but did very nasty things themselves, like wearing their shoes when they were sitting on their bed. And we had to eat their food. I still will not eat macaroni and cheese." A number of hosts also were glad when the Cambodians were able to move to their own quarters.

With limited resources, volags and sponsors initially placed Cambodians in inexpensive apartment complexes located in inner-city areas, assuming that this was the housing refugees with minimum-wage jobs or public assistance could afford. The inexpensive housing meant refugees were often living in shabby, even dangerous, conditions, afraid to complain because of their gratitude to sponsors, lack of English, and unfamiliarity with housing regulations or fear of eviction. As the number of Khmer arrivals increased, Cambodians gathered in metropolitan developments that often housed one hundred to three thousand people where generations of immigrants had lived before. In East Boston, Cambodians were clustered in neighborhoods of battered triple-deckers, each housing twelve families amid tiny family-run corner markets and delis, few trees, and congested traffic (Hansen 1988). In Sacramento, housing complexes previously occupied by African Americans, Hispanic, and Vietnamese were subsequently occupied almost exclusively by Cambodians. In the East Bay area near San Francisco, Cambodians occupied a fifty-unit building, with as many as twelve people living in two or three rooms.

Many buildings had inadequate heat, leaking ceilings, doors without locks, frayed wiring, decaying walls, rotting stairs, and puddles of sewage standing in bare dirt yards, and numerous apartments were infested with cockroaches and mice. In addition, many Cambodians were hesitant to leave the safety of their apartments, however mean, for the larger world of poverty, with few job opportunities and poor schools, and surrounded by hostile neighbors, drugs, and criminal activity. In other regions, refugees were encouraged to apply for low-cost public housing. While many Cambodians have done well for decades in public housing, often sought after as being model tenants and neighbors, others said service providers tended to view residents as having low potential and claimed public housing encouraged dependency and criminality. Over the long term, Cambodians who sought housing outside the realm of public housing did better economically than those in public housing, saying they were pushed by circumstances and neighbors to gain self-sufficiency and, eventually, education for their children.

Refugees and Sponsors

Relationships between Khmer refugees and Americans were unprecedented for most because they involved immediate intimacy between strangers who came from differing cultures and spoke different languages. The sponsor-refugee relationship itself was so new there were few appropriate terms for it. Americans struggled with what to call the refugee counterpart to sponsor; while "sponsor" was in common use among both Cambodians and Americans, "sponsoree" was seldom used by anyone. Refugees speaking of "their" sponsor seemed appropriate, as one speaks of one's teacher or mother, but sponsors talking about "their" refugees seemed much less appropriate, implying an unequal relationship. Many sponsors went out of their way to avoid such phraseology and instead spoke of "the family they sponsored" or "the man we sponsored." Other sponsors did not, and refugees sometimes took offense. "I am not *her* refugee," Thom said indignantly one day several months after his arrival.

Refugees and sponsors often clashed over the length of sponsorship and its terms. Khmer refugees recognized they needed long-term assistance but wanted independence as quickly as possible. Most Cambodian sponsors watched the growing independence of those they sponsored with relief, since they had their own resettlement struggles. Having the same cultural assumptions about mutual obligations, living arrangements, and gratitude, Cambodian sponsors and arrivals more easily lived together and parted ways. Some American sponsors, however, had difficulty judging when to let refugees be on their own. Some assumed the refugees' immediate material and institutional needs were satisfied by a few months' assistance and withdrew assistance too early, leaving refugees stranded. Others did not hear from the refugees they sponsored and so concluded they no longer needed assistance, not realizing that many were unable or unwilling to admit or communicate their needs.

Some American sponsors, in contrast, complained that refugees expected a limitless commitment from them or were piqued when they felt refugees were not sufficiently docile or grateful, ignored their advice, refused their services, or rejected their religion. Tensions between American sponsors and Khmer refugees often increased when contact became more frequent, and a number of sponsors increasingly viewed Cambodians as uncooperative, unworthy of services, or too ignorant to benefit from the assistance being offered. Many sponsors were displeased by refugees' money decisions, calling the purchase of a color television a month or two after arrival irresponsible. New arrivals, on the other hand, saw a television as an aid to understanding Americans and a buffer against loneliness. Cambodians should save their money, sponsors said, to buy a house or put their children through college. Sponsors often had difficulty understanding that many Cambodians were not much interested in "becoming Americans," other than being able to support their families and live peacefully.

Refugees had their own grievances. Some expected their sponsors to do much more for them than they did; others worried about repaying their sponsors for their generosity. Some Cambodians resented their sponsors' control over them (also Horng Kouch 1989). Many refugees, however, were happy with their sponsors. One woman said she continued to attend her sponsor's church because it "makes my sponsor happy." Some Cambodians said they could not be displeased with their sponsors because the relationship was the result of karma: a good sponsor meant one had earned good karma, and a bad sponsor meant the opposite.

Cambodians had numerous ways to resist unwelcome sponsor interference. One sponsor complained just months after "her" family arrived that she "used to see them all the time but now, whenever I go to their house, they are not there." I was visiting the family one afternoon when she knocked on their front door. Family members sat motionless until the sponsor left. Seeing my surprise, the husband said, "We are thankful for her help, but now she just stops by to see what we're eating." Some Cambodians ended their relationship with sponsors by moving to another city, a few departing without saying goodbye and leaving sponsors to dispose of apartments and possessions they had acquired for the refugees. Several refugees spoke of "divorcing" their sponsors because they offered little assistance (also Ly Y 2000). A few sponsors reacted bitterly at what they viewed as refugee abandonment of their hard work and financial contributions and stopped assisting refugees.

While some sponsors remained in contact for years with the refugees they sponsored, others faded away, became friends or occasional acquaintances, or disappeared entirely from refugees' lives. Some observers note that despite intense contact between Cambodians and Americans, few personal friendships were formed; Americans aided refugees out of duty or to serve their own needs, and Cambodians in need accepted help from Americans they viewed as patrons. Other observers disagree, saying that many refugees and sponsors became friends. When Cambodians and Americans were able to choose associations, they formed strong relationships, with Cambodians becoming friends with American teachers, fellow students, neighbors, and colleagues. Despite cultural differences and misunderstandings, Cambodians and Americans talked frequently of their affection for one another. Some called their sponsors "Mom" or "Dad," others "Brother" or "Sister." Whatever their eventual relationship, curiosity about one another's sponsors and refugees was constant. Cambodians asked one another, "How are your sponsors?" and Americans asked the same about one another's sponsored families.

Among the Southeast Asian refugees resettled in the United States were approximately 160,000 Cambodians, over 1,120,000 Vietnamese, 200,000 Hmong, and 135,000 Lao from Laos. Four waves of Cambodian refugees have been resettled in the United States. Most Cambodians accepted for resettlement in America left Thailand in the early 1980s. Between 1979 and 1981, approximately 630,000 Cambodians left Cambodia for Thailand, and in the following years, 208,000 were resettled in other countries, including 136,000 in the United States, 32,000 in France, and 13,000 each in

Australia and Canada. The first wave consisted of approximately 6,000 Khmer who came to the United States in 1975 when Cambodia fell to the Khmer Rouge (Gordon 1987). Another 1,300 Khmer refugees were resettled in 1978, sponsored by relatives or former American colleagues who had worked in Western corporations or with the American government or military. By 1979, approximately 14,000 Cambodians had been resettled in America (Coleman 1987). Most came with no resources, and the assistance given them was often sporadic because their arrival dates and destinations were unpredictable, conditions that continued throughout the migration of Cambodian refugees. Phala's family expected to stay in California but were told in flight that they were going to Arkansas. They were actually resettled in Virginia without ever learning why or who was making decisions about their lives.

The more Americans knew about Cambodians' experiences, the greater their concern for them. Emblematic of many Americans' welcoming attitude toward Cambodians was First Lady Roslyn Carter's visit to Khmer refugees in Thailand in 1979 and Massachusetts governor's wife Kitty Dukakis's advocacy for Cambodians before Congress. Other Americans were not so welcoming. A Massachusetts demonstrator held a sign in front of Governor Dukakis's residence proclaiming, "Okay, why don't you take these refugees into your home?" (Chan 2003: 113). At the height of public awareness of Khmer refugees' plight, two out of three Americans did not want them in the country. Politicians tried to limit admission numbers and services, and Senator David Durenberger asked the State Department in 1986 to curtail refugee resettlement in Minnesota, arguing that refugees "have proved economically difficult to assimilate" (*Rochester Post-Bulletin* 1986).

Americans were particularly worried that refugees were competitors for jobs and benefits. One man said of a Khmer neighbor, "They aren't even Americans, but they live better than we do and both my wife and I have good jobs." Rumors spread that refugees received cash incentives and social services and resources. Americans wondered why Cambodians received government money to open restaurants when they were unable to get loans, and they worried that Cambodians would lower property values with too many cars or untended yards. Seattleites were concerned when they heard Cambodians were growing poppies outside their apartments to make illegal drugs, unaware they were talking about Hmong from Laos who were growing the poppy for medicine and religious ceremonies.

Although decisions about refugee admissions and placement were made nationally, the costs for meeting their needs fell on local governments and neighborhoods, influencing the reception refugees received.

Americans considered small groups of refugees "manageable" when they arrived in homogeneous neighborhoods like Rochester, Minnesota (Hein 2006). When Cambodian refugees arrived in large numbers, however, as in Chicago, they did not stand out as they did in predominantly white neighborhoods but were greeted with hostility by many dark-skinned neighbors. Despite the lack of welcome, Cambodians in diverse neighborhoods were freer to establish ethnic communities that provided them with refuge and resources. The welcome of smaller communities quickly eroded when Cambodians arrived in larger numbers and appeared at hospitals and agencies without sponsors, interpreters, or advocates.

As American resentment grew over the increasing number of refugees being resettled, some Americans reacted to their presence with glares and insults. Americans called Cambodians "Bodes," "Bodees," "FOBs" (fresh off the boats), and "JOJs" (just off the jet) (Krich 1989). A reporter friend said that every time she visited a bar in a small Washington coastal town, customers made discriminatory comments about "Cambos" living there. Epithets such as "gook," "spic," and "chink" were common. A supervisor repeatedly said "gotdam pepo" when he talked to a Khmer worker, who asked his family and friends what it meant (Fiffer 1991). No one had any idea, and it took some time to learn his boss was saying, "You goddamn people."

Americans worried that large numbers of Cambodian refugees would undermine America's "shared culture" and "national unity" and wondered why Cambodians still acted like Cambodians, a social worker saying in 1994, "They've certainly had long enough to learn to act like Americans!" Cambodians were accused of eating cats and dogs, and refugee offices received calls asking if "some of those refugees" had swiped their pet for dinner. In Rochester, Minnesota, Americans accused Cambodians of bringing "big city" problems of gang activity and petty crime into the community. Hostility toward Cambodians has continued over the years. A white male called Khmer immigrants "violent, dangerous, rage filled, drug dealing, lazy, and welfare dependant" [sic] in his blog and blamed their presence on "LBJ and RMN for losing the Vietnam War," referring to Lyndon Johnson and Richard Nixon (Federale 2011). He described one family as "the ever giving gift of immigration," saying the parents returned to Cambodia, leaving their children to fare for themselves and calling the son a "ghetto thug" "assimilating downward" by "imitating the social pathology of black Americans." He concluded by asking why America is bringing "people like this in."

Some educated Americans have agreed. A scholar in the 1990s said immigrants in America had been valuable in earlier centuries but were no longer needed (Hardin 1995). He suggested that advocates whose jobs are not threatened by migration use phrases like "a nation of immigrants," "the open door policy," and "my brother's keeper" to induce other Americans to feel guilty for worrying about their own interests, and he concluded that immigrants *do* present a threat to Americans' interests. Experiencing compassion fatigue as they grew weary of newcomer problems, Americans grew stingy with their sympathy, often saying of Cambodians, "It's better for them to be poor in America than to stay in Cambodia." One scholar noted that Cambodians were living among Americans who were "fascinated by violence but bored by suffering" (Fujiwara 2010: 318). As the number of Khmer arrivals slowed and American attention to their plight faded, agencies found sponsors increasingly difficult to recruit. As early as the 1980s, when 150 refugees were expected to arrive in Pittsburgh within a few weeks, a refugee resettlement office was "scouring the city in a desperate attempt to find them sponsors" (McMillian 1981).

Americans became inured to reports of disaster, destruction, and death and the plight of Cambodians as tales, statistics, and photographs of them lost their power and were overshadowed by those of other refugees and natural-disaster victims. Many Americans have been oblivious to the consequences of America's international activities. A pilot who directed air attacks in Cambodia described friendships between American and Khmer military men during bombing raids over Cambodia and ongoing efforts to help Cambodia but neglected mention of damage done to people, villages, fields, and stock (Wood 2002).

Relationships between Cambodian Refugees and Americans

Americans and Cambodians turned to familiar terms for relationships between them: parent-child, teacher-pupil, host-guest, and patron-client. Because Cambodians came with few resources and little familiarity with American ways, they tended to be treated as children needing food and shelter, safety, and basic information. One American said, "A child who does poorly is the one parents pay attention to. This is like the poor Cambodians, who need attention." Some sponsors saw refugees as teenagers who need firm parental guidance to become independent. Others likened sponsorship to being a godparent who maintains an interest in the child. Many Cambodians were content to act as children in the first weeks of resettlement, acknowledging that new-arrival problems were similar to those of babies needing shelter, sustenance, and clothing.

Refugees referred to many of their American sponsors and teachers as fictive kin, addressing them as "brother," "sister," or "mother." Fictive kin relationships were marked by exchanges of money, food, gifts, visits, and occasional attendance at celebrations and family events. While most fictive kin relationships were brief, some were not. One man's American mother paid his way through college and attended every important celebration with his family for over thirty years. Another Khmer introduced his bride's American family to his family and his American sponsor; he said, "I want my in-laws to meet *my* extended family."

Cambodians and Americans found teacher-student relationships less fraught with potential offense than parent-child relationships. Cambodians displayed great respect for teachers, as they had in Cambodia. Cambodians gave Americans who taught them how to light a gas stove, adjust a thermostat, or mail a letter the respect they gave teachers, although they sometimes thought American agencies, schools, and churches set up classes that were unnecessary, such as teaching Khmer women to bake chocolate chip cookies, teaching Khmer children to demonstrate respect to their parents or sing "Old McDonald Had a Farm," or teaching parents how to praise their children, give allowances, or take out the garbage and mow lawns (Murakami 1993). In reaction, one Khmer said, "We teach respect for elders and we have our own tales."

Americans expected Cambodians to be attentive, obedient, and eager to learn, and most Cambodians maintained an attitude of respect toward American teachers, despite the lack of respect Americans sometimes displayed to them as students. Americans often had low expectations of Cambodians. Health officials announced at a meeting in 1982 that they would offer classes only to younger Cambodians who could learn English, were mentally stable, and still had their teeth. A Khmer colleague in his forties leaned close, stretched his lips to cover his teeth, and whispered, "I guess we are very stupid." When American sponsors viewed Cambodians as guests, they expected company manners, respect for the host's privacy, and compliance to house rules, not realizing Cambodians observed their own, often different, "company manners."

Coming from a country in which a hierarchical system of patronage has operated for centuries, many Cambodians saw Americans as patrons, usually without the awareness of Americans. In one Cambodian's words, "There are those who are high and those who are low, and those who are high use those who are low." In Cambodia, patrons with greater power, wealth, and knowledge than their clients provide them with protection, resources, services, and connections. In return, clients provide loyalty, labor, and support to their patrons, who themselves serve as clients to patrons with even greater resources and power. Cambodians found patrons in the camps and often sought their assistance in finding sponsors. One resettlement office received numerous letters in the early 1980s, some addressed to "Mr. Archdiocese of Seattle," promising loyal cooperation if he sponsored the family. A Khmer worker in another refugee office completed sponsorship forms for hundreds of Cambodians, assuming kin relationships with many and filing papers as a "cousin" or "sibling." Many eventually became his clients.

Influenced by their contact with mild and gracious Khmer refugees, Cambodians' reports of prewar Cambodia as a peaceful land, and stories of the brutal Khmer Rouge fratricide, many Americans saw Cambodians as "survivors," "victims," and "remnants of the killing fields." Americans were drawn by their stories, the horror of their experiences, and the questions they raise about human nature. A number of sympathetic Americans saw Cambodians as having been victims of history, with arrogant politicians, cruel rebels, ignorant foreigners, oppressive bureaucracies, and, after resettlement, overbearing sponsors, greedy landlords, supercilious welfare workers, or patronizing teachers abusing them. In American descriptions of Cambodians, there was a sense of Americans' invulnerability to collective tragedy, in part because of the differences between Americans and Cambodians.

Americans said they did not recognize how different Cambodians would be from them, and some aid workers clumped them with Southeast Asian tribespeople as the strangest of newcomers. Many American service providers saw Cambodians as the most ignorant, helpless, and needy of refugee groups; even Americans in "kin" and "friend" relationships with refugees frequently displayed disdain for them, rebuking them not only for their purchases of "native" foods or putting their money in the temple rather than savings but of continuing to act as foreigners: tying the bottom of their curtains into knots, pounding spices in a mortar and pestle, hacking a chicken to pieces with a cleaver on the floor, or spitting betel juice into a coffee can.

Politicians and reporters called Cambodians foreigners, and many Americans saw their differences as dangerous and polluting. One sponsor said Khmer music and dancing seemed "un-American" to her. "Why don't they act more like Americans?" was a common refrain, and after listening to other tenant complaints about strange music, cooking smells, or children not respecting yard boundaries, landlords pleaded with refugee workers, "Could you tell them not to do that?" One American asked, "Why don't they go back to Cambodia, where they belong?" Many Americans were unashamed of their attitudes, like one who identified herself and was quoted as saying, "I don't think anybody likes them around here. It's a pretty nice neighborhood otherwise" (Andrist 1983).

Americans continue to know little about Cambodia. Many think it is in the Pacific Islands, and others wondered what Cambodia had to do with the Vietnam War. What they do know they often use in peculiar ways: although Cambodia is not the natural habitat of Bengal tigers, the tiger exhibit at the Miami zoo consists of a Khmer temple replica containing cages for five Bengal tigers (Croke 1994). Neither did ignorance of Cambodians stop Americans from offering explanations for Khmer behavior. Americans said their behavior was culturally caused, saying repeatedly, "This is just the way Cambodians are." Americans said successful resettlement depended on getting Cambodians "unstuck" from their "cultural baggage" including ideas about parenting and schooling, hierarchical relationships, and Buddhist beliefs. Americans said they needed to "slice away" their original knowledge and ignorance to "become Americanized" as soon as possible.

Not realizing Cambodians were wearing clothes they had been given by larger-sized Americans, donated for tax purposes and often fit only for the garbage bag, Americans saw their attire as evidence of bizarre Khmer tastes and criticized it for being too loose or too tight, threadbare, stained, out of fashion, and mismatched—wearing checked pants and striped shirts together and combining colors few middle-class Americans wore in the 1980s. Discounting the difficulties of learning unwritten rules as adults, Americans later ridiculed Cambodians for wearing dresses with price tags attached and suits with the maker's name still on the sleeve.

Cambodians' difficulty with English was especially irksome to Americans, who saw the acquisition of English as evidence that Cambodians were trying to act like Americans and get good jobs, but most Cambodians spoke English in a nervous, fragmented, and unconvincing manner, reinforcing American perceptions of them as ignorant. Americans complained Cambodians were not working hard enough to learn English or had given up on learning it at all. "They live here now," Americans said. "Why won't they learn English?" Claiming their immigrant ancestors had "pulled themselves up by their bootstraps" and received no government help, Americans ignored the reality that many ancestor immigrants already spoke English, while others attended classes not available to many Cambodians or found employment with others who spoke their language. Many of our ancestors never learned English.

Recent immigrants to the United States were often especially critical. An immigrant from Singapore who speaks fluent English was outraged that Cambodians after thirty years could not speak English, dismissing Cambodians' background and her own four years at an expensive language school, and saying what Americans often say: "If I can learn English, anyone can." A friend from a well-educated, liberal, and famous family returned frequently to the topic before her death, emphasizing that she could not understand why immigrants do not try to learn English. She was friendly with a Cambodian who has successfully run a business for many years but took her heavy accent as a personal affront.

The language Americans used with and about Cambodians revealed their attitudes toward them. Americans often discussed Cambodian capabilities and potential in disparaging terms even in their presence and when Cambodians knew what was being said. Americans saw Cambodians' lack of English fluency as a deficiency, even a demonstration of their lack of intelligence. When Americans communicated with Cambodians by speaking loudly, Cambodians cringed or muttered in Khmer that they were not deaf. When Americans did not want to communicate clearly with Cambodians, they frequently obscured issues by using complicated bureaucratic, religious, or academic language, talking in an indirect and circular manner, using diffuse and ambiguous words and phrases such as "in terms of" and "staffing-wise."

In agency meetings, Americans often treated Cambodians as invisible or irrelevant to the discussion. In one meeting, American agency personnel wanted to apportion funding among American-led rather than refugee-led organizations and did not want to explain exactly what was at issue or listen to refugee input. Americans used "industry" to mean language teachers and classes and "shop" to mean a local refugee office; the chairperson said cooperation between the two "was an open," meaning it was a possibility. The Cambodian sitting next to me, who thought his English was excellent, could not say later what the meeting was about. Several Americans suggested changing meetings to allow refugee input and taking periodic breaks so refugee participants could be certain they understood the discussions and decisions to be made. Most Americans were resistant, saying they lacked time for such tactics, suggesting instead that breaks come after decisions had already been made.

Cambodians said they understood that Americans often ignored them but saw that as the privilege of having greater power and resources than refugees. Although they often resented American attitudes, Cambodians needed their help and so were willing to act as inferior clients by agreeing, smiling, nodding, and declaring love and gratitude in exchange for assistance, advice, and gifts. One woman complained that her sponsors gave her too many old clothes and not enough furniture, made her go to church, and forced her to look for a job. When the worker offered to talk with the sponsor, she replied, "Oh no! They are my parents. I can't talk against my own family." Cambodians resisted Americans' advice by feigning lack of comprehension or agreeing with them and then doing as they themselves wished. In the presence of authority figures, such as health providers, welfare workers, or police, Cambodians said that incomprehension and agreement was easier than trying to explain themselves. Khmer refugees also used silence and smiles to protect them from divulging information they wanted to keep to themselves, and noted that their smiles can have multiple meanings. After the 2010 Deep Horizon oil spill, a Khmer shrimp fisherman's wife talked about a reporter who said she did not have a real smile. Later, she said that was true; she said she had instead an "unhappy smile" that hid her distress over the oil spill (Roosevelt 2010).

Whether relationships between Americans and Cambodians were parent and child, teacher and student, host and guest, or patron and client, both Cambodians and Americans said they were often frustrating. Cambodians wondered why sponsors did not get them jobs, teachers neglected giving them valuable information, hosts threw them out, or patrons abandoned them. Americans who had given resources and time to Khmer refugees were surprised at their inattentiveness, lack of compliance, ingratitude, or servility. When weariness with one another set in, their relationships shifted, often becoming strained. Cambodians knew Americans saw them as foreigners and, as the years passed, said they felt foreign. They felt, in one man's words, like "forever foreigners."

While most Cambodians did not see themselves as victims, many were willing to use their experiences to gain sympathy and ongoing benefits from Americans. Some Cambodians, on the other hand, resented being viewed as victims and saw themselves primarily as survivors, not victims. Even those receiving public benefits looked to the day they would be free of welfare, and most struggled to learn English and find better jobs. As the years passed, they have continued to struggle for better jobs and options for their children, one man saying, "We are survivors. We are resilient. We are alive." Even when Cambodians spoke of themselves as victims, many acted as if they were not.

When Americans suggested Cambodians' experiences made them resistant to certain types of learning and risk-taking, Cambodians admitted they knew little about life in America when first resettled but have since learned from each person they meet. Since few Cambodians visited Americans or talked with them in other than an official capacity, they learned from television and observation. Cambodians asked questions constantly and listened to those around them, using what they heard to guide their behavior. When I asked a young girl what she meant when she talked about "spans," she said fellow students used the term to refer to Hispanics. Learning it was derogatory, she exclaimed, "Oh, that's why Carlos got angry when Bong called him that." Parents learned from children, who themselves were learning rapidly at school and from peers.

Amazed at Americans' ideas and behaviors, Cambodians were astonished at Americans' ignorance of knowledge Khmer considered basic. Women in the 1980s were surprised that doctors did not know suspending scissors or a knife over a mother's head during childbirth "cut" the mother's pain. The staff at one hospital solicited donations from local churches because Cambodians did not bring infant clothing, asking one another, "Didn't they know they were going to have a baby?" When an American asked him the same question, a Khmer man said indignantly, "Don't Americans know that the Khmer way is not to prepare anything before the birth? We get the baby clothes after we know everything is okay." Since Americans seemed to know so little about childbirth, Cambodians said they were not surprised at their ignorance of other physiological facts, such as the fact that men who make love to women with pear-shaped breasts will die. Cambodians said Americans were also ignorant of basic Buddhist concepts; one Khmer monk thought it strange that "Americans call a man a monk if he wears a robe, even if he sleeps with women."

They felt humiliated when Americans assumed they were ignorant about hygiene and cooking and handed out brochures that seemed to imply that Cambodians were damaged or diseased. They said they disliked feeling invisible and beneath notice and hated Americans' contempt of them. Several Khmer told me they had come to expect contempt and arrogance, even from many of those who assisted them. An American living with a Khmer family said, "Have you seen how dirty they are, how many cockroaches there are? Cambodians don't know anything about our culture." The American did not realize family members were being nice to him, although they did not like him. Many Cambodians were hurt when Americans said they were not welcome in America, did not deserve public assistance, were displacing Americans in college and jobs, and were causing inner-city problems. Cambodians complained that media accounts sensationalized Khmer misdeeds and gang activity and minimized stories about successful Cambodians. Cambodians were also angered when they felt slighted. Complaining about a visiting American student, a temple board president said, "He was not respectful to our monks. He should not come to our temple again."

Cambodians were surprised by what they said was American naiveté. When a young Khmer woman told compatriots, "There are small farm stands where you take the vegetables and just leave your money in a pot," her disbelieving listeners said that was unlike the Americans they knew. Cambodians spoke approvingly of the lack of corruption in America (Bruno and Kuras 1984), admired American bureaucratic efficiency, and spoke highly of American generosity, but were shocked at the lack of etiquette, saying Americans are too loud and direct and exaggerated in their gestures, swinging their arms and stomping around carelessly. Cambodians mocked the gracelessness of American women, who walk noisily and clumsily, "like horses." Their greatest dismay was reserved for

American sexual mores. Cambodians contrasted Khmer with American women, noting the reserve, gentleness, and purity of the former and the brashness and promiscuity of the latter. Cambodians said men want to marry a virgin who is quiet, will stay home, and take care of the home, not women who are selfish and ignore family and propriety, suggesting that Khmer women had the first characteristics, and Americans the second.

Cambodians also expressed surprise at Americans' innocent perspective on male-female friendships, which Cambodians said are impossible. One woman told how her husband regularly came home late, saying he was with an American woman with whom he was "just friends." Spitting out her words, she said, "Whoever heard of a man who has a 'friend' who is a woman?" Cambodians pointed to abortion as further evidence of American immorality, saying it is the same as "killing a baby." Cambodians saw sexual abuse as even more indicative of American immorality, saying they drove miles to place their children with trusted relatives or friends who "don't do that kind of thing" rather than leave them with American babysitters or day-care workers. Every account of sexual abuse set off a fresh burst of dismayed comments from Cambodians I knew.

Cambodians also say their emphasis on cooperation is preferable to Americans' focus on competition and pointed to the smugness of resettled Khmer children when they won and their bitterness when they lost at New Year games as evidence of American influence. Cambodians claim they value friends more than Americans do, saying friends are like relatives who are trustworthy and dependable, and friends must be loyal, even when their friends are wrong. When a woman asked her American professor friend to write a college paper for her, she was shocked at the professor's refusal. When the professor sought consolation from a highly educated Cambodian long in America, he told her that by refusing to write her friend's paper, she had ended their friendship, saying, "Between Cambodians, you have to do anything a friend asks." Many Cambodians agreed, but others said his comment was nonsense, saying they would not comply if a friend asked them to commit an immoral or illegal act.

Cambodians frequently say Americans are hard. A respected monk, Venerable Maha Ghosananda, said American culture "is not very good for Buddhist people because Buddhist people are very gentle, very soft, and here very hard, not so soft, and not so gentle" (Levin and Hott 1991). Some Cambodians conclude Americans are not religious because they act so poorly to one another. They speak of American cruelty, saying it is frequently displayed in public. An educated Khmer described his first contact with Americans while sitting at dinner his first week of school in the 1960s. When fellow diners asked about his life, he said his mother died when he was six, and although he found the telling difficult, he smiled through the story. An American misunderstood his smile and asked how he could be so unfeeling about the death of his own mother. Twenty-five years later, he asked, "How could this woman be so cruel?" He could not understand why the woman did not realize his smile masked his grief and said he has not liked Americans since that day. Cambodians wonder why Americans are also cruel to people they know. A few days ago, a Khmer woman called to ask, "Did you hear about that American woman who cut off her baby's head? How can she do that?" Her own three children died during the Pol Pot years.

Cambodians and their traditions benefit from their comparisons of themselves with Americans. Although they admire Americans' techno-logical advances, most first-generation Cambodians see much of Khmer culture as more complex, interesting, and insightful than American cul-ture and their values more useful. After resettlement, Americans became potent symbols of how life should not be lived, but what Cambodians feared they and their children were becoming. Cambodians often expressed delight and relief that they were not like Americans, and in the earlier years of resettlement, Cambodians suggested American problems could be dealt with by using Khmer ideas. One man suggested America's drug problem could be solved by putting drug addicts and dealers in pris-ons in the forest. Another suggested that Khmer construction is preferable to American work because it is simpler, explaining that in Cambodia, "Nobody hires a carpenter. You do it yourself. You don't have to follow all the rules and make it so difficult." Despite their disappointments with Americans and occasionally despairing of being understood, Cambodians never stopped trying to explain themselves to anyone who would listen, particularly sponsors, teachers, and friends.

Gratitude was a theme that ran through refugee and American discus-sions of their relationships with one another. While often grateful for their relationships, Cambodians and Americans frequently viewed one another as ungrateful, especially in the first years of resettlement. Americans said they gave resources and services to Cambodians out of a sense of char-ity and wanted nothing in return, but most expected gratitude and were irritated when they did not receive it. When a Cambodian explained that Cambodians often do not express gratitude verbally because they see relationships as reciprocal, with favors to be returned in the future, or con-sider respect and obedience sufficient gratitude, one American responded, "They should at least say 'Thank you.'"

Cambodians were also annoyed when Americans did not recognize their efforts on Americans' behalf. One woman said her colleagues con-stantly ask her to contribute egg rolls for potlucks but do not appreci-ate how much time it takes to make them. Yet both Cambodians and

Americans talked about their gratitude for the other. Cambodians said they were grateful to America for resettlement and to all those who assisted them and said they were honored when Americans recognized their suffering. When Khmer children were killed in Stockton, their families said they were honored when the governor and other officials attended the funerals (Kam 1989). A monk and PhD candidate at Brandeis University said that despite his suffering from American bombing, he had come to love America for its beauty and "open-minded, very honest people" (Nealon 2001).

After a Khmer temple was vandalized in Minnesota, Americans helped clean up. In reaction, one Cambodian said, "I was getting goosebumps because I was so happy" (Russell 2010). Modesto Cambodians were appreciative of American assistance in gaining permits to build a temple, one saying, "I was overwhelmed with joy and my heart was touched like never before when many different groups of people from different faiths came to support our cause" (Ry Kea 2010). Cambodians were grateful to neighbors with whom they shared information, assistance, childcare, and food and possessions. A Haiti and a Khmer woman who could not speak to one another shared bread and laughter as they watched their children play, lent one another food and kitchen items, and walked to language class together, and their relief was obvious as, over the months, they were increasingly able to communicate and share their gratitude for one another's assistance during their struggles.

The first struggle of Khmer refugees in America was economic survival.

Chapter Two

Economic Survival

After arrival in the United States, Cambodians needed to find employment in order to survive, although their definition of adjustment differed from that of Americans. Cambodians wanted to return to living *as Cambodians,* while Americans wanted Cambodians to become *like Americans.* The 1980 Refugee Act provided three years of cash and programs to assist refugees in becoming self-sufficient, defined as families being able to meet their basic needs without reliance on outside assistance. States differed in their approach to assisting refugees in achieving self-sufficiency. Work-first advocates said refugees should find work immediately and access language and vocational training courses in their nonworking hours. In contrast, training-first advocates said ill-prepared and traumatized Cambodians did better gaining English and American job skills before they sought employment.

Khmer Expectations and American Marketplace

The work-first philosophy prevailed in the South, one minister saying, "It is God's will that we work for our living," while the training-first philosophy was used in many northern and western states. Increasing numbers of refugees arrived in the early 1980s as the American economy weakened, and government and agency pressure grew for refugees to quickly find jobs. Funding increasingly focused on assistance that aided employment: job training and language programs supplemented by childcare, transportation, and tuition (North, Lewin, and Wagner 1982).

Cambodians were surprised to learn their refugee camp classes imposed no obligation on American employers to hire them. Heng's certificate that recommended giving him "the highest consideration for any position which he may choose to seek upon his arrival" carried no weight when he applied for work. His GED scores revealed why he was not qualified:

in the science and math courses he had taught in Cambodia, his scores as a student in America were much worse than those of his American classmates. Americans were dismayed by Cambodians' lack of education and often overlooked their abilities. One American volunteer was disheartened by an illiterate man's single year of schooling. Muttering one day that it was difficult to get competent workers in her shop, he replied, "Yes, I had that problem, too." Thinking he had misunderstood her, she asked, "You had employees working for you in Cambodia?" "Yes, in my fruit garden," he replied. Initially concluding he was an orchard foreman, she subsequently learned he had employed hundreds in his own orchards and factories. He used his management skills to operate a janitorial service business in America for over twenty years.

Cambodians frequently knew better than Americans the paths appropriate for them. A nursing aide student told me in 1982 he was quitting to go to California. I urged him to stay with the course, since jobs were promised to graduates. Despite my advice, he found work in California and, three years later, proudly told me he was making "four times what you earn, Carol," producing pay stubs to prove it. When another man said he was moving to California to open a doughnut shop and refused the job found for him in a tight job market, I pointed out the risks and urged him to stay. He politely refused, moved his extended family to Southern California, and a decade later owned four shops and a restaurant. While Americans generally knew better than refugees the realities of the American workplace, Cambodians knew more about their own capabilities and had access to immigrant knowledge.

Cambodians quickly realized that finding employment was not easy. Most were former farmers who had cultivated rice and vegetables; plowing and harrowing fields by oxen; fertilizing the soil with cow dung or salt; repairing dikes; transplanting seedlings; chasing away crabs, caterpillars, grasshoppers, and birds from the crops; and weeding, regulating water, and conducting rituals to ensure a good harvest before harvesting the rice by sickle and threshing it by hand. America's enormous fields, straight furrows stretching beyond sight, massive machinery, and extensive irrigation systems were nothing like the fields at home. Cambodians remembered a homeland where food was abundant, easily grown or caught, inexpensive or free, and an individual working diligently could cultivate food adequate for an extended family. In America, Cambodians said one person's wages was inadequate to support even one person without public assistance.

Differences between urban jobs in Cambodia and America were also stark. Darany's former job as a bank clerk included selling lottery tickets. Piseth had sold fuel by purchasing two liters of fuel at the distributor's home, walking to his downtown Phnom Penh corner to sell small plastic bags of gas for a few cents, and repeating the steps when he sold out. Unable to convince a Detroit gas station owner that he had relevant job experience, he washed dishes, describing it as "woman's work" he would never have done in Cambodia. Samnang drove a taxi in Phnom Penh but could not read a map or comprehend road signs in Los Angeles. Those more prepared to enter similar occupations adapted more easily than refugees who did not (Stein 1979), but they were few in number. Some Cambodians refused employment they considered beneath them, resented working long hours for low wages, or felt they were owed for their suffering, but most worked at anything to survive. Some made spectacular gains: one Cambodian became a presidential aide, another a MacArthur Fellow, and a number became doughnut franchise owners. Most Khmer refugees, however, remained in low-wage jobs.

Contrasts between refugees' lives in pre-Khmer Rouge Cambodia and after resettlement were startling. Rice farmers polished furniture in Massachusetts, packed plastic bags in South Carolina, stacked pizza boxes in Florida, slaughtered chickens in Kansas, made air conditioners in Texas, assembled computer boards in California, and processed peas in Washington and salmon in Alaska. In Cambodia, Phinh was a utility office clerk until 1971, a soldier until 1975, a canal-digging slave until 1978, and a refugee camp medical aide until 1981. In America, he worked as a janitor and a social worker. In Cambodia, farmers followed the sun's course to determine activities, rising when it rose and resting when it reached the treetops, but in America, Cambodians were surprised at rigid work schedules calculated to a fraction of an hour.

Cambodians complained that work in America seldom stops, saying repeatedly, "There's no time to rest!" They wondered why Americans chose work over family activities, yet did not seem to enjoy their work, spending their weekdays waiting for weekends. Cambodians recalled interspersing the hard labor of plowing and transplanting rice with singing, talking, and laughter in Cambodia. Roth said that in Cambodia, "I worked at the factory and made a good income to support my family. I was never worried about being homeless or not having money." Cambodians also emphasized how hard they had worked. One woman said Americans work eight hours and say they are tired, disdainfully adding, "They don't know anything about hard work." She said that in Cambodia women pounded rice, carried water, cooked food and hauled it in large pots to the men, and worked in the fields.

Because white-collar workers in Cambodia did not work with their hands and considered themselves superior to those who did, resettled Cambodians were confused by white-collar–manual-labor distinctions:

manual workers making higher wages than some white-collar workers, plumbers or contractors making more than receptionists or professors, and welders or electricians requiring more training than clerks or ticket takers. Cambodians were surprised that advancement to white-collar work often includes a period of manual labor and by Americans' lack of shame in laboring manually for wages or leisure—a professor repairing her car or a businessman with a Mercedes cleaning his home. Cambodians were especially surprised when Americans expected them to do manual labor. When I strung Christmas tree lights, moved office furniture, or cleaned up after a festive event, Khmer men were more likely to stand aside than join in, wondering at women who would do such work. Khmer women usually helped, thinking this was woman's work in this country.

Employment Strategies

Social mobility was limited in 'Cambodia; without resources, few could obtain the education and contacts needed for lucrative jobs. A few elite Khmer refugees, most resettled in 1975, had resources and American contacts. In America, a few purchased restaurants or obtained good jobs, although most had to live more frugally and work harder than they had in Cambodia. Others huddled at home, stunned by what they had lost, ignored by Americans, and isolated from other Cambodians. The aspirations of middle-class Cambodians, in contrast, expanded after arrival.

When Cambodians encountered barriers to "sitting down" jobs in their own field, many turned to any white-collar position they could find; professors worked as interpreters, doctors as technicians, and generals as janitors. Humiliated by their work, several said ruefully, "At least I have a job." Family obligations forced many to give up educational opportunities to work. Refugees often misunderstood the workplace. One man refused to apply for a bilingual position he considered menial, although he lacked sufficient English to get the job. He worked for years as a janitor and, when his job title shifted to "custodian," was pleased at what he considered a promotion, although he did not understand why his wages remained the same.

Many Khmer took second jobs. Prak worked days as a church secretary and nights as a custodian, helping countrymen with paperwork for employment, benefits, and school in his free time. His night job brought him money, but his office and volunteer work brought him status. Some Khmer men kept the fingernail on one or both little fingers long to indicate that they were not laborers. Some became bilingual workers, allowing them to care for their families while expanding their personal influence.

Many could not understand why Americans would work as volunteers and interns without pay, although some took advantage of such opportunities to gain experience and contacts that turned into jobs.

Sokha volunteered at his sponsor's fast-food franchise for several months before being hired to be in charge of the night shift, accepting, sorting, and storing supplies and preparing for the next day, a job he held for many years. Chhay's position as a full-time volunteer for a refugee agency led to a full-time job. Some former white-collar workers preferred welfare to manual work, and others moved to find work that did not involve physical labor. Several men avoided manual labor jobs by becoming monks. Cambodians said politely they found it difficult to believe I cut asparagus, grapes, and tomatoes, picked fruit, weeded beets, packed salmon eggs, and worked as a nurse's aide and veterinarian assistant as a student. In Cambodia, children whose families had funds to send them to school did not need to work. While most Khmer refugees agreed with one man who said, "I will do whatever they ask me to do," Cambodians unable to learn English or American job skills often found it difficult to find employment and were usually limited to entry-level, low-paying, and often part-time jobs. The greater the age and the worse their experiences and health, the more difficulty Cambodians had finding employment.

Although some uneducated Cambodians able to learn English found lucrative employment, including as car, insurance, or real estate salesmen, many transferred their employment hopes to their children. One illiterate father asked me in 1985 to complete medical school application forms for his high school daughter and did not understand my explanation that at the rate she was acquiring high school credits, she would not graduate for fifteen years. The daughter realized long before her parents that their dreams were unrealistic and married and took a job at McDonalds. Her father remained saddened that she was not going to be a doctor. Refugees with little English or American job experience found the workplace especially challenging during the 1981, 1991, and 2001 recessions. The 2008 recession struck Cambodians especially hard.

Cambodians sought employment with the assistance of Americans, relatives, and countrymen. Fellow Cambodians sometimes urged others to move to their area for employment. Saran said he could not find a full-time job in Stockton, California, "fitting to me," so he moved to Bakersfield and was soon working in the restaurant where his cousin was employed. Some field, factory, and restaurant managers hired English-speaking Khmer supervisors to oversee Cambodians doing low-paying, repetitive work. Aided by his American sponsor, one man found employment at an electronics assembly plant and helped twelve non-English-speaking

Cambodians get jobs there. Cambodians often found work at locations where refugees had established a good reputation; Khmer Cham in one town easily found jobs in clam processing plants that already employed Cham. One employer said, "Cambodians are wonderful workers. If you let them go to the temple on special days, they will do anything for you on the job." His Khmer workers said they did not mind his stereotyping, saying, "We get lots of freedom."

In the Northwest, Cambodians working in casinos drew others to the work; although demanding, many positions required minimal training, paid good wages, and quickly awarded promotions, and a number of Khmer kitchen aides and cleaners became supervisors. An advertisement posted at several Khmer temples in 2010 announced in Khmer and English that the Northwest Casino School offered eight weeks of training for jobs paying between $40,000 and $60,000 a year. Numerous second-generation Cambodians found casino employment; although many were poorly educated, they spoke English, understood American customs, and interacted easily with customers.

Cambodians often stayed with their jobs for years. One woman did the same hospital work in 2016 she was doing in 1981, folding and distributing bedding to linen closets on each floor. One man said he remained at the same job because "Cambodians don't move away from their families." Some stayed, afraid they could get no other. Other Cambodians sought economic advancement by increasing their English or job skills, seeking better jobs, or creating businesses. They imitated Americans, learning to give firm handshakes and direct gazes, wearing similar clothing, and reserving sarongs, scarves, and head coverings for nonwork hours. Some worked two shifts a day every day of the week for years on end. An assembly parts worker in 2016 continued to work seven days a week, at least ten hours a day. Although he owns six rental houses, he says he cannot rest because "I am worried about my future."

Khmer refugees without time or money for training also sought to improve their work situation. Nakry worked long hours at a shrimp-packing machine. Talk was forbidden, the smell was overwhelming, and the spraying liquid turned her face dark; finally, she said, "I just couldn't work there anymore." She then found work boxing medicine bottles; there was no heavy lifting, but the bottle tops burned her fingers. Tiring of standing all day at an assembly line, she continued to seek better working conditions. One man was a waiter, cook, janitor, insurance salesman, teacher, factory worker, and vending machine distributor interspersed with unemployment as he sought a position that would give him "money, importance, and friends." His wife's fourteen years at the same restaurant sustained them during his search.

Typical of many Khmer refugees, one extended family who had limited education and employment in Cambodia consisted three decades later of three janitors, two orderlies, a cafeteria supervisor, and an elementary school paraprofessional. Four family members resettled as teenagers, and their spouses, after studying English and attending job training courses in America, became employed as hospital technicians. Family members who arrived as children attended college and became a pharmacist, nurse, computer consultant, and biologist. The family's grandchildren are in high school and college, several on full scholarships, and all are planning on extensive schooling and professional careers.

Supplemental Income

To support families, some Cambodians added part-time work to full-time jobs. Families pooled wages, welfare, and food stamps and staggered their work shifts to care for children and gain work skills. Mothers took classes or found work when their children began school, those without English often in ethnic restaurants or on assembly lines with Khmer supervisors. Vithu worked as a hospital orderly, caring for his children after work while his wife attended classes and later became a medical technician. Kesor stayed home with her children while her husband, Chann, worked as a dishwasher. When the children entered school, she became a waitress, and Chann shifted to part-time work while attending vocational school. When he found work at a shipyard, Kesor took computer programming classes and worked as an electronics programmer after Chann was laid off. Anticipating the layoff, he made double payments on his house and saved $20,000; he received unemployment compensation while learning computer programming and advanced rapidly when rehired.

Many women worked as seamstresses, tailoring Khmer-styled clothing for everyday wear, weddings, and other special occasions; sold Khmer silk, earrings, belts, and ankle and wrist bracelets; rented wedding jewelry and costumes; prepared baked goods and traditional sweets such as coconut jelly, shaved ice, or fried bananas for Khmer restaurants; sold noodle soup, homegrown vegetables, and spices at Buddhist events; repackaged fruit and fish purchased wholesale for sale to neighbors; and produced wedding photographs and videography. Households rented rooms, often to college students or young working singles. A man with a bad leg and arm and no relatives in America lived with a Khmer family for many years, contributing money from his social security check for food, cigarettes, and a weekly bottle of liquor and spending most of his time in his room listening to Khmer music.

Numerous women did piecework for American companies, allowing them simultaneously to care for children and homes and contribute financially to the family. In a scene similar in dozens of cities, a woman or two sat at home on the couch or at a table with a baby or toddlers at the feet, often joined by family members as they sewed by hand or with industrial sewing machines. Surrounded by plastic bags or cardboard boxes filled with cuffs, collars, pockets, or sleeves, they worked with the television usually on. Delivery men transported materials back to the factory, where they were sewed onto garments. Piecework was tedious, often done in poorly lit or ventilated apartments, and frequently led to expensive repairs of equipment, high utility costs for their homes, and neighbors complaining of blown fuses and noisy machines.

Pay was low, so working rapidly and for long hours was important. Khmer women in the Bronx in 1984 were paid five cents for each stitched pocket. Some merchants provided women with sewing machines, which they paid off by making hair clips and scarfs (Bruno 1984); after machines were paid for, workers received seventy cents per dozen items. Two decades later, a Cambodian in Los Angeles earned ten cents for each basted necktie, completing between twelve and fifteen dozen every few days. She was fortunate if she earned seventy-five to one hundred dollars a week when working, but the factory often sent her no work at all. Other Khmer supported themselves by working seasonally at landscaping, cleaning, moving, and construction jobs that required little English, but the work was physically demanding and undependable.

Harvesting forest products in the Pacific Northwest has sustained numerous families for decades, not only first-generation refugees unable to learn English, but many of their English-speaking children. Mushroom season extends from September until snowfall in November, with mushrooms producing in abundance every three years but only for a few days. They are also difficult to find and must be sold immediately to buyers. Prices vary from fifty cents to six dollars a pound, and some pickers can gather two hundred pounds a day. When prices are high and picking plentiful, Cambodians earn as much as $6,000 weekly—a rare event, but when it happens, one picker said, "We sing and dance and are very happy."

When prices are low, pickers also collect smaller mushroom buttons in the forest duff, and when mushrooms are unavailable, Cambodian pickers gather bear grass, salal, moss, shrubs, ferns used in flower arrangements, and cascara bark used as a natural laxative. Less profitable than mushrooms, they are available more months of the year and are more easily found. In the mid-1990s, a salal bunch fifteen to eighteen inches in length with good leaves untouched by caterpillars brought about $1.60.

Women add to the family's profits by tying bear grass into bundles at home, earning as much as $300 to $500 a day.

Pickers often work twelve hours a day, traversing steep inclines through heavy brush to find yellow, white, oyster, and pine mushrooms in old growth timber. Men pull themselves up and down the mountains hand over hand, tree by tree, returning with large bags of mushrooms on their backs. Pickers speak of traveling to forests in car convoys and living in their cars for several days. Women accompany them to prepare food, or pickers purchase soup and noodles from food sellers in the parking lot. Pickers say permit systems are difficult to follow because regulations differ for each forest product, and violations are common. The work is dangerous; pickers told of three men dying from exploding propane heaters used in cars for warmth and of families driving off mountain roads.

They also face violence from other pickers when Khmer, often unknowingly, ignore forest boundaries and neglect unwritten agreements. Native or white Americans lead Cambodian pickers who cannot read maps or signs to trespass on restricted land, leaving them to be caught by rangers. One Cambodian said he would like to get "the book Americans use for finding mushrooms," but it costs $80 or $120 and, he added, "I can't read English anyway." Some retaliation is deadly. A Cambodian was robbed of his cash and matsutake mushrooms and shot to death in October 1992 in southern Oregon, and another was killed in eastern Oregon in June 1993, probably for his morel mushroom earnings (Cockle 1995). In 2008, pickers were attacked when gathering morel mushrooms after a forest fire (Kimball 2008). Some Khmer pickers carry knives and guns for protection. Yet considerable cross-cultural communication and cooperation have occurred. In 2008, pickers converged on Boise National Forest to harvest mushrooms, share information and food, sing karaoke, and watch movies on a big-screen television run off a generator buried in the forest to muffle its sound (Hoffman 2008).

Muslim Cham have been harvesting forest products for over thirty years, at first because they could not speak English, they could be together, and the forests reminded them of Cambodia. In 2014, a leader speaking fluent English said forest products are his major source of income, adding that Cham are proud they can support their families, live in a close community, and observe their traditions. He noted also that no one is on welfare. Pickers can follow their own schedule, the whole family can participate, and the harder they work, the more they make. He noted, however, that some pickers are wearing down from the physical demands of the work and wonder how long they can continue.

Creating Businesses

Since the early 1980s, Cambodians have talked of owning a restaurant, laundry, or store so they would not have to work for someone else or rely on undependable jobs. A number succeeded, opening restaurants; food, video, flower, jewelry, and clothing stores; currency exchanges, bakeries, hair salons, and pharmacies; and sewing and alteration, auto repair, and pawn shops. Business areas developed around Anaheim Street in Long Beach, California, and Chelmsford Street in Lowell, Massachusetts, both areas officially referred to as "Cambodia Town," and in Chicago's Uptown district. After the early 1990s, Cambodian Americans educated in America found employment that providing technological and management skills to businesses, government, and nonprofit organizations in Cambodia.

Many Cambodians said Chinese Cambodian refugees are more successful than ethnic Cambodians in opening businesses because they have family ties, business expertise, and access to capital. They also funnel profits back into the business, while ethnic Cambodians are more interested in buying a house, making contributions to the temple, and sponsoring religious and life-cycle ceremonies. In the 1990s, Chinese Cambodians composed 6 percent of Boston's Khmer population but accounted for approximately 85 percent of Khmer business activity (Smith-Hefner 1995), and since 2000, over 80 percent of Khmer businesses in Long Beach are owned by Chinese Cambodians. While Chinese Cambodians tend to own restaurants often staffed by extended family members, ethnic Cambodians prefer to own hair and nail salons and small stores, usually run by women.

Although many Chinese Cambodians have been successful, many want their children to find jobs that free them from long hours, backbreaking labor, and lack of status. Several Chinese Cambodians mentioned Cambodia's former ambassador to Taiwan who established a restaurant in America after resettlement, saying his status did not assist in his business's success, nor did his restaurant enhance his status. Cambodians often saved money for years to open their own businesses. Oregon Cambodians saved wages earned in entry-level jobs to purchase businesses from Cambodians in California, who themselves then moved to Oregon for peace and quiet (Chan 2003). Other Cambodians received start-up funds from government and nonprofit agencies. A refugee office in Tacoma utilized federal funding and staff technical support to help set up a Khmer-owned janitorial service that remained in operation into the 2000s.

More commonly, Cambodians borrowed money from family and friends. Chinese Cambodians utilized a rotating credit system, in which participants contribute small amounts of money to a pool on a weekly or monthly basis (Flinn 1995). When the pool holds several thousand dollars, the total is loaned to a bidder, who opens a business. His repayments replenish the pot, which is then loaned to another participant. Others began with smaller sums.

Cambodians from Florida to Southern California purchase fish and seafood from fishermen and sell to Asian restaurants and markets. Learning a few words of Spanish, Vietnamese, and Lao, a Khmer woman named Rasmeay followed Northwest crops from berries in June to cucumbers in August, selling food to migrant workers from her van. Up at three in the morning to fix food for the day, she drove to the fields to make her sales, selling a can of soda she purchased for ten cents for seventy-five cents. With expenses of $300, she cleared more than $1,000 a day. With her summer's profits, she began selling Mary Kay cosmetics and continued until her sample case and $10,000 worth of products were stolen from her car. Another Cambodian purchased bananas, long beans, cucumbers, persimmons, papayas, Fuji squash, and oyster mushrooms each morning in Los Angeles, then drove slowly through refugee neighborhoods in Orange County selling his wares from his "Cham Produce" white panel truck.

Numerous first-generation Cambodians achieved their "American dream" with doughnut shops that require little space to make and sell doughnuts. Cambodians needed no certification, previous baking experience, or English fluency to sell doughnuts, one Khmer saying, "You don't have to explain the product, and you don't have to close the sale" (Flinn 1995). A "good morning," a gesture to the desired doughnut, and a "thank you" and smile suffice. Flour, sugar, and shortening are inexpensive, and baking doughnuts is easy to learn. Profits are thin, however, usually about ten cents on a fifty-cent doughnut, and hours are long and grueling, with bakers typically rising at two or three in the morning to bake for the morning trade. Cambodians frequently note the doughnut business is good for large families, since family members can provide much of the labor pool.

A Chinese Cambodian named Bun Tek Ngor was the Khmer doughnut pioneer, making a fortune selling doughnuts and helping other Khmer open doughnut shops (Quinones 2005). A former army officer, Ngor worked as a janitor before getting a job at a Long Beach Winchell's doughnut shop. He saved and borrowed enough in a year to buy his first doughnut shop, then borrowed money from a loan society to purchase additional stores (Ardery 2008). Exhausted by the work, Ngor began leasing shops to refugees arriving in the early 1980s, teaching baking, marketing, bookkeeping, and application procedures, co-signing loans for supplies and equipment, and helping new owners find housing and apply for social security cards. According to Ngor, none of the refugees who entered into handshake deals with him failed.

Ngor became a respected millionaire, owning shops from San Diego to San Francisco, multiple homes, and Mercedes-Benz convertibles (Flinn 1995). He met former presidents Reagan and Nixon, held fundraisers for George HW Bush, and urged other immigrants to support Republicans. As his tenants prospered, however, Ngor took up gambling and eventually lost his fortune, his first wife, a political career in Cambodia, and a second wife. Meanwhile, his legacy continued. Cambodians continued to buy shops; in the early 1980s, shops went for $20,000 to $30,000, and by the late 1990s, opening costs had increased to over $50,000 (Ong 2003). By the mid-1990s, Cambodians owned an estimated 80 percent of California's twenty-four hundred doughnut shops.

In the twenty-first century, Khmer-owned doughnut shops are also located in Texas, Louisiana, Tennessee, Kentucky, the Northwest, and New England. A woman posted in March 2012 that she was opening a doughnut shop in Attalla, Alabama, although, she writes, "Don't know any cambodians [sic] in Alabama" (BaoChannara 2012). Competition between Cambodians is stiff, even in small towns such as Gladewater, Mount Pleasant, Athens, and Alvin in Texas. Initially not familiar with doughnuts, Cambodians have expanded their repertoire of ethnic American food to include central European puffy dough fruit pastries known as *kolaches*, popular in Texas, and tamales, popular in California.

After the 2008 recession, some Khmer-owned doughnut shops closed (Robbins 2010), while others added Chinese food, one shop advertising "Cambodian, Thai and Laos Cuisine and Doughnuts" with doughnuts on one counter and Khmer and Thai curries, salads, and noodle dishes on another. Some owners make doughnuts for the breakfast trade and Chinese food for lunch; others buy doughnuts and cook their own Chinese food. Owners point out that both doughnut and Chinese ingredients are inexpensive, familiar, and simple to cook, and customers need not speak English to buy food they can quickly carry away.

Some Cambodians doubt Khmer doughnut shop ownership will endure, claiming shops are not being taken over by the second generation because they want education and professional jobs. However, the recession convinced a number of second-generation Cambodian Americans to reconsider, and other owners continue because family members are still migrating from Cambodia to join families with the resources to provide business capital. Cambodians sometimes accuse doughnut shop owners of caring more for their families than the community. One owner who was once a strong advocate for refugees was criticized for refusing a doughnut to a street person, saying he was not a shelter, food center, or the Salvation

Army, and he did not want to pay taxes twice (Chan 2003). Some saw his red Jaguar as evidence of his avarice.

Public Assistance

A number of Americans encouraged Cambodians to utilize public assistance because of the trauma they had endured under the Khmer Rouge, in the refugee camps, and during resettlement. Thinking they needed time to gain English and American job training or were unable to find work, Americans helped Khmer apply for benefits. Other Americans discouraged welfare utilization and assisted Cambodians in finding jobs. Bilingual workers discouraged or encouraged welfare use according to the attitudes of the welfare office, community, and worker. Bopha was instructed by her supervisor in 1981 to encourage refugees to apply, while Thom was instructed by his boss in 1983 to tell Cambodians to find jobs or they would be returned to the refugee camps. Bilingual workers often decided on their own whether to encourage or discourage use, well aware that an increase in the number of clients provided job security in a relatively good-paying job, while a decrease meant probable job loss.

Cambodians were often critical of bilingual workers, distrusting their position of power, accusing them of not distributing resources fairly or of spreading client information with others in the community, and responding by exaggerating their needs. Some bilingual workers saw themselves as patrons, thus authority figures, rather than public servants serving their clients. Some had insufficient English to provide good assistance, lacked compassion, were patronizing or intimidating to clients, were competitors with the client's own patron, or did not fully understand American procedures and values. Others shielded themselves from emotional involvement because they could not meet all their clients' needs. Cambodians often expressed jealousy of bilinguals; since bilingual positions were filled on a first-come basis, later arrivals were often better qualified to hold the position than the first refugee to acquire it. Other refugees said it was inappropriate for young females to occupy positions of authority or male workers to assist young women and were displeased when bilinguals pressured them about marriage, reproduction, housekeeping, or child-rearing. Cambodians distrusted some bilingual workers because they had not lived through the Khmer Rouge years.

Yet many Khmer bilinguals provided invaluable information and assistance to their clients, saying they understood that refugee hostility often resulted from their continued dependency and sense of helplessness. The burden of client needs and demands caused a number of bilinguals to weary of clients' needs and demands. Their families complained of ever-ringing telephones and absent husbands or wives. When refugee services and resources were generous, tensions between bilingual workers and clients were low; when clients increased in number and funds ran low, tensions heightened. Many bilingual workers found it difficult to negotiate between the cultural expectations of American supervisors and client needs; Khmer needs were greater than many Americans could comprehend, as was the resistance of many clients to the regulations and demands of Americans. Tension was also common among staff. Expecting protection from American and Khmer supervisors, bilinguals were often shocked when told to improve their work or stop committing certain infractions. When one staffer was fired by her Khmer boss, she refused to look him in the face or greet him, even when they passed one another at the temple. An interpreter who learned an American was trying to get him investigated on charges of corruption said the American was trying "to kill him."

Many Cambodians welcomed public assistance, although they said they hated feeling helpless. Some new arrivals expected benefits, and even Cambodians with little English knew welfare lingo: AFDC (Aid to Families with Dependent Children, replaced by Temporary Assistance for Needy Families in 1996), social security, SSI (Supplemental Security Income, stipends to low-income people who are aged, blind, or disabled), GA (assistance for people without children), and WIC (offering supplemental foods, health care referrals, and nutrition education for women, infants, and children). One woman said she was not surprised to receive high-protein biscuits and vegetables for her baby and toddler because she had queued up for them in the camps.

Many Cambodians said they were entitled to get whatever America gave them because America owed them for not rescuing them from the Khmer Rouge. In the 1990s, some said they found it ironic that the United States assisted Kuwait, Somalia, and Iraq but failed to do the same for Cambodia. "If the United States was concerned about human rights, why didn't they help free Cambodia from Pol Pot or the Vietnamese?" a Khmer graduate student asked. Some said Americans recognized their obligations to Cambodians by offering them resettlement, and they expected welfare benefits as an extension of their resettlement. Although many Cambodians realized that most Americans saw welfare recipients as lazy and exploitative, they also knew many Americans saw welfare as an honorable alternate for refugees without relevant skills.

While a number of Khmer also viewed welfare as a welcome option, other Cambodians saw welfare as a travesty that encouraged dependency and laziness, discouraged Khmer from achieving self-sufficiency, depriving them of independence and pride, and counter to Buddhism's teachings on individual responsibility. Other Cambodians worried that second-generation Cambodians were becoming welfare dependent. One community leader said he repeatedly encouraged Cambodians to get off welfare, telling "his people the community would help anyone who gets a job and tries to help himself, but will not help anyone on welfare." Some Cambodians said they were proud they had never received welfare and instead had sufficient assistance from sponsors or relatives or found employment quickly.

Many Cambodians said they avoided welfare because they did not want to be viewed unfavorably, and many who had received benefits emphasized that their utilization had been only until they found employment. Many found public assistance a necessity. Households headed by widows or uneducated Cambodians with no English or American job skills had little recourse but public assistance, while others found that minimum-wage jobs provided insufficient family support. As children grew to adulthood, many also lacked the language, skills, and contacts to gain well-paying jobs and consequently dropped out of school, married early, and found entry-level work to help support parents and new families; many also needed to utilize full or supplemental public assistance.

Cambodians went to extraordinary lengths to comply with welfare requirements, waiting for hours in welfare offices, attending classes they did not understand, and revealing family information. One young woman waited an average of three hours every welfare visit. Others, however, became bitter when agencies were unable to satisfy their requests and saw aid as an attempt to subjugate them rather than as genuine charity. Most Cambodians wanted only to receive what they deserved or avoid losing what they were receiving, often for fear of being unable to pay for health care. Discouraged that their disabilities did not qualify them for SSI, others attempted to demonstrate their inability to work, undergoing surgery or visiting doctors, chiropractors, and mental health workers they hoped could document the consequences of life under the Khmer Rouge. Although reluctant to be considered "crazy," Cambodians accepted mental health services when they learned they could qualify for disability if mental distress prevented them from working.

Many Cambodians said they were "working the system" by imitating Americans. They moved to states with better benefit and training options, with California a favored destination, although they often found their situation worsened. Dom moved to Long Beach after a friend told him agencies paid their staff hefty wages. Since Dom spoke good English and had office experience, he applied for an agency position. After discovering

Long Beach refugee offices were actually stretching their dollars to assist refugees by paying low wages to overburdened and stressed employees, he returned to his previous town and job. Cambodians with satisfying jobs in states with few benefits, strong sponsors, and family or Khmer community nearby were more likely to remain in place than those who lacked employment or were receiving generous benefits.

Some responded to welfare requirements by marrying in a Khmer ceremony but not applying for a marriage license; women could then receive benefits as unmarried women. Some widows and unwed mothers retained their benefits by concealing relationships, living arrangements, or employment, disguising children's ages, presenting false addresses, getting pregnant, or distributing welfare checks among several households. A number of women eligible for WIC were glad for the inexpensive food but regretted the coupons could be exchanged only for specific items and complained that, unlike the refugee camps, they had to follow rules to receive food. Requirements for receiving benefits were often difficult to follow; one woman picked up bread at the market and said, "How can I read if it's okay to buy it? I can't even read the book my second grade son brings home." Following the advice of other immigrants, some refugees sold, traded, or gave away items that did not fit their lactose-intolerant diet or preferences, thus exchanging milk, cheese, juice, and peanut butter for money, status, gratitude, and the knowledge they were supporting their families and acting as members of a community.

Cambodians with benefits went to great effort to maintain them. Maly was careful to put her car's title in her daughter's name so it did not affect her benefits. Rachana was irritated when public housing increased her rent after she obtained a job teaching Khmer at the local university; her delight with winning a prestigious job over a disliked rival was replaced by dismay over her reduced benefits. Many Cambodians saw welfare as a field of opportunity and tried to get what they could because "one never knows what will happen." One man said in 1984, "Before, I suffered, and now things are better. We may suffer again, so we'd better go for all we can get now."

When a man said Cambodians should leave welfare as quickly as possible, his wife reminded him that when he said that to Cambodians, they "jumped all over us. They tell us, 'It isn't your money. Why do you care?'" Cambodians said Americans were naïve to set up easily exploited programs. In Khmer, "exploit" is literally "to eat," and Cambodians call welfare "what the king eats." Cambodians said they would "eat" the benefits until the government's money is gone, one man adding, "America is a golden mountain, yes, but it will eventually melt away." Many Khmer said they doubted they would be punished for their deeds, because the

Khmer Rouge were not punished for theirs. One man said, "In America, it seems no one's evil acts are punished. So why not take everything welfare has to offer, even if you have to lie for it?" Many thought they were less sinful for receiving welfare benefits than Americans who stole, hurt people, or used drugs, and some Khmer said stealing from the government was not as serious as stealing from other people; in Chamroeun's words, "America is very rich and there are many people. How can just a small number of Cambodians harm the money of this big country?"

As the welfare system expanded into the mid-1990s, so too did Americans' concern over a system that consumed billions of dollars and that many thought was supporting millions of nonproductive recipients. Benefits to refugees had already been reduced over the years, from three years to eighteen months in 1982, twelve months in 1989, and eight months in 1992. In August 1996, President Clinton signed the Personal Responsibility and Work Opportunity Reconciliation Act (PRWORA), ushering in the most significant and wide-sweeping welfare reform since the New Deal. The act shifted welfare programs from the federal to state level, and replaced Aid to Families with Dependent Children with state block grants. Policies shifted from improving opportunities to preventing welfare dependency through time limits, mandatory work requirements, and the reduction or elimination of in-kind food and medical assistance. In Los Angeles County, Cambodians were shifted from job training to immediate employment, and their grants were reduced for nonparticipation. As reform rumors circulated, refugees grew increasingly fearful, especially on hearing they faced deportation if they became public charges, one rumor that was untrue.

Many Cambodians could not understand requirement notifications and found regulations difficult to follow. They also worried about learning English, finding work, or passing the citizenship test; illiterate and unfamiliar with being students, many had already failed at becoming citizens or learning English. Application forms were available in Khmer but were useless to illiterate Cambodians. Many Khmer lost their benefits because they lacked transportation to the welfare office or were unable to keep appointments due to other mandatory obligations such as medical or school appointments. Some Cambodians considered moving in with relatives or roommates or returning to Cambodia, although money prevented most from doing so. A number of Cambodians thought the laws were intended to increase their hardship until they no longer wanted welfare (Applied Research Center 2001). In a sense, they were correct; welfare reform was a retreat from the support, policies, and goals of the 1980 Refugee Act, and for Americans, the victims of communism deserving of rescue in the 1970s had become welfare moochers in the 1990s.

The disciplining rules of welfare reform forced clients into demeaning, minimum-wage jobs without benefits or advancement potential. Cambodians struggling to find job training and jobs that satisfied requirements instead had to accept low-paying food service, light manufacturing, or home care jobs that were without benefits or part-time, with irregular shifts, limited opportunities for promotion, and high labor law violations. A California program prepared women to be caretakers for family members but paid them less than minimum wage to perform work costing far more in institutional settings. When caretakers were assigned less work, their cash grants were reduced because they had insufficient hours. New York welfare workers acknowledged but then ignored many Cambodians' lack of English and placed them in jobs that required them to read job duties, schedules, and instructions on cleaning solutions.

Non-English-speaking welfare recipients were given the dirtiest jobs or inadequate tools, were often unaware they could challenge unfair or unsafe labor practices, and were unable to speak out against injustices. One woman worked outside in freezing weather without gloves, boots, or heavy coat and received no redress when she complained. Several women described their situation as "lose-lose"; they worked for low wages doing piecework or preparing food for restaurants, but competition from others was steep, and "under-the-table" earnings did not fulfill work requirements. Communication by gesture led to poor work performance, ridicule from fellow workers, and unfair treatment, one worker saying that when he was sick, "The supervisor told my son that if I took a day off I would definitely be sanctioned" by welfare (Applied Research Center 2001: 29).

PRWORA curtailed clients' reproductive rights, condemned single parenting, encouraged birth control, and required clients to identify fathers, frustrating Cambodians eager to replace lost family members. Elders also suffered, for legal immigrants were barred from receiving SSI benefits until they became citizens or earned forty quarters of qualifying work, nearly impossible for most Khmer elders, especially those who were illiterate. Many lost their grants, while others substituted medical care with home remedies, moved in with family, or sought health treatment for physical or mental ailments in order to get benefits restored. Anxiety was the by-product of reform: working long hours at low-wage and demeaning work kept workers away from their families, and the ongoing worries about being able to support families and lack of hope for the future were dismaying for many. Cambodians spoke occasionally of those who succumbed to their despair by committing suicide. The burden on refugees was eventually acknowledged by the restoration of welfare benefits in 1997 to refugees who arrived prior to 1996. Despite the decision, a number of Cambodians had difficulty getting benefits restored, and fear of future cutoffs remained.

The use of welfare by refugees has been a constant topic of debate over the past decades, with numerous American citizens, officials, and refugee workers espousing a "myth of welfare dependency" for Cambodians. Not recognizing that many Cambodians were unable to find jobs or earn wages sufficient to support their families and were often encouraged by Americans to utilize benefits available to them, Americans resented supporting dependent refugees "looking for handouts" and criticized refugee programs for creating a new "underclass" of welfare dependents. However, refugee dependency as a characteristic of Khmer refugees and Cambodian Americans is a myth. Cambodians did not come to America valuing dependency, used welfare as sparingly as possible, and have done everything in their power to become self-sufficient. Welfare utilization has been high among Cambodians because of their situation: most Khmer refugees had little education and were hampered by their experiences, health, and resettlement itself, and their children have suffered from their parents' experiences and their own resettlement.

However resettlement was going for Khmer refugees, they said the past was always in their thoughts.

Chapter Three

Refugee Litanies

First-generation Cambodians told stories about life in Cambodia to explain their presence in the United States, saying they are here because of "Pol Pot," who forced four years of hell (*norok*) on them. They divide their lives into before, during, and after the Khmer Rouge. Although Cambodians put great effort into new lives in America, they were drawn repeatedly to the past: metaphorically facing the country they had left, and most trying to retain their identity as Khmer. Narratives are a way to do that, providing a bridge between the catastrophe that hit them and their lives.

After resettlement, Khmer discourse reflected complex memories of atrocities relayed in bits and pieces, their stories only later coming together in chronological order. Some told of their experiences soon after resettlement, others decades later, many saying they had no idea why they talked when they talked. Many found their words inadequate for description, and their experiences irreconcilable with a sensible world. Although Cambodians said their words were inadequate to decide their experiences, they kept trying, describing the Pol Pot time as staggering for its evil. Repeatedly, Cambodians said the Khmer Rouge were like the monsters of Khmer legend: Pol Pot's soldiers ate human livers, roasted fetuses, and impaled toddlers on knives.

Telling Stories

In 1981, an American introduced me to a Khmer arrival, saying, "Tell Carol what those communists did to you." He recoiled, laughed nervously, and said, "I don't understand what you say." Later, he said he understood the American but could not talk about his life on command. Grateful for the lesson, I resolved not to ask questions about Cambodians' experiences but to listen when they talked about them, and in the years after resettlement, they did so incessantly. Discussions on any topic turned into storytelling events as Cambodians recounted their experiences. Conversations began with one person and jumped to another, new voices rising over the first. As voices rose, they became more insistent, softening, grower louder, turning sometimes to tears, sometimes fading to silence.

Just as one Cambodian's story inspired the story of another, so specific smells, sounds, and sights turned Cambodians' thoughts to their past. One man said the taste of a dish recalled his father's death at the hands of the Khmer Rouge, and a mother said the smell of fire brought back the memory of her children's deaths. Two youth watching a video became upset at the sound of metal striking metal, saying it reminded them of being called to eat during the Pol Pot years, one teenager saying it caused "terrible feelings to my stomach." Walking outside to see a neighbor banging on his car's bumper did not assuage the boys' disquiet. Cambodians said certain songs brought nostalgia and grief, and listening to the car radio stirred up childhood memories of the years before the Khmer Rouge. *The Killing Fields* actor Haing Ngor (1987) said he was terrified by the resemblance of a young actress to his actual Khmer Rouge tormenter. The movie itself became a model for Khmer narratives, Cambodians saying it removed some of their shame as survivors and made Americans more sympathetic, but they also said it was not as bad as their own experiences, nor was there an American waiting in Thailand or a sponsor, job, and secure future awaiting them in America.

Cambodians' stories described their own experiences, knowing little of what had happened elsewhere. They told of being forcibly moved from one place to another, working on labor teams, worrying they would die, and more hesitantly, what they did to survive. They spoke of loved ones, what they suffered, and how some had died. Cambodians described the actions of the Khmer Rouge and their leader Pol Pot as a personal attack on them, saying, "Pol Pot killed my son," or "The Khmer Rouge made my mother starve to death." Because their stories were so incredulous, Cambodians occasionally expressed doubt over the truth of their own stories. "Did that really happen?" one woman asked after describing a horrific experience. Another said, "Sometimes I wonder if it was a dream." For most, there were no doubts, and Cambodians were offended by Americans who thought they exaggerated the horrors they had endured. Just as Khmer refugee reports of atrocities were initially dismissed by outsiders, although they were eventually found to be inaccurate only in having insufficiently described Khmer Rouge misdeeds, so many American listeners found Khmer tales unbelievable, not only for their details but by the way they were told: in jumbled bits, at unexpected moments, and often without affect.

Cambodians sometimes told stories with emotion, sometimes without. With no intonation in his voice, a colleague in our refugee office said one day, "I had a foster father. He killed himself. His wife was a student, but I don't know if she is alive now. Maybe they all died. She probably died. She had one baby, also, but maybe it died." He turned back to his paperwork. After listening to a refugee's story a few weeks later, he said it was hard to bear everything that had happened to him and proceeded to calmly describe his brother starving to death, despite his attempts to keep him alive. Gazing at me, he began to smile with cheek muscles clenched, tears welling in his eyes, and his face growing flushed. Over the months, he took less care to hide his grief, revealing it in ways and times that allowed us to continue our daily work. Meanwhile, he continued to listen to refugees' stories day after day, offering what comfort he could.

Other Cambodians also spoke of their experiences at unexpected moments. A teenager suddenly began describing the distress she experienced when wedged among people in a Khmer Rouge truck, trying not to become sick from the stench of feces and vomit. She ceased talking as abruptly as she began. Despite their spontaneity, Cambodians did not talk easily about the Khmer Rouge. Often in the middle of a story, the speaker paused, grimaced, or shrugged before continuing. Some had few words. One woman said, "They killed a lot of people. There wasn't enough water to drink or food to eat." She stopped and said nothing more. Others were unable to stop talking, and some who spoke compulsively at one moment were reticent at others.

After a few years, few Cambodians were telling their stories to Americans, explaining that Americans knew little about Cambodia, were too busy to listen, or found the stories they told in halting English jarring and difficult to comprehend. Cambodians said Americans cried, then forgot their tales or avoided them. "Maybe they think I am lying," one man told me, "or maybe my story is too sad." Although disconcerted when Cambodians talked dispassionately of their experiences, Americans were also disturbed by passionate descriptions. Their response was often that Cambodians needed to "get on with life." In response to specific stories or a general awareness of what Cambodians experienced, some Americans said they felt guilty for not protesting the war earlier or not helping Khmer refugees. Americans, including a prominent historian at a Halloween party in 1985, thanked me "for doing what we all should be doing."

Other Americans became inured to reports of disaster. A sociologist said in 1992, "That Cambodian thing is so old now; I'm surprised people still talk about it." A prominent anthropologist and refugee resettlement administrator explained his absence at a film on Cambodia on one early conference morning, saying, "That's too hard to take at 7:30 in the morning. It's a real downer." Americans initially willing to listen to Khmer survivor stories lost patience, one sponsor saying, "Oh, I just can't bear to hear it anymore." Some did not want to be reminded of suffering, irrational or brutal behavior, or the possibility that such things could happen to them.

Cambodians appreciated willing listeners. When a Moroccan immigrant described his Khmer wife's experiences as though they were his own, his wife said his tears and support help her "carry my memories." Others said they try to forget their experiences rather than relate them, sometimes avoiding dance and music or those who talk about "those times." Even in the cacophony of people describing their experiences in the early years, there were always people sitting silently, saying nothing, looking at the floor, often motionless. Many Cambodians did not talk even to their children. Others began talking but then said it was too painful to continue. Although Cambodian silence about their experiences during the Khmer Rouge years intensified over the years, the memories did not stop; many survivors sat silently at home trapped in their past.

Eventually, storytellers' tales became simpler. Some memories faded as others grew in importance. Cambodians' stories became litany, a recitation of events. Descriptions of their chaotic memories were replaced by recitations of a reduced number of ritualized memories of food scarcity, endless work, inhuman treatment, and dying loved ones. Reciting the litany made the words easier to say. Cambodians' recitations brought them camaraderie with other survivors and identified them as a unique people.

The Litany

Cambodians' litany consists of three parts: the brief beginning about the evacuations; the lengthy middle body that endured for years; and the conclusion that covers the abrupt end of the Khmer Rouge, flight from Cambodia, and life in Thailand's refugee camps.

The beginning litany dealt with evacuations that began on 17 April 1975 and continued for days or months, depending on the region and specific Khmer Rouge leaders. Telling residents that Americans were going to bomb the city, the Khmer Rouge forced two and a half million Cambodians to leave the capital of Phnom Penh. The Khmer Rouge also evacuated Cambodia's other cities, including Battambang and Kampong Cham. Cambodians left by car, on bicycles, on foot, or were carried, taking what they could or going empty-handed, thinking they would soon return. Cambodians hated talking about the evacuation, one man saying it reminded him that he was just beginning his years of horror. Descriptions of terrible evacuation moments were common: abandoning dying or dead loved ones, grabbing food from the weak, pushing past the injured, stepping over the dead. Cambodians said they could not turn back, only go forward.

The body of Cambodians' litany dealt with the events that followed the Khmer Rouge takeover and their evacuation of urban areas. Despite variation in their experiences, the middle body of Cambodians' litany dealt with Pol Pot atrocities, focusing on destruction, control, cruelty, work, hunger, fear, and loss. Destruction was a major theme, and refugees spoke often of the devastation wrought by the Khmer Rouge. Over the next years, after displacing the population from urban to rural areas, the Khmer Rouge destroyed Cambodia's transport, postal, financial, educational, religious, artistic, communications, trade, and political systems and abolished traditional ownership, money, taxes, and laws. Unlike some Khmer Rouge cadre who had motorbikes, bicycles, radios, watches, fountain pens, and special scarves, most Cambodians had no more than a spoon, fork, and two sets of clothes.

Cambodians said Khmer Rouge destruction included trying to eliminate the past. In one man's words, "Everything that we had, we had to burn or throw away," including traditional marriage rites. Instead "Pol Pot stood couples up together and had them shake hands." Hanna, who was married with thirteen other couples, said bitterly, "Never, never in Khmer culture before was it like that." Some said soldiers forbade the Khmer greeting of joining palms together (*sathu*), although others told of using the gesture frequently with cadres in their supplications for mercy. Despite Khmer Rouge efforts to abolish the past, tradition persisted. Cambodians surreptitiously tried to observe rituals, and almost everyone prayed, many constantly through the endless days, one woman exclaiming, "The Khmer Rouge couldn't stop the inside of my head!" Several said that after a group wedding, they wanted desperately to sanctify their marriage, even if their prayers were without candles, incense, or family, so they secretly notified the ancestor spirits of the marriage and asked for their protection.

Control was another frequent topic in descriptions of the Khmer Rouge. Usual Khmer activities, relationships, and goals were replaced by responses to Khmer Rouge directives. The Khmer Rouge told Cambodians when to sleep, eat, or relieve themselves. In the reversed world of the Khmer Rouge, everything Cambodians said they respected and desired became despised by the Khmer Rouge and dangerous to Cambodians, including education, position, possessions, and social mores. The Khmer Rouge divided the population into "old" people, comprised of peasants, rural farmers, and those under Khmer Rouge rule before 1975, and "new" people, who came from urban areas the Khmer Rouge considered non-productive and Western-influenced. Many urban people were moved to "new economic zones," actually jungle and mountainous areas difficult even for local villagers to farm. Old people fared better than new, but also owed complete obedience to the Khmer Rouge, and suffered from lack of food, labored without rest, and faced death on a daily basis (Kiernan and Boua 1982).

Cadre taught children to have disrespect for parents and elders and defined family to include husband and wife and exclude children. They separated family members from one another and replaced hierarchical language with status-neutral language, thus "mother" and "father" with "friend." Treating adults as animals and children as adults, the Khmer Rouge formed children into mobile labor teams. Older children labored as adults, often at tasks beyond their strength, and smaller children were also put to work. The Khmer Rouge encouraged children to spy on their families, gave them rifles and authority to punish people for disobedience or questioning authority, and occasionally ordered them to urinate on their elders' heads to display contempt. Some Cambodians reported seeing children bury adults alive.

The Khmer Rouge directed every aspect of Cambodians' lives through loudspeakers mounted on poles and bicycles and constantly called people worthless, saying they recognized only the "certificate of the rice field," rice fields being square in shape like pieces of paper. They told people that "only the work you do by your hands" is important. At communal meetings, cadre repeatedly said, "We will effect a real Khmer pure community society as a world model, and we will continue our revolution until the last remaining Khmer person" (Hin Sithan 1992). People were to "rebuild" their thinking, and not allow "memory sickness" of their pre–Khmer Rouge lives to interfere with their work. The Khmer Rouge dictated everyone's appearance: forbidding jewelry and allowing only bobbed hair. They tracked female reproductive schedules to encourage people to have more children, yet separated couples and starved women until many stopped menstruating.

Khmer Rouge cruelty was a common theme. Refugees told of soldiers shortchanging them on rice soup even when it was available, keeping some working hour after hour after others were allowed to rest, refusing to let them relieve themselves, or withholding white cloth in which to wrap a deceased child. Some Cambodians said female soldiers were meaner than male, and child soldiers crueler than adult soldiers. Cambodians very rarely described a kind Khmer Rouge act. A woman looked up to see a soldier watching her catch a grasshopper. To her surprise, he smiled and walked away, leaving her worried he would eventually hurt her. She remembered the fear more than his brief kindness and, like others, found cruelty much more common. Cruelty was often accompanied by frugality, one man saying, "The Khmer Rouge used the cheapest things to kill us." To save bullets, they suffocated Cambodians with plastic bags, hung them with clothing or string, or beat them with bamboo stalks or gun stocks. Cambodians told of stumbling into decaying corpses in pits or muddy piles of leaves, hearing the sounds of bayonets hitting ribs and axes striking heads, and cadre complaining of exhaustion and soreness from their work.

Especially horrendous to Cambodians was attacking the head, the home of the soul, with either a hoe or an axe, the basic tools of rural life. Between the slats of a wall, Saran saw one thousand Khmer Muslims herded into a trench, forced to remove their clothes, and beaten with shovels and axes. Saran said the soldiers, returning with the clothing and covered in blood, "looked like vampires." The scope of violence and death was startling; Khmer author Soth Polin wrote that living things were reduced to ashes, and death was written into matter (1980).

Cambodians said they had little interest in anything but relief from their travail, one young man saying, "I guess you can see we were miserable." A girl said, "I never saw my friends. When we worked, we didn't dare talk. I was so unhappy." The Khmer Rouge thought people were barely human and said people were "soil for the rice field" (Khuon Kiv 1997: 102), "slaves of the rice field," and less important than slaves. Sokun said, "Pol Pot thought the cow was higher than people." One man overheard a soldier say that with slaves and animals, "you can beat them, but you cannot wound them." An older rice farmer said, "The Khmer Rouge idea was okay, that everyone would be equal with no one high and no one low. But they took everything away, so everyone was equally low." After a pause, he said, "Except them."

Work was another major theme. In what a Khmer rapper calls the "camp place" (May 2004), Cambodians were forced to work on an extreme schedule: six or seven days a week for months, stopping only for meals. City folk were grateful for any rural knowledge they had, several saying they survived only because they had learned as children how to yoke water buffalo, transplant young rice seedlings, and wield a hoe. Even those used to physical labor found work under the Khmer Rouge inhumanely difficult, one man saying, "I worked like an animal in the fields plowing and planting rice." Some had dug canals before, but never up to twenty hours a day through the hot sun.

Cambodians' recitations always referred to their hunger throughout the Pol Pot years. They spoke of the inadequate water and nourishment Cambodians received despite the work they did. "We had nothing to eat but rice soup" was a common refrain. Khmer refugees said they thought always of food. One man said, "When my fiancée and I lived together, we never touched. We just thought about working and finding food." Within weeks, no one looked as they had before, and within months, heads and knees looked huge. One man said, "The young became too old, and the old people all looked like ghosts' faces." Cambodians said the rice and vegetables they had grown was loaded on trucks and hauled away, one old man lamenting, "All that work, and they took the crops away." Cambodians ate what they could—papaya stumps, small fish, snails, grasshoppers, snakes, crickets, crabs, insects, mice, and bats—and stole pumpkins, potatoes, watermelons, lilies, cassava, and chaff, the scaly protective casings of cereal grains, usually fed to animals. Still they were hungry.

Every food-finding story mentioned cadre retaliation. Cadre slit open people's stomachs to see if they contained stolen food, and one soldier chopped at a child's hand when he tried to catch a crab, "but luckily only my middle finger was chopped off" (Boreth Sun 1989: 117). Despite the horror they attach to cannibalism, survivors said some people dug up and ate dead people. While they tried to secure food for themselves, Cambodians went to even greater lengths to save their children. A woman sold her hidden jewelry and bought stolen rice she secretly cooked for her daughter, who died anyway. Staring at the floor six years later, she looked up, shook her head, and muttered, "So much waste. Such loss." Another mother said she was not sad when her children died of starvation, because they were no longer suffering and she did not have to listen to them plead for rice. A young man said his grandmother secretly cooked spilled rice for him, and when he was taken to a youth labor camp, she walked miles to give him a few extra grains of rice. "She was willing to give her life for mine," he said.

Many Cambodians spoke of help they received from fictive mothers and aunts; Pin said a woman who called him son saved his life by hiding, feeding, and healing him. In spite of Khmer Rouge efforts to divide families, Cambodians tell of in-laws becoming as close as siblings, older brothers and sisters taking on the role of parents, children caring for parents and grandparents, and friends forming ties that endure to the present. A Cambodian whose child died during those years wrote that the Khmer Rouge "killed a generation of our children" (Ly Y 2000: 80). Cambodians also said they disliked being unable to eat together as families. Instead, they lived in communes of between fifty and one hundred families and ate collectively; those who gathered, cooked, or consumed food on their own were called "traitors of collectivism" and were killed (Hin Sithan 1992).

Fear was another litany theme. Cambodians said they feared hunger, sickness, and torture; those who lost hope for themselves and assumed they would die were afraid for family members. Many talked of fearing darkness, nightmares, waking up, or any change or rumored changes: that they were being moved, work was shifting, or leaders were being replaced. One man's fear of death came perilously close when soldiers threw him in a pit and shoveled dirt over him. Too weak to move, he remained buried until a friend dug him out. Cambodians also spoke of their fear of trips to what the Khmer Rouge called "hospitals." Also called "dying places," Cambodians dreaded seeing sick loved ones carried away, knowing they would not see them alive again. A few Cambodians said medical experiments were conducted on patients, but they refused to say more.

Cambodians said they worked in fear. One man spent a long time trying to lead an uncooperative buffalo to its plow under the glare of a teenaged soldier. When he finally succeeded in attaching the two, "I was shaking so hard, I fell to my knees and threw up." He added, "But nothing came out," thus mentioning another bane of Khmer Rouge existence and a major theme of Khmer litanies, hunger. Cambodians said they feared their language or soft hands would lead soldiers to discover they were educated, had worked in the previous government or army, or had Western connections. They told of cadre recognizing family, friends, and acquaintances and permanently marching them away. Samroth met a soldier who was an old friend, saying, "He was probably an official, since there were some young men with guns protecting him. He called me by my name and asked me how I was. I told him I was not who he thought. He said he knew me well, that we had been classmates." Assuming he would be killed, he went on his way. Nothing happened, but the incident remained one of his most vivid and terrorizing memories, and he continued to fear again meeting his former mate.

Some Cambodians lived because the Khmer Rouge considered their skills useful, but that did not prevent their constant fear. A grim-looking soldier came to take Chung to the village leader. Thinking he was going to be killed because cadre had learned he was a teacher, Chung sat paralyzed as the cadre talked. After being ignored for several hours, the leader asked him to repair a dry-cell radio. So frightened he could not concentrate, it took him an hour to realize the battery had been inserted incorrectly. He reinserted it and the radio worked. He was then told to find the channel "with the American voice speaking Khmer." Thinking they knew he was secretly monitoring Voice of America broadcasts while doing his repair work, Chung spent another terrified hour finding the channel before being returned to his work site, exhausted but relieved that he was still alive. Another man endured years of fear because former students kept calling him "teacher," and if overheard, he would be killed.

Even language suffered, as the Khmer Rouge turned an eloquent and subtle language into a weapon of fear. Khmer Rouge called their organization Angka, an all-knowing, all-powerful entity, and used the pineapple eyes as a metaphor for seeing everything anyone did. The Khmer Rouge spoke with "diabolical sweetness" (Soth Polin 1980), speaking charmingly while acting vilely, "suggesting" action rather than demanding it, but backing up their "suggestions" with violence. They forced people to use egalitarian words, such as "friend" or "comrade" (*mitt*) rather than status terms such as "mister" and "sir" (*lok*), and entwined gentleness with cruelty until even Cambodians were confused by their words and actions (Marston 1997).

Cambodians say there are "a thousand and one ways" to describe eating, drinking, or smoking in Khmer, depending on a person's rank, age, and relationship, but the Khmer Rouge collapsed these distinctions. They often mandated silence, and Cambodians advised one another to act as deaf mutes, hearing and saying nothing, citing the proverb "Plant a deaf tree in front of oneself if one wants to survive." Cambodians said it was always wise to restrain one's tongue; many ceased talking, afraid of being killed if they said the wrong thing and were overheard or reported. One man said that no matter how small the portion of food or how great the quantity of work, "we could not complain. If you did, they took you away." Another added, "How could they know about your complaints? They knew. There were informers and spies." "Trust no longer existed," Cambodians said, so they looked away, appeared disinterested, and thought and said nothing.

A final theme in Cambodians' litanies was that of loss. Cambodians talked often of their loss of health at the hands of the Khmer Rouge and the conditions of their lives during those years. Many survivors described the pain they continued to suffer from torture and beatings they had received, ever-present reminders of their past. Thinking Thom was hiding an insect in his hand, a Khmer Rouge soldier twisted his hand until it broke. Looking at the misshaped and useless hand that had caused him excruciating pain for decades, Thom said ruefully, "I was trying to catch a cricket, but I missed it." Another man had muscle cramps from being jailed in a small space and swollen legs from working in waterlogged rice fields.

Many Cambodians did not survive the Khmer Rouge years. The destruction effected by the Khmer Rouge echoes that of five centuries earlier, as Khmer Rouge leaders emulated Angkor kings in multiple ways.

Famous for his promotion of Buddhism and massive irrigation and construction works, Jayavarman VII in the 1100s forced hundreds of thousands to labor on his projects and in his armies, straining the country's resources. In both eras, a small group controlled the labor of a multitude of workers, resulting in disaster for the country and the death of many. Under the Khmer Rouge, Cambodians died from execution, exhaustion, starvation, and illness—older people dying first, then children, men, and women—and most Cambodians lost family members and friends.

In the first decade of resettlement, Cambodians estimated that millions of their countrymen had been killed. A freshman at Cornell said three million (Vaddhana Kchao 1989), and another claimed two million dead in "just three years and nine months" (Reasey Poch 1989: 17). In 2010, the Cambodian Genocide Program at Yale University reported that at least 20 percent of the population, close to two million people, died during the Pol Pot regime (Kiernan 2003). The "one million," "two million," or more Cambodians who died during the Khmer Rouge years is difficult to comprehend, as is the number of those who died before they came to power. The number of days in the lifetime of a person who lives to eighty is less than thirty thousand, and the number of days since the birth of the Buddha is less than a million, both numbers considerably smaller than the number of those who lost their lives during the Khmer Rouge years.

The Khmer Rouge targeted some for elimination, and 80 to 90 percent of artists, musicians, actors, and dancers died; only fifty of five hundred doctors and seven thousand of twenty thousand teachers survived (Vickery 1989). Hin Sithan (1992) was one of six survivors out of forty-six fellow teachers at Net Yang High School in Battambang. The Khmer Rouge also targeted minorities; the Cambodian Cham Muslims had between a 36 and 50 percent death rate, in comparison to 15 percent for rural Cambodians (Kiernan 1990). The first wave of violence came with city evacuations, as abandonment, injury, illness, hunger, or murder took many, including officials, businessmen, and military personnel with ties to the previous government. Overwork and starvation over the next years took large numbers of city folk, and illness was endemic. The Khmer Rouge also punished Khmer Rouge cadre and officials who failed production and distribution goals, particularly in 1977 in areas resettled by urban people (Kiernan 1996). Pol Pot himself survived several coup attempts and ruthlessly retaliated with torture, killings, and purges.

The end of the Khmer Rouge years came abruptly for many. During the work, hunger, fear, loss, and powerlessness, many felt conditions would never change, that only death remained. Others said they had no idea if their torment would end, had become used to death, hunger, and constant fear, and concluded there was nothing to do but continue living. They felt numb about their own situation, one saying, "I no longer had any feelings" (Theanvy Kuoch 2000: 427). One man told how he distanced himself from his situation because the Khmer Rouge said they would kill him if he showed emotion. He wrote, "I can shut off everything in my body, practically, physically. I saw them killing people right in front of me, the blood was there, but I didn't smell it. I made myself numb" (Simms and Arn Chorn-Pond 2002: 28). Another man who was repairing bicycles for cadre near the village "killing place" said, "That's exactly what I felt."

Some Cambodians found relief in no longer caring what happened to them. Some said they no longer felt human. Others told of doing terrible things, but I did not ask what, and few elaborated. One man said he stuck toothpicks in captives' ears or pistols in their mouths to get them to talk, a woman said she took food from her brother, another admitted informing on others in her commune, and a man admitted killing a friend knowing he himself would die if he did not do as the soldiers instructed. Some Cambodians said they were angry, some hopeless, but they carried on.

Flight

Suddenly, everything was different for Cambodians living under Khmer Rouge control, and their recitations of the end were short, reflecting its abruptness and confusion. After the late 1978 Vietnamese invasion that ended Khmer Rouge rule, Cambodians fled their villages or work sites, some with the invading Vietnamese, some forced to accompany the fleeing Khmer Rouge who were themselves fleeing Vietnamese troops. As the Vietnamese struggled to restore security in the country and free it of the Khmer Rouge, some Cambodians woke in villages emptied of Khmer Rouge cadre or occupied by Vietnamese soldiers. Other Khmer watched Khmer Rouge flee and the Vietnamese appear, leaving them to scrounge for food, search for family and safety, or return to their home villages. Crop yields had declined under the Khmer Rouge, and the chaos that followed their overthrow resulted in the neglect of winter rice crops and spring plantings. Not only food but assistance was scarce in a country without infrastructure, services, or governance (US Committee for Refugees 1982). Hundreds of thousands of Cambodians began an exodus to Thailand within months of the invasion.

Many Cambodians said they did not like talking about this period, and others said they did not remember much about it except being hungry, frightened, and uncertain about what to do. Cambodians usually skipped descriptions of the Vietnamese period and then went on to their flight stories, which they recited eagerly. Flight began Cambodians' lives as strangers and, in retrospect, began another set of unimaginable experiences. Cambodians said talking about their flight from Cambodia reminded them they were survivors. Now they had more danger to face. Most Cambodians described flight as frightening and dangerous. Flight was an interlude between Khmer Rouge rule and refugee camp life, and unlike the endlessness and powerlessness of both, flight was brief and usually voluntary, involving their own desires and actions. Although frightened, Cambodians said they felt brave, even heroic, actively seeking relief from all they had known and hopeful at last for their future. Asked about camps, Cambodians spoke instead of flight.

After describing the years following the Khmer Rouge, one man said, "The camp was in Thailand, and we ran there from Cambodia." He then spent twenty minutes describing his two-week flight. When asked where he met his wife, he answered, "In Khao I Dang camp," and returned to discussing his flight from Cambodia. When Sovann was asked if he wanted to talk about his time in Thai camps, he said, "No," and without pause continued, "We found a guide to take us to Thailand," and told his flight story. Asked about camp life, a girl said, "I lived in three camps, but I don't know the names," and went on to spend ten minutes describing her flight from Cambodia.

Flight stories included reasons for leaving Cambodia. The decision to flee was momentous in its consequences, with implications for those leaving and those left behind. Some Khmer said they left on a moment's notice; others that they left after weeks of speculation or feelings of hopelessness. Several thousand Cambodians fled before the April 1975 Khmer Rouge takeover of Cambodia. As the Khmer Rouge advanced on Phnom Penh, increasing numbers of Cambodians with resources and opportunity joined the escapees, some on commercial or private airplanes, many taking family and wealth with them. Some Cambodians living near the Thai border, fishermen with boats, and air force pilots fled by ground, sea, or air. The closer the Khmer Rouge takeover appeared, the more Cambodians fled Cambodia. They left, they said, because they were suspicious of Khmer Rouge intentions or worried about the protection a new government could provide.

A former army general who fled Phnom Penh with his immediate family said he did so because he feared Khmer Rouge reprisals against him. He fled with a planeload of purloined medical supplies donated by the United States, his insurance, he said, "that the Thai will let me live in Thailand." Those who fled after living through the Khmer Rouge years said they fled Cambodia because they were worried about continued violence, the worsening Vietnamese occupation, and the lack of food. Some Cambodians said they tried to reestablish lives, but they were exhausted, kinfolk had died, their homes were destroyed, and famine was imminent. Some said they just wanted away from Cambodia, and although many were forcibly ejected from Thailand, they escaped again and again; in Rhaun's words, "They cannot stop me from freedom." Many Cambodians said they fled in hopes of resettling in a third country, preferably France or the United States.

Flight stories also included descriptions of Cambodians' preparations to cross the border: finding a route and guide, and the hardships they encountered crossing the border and gaining admittance to a camp. The border approach and crossing were often brutal. Knowing only that Thailand was west, Cambodians waited weeks or months to join a group or a guide to accompany them across the border, through unfamiliar hills and forests filled with bandits, and Khmer Rouge, Vietnamese, Thai, and Khmer resistance soldiers fighting one another and preying on Khmer escapees. Other Khmer wandered for weeks looking for the border, avoiding or stumbling into danger, or returning to Cambodia to try again later. The trip lasted from a few days to weeks, and the refugees faced heartbreak at every turn. Some escaped with family members from whom they had been separated for years, only to see them die from disease, accident, land mines, or violence. Cambodians said their distress was so great that occasionally babies were abandoned because parents were unable to feed them or, in extreme cases, were smothered so their crying did not betray the group (Roeun Chea 1989).

Mothers often lacked sufficient milk for babies, and fathers and older siblings toiled to carry debilitated children. Cambodians feared animal and human attacks, but most could not avoid the smugglers or soldiers who took their few valuables and sometimes their lives. Kravann said, "There were many people in the jungle looking for us to steal things. They had guns, and we were scared," and Sam recalled hearing "gun batteries shooting from behind us, and bullets flying over us." Separated from others in his group as they ran in all directions to escape the robbers, he forged ahead with his children and brother. He and his family fled safely but never saw the rest of the group again.

Unfamiliar with the terrain, and already weakened by injury or disease, Cambodians suffered additional injuries and death from accidents, land mines, and sporadic battles. Some suffered dysentery that caused them to stop again and again and then struggle to catch up. After Rann broke his leg, he leaned on his brother the many miles left to the border, and in numerous repetitions of his flight story, Rann repeatedly grimaced as he remembered the pain of walking on a splinted, broken leg. Rape was common, although Cambodians said it was difficult to talk about it. Women talked of other women being raped, or being kidnapped to be raped, or raped and then killed, but seldom in reference to themselves or their relatives. Men were more open, saying they had witnessed rape and knew women who had been raped, always concluding by talking about their own feelings of helplessness.

Cambodians occasionally told flight stories to justify leaving Cambodia, especially after the country became stabilized and Cambodians in Cambodia were rebuilding their lives. Cambodians resettled in America who found themselves stranded in a foreign land facing never-ending challenges and a sense of loss said they sometimes wondered if they should have left their homeland. Their occasionally sense of resettlement doubt was relieved by recitations of flight stories, reassuring them of the reasons they had had to leave, and they often ended their stories with assertions that Cambodia was still threatened by communists, neighbors, or corruption. Their separation pain was also eased by their increasing ability to communicate and share videos, tapes, photographs, and resources with relatives in the homeland and, later, to travel there.

Despite the difficulties of crossing the border into Thailand, Cambodians kept fleeing; by September 1979, there were half a million Cambodians on the Khmer-Thai border. Khmer arriving at the border in October 1979 were dehydrated, starving, diseased, and dying (Shawcross 1984), and as a result of the stories they were telling, Cambodia soon became known as "the killing fields." Thailand, however, was hesitant to allow hundreds of thousands of Cambodians, whatever their pitiful condition, to remain on its borders without international assistance and pressed Western countries and the United Nations to support refugee and border camps for the short term and to provide a permanent solution to Thailand's refugee situation through resettlement to a third country or repatriation back to Cambodia (Thompson 2010). To strengthen its demands, in June 1979 the Thai forced forty-two thousand Cambodians down a two-thousand-foot escarpment to the plains below, on which the Khmer Rouge had laid land mines (Vickery 1990b). As Thai soldiers pushed large rocks over the cliff at them, survivors climbed down vines with children strapped to their backs or chests and then followed a path left by mine-exploded bodies, using the dead as stepping-stones.

This single pushback resulted in an estimated three thousand Khmer dead and seven thousand missing, but Thailand's efforts did not stop Cambodians from fleeing Cambodia. It did create an international furor as journalists wrote about Thailand's pushback efforts, and humanitarian organizations urged their governments to pressure Thailand into assisting rather than oppressing fleeing Cambodians. In response to international dismay and with nations guaranteeing support and resettlement, Thailand shifted its position. Viewing Khmer refugees as a buffer between Thailand

and the Vietnamese troops occupying Cambodia, Thailand created "holding centers" supported by the United Nations High Commissioner for Refugees (UNHCR) and international organizations and administered by the Thai military.

Thailand established a number of "official" camps. Within weeks, one of them named Khao I Dang had a population of 130,000, becoming the largest settlement of Cambodians in the world outside Cambodia itself. By May 1980, Khao I Dang was also the world's most elaborately serviced refugee camp, with thirty-seven nongovernmental organizations providing resources, nutrition, medical attention, and a variety of other services in just the first two months. There were also temples, churches, and Thai and Khmer shops. Over the next decade, Khao I Dang remained a primary depository for Cambodians waiting for resettlement, although most were never resettled in another country.

In addition to opening official camps, Thailand allowed "unofficial" border camps to be opened on the border between Cambodia and Thailand, an area that had never been adequately surveyed and that Thailand was now considering Khmer land (US Committee for Refugees 1982). The resistance groups included an anticommunist, pro-Western group opposed to Cambodia's Vietnamese-installed government, a royalist group devoted to Prince Sihanouk, and the Khmer Rouge. While many Cambodians who came to the border returned to Cambodia, over half a million remained in either official or unofficial border camps, most in unofficial camps and some for many years. Since the opportunity to apply for resettlement was available only in the official refugee camps, Cambodians often made desperate attempts to avoid or escape the border camps and spoke of their relief at reaching a "real" refugee camp.

The UNHCR and the International Committee of the Red Cross also established a "land bridge" program on the border to provide food, tools, and seed rice for Cambodians in Cambodia. Cambodians went to the border to exchange scavenged goods for food, drugs, and clothes they transported by truck, boat, oxcart, bicycle, and human porter into Cambodia for family use or resale. The US Committee for Refugees estimated in 1982 that the land bridge saved a million and a half Khmer lives. While the land bridge brought relief to many, it also drew Cambodians to the border to serve as resistance soldiers or seek resettlement (Osborne 1980). As more Cambodians learned about resettlement possibilities or of relatives leaving for other countries, more were inspired to leave Cambodia.

Refugee Camp Life

On reaching a camp, Cambodians were first relieved. Vibol said that when he reached Khao I Dang camp, "I thought there will be no problem with anything. Now that we are out of Cambodia, we don't have to think about anything." He quickly discovered that was not the case. While refugees who arrived in 1975 were free to move around locally and were soon resettled, those who arrived in the late 1970s faced hostility from Thai, who resented their intrusion and need for assistance. A Thai student said, "The Khmers are like snakes. If you put out your hand to feed them they bite you" (US Committee for Refugees 1982: 2). The feelings were mutual, and Cambodians' relief soon turned to dissatisfaction. They described poor treatment by Thai government workers, soldiers in particular. Restricted to overcrowded camps and tightly regulated, Cambodians saw people shot as they approached a boundary fence, even if they did not appear to be fleeing. One refugee saw a Thai soldier shoot a young boy who was climbing the fence to retrieve a hacky sack ball: "He just shot him. Then he was dead."

Although Cambodians in refugee camps could apply for resettlement in a third country and regularly received food, chlorinated water, and limited health care, life was difficult. Rations of rice, a little fish, and salt were more plentiful than in the border camps, but residents had to queue for everything. Shelter was minimal, with residents living in cramped wooden and bamboo shelters in overcrowded neighborhoods with little privacy. Education was often unavailable, and English-language classes were forbidden to discourage refugees from seeking resettlement. Many circumvented these stipulations by setting up private classes and charging small fees, and refugees who could not afford to pay said they were chased away when they stood outside classrooms to listen to the lessons. Cambodians had to submit to strict regulations dictated by Thai officials and soldiers, UNHCR personnel, and aid workers from around the world. Strangers were in control of their lives, defining how they received food and water, where they could go, and when they would leave.

Cambodians said the complex and ever-shifting rules, organization, and personnel and a confusing system of assistance further emphasized to them that they were controlled politically, economically, and socially. They had few possessions and virtually no distinguishing marks of status. Most were unable to work, and the few who had jobs had limited work hours. There was little recreation, farming was usually prohibited, and boredom was ever present. Cambodians were treated alike and were involved in similar activities: waiting in long lines for food rations, water, and medical care, which they said made them feel like animals. Camp inmates could do little about the insufficient food they received or the donated clothing that they described as lasting barely three months.

Camp stories emphasized the endless waiting and the "smell of waiting." Cambodians said a day in the camps was as long as a week, others said a year, and one described a day in a refugee camp as "a thousand years long." Ponleu resented being a "nobody" in the camps, in charge of nothing and no one. Cambodians said they were pawns for the government, military, merchants, and aid organizations of many countries, with little to do. Nothing they had endured prepared Cambodians for the camps' strange limbo. One described life as "fields of killing time" (Robinson 1996), with boredom the daily ration. Some were alone for the first time in their lives, most had lost family members, and all missed loved ones. One man said, "I had no family, only me and my baby daughter were left. I carried her everywhere I went, anything I did. I didn't have any milk, so I just fed her rice soup." Having practiced subterfuge, disguise, lying, and silence to survive the Pol Pot years, it was difficult for Cambodians to distinguish between victims and victimizers, and they said they trusted no one.

Cambodians said the loss of freedom and status left them feeling isolated and humiliated. Aid workers lived in neighboring towns, and visitors were tightly supervised, leading one refugee to tell an observer, "You cannot get in and we cannot get out." The widening gap between parents' and children's memories and experiences caused additional strain on family relationships. Adults were distracted, weakened by their experiences, frustrated by their living conditions, and fearful of the future. Many felt apathetic, helpless, or aggressive. Cambodians described being overwhelmed by the discomforts, tight quarters, conflict, and stress of the camps. Families were fragmented, and children often displayed habits learned from the Khmer Rouge rather than traditional respect. Many families were without male members, who were dead, absent, or serving as resistance soldiers.

It was in the refugee camps that the enormity of what had happened struck most refugees. In their relatively safe asylum, Cambodians came to realize the consequences of their decision to leave Cambodia, some saying they felt midway to nowhere, with few options (Kunz 1973). They could return voluntarily to Cambodia. Thailand and other countries were urging them to do so, and Cambodia was willing to have them return. Their return would legitimize Cambodia's new Vietnamese-influenced government, relieve Thailand of its refugee burden, and free other nations of the burden and expense of resettlement. The second option of resettlement was available to only a few. The third option was to remain in the refugee camps, a dour alternative that some Cambodians endured for the decade it took Vietnam to retreat from Cambodia.

The shorter the stay in the camps and the greater their involvement in work, ritual, and helping others, the better Cambodians described their lives in Thailand. In spite of obstacles, most Cambodians began reconstructing their family and neighbor relationships, buying and reselling goods, planting small patches of garden when possible, and sewing for one another. They put together dance and music troupes, built temples, and participated in Khmer Buddhist ceremonies. They cooperated in defending their communities and worked to resist feelings of powerlessness. Although removed from most webs of kinship, alliance, proximity, and friendship of traditional life, Cambodians continued to frame their camp lives in terms of their former lives.

Western writers have variously described refugee camp life for Cambodians, some emphasizing the desperate shape in which Cambodians arrived in Thailand, the violence and unpleasantness of the camps, the corruption and cruelty of the Thai, or the self-serving and competitive nature of the international agencies there to assist refugees (Robinson 1998; Mason and Brown 1983). Others describe the compassion of aid workers, the generosity of the international community, or the resources and relief received by refugees. Thousands of aid workers assisted hundreds of thousands of Cambodians who described being grief-stricken, in pain, and anxious. Refugees were touched by brutality, selfishness, and violence but also by compassion, grace, and assistance. In hundreds of conversations with both critics and Cambodians familiar with the camps, Khmer litanies of complaints and criticism were followed by expressions of gratitude for the sustenance and support they received.

For many camp residents, applying for resettlement became a primary activity. Hoping to improve resettlement chances, some sought patrons among aid workers and other residents, while others converted to Christianity. Some Cambodians said they constructed identities they hoped would please superiors and manipulated information about family relationships according to their understanding of the family units favored by Western immigration officers. Cambodians able to do so united with family members, and others joined together as fictive kin, claiming friends as brothers, second wives as sisters, and orphaned children as their own children. Cambodians also said they tried to appear healthy enough for resettlement but sufficiently damaged to be worthy of resettlement, and they managed information and responses to interviews with great care to promote their constructed view of themselves and to prevent mistakes that might lead to resettlement denial.

Stories of camp life focused on the camps' monotony and refugees' grief over what they had lost and their anxiety for the future. In contrast to the Khmer Rouge years, cruelty in the camps was less extreme and seldom life-threatening. Cambodians' flight from Cambodia had been brief, but their flight stories were long; while camp stays were long, Cambodians' camp stories were brief. While flight stories focused on what Cambodians did to escape their situation, refugee camp stories emphasized what was done to them. Cambodians had food, safety, and hope, however mini-mum, but remained at the mercy of others—imprisoned by fences, rules, administrators, and soldiers.

Many hated what they did to survive; Sokhem said he stole only once in the camps, taking a pair of shorts because "my own shorts had so many holes I was ashamed." In response to the conditions of the camps, most narrowed their circle of concern to immediate family members and old close friends. Worried about the future, Cambodians were weak and starved for information, one recalling, "We were thinking maybe we could go to France or America. We talked every day about where to go. Would they accept us? What country was better? What would happen if no country took us?" In retrospect, some Khmer accounts of the camps became more glowing, especially those of older Cambodians, who came to see their camp time as a period of relaxation after experiencing the uncertainty and discomfort of resettlement. Some said they wished they could return to live in the camps, where they had friends and food, no anxiety about husbands or children, and everyone spoke Khmer. And, said several quietly, not wishing to offend, the camps were not filled with Americans.

Memoirs

After resettlement in the United States, numerous Khmer refugees expressed a desire to write about their experiences so their people's suffer-ing would not be forgotten, and they frequently urged Americans to write for them, saying they were too busy or wounded or their English was insufficient. Many insisted Americans would listen to a fellow American before they would listen to Cambodians. They wanted Americans to know why they were in America and understand what they went through.

"Tell them about how my wife was killed," one man said pleadingly. "Tell them about how Pol Pot killed my brother." Cambodian American scholar Lee (2010) writes that he feels responsible for bringing the kill-ing fields to public attention. Cambodians wanted to emphasize what Americans wanted to forget, that this could happen to them, too; in Loung

Ung's words, "If you had been living in Cambodia during this period, this would be your story too" (2000a: ix). Cambodians soon began writing about their own experiences. Unpublished writings by students were passed from teacher to teacher, read before a class or student body, or put in the school newspaper (Chandakhan Nuon 1983).

As the years passed, a number of memoirs were published. One of the first in the 1980s was Vek Huong Taing's memoir, *Ordeal in Cambodia: One Family's Miraculous Survival—Escape from the Khmer Rouge* in 1980. *The Death and Life of Dith Pran* by Sydney Schanberg, on which the movie *The Killing Fields* is based, first appeared in the *New York Times Magazine* in 1980. Haing Ngor, who won an Oscar for his portrayal of journalist Dith Pran in the movie *The Killing Fields*, wrote his own account of his experiences, *A Cambodian Odyssey*, published in 1987. It was republished in 2003 as *Survival in the Killing Fields* by his coauthor, Roger Warner, and includes an epilogue in which Warner discusses the murder and last years of Haing Ngor. Several Americans in intimate contact with Khmer refugees wrote accounts, including *Spirit of Survival* by Gail Sheehy in 1986 and *To Destroy You Is No Loss: The Odyssey of a Cambodian Family* in 1987, the perspective of both American sponsor Joan D. Criddle and Khmer refugee Mam Teeda Butt. In 1992, Criddle's *Bamboo and Butterflies: From Refugee to Citizen* was published.

Other early published accounts included *Cambodian Witness* by Someth May, *The Murderous Revolution* by Stuart Fox-Martin and Bunheang Ung, and *The Stones Cry Out: A Cambodian Childhood, 1975–80* by Molyda Szymusiak in 1986; *Stay Alive, My Son* by Pin Yathay in 1987; *Beyond the Horizon: Five Years with the Khmer Rouge* by Laurence Picq in 1989; and *The Far East Comes Near: Autobiographical Accounts of Southeast Asian Students in America* in 1989, edited by Lucy Nguyen-Hong-Nhiem and Joel Martin Halpern, a collection of autobiographical essays written by college students who fled Southeast Asia as refugees. Memoirs published in the 1990s included *Children of Cambodia's Killing Fields: Memoirs of Survivors* in 1997, edited by Dith Pran, accounts by refugees in the United States who were children during the Khmer Rouge regime; and *Beyond the Killing Fields: Voices of Nine Cambodian Survivors* by Usha Welaratna in 1993, more accounts of Khmer survivors.

Memoirs in the twenty-first century have included *Heaven Becomes Hell: A Survivor's Story of Life under the Khmer Rouge* by Ly Y and *Never Come Back: A Cambodian Woman's Journey* by Darina Siv in 2000; *The Price We Paid: A Life Experience in the Khmer Rouge Regime, Cambodia* by Vatey Seng and *Escaping the Khmer Rouge: A Cambodian Memoir* by Chileng Pa and Carol A. Mortland in 2005; *Soul Survivors: Stories of Women and Children in Cambodia* by Bhavia C. Wagner in 2008; *To the End of Hell: One Woman's Struggle to*

Survive Cambodia's Khmer Rouge by Denise Affonço, *Alive in the Killing Fields: Surviving the Khmer Rouge Genocide* by Nawuth Keat and Martha Kendall, and *Golden Leaf, a Khmer Rouge Genocide Survivor* by Kilong Ung in 2009; *Facing the Khmer Rouge: A Cambodian Journey* by Ronnie Yimsut in 2011; and *The Years of Zero: Coming of Age under the Khmer Rouge* by Seng Ty and *The Elimination: A Survivor of the Khmer Rouge Confronts His Past and the Commandant of the Killing Fields* by Rithy Panh in 2014.

The number of self-published memoirs provides additional evidence of Khmer refugees' desire to tell their stories. They include Sopheap Ly's *No Dream Beyond My Reach: One Woman's Remarkable Journey from Cambodian Refugee to American M.D.* in 2009 and *Shoulders to Freedom: A Cambodian Diaspora Memoir* by Mai Bunla in 2013. Not surprising, considering the extreme and chaotic conditions under the Khmer Rouge and the nature of survivors' memories, narratives contain confusion, inconsistencies, contradictions, and inaccuracies. Cambodians portray themselves and others as they wish to be seen by readers, and while most accounts are respected for relaying experiences difficult to describe, Cambodians have expressed doubts about the credibility of several memoirs, saying it is a disservice to all who survived the Khmer Rouge to tell false stories.

Some Cambodians accuse Loung Ung, author of *First They Killed My Father: A Daughter of Cambodia Remembers,* of writing an inaccurate and fantasy-filled book biased against ethnic Khmer. Critics suggest the subtitle is doubly false: that Loung Ung does not remember, and that she does not consider herself a daughter of Cambodia, since she emphasizes that she is Chinese Khmer. The Khmer Institute (2000), cofounded by lawyer and scholar Sody Lay, claims her book's misinformation outweighs the positive attention the author has brought to Cambodians and says its lack of veracity throws doubt on other survivors' tales.

Sody Lay (2001) calls *First They Killed My Father* a "blatant sensationalization and over-dramatization of the Killing Fields experience," claiming the book is based on imagination rather than memory, because the author was only five in 1975. He says her story is not historically or culturally accurate; that Loung Ung remembers detailed conversations, but seems oblivious of the upheaval around her, and neglects to emphasize her family's wealth, her father's position in the country's secret police, and the corruption, war, refugees, and poverty. Most offensive to many critics is what they perceive as her preference for light-skinned Chinese Cambodians over darker ethnic Khmer.

Sody Lay claims a memoir based on lies lacks teaching value; "demeans the experiences of survivors"; offends the dead, including his relatives, "contemptuously dumped into mass graves"; and misleads those who want to know what happened in Cambodia. He accuses Loung Ung of writing for profit and cycling through media outlets and universities with her "con" story. That people have been moved by her story does not negate her duplicity, in his eyes. In contrast, he says, two memoirs published in 2000, *Music through the Dark*, written by Bree Lefreniere and narrated by Daran Kravanh, and *When Broken Glass Floats* by Chanrithy Him, devote attention to detail and demonstrate the authors' love for Cambodians, thus exhibiting their need not for profit but to tell what Cambodians endured.

In response, Loung Ong says she modeled her story on *To Kill a Mockingbird* (Harper 1960), in which a six-year-old speaks with the intelligence and wisdom of a forty-year-old man (Loung Ung 2000b). She explains that she does not hold the same views as an adult that she held as a child and gives as evidence of her good-heartedness her work on behalf of her nonprofit organization, Campaign for a Landmine Free Cambodia. In an attempt to discredit her critics, Ung told the *Boston Globe* in 2001 that she received death threats from Cambodian Americans who "continue to deny the genocide's existence" and from others "for being half-Chinese while writing on behalf of Cambodians." The Khmer Institute responded with a letter to the editor to the *Boston Globe* stating in part, "The notion that we would deny our own tragedy is not only absurd but perverse," writing, "Members of the Cambodian community are not outraged with Ung and her book because it has been written by a Chinese-Cambodian, but because it is such a gross distortion of the real Cambodian experience" (Khmer Institute 2000).

Critics have also called another memoir, *On the Wings of a White Horse* by Oni Vitandham (2005), unbelievable, expressing doubt that she is the daughter of Prince Chan (page 33), broke her jaw when she was three trying to chew jute ropes that bound her adoptive mother (44), was forced to eat sweet potato soup mixed with corpse parts (60), fled to Laos and traveled on the Ho Chi Minh trail (69), was imprisoned in Hanoi, fled by boat at the end of 1978, and was harshly treated as a servant in a Phnom Penh household. She describes sleeping and being fed miraculously at Angkor Wat (84), being kept safe by a tiger and snake (85), and realizing the importance of Angkor Wat to Cambodia's future after seeing a bright light (85).

Oni Vitandham writes that it "may seem strange that a seven-year-old girl would have such deep thoughts," but she says it seemed natural to her then (2005: 86). In early 1980, she walked west toward Thailand alone at age eight (91). Oni Vitandham also claims the Vietnamese imprisoned American soldiers in Lao caves, saying many were never released (68). She says she was abused by an American foster family and lived on the streets while going to school (Ellis 2006). Her philanthropic work has been criticized as a chimera because there is little evidence of it, and one critic accused her of "making a living by collecting money from people on SSI or welfare in a few cities in California" (*KI Media* 2006). The severe criticism has not stopped either author, particularly Loung Ung, from gaining international attention.

I am neither Cambodian nor survivor of the Khmer Rouge, but I have been listener and witness to the testimonies and suffering of Cambodians for over three decades. It is an insult not only to survivors and their heirs but to listeners and witnesses when stories presented as actual are in fact fiction. In contrast, stories about the reality that occurred told as well as survivors can recall are painful gifts to those fortunate enough to have escaped such suffering.

Bunkong Tuon (2013), however, argue that historically inaccurate portrayals can be valuable in bringing awareness to readers of the destruction wrought by the Khmer Rouge on the Cambodian people. The atrocities of the Khmer Rouge have been called incredible, unbelievable, inconceivable, and beyond imagination. The words imply the events and suffering could not have occurred, but the weight of evidence and the words of millions say it did. As Cambodians have said repeatedly, the words of no language can adequately describe what happened to Cambodians in the 1970s.

As Khmer refugees were pulled from their economic struggles by their memories of the past, so the realities of resettlement in the United States continued to challenge them on a daily basis.

Chapter Four

Resettlement Realities

After their initial relief at being in America, Cambodians said they began to realize the difficulties of resettlement. They said often that everything in their lives was upside down, in one man's words, "In America, up is down, down is up." Over the next several years, some Cambodians spoke of their regret that they had left the homeland, and others said they wished they had returned to Cambodia from the camps rather than accept resettlement in the United States.

Resettlement Reactions

Surprise

In America, Cambodians said one of their first reactions was surprise. Cambodians expressed astonishment at America's size, stretching over ten times the width of Cambodia, with a population thirty times greater. Buildings, highways, houses, and cars are larger in size and variety in the United States than in Cambodia, and Americans themselves display greater size and diversity than Cambodians. Cambodians often compared distances between America and Cambodia, where travel was by foot, water buffalo, or oxcart at a speed of about ten miles a day, and only a few people traveled by train or vehicle. Many Khmer said that in Cambodia they had never gone far beyond their villages or urban neighborhoods; they had known their relatives and neighbors, as their parents had known theirs and as they had assumed they and their children would know them. In America, however, distance is on a different scale, often becoming a barrier to refugees' contact with family members and countrymen.

A Khmer man in Kansas was dismayed to discover his sister in San Francisco lived over a thousand miles away and asked, "How will I ever see her?" He was relieved a few months later when his brother-in-law drove east to relocate him to California. Describing the trip back to San

Francisco, he said, "We only stopped for gas, but we had to drive all day and all night and all day again." In 1985, a rice farmer told me that Thailand was two hundred miles from upstate New York, although he was not certain because he slept during the flight. He had no watch nor did he know how to read one. Although his geography differed from that of most Americans, his resettlement brought him awareness that the world was much larger than he had previously thought. On a cross-state trip through Washington, Cambodians repeatedly expressed surprise at the size of alfalfa, timothy, mint, potato, and corn fields, irrigation systems, and machinery, and the fields so different from the flat, un-terraced, and diked rice fields of Cambodia. Khmer refugees also said they were startled to find that most food in America is grown and prepared by strangers in far-off fields and factories. Most Khmer refugees had been rice cultivators who grew up surrounded by rice fields, gardens, and livestock; the rest were urban dwellers who had kinfolk living in the countryside or who were familiar with rural life.

Realizing that, in America, they were a small group among many others in a large land, some Khmer refugees said the realization made them feel small, as individuals and as Khmer. Cambodians said they could not return to knowing little beyond their own world. Their doubts about themselves did not stop their efforts to reestablish traditional ways, but many Khmer said they remained plagued by questions. Like other immigrants who migrated to live in very different circumstances (Massey and Sanchez 2010; Wiley, Perkins, and Deaux 2008), Cambodians spoke of questioning who they were and what their role was to be as they prayed to the Buddha and paid homage to the spirits.

For Khmer refugees, Cambodia and America were literally and figuratively worlds apart. With few resources and American job skills and little English, they also talked about the challenges of weather, discrimination, unfamiliar technology, and grief. Some described themselves as "below zero." In reaction to their new circumstances, some Khmer felt they were owed something and became "aggressive, demanding, and suspicious" to conceal their "confusion, uncertainly, and a need for guidance" (Stein 1981: 69). Some Cambodians became disillusioned, finding resettlement life a roller coaster of raised and dashed hopes. The majority of Khmer refugees, however, said that although they found resettlement difficult, they had to keep struggling. Narith said, "What else can I do?"

Other Cambodians said that while they recognized they had been transplanted from a small to a large country, their realization of the two countries' relative size did little to shake their view of themselves as heirs of an empire great in size and power and to a magnificent tradition. They often mentioned the superiority of Khmer traditions and practices over those of Americans. Cambodians said the poorest Americans lived better than they had in Cambodia, but they wondered about food choices in a country with such bounty. Saung asked, "If Americans are so rich, why do they eat pancakes, mashed potatoes, dried-out turkey, orange juice, and milk?" She wondered why Americans did not eat delicious food, "as we do."

Amazed at America's opulence, Cambodians said their land, homes, and possessions lacked the warmth, aromas, and richness of Cambodia. American plastic and metal replaced Khmer thatch and wood; American buildings and objects were sharply angled and garishly painted rather than rounded and of natural earthen colors. Cambodians said they knew language would be different but found even survival English difficult. Nimith loved the complexity of English, saying, "It's a game and I enjoy it a lot," but few countrymen echoed his sentiments. Many Khmer wondered if they would ever be able to talk with Americans. One man said things were so strange in America, he often wondered if "maybe they are tricking us, and we are really back in Cambodia."

Familiar with spending much of their time in the open, leaving windows and doors ajar to chat, and calling out to passers-by, "Come eat with us," Cambodians said they were surprised that Americans spent most of their time invisible and inaccessible inside buildings and wondered whether weather, work, or business was the reason. Cambodians also said they found American distinctions of safe and dangerous areas confusing. Cambodians had traditionally viewed cultivated areas as settled, civilized, and safe (*srok*), and forested hilly areas as uninhabited, uncivilized, and dangerous regions where "savage men" live (*prei*) (Chandler 1982b). The dichotomy between cultivated and wild was shaken during the Khmer Rouge period, when cultivated lands became unsafe and the forest was often a place of refuge, and that confusion continued in America, where the most inhabited areas were often the most dangerous.

In other arenas, also, what Americans considered dangerous some Cambodians said was silly, such as tap water, lead paint, or metallic dirt that allegedly caused cancer, one woman noting that children in Cambodia were less clean than in America and did not become ill. Instead, some Cambodians mentioned being frightened by the unfamiliar sounds of English, water sprinklers, or backfiring cars. Many Cambodians feared animals. Kosal sat up through the night to catch rats biting his children in his rundown tenement apartment. Many were frightened by dogs and wondered at Americans who lavished affection and money on them, although over the years many acquired their own dogs for companionship and protection against another kind of danger: human predators. For certainly, Cambodians said, the greatest danger in America were people.

Coming from Cambodia, where strangers had been considered threatening and dark-skinned people brought to mind dangerous and otherworldly beings, resettled Khmer had little affinity with darker-skinned neighbors in America. Resettled in urban areas characterized by violence, Many Khmer refugees lived in fear as they negotiated their way, in the words of one Khmer group, "amidst gangs, drugs, urban violence, inadequate housing, and poor schools," feeling they "had been transported from one war zone to another" (Cambodian Association of Illinois 2000). Keeping money and jewelry under mattresses and neglecting to lock doors, close windows, or draw curtains, as few people had done in Cambodia, Khmer in some areas were robbed so frequently they resolved never to leave their homes unattended. Revealing the fear some refugees had of brown-skinned Americans and others they did not trust, one Khmer woman said white Americans did not know about the valuables they had hidden, "but Vietnamese and Hispanics do. They know, and they will steal it off you." Cambodians were targets of rudeness, harassment, arson, and gang violence, and women avoided dark streets for fear of being robbed, raped, and killed.

Cambodians said they hated the random violence in their neighborhood, which they thought they had left behind. Over time, many exchanged fear of specific groups to identifying violence as a characteristic of some neighborhoods and individuals, and they moved to safer areas or transported children to and from school to keep them safe. Others continued to witness or experience violence for decades. Cambodians said they were especially disturbed by the death of a Purple Heart Khmer marine who survived an explosion in Iraq but died after being hit by a bullet from the street while he was at a backyard barbeque in California. Even more distressing, Cambodians said, was violence committed by Khmer against other Khmer.

Both Cambodians and Americans expressed surprise at the number of Cambodians committing suicide; in one town, a man in his fifties and another in his twenties killed themselves in the same week. Several men committed suicide after killing their wives, girlfriends, or children for real or imagined faults. Cambodians said other men killed themselves from feelings of hopelessness about their economic situation or shame over the behavior of a family member. One man killed himself after hitting his daughter when she returned home late from a date, and the family of another man said he committed suicide because his son was imprisoned for assault; others committed suicide on hearing their welfare benefits were being eliminated. Cambodians also said Khmer young people were demonstrating their distress by being violent to themselves or others.

Parents were appalled to see their children exhibiting what they called "Khmer Rouge poison" by using intimidation and violence to solve their problems. American-born Cambodians have one of the highest rates of incarceration in the United States (Ahuja and Chlala 2013; Rumbaut et al. 2006); in the 1990s, 40 percent of the sixty-four Cambodians in jail in California were serving sentences for killing someone, often a family member. A Khmer writer describes a seven-year-old child who, having witnessed his brother's death in Cambodia, held so much anger he wanted to kill everyone (Ng 2001). Some Cambodians said they blamed the violence on the experiences Cambodians had endured. One youth spoke of being dismayed that his brother justified his crimes by saying he had learned how to act from the Khmer Rouge. Other Cambodians said they shared their fellow Cambodians' anger, if not their use of violence. A number of Cambodians said many young Cambodians were influenced less by prior experiences than by having been resettled in neighborhoods where violence was common. Cambodians also said some Khmer youth who became involved in criminal activity did so because they were poor, did not do well in school, and most importantly, lacked parental guidance because there was no male presence in the home.

Grief and Anxiety

Grief was a primary Khmer reaction to resettlement, and Cambodians spoke often of the difficulty of living with their sadness. Most Cambodians had lost loved ones to violent death during the Khmer Rouge years and had left other family and friends behind in camps and Cambodia. Cambodians said they were glad for what they had been given and what they had achieved in America, but people "don't just bounce back from genocide" (Moore 1992: 1). Many said they grew sadder over the years, thinking of their losses when awake and dreaming of death and the Khmer Rouge when asleep. Cambodians who had lost "properties, home, natal village, belief, culture and their country," in one woman's words, continued to get news of additional losses.

Some Cambodians who had lost hope during the Khmer Rouge years lost it again as they saw their aspirations for the future and hopes of seeing family or home again fade. When his eight-year-old daughter was murdered in California, her father wondered how he could go on. When a woman who had lost her husband during the Khmer Rouge years saw her son shot to death in New York, a friend said, "Her two children are like eyes to her. Now, one eye is blind." Cambodians said they also felt loss when their youngsters turned to peers for the support that was traditionally provided by family or devoted themselves to

American interests rather than respecting Khmer tradition. Most parents decided they had no option but to continue teaching their children as best they could.

Anxiety was also common among resettled Cambodians. Physically and psychologically displaced and worried about survival, Cambodians talked of feeling as numb as they did during the Khmer Rouge years. They said they tried to control their emotions, saying they had to deal with both their memories of the horrors of the Khmer Rouge years and the pressures of adjustment. They frequently spoke of feeling isolated, lonely, and depressed. They missed kinfolk and friends not living nearby and said that even when they lived with family members, they often felt insecure and distrustful of others. Several Cambodians said they had been frustrated by their lack of control over their own lives from the first days of resettlement, since placement locations and resources, information, services, and access to them were provided by sponsors and workers with little input from the refugees themselves. Cambodians said they were increasingly eager to make their own decisions. Some revealed their anger and resentment by refusing help or moving away from the Americans helping them. One man said fifteen years later, "We were mean to our sponsor, but I don't care. He didn't understand or respect us."

Cambodians worried that ill fortune stalked them, many ascribing it to the Khmer Rouge. One woman said, "I feel like the Khmer Rouge hand is waiting for me. It is waiting to jerk me back to something bad." A Khmer mother and father were understandably distraught when their son was sentenced to life in prison for murder, saying they did not understand how this could happen "to our family" in America because they had never received public assistance, had ensured their children received a good education, and tried to "live like Americans." Now they were living alone, their other children, a lawyer, engineer, and teacher, having isolated themselves in other states to escape the family's shame.

Cambodians spoke of the guilt they felt for surviving when so many died or for being accepted for resettlement when so many were rejected. They also said they felt guilt over what they had witnessed. When Kesor saw a soldier rip out a woman's fetus and Leap saw two women being raped by cadre, each said, "There was nothing I could do," and each hid and then ran away. Some said they suspected the death of others had contributed to their own survival and regretted their inability to assist those who had suffered. Weeping, one man said, "I was so afraid of the Pol Pot soldiers, I didn't even try to help other people, even my wife. She died." He paused, then said, "But if I try to help her, I die." Saying that he was worried that his good fortune in America had come at others' expense, one man regularly carried money and gifts back to his home village in Cambodia. Another man who said he felt guilty for "not help-ing Cambodia more," plans eventually to return to Cambodia to help "his people."

Resettlement brought continuing unease in Khmer lives with earlier traumas causing pain that was revitalized by each additional trauma: earthquakes, Hurricane Katrina, the 2008 recession, the 2010 Deep Horizon oil spill, Hurricane Sandy, and particularly the events of 11 September 2001. Cambodians commonly shrank from thunder, backfiring cars, and fireworks, several commenting that loud noises are often forerunners of desperate events. Cambodians said they knew catastrophe would even-tually strike them and wondered when it would happen and said they would never again take life for granted. They said repeatedly that they never wanted "to live under the Khmer Rouge again." Several Khmer men said they were not surprised by the 2008 recession. "We know some-thing bad is always going to happen to us," a woman said, her husband adding that he thought Cambodians had suffered enough in their lives. Although they expected misfortune, they did not know why it occurred. After a car accident left several Cambodians dead, one Khmer woman kept shaking her head, saying, "Why does this happen to us?"

Cambodians said earthquakes were especially frightening. When a quake struck the greater Los Angeles area in 1987, thousands moved to central California, Oregon, and Washington to be safer, several saying the earthquake made them remember the Khmer Rouge, and all they wanted to do was escape as soon as possible. Cambodians who experienced the 1989 San Francisco earthquake said they did not at first realize what was happening, and some thought they were back in Khmer Rouge Cambodia. Others knew something was wrong, one woman saying, "We don't have such things in Cambodia, so I thought I was sick." Many Cambodians fled to a nearby park and spent several days on mats under plastic tarps, before moving in with other Khmer, usually into one-story homes they thought safer than multistory apartments. Some concluded earthquakes were worse than war, one man explaining, "In war, you hear where the gunfire, the artillery, or the B-52s are coming from, and you can run away. But with an earthquake, you don't hear any warning." Some said they could no longer "trust in the earth."

One family moved from Washington to California when they heard of the destruction caused on the nearby coast by the 2011 Japanese tsunami. After relocating, they were dismayed to learn that the same tsunami had just caused $50 million in damage in California and killed one person, but they could not afford to relocate again. Flooding caused by Hurricane Katrina in 2005 brought loss and upheaval to a number of Cambodian fam-ilies, as did the 2010 Deepwater Horizon oil spill. Some shrimpers living southeast of New Orleans were still recovering from Katrina and living in trailers provided by the Federal Emergency Management Agency. When the oil spill occurred, Khmer fishermen were unable to fish because of the oil spill and could not obtain assistance from British Petroleum (BP), the corporation responsible for the spill, because they could not understand the paperwork. Some eventually obtained cleanup work, including a man who was grateful but appalled by the filthy work, comparing it to labor he was forced to do during Pol Pot times. BP gave them equipment without instructions or schedule, and payment was sporadic. Like many other families, Khmer families said they worried about what they would do when BP compensation funds ran out. Cambodians involved in a class action lawsuit did not know their lawyers or how to contact them and knew nothing of its progress.

Cambodians said the experiences of the Khmer Rouge years had subsequently led a number of their countrymen to engage in disruptive activities; they estimated that many were having problems with gambling. While many Cambodians see gambling as a problem, some said they think gambling is a strategy for success because it offers them a chance to become rich. Cambodians often speak of what they will do with the winnings: "I will buy a Hummer for my son," one mother said, and another, "I will go see Angkor Wat." One man wanted to "buy a house big enough for my whole family." A woman said she bought lottery tickets every week for years in order to "take care of my family, and so I won't have to work." Told lottery officials put jackpot winning odds at 1 in 176 million, she shushed the speaker, saying the chances of winning depend on fortune, not American statistics. When a doughnut shop sold a winning national lottery ticket worth $133 million, both the Khmer owner and his customers considered the shop lucky. They were confirmed in their belief when they learned that lottery officials said the shop sells an unusually high number of tickets. Cambodians continue to drive for miles to purchase tickets at the shop, saying fate will eventually reward them for their suffering and struggles.

Resettlement Strategies

One adjustment strategy Cambodians utilized after resettlement was to reestablish the traditional Khmer lives they remembered from an idealized pre–Khmer Rouge Cambodia. Many resettled Cambodians recalled the period between independence in 1953 and the early 1970s as the "good old days." One man described those years as the "time of Sihanouk," saying his family had lived in a large house and had many animals and servants. He claimed that "not only my family, but all the people were very happy with the government, and many things grew very well." Another man said, "My family lived a good life, always smiling, having fun." A former vegetable farmer said, "We had friends and family, play and work, songs and stories." While adults recalled the contentment of their lives during those years, youngsters remembered school, treats, soccer, and hopscotch. Cambodians also claimed the "good times" had extended back in time, and an older woman spoke of her family's happiness in her great-grandmother's time, "even before King Sihanouk." Others extended the nostalgic past to ancient Angkor, emphasizing its former glories as evidence that Cambodia was a "good country" populated by "good people."

Resettled Cambodians attempted to reestablish the "good old days" they had known in Cambodia by enjoying the company of other Khmer on special occasions, such as religious celebrations and life-cycle events, particularly weddings. Musicians and dancers began crafting musical instruments and putting together dances and costumes in order to perform traditional music and dance, and other Cambodians delighted in their efforts. Khmer refugees also made every attempt to listen to Khmer music on tape and, later, discs and to view familiar Asian movies and, later, videos from Cambodia.

Cambodians also recounted memories of the closeness and values family members shared. One woman said that before the Khmer Rouge took over Cambodia, her family had loved one another and never quarreled. Cambodians said their community had also acted as a family, with neighbors being generous, joyful, and helpful to one another. One older woman compared the comfort of participating in family rituals in "the old days" to the sorrow that accompanied their absence during the Khmer Rouge years, and another woman spoke exuberantly of her happy family "during Sihanouk," then added, "Pol Pot took all of Cambodia's peace and all prosperity." Cambodians also described their previous lives as easy, one saying, "There was "plenty of fish," and another, "No one went hungry." They spoke of hoping one day to again see the beautiful gardens of hibiscus, roses, mangos, coconuts, and bananas of Cambodia. One girl compared her thatched stilt house in an evening breeze beside a languid river of splashing fish in Cambodia to a mustard-colored, aluminum-sided trailer in Texas, sitting in a tiny yard of dying grass and thin tomato plants propped up on twigs (May-lee Chai 1994).

Their idealized remembrances reflected well on Cambodians, who described their tradition, language, religion, and values as matters of great pride. Some Cambodians said their history reminded them they were not inferior, as so much in America seemed to indicate, and their presence had value and purpose. In America, resettled Cambodians emphasized the importance they placed on family and the closeness they were again experiencing. They expended great efforts to gather together with family and friends, moving to live with or near them or keeping in touch with loved ones they could not rejoin physically. They were also concerned with keeping in contact with relatives and friends in the refugee camps in Thailand and, when contact became possible, in Cambodia.

Although intent on reestablishing their traditional Khmer values, Cambodians said their dimming memories were becoming a concern to them. The years of Khmer Rouge rule and refugee camp life had separated Cambodians from the annual round of religious ceremonies, life-cycle celebrations, festivals, school lessons, and storytelling that had occurred in the years before the Khmer Rouge takeover. In addition, there were few opportunities in America for listening to traditional Khmer recitations, songs, storytelling, and sermons or to engage in traditional dancing or games. Cambodians said their cultural knowledge was fading as a result. Instead, younger people were learning American language, history, and values. Cambodians lamented that increasingly their memories of Khmer traditions consisted of fragments of chants, stories, and songs they had learned in childhood. In addition, they said their children were learning little about their Khmer heritage.

Most Cambodians were intent on reestablishing hierarchical Khmer relationships, with parents superior to children, men to women, teachers to students, managers to workers, and the wealthy to the poor. Khmer tradition defines the appropriate behavior for each hierarchal level, and the Khmer language reflects hierarchical relationships. Cambodians say their use of language facilitates their communication with one another, and the traditional etiquette that reflects relative status helps maintain harmony in Khmer relationships. Cambodians typically greet superiors with downcast eyes, a bow, and palms pressed together in front of the chest, neck, or head; the higher the status of a person being greeted, the deeper the bow and the higher the bower's hands. Superiors return the gestures, but in reduced measure.

The hierarchical order is legitimized by Khmer Buddhism, which teaches that Cambodians are to accept their place in the social order because human beings exist on a spectrum of relative merit that persists from previous lives; the more merit a person accrues, the greater his or her social status and power. Maintaining and increasing one's standing is dependent on earning merit (Lester 1973). Cambodians say that people who have high status in their current lives earned that status during their previous lives and thus deserve the status they possess. It follows, Cambodians say, that a Khmer king is "one who has merit" and that

Khmer refugees who were successful in adjusting to America had earned their success in previous lives.

After resettlement, Khmer refugees said that a person's status is evident in his or her appearance and gestures and that even the way someone greeted them at their front door indicated their position in life. Cambodians described higher-status Cambodians as stepping forward confidently to shake a visitor's hand, practice their English if the visitor was American, and immediately ask visitors how they were doing. Persons of low status, said Cambodians, were reticent and quick to offer a greeting characterized by downcast eyes, a lowered head, and palms held high before one's face. Although both high- and low-status Cambodians offered their visitors refreshments, the first did so immediately and with confidence, the second hesitantly and with tentative gestures.

Cambodians also said previous occupation said much about refugees; a rice farmer probably had no more than a few years of schooling and had been unfamiliar with urban life, was relatively poor, and had little status. Cambodians described an urban dweller, on the other hand, as someone who probably spoke French, was educated, and undoubtedly belonged to a family with more resources than most rural families. Cambodians also judged a person's class by appearance, saying the lighter one's skin, the greater the chance one was an urban dweller; the darker the skin, the more likely a person had a rural background.

An educated Cambodian familiar with Americans ideas of equality said with a bemused look, "Mr. Thomas Jefferson's claim that all men are created equal confuses Cambodians. They know that isn't true." Higher-class Cambodians indicated that in the years after resettlement, class distinctions were more important to them than to lower-class Cambodians, particularly high-class Khmer whose lives held few signs of their former privilege. On meeting Americans, they often included information on their family's background and possessions to enhance their own status. Several said their families owned slaves "when Prince Sihanouk was king," adding that they understood such activity was unacceptable in America but was evidence of their position in Cambodia before the Khmer Rouge years.

Acknowledging that Americans were superior to them in understanding how to act in America, Cambodians said they adjusted to their new lives by imitating the behavior of Americans. Khmer refugees modeled their behavior on their American neighbors, fellow workers, people in public settings, and what they saw on television. Cambodians gradually shifted from exchanging traditional Khmer gestures to those used by Americans, such as shaking hands firmly and gazing directly at another person's face. Cambodians said they tried to be direct in their conversation and gestures with Americans but said it was difficult. Heng said, "I think I am not polite when I talk like Americans." Several Khmer men said they tried to walk like Americans but could not figure out how to do it. When Pich learned his colleague was saving money for his children's education, he began doing the same. He could afford only two dollars a month, but said saving money made him feel "more like an American." One woman bought a planner because her sponsors had them and said she did nothing without checking "her American book." Appointment books became status symbols among a number of Khmer interpreters and staff. One colleague said in the 1980s he would not go into a refugee's home without his "book" because it informed them "I know what I'm talking about."

One couple practiced American gestures, looking into each other eyes, but said they dissolved in giggles from their feelings of discomfort. A teenager noted the contradictory American and Khmer cultural demands by saying, "When I don't look at Mrs. Wilson in social studies class, she gets angry with me. But when I look my father in the face, *he* gets angry at me!" Cambodians in 1994 said they had more contact with Americans at work than in 1984 but said they still felt uncomfortable; twenty years later, they said that remained the case, and one man said, "I'm glad I'm going to retire next year." Some American-Cambodian relationships did not weather the shift in Khmer gaze. Sponsors in the late 1980s complained that Cambodians they sponsored in the early 1980s had become disrespectful to them, no longer lowering their gaze but looking directly at them. One sponsor said, "I know enough about Cambodians to know what that means." The refugee she sponsored told me later, "I love my sponsor. I don't know why she thinks I don't respect her."

In the early months of resettlement, Cambodians were often surprised when Americans suggested they change their names. "They call me 'Joe' at work," said Sovann, "but I don't know why." His American colleagues explained that they could not pronounce his name. Sponsors suggested that the Tith family change the pronunciation of their name from "Tit," as it sounded to Americans when Cambodians said the name, to "Tith," to emphasize the "th" sound. The family quickly agreed after their children told their parents some of the comments they were hearing from their peers at school. As time went on, Cambodians said they understood why Americans were occasionally changing their names, and they began doing it themselves, saying they wanted to make their lives easier and ease their children's adjustment at school. Several Cambodians pointed out that it is not unusual for Cambodians to change their names, particularly when they undergo changes or want to change the direction of their lives. A number of Khmer said they changed their names after the years of Khmer Rouge to mark the end of a terrible time.

Some Cambodians choose names that are easy for Americans to say, such as Nan, Lisa, Zim, Lam, Kim, or Yan, or that are common in both languages, such as Sam, Danny, or Ron. Other Cambodians give their children names that sound alike or similar but are spelled differently in Khmer and English: Phal to Paul, Phala to Paula, Ranny to Ronny, and Thom to Tom. Some choose names of helpful Americans; Yon named his son after his employer, Mr. Johnson, who then became, in the Khmer style, Yon Johnson (Teteak 1992). Others choose names that "sound good" or important. One man named his child "Hillary" because "it is a name for important women" and was the name of his teacher and boss's wife. Jennifer, Kimberly, and Michelle are especially popular names for girls, and Michael, Henry, and John for boys. Some Cambodians changed their own names; Sophal and Bong took their sponsor's suggestion and became Mary and John. Some changed their own names but gave their children Khmer names. One man changed his name to Joe Cook to ease his work at a restaurant, but he named his ten-year-old son Ankorwat and five-year-old daughter Sumuri, traditional Khmer names (Baxter 2008).

Cambodians used many of the survival tactics in America they had used during the war years. Saying they had learned Americans expected them to be dependent, silent, and inconspicuous, despite their emphasis on independence and equality, Cambodians acted accordingly. They were often silent, unobtrusive, and passive with Americans in positions of authority, often neglecting to request services or resources out of deference for Americans. "We feed the baby who cries for milk," a Khmer agency director said. "Whoever doesn't cry, we think they're OK," said another (Chan 2003: 170). While most Cambodians said after resettlement that they considered their culture superior to that of Americans, they acknowledged Americans' dominance over them in class, education, and economics and responded by subjugating themselves to them and keeping their actual thoughts to themselves.

Television quickly became an adjustment strategy that allowed Khmer to explore America without leaving their own homes. It was usually one of the first items Cambodians acquired after resettlement, and Cambodians quickly learned its operation, although some older women said they watched the same channel all day because they had difficulty using the remote. They did not long remain ignorant of its operation, however. A ubiquitous, undemanding companion, Cambodians said television gave them a diversion from their struggles and memories and taught them what to wear and how to find items on sale. Many first-generation Cambodians enjoyed wrestling, cartoons, and action movies because, they said, they could most easily understand the gestures, facial expressions, and often slapstick actions.

One woman said soap operas kept her company while her children were at school, and she could see "inside Americans' houses." She was pleased with her ability to recognize actors, saying, "They are like my friends." She was especially fond of Katherine Chancellor, the iconic fictional character on *The Young and the Restless*. Some Cambodians were disturbed by the amount and explicitness of sexual activity on television, and many said they saw television as a threat to their culture, since Cambodians are spending more time on American entertainment than on Khmer music, dance, and drama performances. Many Khmer who viewed television as indecent and a threat to Khmer culture, however, had their television set on much of the time.

Just as Cambodians sought out Americans as patrons, seeking their assistance as people with more resources and knowledge than they had as newcomers and giving them loyalty, labor, and gratitude in return, so Cambodians sought patrons from among other Cambodians. Cambodians' strategy of utilizing both American and Cambodian patrons allowed them to deal with issues in their lives, such as unfair landlords and employers, and with an unfamiliar American bureaucracy. Cambodians often expected that their patrons could assist them more than they actually could, since American bureaucracies utilize standardized criteria in determining eligibility for resources and services rather than responding to the personal ties and rewards that facilitated access to services and resources with which Cambodians were familiar. Khmer refugees did benefit, however, from having patrons who could advocate for them, because they spoke English and understood American regulations and restrictions, and thus assist them in gaining resources and services.

Some Khmer patrons were diplomats, soldiers, and students already living in the United States before Cambodia fell to the Khmer Rouge, and others arrived in America as refugees before their clients; thus they had more familiarity with English and American customs and more contacts with Americans and Cambodians in positions to assist newly arrived Khmer refugees. Others were Cambodians who spoke English and knew Americans before they came to America as refugees. Some Khmer refugees serving as patrons to their countrymen were hired by government and private agencies as bilingual workers, expanding their knowledge and resources and, subsequently, the number of their clients. A number of ambitious young refugees who arrived in the early 1980s quickly learned English and American ways and gained American contacts also became paid agency workers and unpaid patrons.

Articulate and personable, one young man in 1981 became an apprentice to a patron who had arrived in 1975 and, within two years, had gathered his own clients and broken with his patron. He started a Khmer organization, sponsored monks from the camps, and became the president of the city's first Khmer temple. He eventually had hundreds of clients, supervised a small army of young men also assisting new arrivals, and was popular among service providers. Patrons funneled resources to clients and brokered relationships between clients and other Americans who also acted as patrons to both Khmer patrons and clients. Although Americans had little understanding of Khmer patronage, they benefited from it. In return for providing Cambodians with transportation, housing, and jobs, Khmer refugees prepared food and did other tasks for their American patrons, although they seldom recognized they were doing so (Mortland and Ledgerwood 1987a). When Cambodians brought refreshments to American celebrations, Americans seldom recognized that they were working on behalf of a patron.

A few Khmer patrons were women, some benefiting from American affirmative action initiatives. With Khmer women often learning English and American customs more rapidly than men, government and private agencies were soon hiring female caseworkers, interpreters, and paraprofessionals, and a few used their positions to act as patrons. Although few women took leadership positions in the community, several female agency workers in Stockton, California, became community leaders. Patrons had to fulfill promises to their clients and their own patrons in order to keep their clients and their position in the community. They often worked far into the night and through the weekend relaying information to clients about resources and services, assisting with paperwork, filling in when clients failed in their duties, and handling emergencies.

Cambodian patrons competed with one another to acquire and keep clients, often setting up their own temples and organizations. Two young, smart, and attractive friends glad to be resettled together both found it easy to learn English and impress Americans. Both were hired by agencies to serve as bilingual workers, and realizing they could "be somebody," in one client's words, they soon became patrons. They quickly grew into rivals. Although they were civil to one another in agency meetings, clients said their enmity was obvious in their wives' behavior. One woman told me to "watch their wives. They take every opportunity to offend the other in public." The two young patrons and their families remained enemies to their deaths many years later.

Cambodians acknowledged their need for patrons and said they deserved the status they held. They said of a thriving but unpopular countryman that he must have done something right in his previous life because he was certainly doing well in America. They also saw themselves as powerless, one man describing clients as "frogs in the well," seeing only the bottom of the well and unaware of the world above. One client said, "We are refugees. We cannot win over the patron." One man explained his position as a client by saying, "I must have done something horrible before, because my life is not good now." Patrons had their own struggles. They were occasionally, often frequently, at cross-purposes with providers, wanting to provide services that enhanced their own power rather than the goals of agencies. Some Khmer bilinguals were fired when agency personnel became aware of their activities. Other Khmer bilinguals said they felt enormous pressure from American colleagues who did not understand the demands Cambodians made on them and from Cambodians who expected more from bilinguals than they had the power to deliver.

The greater a patron's knowledge, contacts, and number of clients, the greater his ability to provide resources and services to them. The relative power of patrons and clients led some patrons to pay less attention to their clients' concerns, and some patrons to become arrogant. As a result, some patrons lost clients. Clients usually complied with their patrons' requests, although their compliance was often minimal and sometimes declined over time. Poorly educated Cambodians were the least likely to leave patrons, because they were most in need of assistance. One couple who were rice farmers with little education in Cambodia said they disliked their patron but needed his services, so they were going to obey him until they had full-time jobs. The wife explained, "It makes too much trouble to fight him. Just let him have his way now. I will win tomorrow." Over time, clients gained a better sense of their patron's actual connections and powers and their own resources, and left their patron. In the early years, clients said the best way to escape their patron was to move away or choose another patron.

As the years passed, an increasing number of Cambodians learned English, gained American job skills, and acquired direct access to knowledge and benefits. By the 1990s, many patrons had quit, finding the work too stressful and the constant criticism tiring. One former patron said, "You cannot carry someone's penis," likening patronage work to helping someone urinate. He said that in the end, being a patron "gets you nothing." Some patrons exchanged being a relatively low-paying patron for providing the same services for pay on a freelance basis. A Khmer health worker opened an office and charged for counseling referrals, transportation, and interpretation; a mental health worker set up a clinic that, for a sizable fee, helped people obtain disability insurance; and a former security guard enhanced his lost power as a patron by serving as a security guard at Khmer events, wearing a uniform and claiming to work for the police department. Other Cambodians were impressed and said he made a good guard because he had the ability to arrest people. Patronage declined further in later years with the increased numbers of Cambodian Americans. By the twenty-first century, patronage among Khmer refugees and Cambodian Americans has been greatly reduced, although it remains vital for some older, illiterate Cambodians.

Migration was another major strategy Cambodian refugees utilized to adjust to life in America. As American concern about refugee impact on institutions, resources, and neighborhoods increased, the American government increasingly dispersed newly arriving Khmer refugees throughout the country, often in American cities and towns where few Cambodians lived. Cambodians were sent to every state, with Alaska alone receiving around one hundred refugees (Baker and North 1984). Although many Americans favored the dispersal, Cambodians themselves soon realized their dispersion hampered their ability to adjust to American life by separating them from other Cambodians best able to understand their situation and assist them.

Khmer refugees responded by moving to join family, friends, and ethnic communities. This secondary migration by Khmer refugees became common, and resettlement personnel soon worried that American sponsors would be more difficult to recruit if they realized refugees might move away (Mortland and Ledgerwood 1987b). Indeed sponsors who had devoted considerable time and resources in preparation for the arrival of refugee families and in resettling them after arrival were often annoyed when they left. Agency personnel increased their pressure on Khmer refugees to stay where they were initially placed, and some Cambodians were surprised when they learned they had the right to move.

Despite government efforts to disperse refugees and then keep them in place, Khmer refugees flocked to areas where Cambodians resided. Policymakers became concerned that local agencies were unprepared to handle large numbers of unexpected refugees. They were especially concerned about Long Beach; by 1980, half of twenty thousand resettled Cambodians had migrated to Southern California, six thousand to Long Beach alone. In response to the number of Cambodians leaving their initial placement site to join Khmer communities, officials increased their efforts to locate new arrivals away from other refugee concentrations. Officials defined regions of the country they said would be "adversely impacted" by additional resettlement and adopted a policy of scatter placement. They hoped that dispersing Khmer refugees widely would lessen their impact and visibility and prevent the formation of ethnic enclaves.

Cambodians were dispersed in locations according to the availability of jobs, housing, and resources, community attitudes, and rates of public dependency. The Cambodian Cluster or Khmer Guided Placement Project attempted to create Khmer communities as Americans thought they should be. The project resettled eight thousand Khmer refugees over a six-month period in twelve "favorable" sites, including New York, Chicago, Cincinnati, Houston, and Richmond, and emphasized self-sufficiency through job training and placement. Long Beach Cambodians were encouraged to be part of the cluster project, or "Khmer Refrigerator Project" as Khmer called it, because many of the sites were in colder regions. Another project with the same goal, the Favorable Alternate Sites Project, resettled 584 Cambodians in Charlotte and Greensboro in North Carolina and Phoenix and Tucson in Arizona. The project was considered a success despite the small number of Cambodians involved, because welfare use was significantly reduced and the sites became home to large- and medium-sized Khmer communities. An additional effort to prevent Khmer secondary migration, the Planned Secondary Resettlement Program, was established in 1987 to assist eligible refugees in high welfare dependency areas to relocate to communities offering favorable employment and resettlement opportunities.

These schemes faced numerous obstacles. Refugees resisted leaving their original sites, and local leaders who benefited from their presence resisted efforts to move them away; in one example, Khmer leaders prevented a movement of Cambodians from New York and California to Phoenix, Arizona. Approximately one-third of the Khmer who moved to Greensboro left the area, typical of the secondary migration that Khmer refugees undertook to leave placement sites arranged by Americans rather than refugees. The Cluster Project was also unsuccessful in preventing secondary migration, with one-third to over one-half of the Cambodian refugees moving away, most of them going to California, New England, and Seattle. In addition, in spite of its success in reducing welfare rates, about a third of the participants left the Favorable Alternate Sites Project.

Cambodians said they saw numerous benefits in secondary migration, despite the anger they sometimes left behind. They spoke of once again being in control of their own destiny and again being able to choose a place of residence. Some moved to warmer climes, many leaving eastern and northern cities for western and southern ones (Cafazzo 2008). One Cambodian said Long Beach weather was a major attraction, observing, "The warmth comforts our own." Cambodians also moved to raise their children in better surroundings; to escape sponsors, disliked neighbors, shame, ridicule, or scandal; or to find more generous public assistance benefits. Older people, widows, and those with numerous dependents were especially interested in obtaining assistance. Cambodians also moved for employment, many saying they had to work to feel good. The primary reason Cambodians said they moved, however, was to join other Cambodians. As families and friends were reunited and ethnic communities developed, refugees had increased access to information, assistance, and comfort.

Paths of Adjustment

In early resettlement years, many Cambodians and Americans concluded that Khmer refugees displayed a dual pattern of adaptation as "haves" or "have-nots," defining "haves" as those demonstrating economic self-sufficiency, and "have-nots" doing the opposite (Portes and Rumbaut 2006). Americans said self-sufficiency for Khmer refugees meant the ability to support a family long-term through adequate wages and health insurance. They also defined self-sufficiency as being able to speak English, follow Americans' written and unwritten rules, and abandon "offensive" foreign behaviors.

Both Cambodians and Americans agreed that learning English and American job skills were important in gaining self-sufficiency in America. Cambodians' ability to do so was influenced by the education, occupation, and family reputation they had in Cambodia and their resettlement situation after arrival. The greater the education, occupation, and status of parents, themselves, and others resettled with them, and their familiarity with Western ways, the better Cambodians' opportunities and success in America. They learned English, gained employment, and improved housing more rapidly, and their children did better than those who came with less education and fewer family advantages.

Cambodians said refugees with better physical and mental health were also able to devote more energy and strength to adjustment, and strong family and social connections in the United States, an optimistic outlook, Buddhist practices, and maintaining Khmer traditions added to Cambodians' ability to adjust to American life. Several Cambodians pointed to the importance of information and opportunity to refugee success in America; a lack of information led to missed opportunities, and one missed opportunity usually led to other missed opportunities. The assistance of helpful teachers or neighbors gave some Cambodians opportunities that lifted them and their families from poverty to economic stability. Several Khmer leaders suggested that successful Cambodians were more interested in acquiring education and accumulating resources, while the unsuccessful were less interested in doing so or thought they had little chance of achieving social mobility. One Khmer said emphatically in 2002, "Many Cambodians don't even know about opportunities. They just don't know."

Cambodians say "haves" include refugees who were professionals, business owners, or students in Cambodia who were able to translate their skills and experience as students into jobs in America. In contrast, Cambodians say most Khmer "have-nots" were rural farmers and urban workers who were less able to learn a new language and job skills, and thus most have become low-wage workers or welfare dependents. Predictions that the gap between the two groups would increase have proved accurate, with the gap extending into the second generation (Schlund-Vials 2012). Khmer refugees with good jobs, houses, and children who are doing well consider themselves fortunate, while those who have low-paying jobs or no jobs at all, live in subsidized or substandard housing, and have children struggling with school, drugs, or the law often describe themselves as unfortunate.

Some Cambodians describe the dual pattern of adjustment as a distinction between educated and uneducated Cambodians, smart and not smart, urban and rural, even proper or improper, with the "haves" the former and the "have-nots" the latter. Several gang members contrasted "gang boys" to "college boys" and said they wanted their sons to go to college. A Khmer social worker said the difference between fortunate and unfortunate is their sense of self-worth, saying women who lack English and American workplace skills have no shame accepting free meals, while those with high school educations and good jobs would be shamed to accept free food. Cambodians said Khmer refugees who considered themselves successful and were considered by others to be successful were a minority, several suggesting approximately 5 percent. Cambodians say the situation in the twenty-first century remains similar, with most Khmer refugees and their descendants continuing to consider themselves economically unsuccessful.

Not all Cambodians fall into a clear have–have-not dichotomy. While second-generation Cambodian Americans whose parents were of higher socioeconomic origin in Cambodia have made greater educational and economic advances than second-generation Cambodian Americans whose parents were of lower socioeconomic origin (Sakamoto and Woo 2007), other second-generation Khmer have also done well. Households with multiple income sources from minimum-wage work, part-time or seasonal work, and social security are often better off than households supported by income from one well-paid job, and they consider their families successful, especially if they have children in college or headed to college. As household wages increased over the years, more middle-class and multiple-income Khmer households were able to purchase homes, move from low-income and public housing sections of town into lower-middle- or middle-class suburbs, and acquire more reliable cars and better furnishings and clothing. Cambodians say they moved primarily because they did not want to live surrounded by gangs, drugs, violence, divorce, spousal and child abuse, and gambling.

Khoeun had few privileges in Cambodia but considers his family successful. His parents had a farm in Cambodia and worked as laborers in Phnom Penh during the non-farming season. After resettling in the United States, his family lived on welfare, food stamps, and trips to food banks and resided in a dangerous section of town; he carried a *nunchuck* in his backpack to protect himself as he walked to and from school. Although his parents had little education themselves, they wanted their children to become educated. His three sisters earned college degrees, and a younger sister graduated from high school. Khoeun went to community college, then to university three hundred miles away because he "wanted to get away from the bad element, including Khmer gang kids." He signed up for mechanical engineering, although he was not sure what it was, graduated as a mechanical engineer, and works as an engineer.

Many Cambodians define themselves as successful by pointing to the educational and employment achievements of their children, their purchase of a home, and their having a comfortable lifestyle as evidence of having survived successfully. Khoeun's father quit his job as a casino dishwasher after a supervisor spoke harshly to him, and he now babysits his grandchildren and assists his physically disabled wife. "My family is a success," he said proudly. A number of other families struggle economically, usually in low-wage labor positions such as maintenance, fishing, farming, factory assembly, food and hotel service, retail, mills, and casinos, or have part-time jobs, temporary or piece work, or subsist on government benefits. They say they are successful, however, because they act appropriately as both Cambodians and Americans: fulfilling their obligations, having obedient children, and avoiding scandal and legal difficulties.

Other families have had varying economic success, with some children graduating high school or college and others becoming involved in gangs, drugs, crime, or early parenthood. Second-generation Cambodian Americans who gained steady employment, moved to the suburbs, and focused on raising their own children often lament the fate of siblings who, in one man's words, "got caught" by the streets. Khoeun's parents, with several children college graduates, also had a son who dropped out of school and served a three-year sentence for drug possession and robbery. Family situations can change rapidly, however. One family's oldest son joined a gang, spent several years in jail, and was "somewhere" in California. The two youngest daughters became pregnant, dropped out of school, and went on public assistance. Ten years later, the son has returned and has a job, wife, babies, and his parents living with him. Both daughters have jobs in food service, are married (not to the fathers of their first babies), and are active in the local temple. One daughter speaks at local high schools, urging girls to complete their schooling and get jobs before having a baby. "You can do it that way!" she tells them, then adds with a laugh, "But it sure is hard."

While first-generation Cambodians continue to see themselves as refugee migrants, carrying vivid memories of their survival and resettlement struggles, second-generation Cambodians and other Americans in the twenty-first century classify Cambodians in the United States according to their economic class rather than ethnicity or ancestors' origin. Like immigrants before them, many Cambodians exhibit middle-class values: expending great efforts to acquire comforts and possessions such as houses, cars, furniture, electronics, and brand clothing. An increasing number of Cambodians are integrating into American society as individuals, not as a group (Haines 2010), devoting more energy and resources to themselves and their immediate family than to extended family and the community.

Although Cambodians and Americans often make a sharp distinction between successful and unsuccessful adjustment, linking it to economic success, Cambodians say that while economic security is important to them, other achievements are also important to successful adjustment. Some have chosen paths they consider successful although they are not financially rewarding, such as working in refugee social work, advocacy, religious work, social justice, or politics in America or Cambodia for low pay or as volunteers. Many support extended families in both the United States and Cambodia and consider family time more important than improving their economic or financial status, and many say success includes establishing and supporting temples or churches and earning merit. Some Cambodians claim the opportunity to live in a free country with public education is more valuable than material advantages and say they are content with low-status and low-wage jobs if they can support their family.

Over time, less economically successful Cambodians struggled to maintain traditions but often lacked the resources to donate to the temple, visit relatives, or purchase traditional foods. Many women in the Bronx were estranged from husbands and living with five or six children "crammed" into single apartment rooms (Chira 1993). For many, time brought increasing personal problems and domestic conflict. Ongoing tragedies, health problems, and mental health issues pushed many families into chaos, lessening children's attachment to the Khmer community and increasing their attraction to violence and drugs.

Many families continue to live in the same low-income neighborhoods in which they were resettled and view themselves as unsuccessful. If they did move, they moved to similar areas, finding that even full-time work does not provide sufficient income to allow them to move to safer neighborhoods. Many have joined America's "new servant class, responding to the demands of an expanding underground service economy" (Ong 2003: 141). They say they are trapped in jobs with little hope of advancement, knowing they are unlikely to find another if they leave. Cambodians continue to suffer in contrast to others; in 1990, 43 percent of Cambodian Americans were living at or below the federal poverty limit, compared to a third of Vietnamese refugees and 10 percent of other non-Khmer Americans.

The 2008 recession hurt Khmer by limiting their chances of escaping crowded, intergenerational households, with little privacy or quiet for children doing homework, and without front or back yards, porches, cars, or fresh air. Public transportation in these neighborhoods is usually inadequate or dangerous, making it difficult to access good schools and supermarkets with less expensive food. Family funds are limited to paying for housing and food, and many are fearful of crime, gangs, and rude shopkeepers. With most refugee assistance offices, Khmer self-help groups, and Khmer-specific services gone, Cambodians say the American dream is far beyond their reach.

Luoth considers himself typical of a refugee who "missed the raft," as he said one day. Resettled in 1981, he took two months to learn the location of English classes and several more months to learn how to ride the bus. With only two years of education in Cambodia, he felt overwhelmed by learning English and depressed by his ignorance of America. Luoth was further upset when told his children could not go to school until they had been immunized. He had received vaccination information but had ignored the "school paper" because he could not read English and did not want to ask for help. Finally taking his children to obtain vaccinations, he missed some of his own classes and fell behind in his coursework. Further depressed and angry when a neighbor told him he had seen Luoth's wife with a Lao man, he beat her and was ordered by the police to leave his home.

Luoth never learned English, could find no work other than gathering mushrooms, salal, and clams, and was thrown out by his new girlfriend. After experiencing multiple problems at school, his children dropped out. His son spent years in jail, and his daughter has had numerous "husbands" and children, themselves growing up in poverty, dropping out of school, and having troubles with the law. Luoth's wife never learned English and has had several abusive husbands. Luoth is an example of the problem of missed information and opportunities; he received too little of the information he needed to succeed, and it always came too late.

Other Khmer came much closer to Cambodians' view of the American dream. Phirum's family of five arrived in 1981. A week after arrival, with his wife watching the children and learning where best to shop, he took the bus to begin daily English classes. Within another week, Americans knew he was a former teacher, and within two months, he was interpreting for other Cambodians. After six months, he began an electronic assemblage vocational training class. Two years later, he found a job at an armored car manufacturing company and moved to suburbia, saying he was doing so to remove his children from a "bad" neighborhood and himself from constant pleas for help from other Khmer. Several years later, with their children in school, his wife completed a training course and began working for the same armored car company. When Phirum was laid off, he studied at employer expense; soon rehired, he progressively acquired promotions and higher wages. After twenty-five years, both continue to work at the same company, have a home and considerable savings, and have put their children through college. Phirum, his wife, and others consider themselves successfully resettled, although they say they have faced numerous struggles; Phirum's own daughters caused their parents years of worry before settling down.

As the children of first-generation Cambodians graduated from college and acquired professional jobs, many purchased their own homes in the suburbs. Some with more resources moved into gated communities, but most moved to developments often many miles from workplaces and previous communities. Most parents who moved with children devote themselves to grandchildren and the home while their own adult children are at work, but many lament their distance from a Khmer temple, ethnic stores, and other Cambodians. A number of other Khmer with less education and lower-paying jobs also moved from inner-city areas to their own homes in safer neighborhoods, usually pooling family resources from several employed adults, youth with part-time jobs, and older family members receiving government benefits. Many of these families remain closer to the Khmer community and temple than do Cambodian Americans with more resources.

Incorporation into American Life

Cambodians' attitudes toward citizenship are testament to their ambiguity about their identity. For many, attaining American citizenship was evidence of America's acceptance of them and their acceptance of America, and Cambodians said citizenship provided them with protection against the capaciousness of events such as they experienced in Cambodia. Other refugees said, however, that becoming an American citizen seemed a betrayal of their ancestors and homeland. A number of Cambodians neglected becoming naturalized because they did not understand the process or feared they could not pass the citizenship test. With the advent of welfare reform in 1996, however, Cambodians rushed to apply for citizenship, particularly the elderly and disabled, fearing benefits would be restricted to legal immigrants. The threat of deportation in the early 2000s set off a new wave of citizenship applications, mostly by younger Khmer who were resettled as children and had never understood citizenship benefits or had the resources to apply. By 2007, three-fourths of those of Khmer ethnicity in America were citizens, many of them by birthright (American Community Survey 2007).

In the 1980s, Khmer refugees often said they were not Americans. They said they were relieved to be in America but emphasized their Khmer heritage. In the twenty-first century, most continue to emphasize that despite their American citizenship, they are Khmer. Their children, however, say without hesitation that they are Americans, and they are proud to display the symbols of America; the American flag flies beside the Buddhist and Cambodian flags over most temples and is displayed at most events, often with a statue of Buddha sitting between the flags. In non-Buddhist settings, the American flag shares decorative pride of place with the flag of Cambodia. Numerous Cambodians have served in America's armed forces. Master Sargent Sarun Sar served in several states and on most continents, including Afghanistan, where he was awarded the Silver Star. Typical of many Cambodians who have done well in America, he has been involved in assisting his homeland, obtaining funds from the State Department to remove land mines in one of the most heavily mined countries in the world (Silliman 2006). First- and second-generation Khmer are increasingly asserting their legal rights, filing lawsuits over temple ownership and other issues. Phanna Xieng sued People's National Bank, saying he was denied a promotion on the grounds that his accented English prevented him from dealing with customers who had been refused loans. The Supreme Court of Washington agreed with him and awarded him $389,000 in 1993. The vigorous rebuttal of a Khmer doughnut shop owner, after the government charged her with fraud for filing false income tax returns, resulted in her being cleared of the charges.

Most resettled Cambodians have had little understanding of American politics; their interest has been in the politics of the homeland. Most have not been interested in voting, but over the years, an increasing number have become interested, particularly as they become aware of the consequences politics have on their lives. In 2003, Long Beach Cambodians asked officials for more help with youth violence and gangs (Needham and Quintiliani

2008), and Cambodians in other communities have requested similar assistance from politicians and law enforcement officials. Cambodian Americans have run for city council and the school board but lack grass-roots support and financial support (Samkhann Khoeun, Thompson, and Strobel 2008). In 1991, Chanrithy Uong, a Cambodian American guidance counselor at Lowell High School, was elected to a seat on the city council, the first nonwhite elected official in Lowell, Massachusetts, and the first Cambodian American city council member in the United States (Nien-chu Kiang 2007).

Cambodians have also became increasingly involved in national events, protesting the 1996 welfare reforms and early 2000s deportations and asking for American politicians to respond to Cambodia's abuse of human rights. There was an increase in Cambodians' support of Republicans after President Bush appointed Cambodian Sichan Siv as deputy assistant to the president in 1989 (whose memoir, *Golden Bones: An Extraordinary Journey from Hell in Cambodia to a New Life in America*, was published in 2008), and President Obama's 2008 candidacy excited many younger Cambodian Americans, who voted and campaigned on his behalf. Khmer Americans gradually realized that completing forms, providing informa-tion, and learning about available resources often determined the flow of materials and services to them, especially victims of hurricanes, oil spills, floods, and tornadoes. Several Cambodians who had served in the mili-tary said they were beginning to understand the political decisions that led to overseas military activities, and others said they were realizing the importance of influencing decisions that affect educational and employ-ment opportunities. A Boeing worker was upset by the North American Free Trade Agreement, worrying with colleagues that they might lose their jobs if Boeing hired inexpensive labor in other countries.

The incorporation of Cambodians into American community life is evident in media representation. The focus on Cambodians shifted from portrayals of Khmer Rouge survivors in the 1970s and 1980s to "rags to riches" or "tragedy to achievement" stories through the 1990s, such as those of survivors Dith Pran and Haing Ngor of *The Killing Fields* fame. In the 2000s, ordinary Cambodians became visible in American obituaries. Typical is an obituary for a 71-year-old reporting that the retired assembly line worker arrived in America in 1981, moved to St Petersburg, Florida, in 1987 from Connecticut, and was a member of the city's Cambodian Buddhist Temple (*St Petersburg Times* 2003). As Americans have discov-ered the financial benefits of Khmer celebrations, their acceptance has grown. Casino billboards advertise "Asian nights," "Cambodian dance troupe," or "Khmer New Year's" in Tacoma, and an annual Thanksgiving event sponsored by a Santa Ana Khmer organization includes turkey dinner with ingredients donated by local businesses, churches, and politicians.

Another obituary gave the birthplace of a man aged seventy-five and said his wife was murdered "in the Khmer Rouge War." The obituary said "he gathered his children and left Cambodia" and was sponsored by a Presbyterian church in Lake Geneva, Wisconsin. He was "a peace activist in the US fighting for Cambodian freedom from Communism" and "spent much of his time writing letters to the United Nations and President Bush for the cause of Cambodian freedom, and established the Cambodian Association of Wisconsin." After listing the names of his children, the obituary said visitation and services would be held at the Khmer temple (*Wisconsin State Journal* 2007). An immigration lawyer was honored at his death by Buddhist ceremonies in both Cambodia and at a Khmer temple in Massachusetts and televised on the local Khmer channel (*Lowell Sun* 2007).

With increased English, Cambodians have had more contact with peers, colleagues, and neighbors, including romantic ties that have often resulted in children, upsetting some older Cambodians, who say disparagingly with a shake of the head, "He had a baby with a Mexican" or "She has a black boyfriend," and view them as white, Mexican, native, or black but "definitely not Khmer" (Linna Teng 2012: 21). Other first-generation Cambodians have been accepting of mixed-race babies, saying, "We are in America now," one woman adding, "And we've been here a long time." Cambodian parents are distressed when their children spend most of their time with American partners and families, although many adult children eventually turn back to their family and community. Other parents, however, are happy with their children's knowledge of American ways. They regret the loss of heritage among Cambodian Americans but are grateful they are healthier and more prosperous than they say they would have been in Cambodia.

Khmer youth are also broadening their involvement in the professional world. Most students initially went into engineering or other technology fields favored by their parents, whose reverence for formal or applied sciences was often greater than for social or natural sciences or humanities, and some young people entered college via the military, thus choosing the more technical fields needed by the armed services. An increasing number of Cambodian Americans, however, are becoming school teachers, journalists, rappers, filmmakers, and even social scientists, including Khieng Un, Leakhana Nou, Khatharya Um, Naranhkiri Tith, Sody Lay, Chhany Sak-Humphry, Sophal Ear, and Jonathan HX Lee.

American incorporation is also seen in the English of Cambodian Americans. Youngsters learn the languages of those around them, and most speak English in the dialects of the cultures and regions in which they grew up: Cambodian Americans speak street language, Ivy League, southern drawl, or Philadelphia, New Jersey, Long Island, Cajun, New England, or Minnesota English. Wright's (2010) description of two Khmer-Mexican American students in San Antonio who speak Spanish and English but not Khmer is not uncommon. Some Cambodians are utilizing their Khmer background in America; they say learning fluent Khmer not only gives them pride in being Khmer and allows them to speak with Khmer elders, but it qualifies them for employment requiring bilingual skills in America and Cambodia. There are fourteen million Khmer speakers in Cambodia and another million overseas, and Khmer is on the list of languages for which the federal government needs advanced-level speakers (National Security Education Program 2015). One Cambodian American proud of her fluent Khmer is Soben Huon, who competed in the 2006 Miss USA Pageant. An accomplished linguist, dancer, and musician who studied international relations in Germany and is now a financial advisor, she said proudly during the competition that she "speaks fluent Khmer" (Hardy 2006). She is the exemplar of "fobulousness" to which many youth aspire.

Although there is interest among some young people in learning Khmer, English-only programs and the No Child Left Behind Act of 2001 have facilitated the loss of Khmer for many Cambodian Americans. The current ideological bias toward immigrants and English-only policies devalues Khmer and other cultures and languages and is counter to American interests by further isolating Americans globally. Some young Cambodian Americans resist American disdain for immigrants, turning "FOB," the derogatory "Fresh Off the Boat" to describe awkward newcomers, to "Fabulous Oriental Beings," some claiming "FOB" refers to immigrants who share characteristics such as "You speak perfect English and you are fluent in your native language" (*Urban Dictionary* 2012b).

Cambodians have increasingly turned English to their own advantage, throwing English words and phrases into Khmer conversations. They borrow English phrases to describe their own experiences, such as comparing the Khmer Rouge to 9/11 terrorists. Khmer refugees resettled in Tacoma, Washington, referred to Saint Joseph as the "hole hospital," because of its round windows, and Mount Rainer standing grandly over the city as the "ice mountain." Cambodians celebrated their new country, *amayrrekaing*, with a multitude of simplified terms; California became "Cali," and an area of one town on Thirty-Eighth Street with a number of Asian markets was called "Thirty-Eight." Cambodians continue to use Khmer metaphors to explain themselves and their experiences to the Americans and other immigrants surrounding them, describing elders as trees on an undercut riverbank whose roots are no longer founded in soil, and youth as a river overflowing its banks and lacking guidance (Silka 2007).

Whatever their experiences of resettlement were and their efforts to adjust to life in America, Khmer refugees spoke often of the importance of family to them as Cambodians and as survivors.

Chapter Five

Family

After resettlement in the United States, Khmer refugees talked often about family, saying the ideal Khmer household is composed of a husband, wife, and children, with primary relationships being between parent and child and husband and wife. Khmer family members are further embedded in a network of kinfolk called literally "older younger" (*bong b'aun*). Family members include the residents of a household, who share shelter and food and may consist of biological, marital, and fictive relatives. Both maternal and paternal kinfolk are potential kin, and family includes deceased ancestors and unborn children. As Cambodians have done traditionally, Khmer often define various Khmer and non-Khmer as fictive kin, addressing and referring to them by kin terms, including them in family activities, and equating them in importance with other kinfolk. Some resettled Cambodians said acquiring fictive kin enabled them to rebuild families decimated by war and the Khmer Rouge and fractured by migration. Others spoke of acquiring fictive kin to assist them with resettlement.

Cambodians described fictive kin they had met during the Khmer Rouge years, during flight from Cambodia, or in the refugee camps who they had learned were trustworthy. One family said they began calling their neighbor in the refugee camp "grandmother" because of her kindness to them, and years later, they continued to treat her as a beloved elder and assist her as she became crippled with arthritis. One Khmer said of the man who helped him during the Khmer Rouge years, "He is always my brother." One man said his "brother" saved his life by hiding him during their flight from Cambodia. Another man called the woman who nursed his motherless baby in the refugee camp his "always sister." After arrival in the United States, a number of Khmer refugees began referring to Americans as family and addressing them by kin terms; sponsors most often fit this role, since they had initial responsibility for refugees.

Importance of Family

Cambodians say family provides them with reassurance, advice, and identity and assert that it is among family members that they reveal, celebrate, and solve their joys and difficulties. Cambodians said life in Cambodia before the Khmer Rouge years centered on family, one man saying that "when one has a family, the world is only them." Cambodians said they considered re-establishing familial relationships after resettlement of utmost importance, and they wanted to do so according to traditional concepts of status, class, and hierarchy. Many resettled Khmer spent most of their nonworking hours with relatives, and many Cambodian Americans continue to do the same. A young married couple, who were seven and thirteen when they arrived in the United States in the early 1980s, said in 2009 that they spend most of their free time with the wife's parents, sister, or other relatives. The wife added, "It seems to me that family is more important to Cambodians than for Americans."

Through the years, Cambodians agreed that Americans do not consider family important and were surprised when Americans found it newsworthy that a young Khmer woman took in seven younger siblings after their parents' death rather than allow them to go into foster care. One man said, "The first thing you must know about us is that it is not the individualism of Americans that is important to Cambodians, but the family." When one young man's girlfriend had his child, his wife and sisters stepped in to care for the infant. While the former girlfriend was at work, the man's wife watched the baby. The child is now in high school and continues to spend after-school hours with his father's family until his mother picks him up on her way home from her job. Although the women never speak to one another, the child benefits from having two "mothers" and scores of indulgent relatives.

Cambodians also say family is important because the behavior of one member can affect any other family member, and the reputation or "face" of a Khmer individual and his or her family is important to them. A Cambodian with a good reputation has a good face, while a Cambodian without has a mean or shattered face, and Cambodians assert that they strive diligently to avoid the latter. Khmer refugees often spoke of one family or another who had moved away after feeling shamed by a misbehaving son or a pregnant unmarried daughter. One man said he moved to another town because he was laid off from his job and he thought other Cambodians were saying he had been fired. Cambodians also worried that any improper behavior on the part of one family member would bring retribution from the spirits on a family member and not necessarily the one who had misbehaved. They explained that fear that an innocent family member might suffer causes each member of the family to be concerned with the behavior of everyone else in the family.

Ideal Husband and Wife Relationships

Cambodians say the importance of the husband and wife relationship is revealed by its permanence, boasting that couples stay together "like Americans do not, because they are Cambodian." Cambodians say husbands and wives should stay together because their marriage has been determined by fate, and young people contemplating marriage often consult a fortune-teller to determine if they are compatible. The marriage ceremony itself is performed in the presence of family and friends and, Cambodians say, witnessed by their ancestral spirits. Cambodians claim the marriage itself binds the couple together, one woman saying, "If you don't get married, it is easy to come together, easy to go apart."

Gender relationships are hierarchical but are also complex and often ambiguous and contradictory. Cambodians describe men as dominant over women, and women as submissive to men, but many also say men and women are equal to one another. The inequality of couples is evident in their respective ages and terminology. A husband is usually older and, respective of actual age, commonly refers to his wife as "younger sibling" (*b'aun*), while a woman calls her husband "older sibling" (*bong*). The same traditions continue in many Khmer households in the twenty-first century, although a number of younger couples are increasingly treating one another as they say American couples treat one another and addressing one another by their first names, although many revert to traditional behavior and terminology when around extended family, with wives using "older sibling" to address their husbands to please their parents. Some Cambodian Americans say they model their marital behavior on the way American couples act toward one another on television. "We don't go into American houses," said one young wife, "so we just watch them on TV and at the store."

Whatever their thoughts about the relationship of men and women, Cambodians claim both men and women are taught to follow the ways of their ancestors in fulfilling their obligations to spouse, children, and relatives and protecting the family's reputation. In the early years of resettlement, they described Khmer girls being socialized in Cambodia prior to 1975 to walk so their skirts did not rustle, while boys learned they would lead their household. Numerous Khmer men said they were the head of their household and responsible for the behavior of everyone in it, and even wealthy and powerful women habitually portrayed themselves as quiet and passive.

Cambodians say they expect husbands to provide shelter and food, while women are to assist men in their work and care for home and children. Discussions of proper Khmer behavior are considerably briefer for husbands than they are for women. Cambodians claim a good husband is physically and emotionally stronger than his wife. Several Cambodians said if one wants to "insult a weak man, call him a woman." He may have a humorous nature, but Cambodians say men must "act like men," demonstrating their strength by controlling their wives and children. After a prominent leader in one community died in middle age, Cambodians frequently noted that his widow sometimes acted improperly now that her husband was no longer around to manage her behavior. "She's out of control because her family is too weak to control her," one older man said.

While his wife is responsible for her children, a husband is answerable to his relatives, ancestors, and the larger Khmer community for the behavior of his wife and children, while his wife is responsible for the behavior of the children. Thus, one man explained, if his child misbehaves, a Khmer man will strike his wife rather than the child. Cambodians say there is no point in hitting the child because children lack reason and are too young to learn from being punished. Another man said, "When wives act badly, husbands can beat them. If they don't beat the wife, the husband has stopped caring for her." Although a husband should be stronger than his wife and dominant over her, he should avoid fighting with her. Sathea said, "If you fight with your wife, that shows you are a weak man."

Cambodians describe male purity as a goal men should attempt, although they say most cannot achieve it. Cambodians also say male purity has less to do with sexuality than female purity has for women. Cambodians describe an ideal husband as a man who is faithful to his wife, avoids alcohol and gambling, follows tradition, and maintains an obedient family. Cambodians say former monks make good marriage partners because they have demonstrated obedience, patience, discipline, and respect for tradition when they served as monks. Conversations about male obligations usually become discussions about females, who must be pure because men find it so difficult to be the same. Cambodians warn that women must always be cautious because of the nature of men. One man quoted a proverb as evidence that men are insatiable, saying, "Ten rivers cannot fill a sea; ten women are not enough to satisfy a man." His wife added, "This is true, but a woman loves only one man."

Cambodians say sex is what men seek because of their nature, and sex is what unmarried women are responsible for avoiding. An older man warned that Khmer men are always trying to trick women into being with them alone, "even American women!" he said laughing, and he urged me to be careful about going anywhere alone with a Khmer man. He said this is probably true of all men, but he knows for certain that it is true for Khmer men. Cambodian men note their own frailties with humor rather than shame, often commenting that it is good their wives are "good" women because they are uncertain about their own proclivities. If a male acts improperly, it is a stain on him and his family's reputation, but if a girl acts improperly, her family's reputation is ruined for generations. "Men are like gold or diamonds, which can be washed clean if dropped in the mud," Cambodians say, quoting a popular proverb, but "women are like white cotton cloth, which once soiled by mud can never be clean again."

Cambodians say a "perfectly virtuous woman" is pure in body and mind (Ledgerwood 1990a). Unmarried girls were traditionally thought to be ignorant about anatomical and sexual matters, were expected to remain chaste, and were seldom out of sight of a family member. Women thought to be impure were treated as outcasts and compared to animals; in America, Cambodian women thought to be impure were described by Khmer refugees as being "like Americans." One woman said sadly about kissing in public, "It must be embarrassing as a human being to do such a thing." Another said Americans do not understand that "the body is not like a toy that you can get on and off of. That is not human." A number of Khmer women said they knew nothing about menses before puberty or sex before marriage. The bride of an arranged marriage said she could not believe what her husband was saying when he explained marital relations on their first night together, saying later, "No one had touched me in my life" and he was "trying to thrust against me like that?" Too embarrassed to ask family members for advice, she did not allow her husband to touch her for a week, finally yielding to him after realizing she was tied to him permanently.

After marriage, Cambodians say the purity of a wife rests on being true to her husband. One Khmer man said, "Whomever a Khmer wife loves first, she loves forever." Another man explained that being a good wife is like weaving beautiful cloth: it must be done consistently. If neglected, both marriage and threads become tangled and the pattern is lost. Thus, Cambodians say, if a woman becomes entangled in bad behavior, the reputation of her family suffers. Women not only bear a greater obligation to be virtuous than their husbands, Cambodians say they have more responsibility when things go wrong. They must accept blame and not shame husbands by revealing private matters. Numerous Khmer men agreed that wives should stay at home, should not worry about thinking, and should be respectful in what they say. Yet many men insist that women have considerable power, including responsibility for household finances.

Cambodians say a Khmer wife handles the family's income, allows her husband a small allowance, and must be consulted by her husband before he makes a major purchase or becomes involved in a business enterprise.

Both men and women claim such a financial arrangement is necessary because, in one man's words, "women save money but men spend it." When students in an adult English language class were discussing a museum field trip in 1983, one man said the cost did not matter. A female fellow student snapped at him, "Of course it doesn't matter for you. You don't have to worry about the house and the children and paying the bills." Excited at the prospect of getting a raise and having more than the weekly ten dollars his wife gave him, a bilingual worker told his boss in 1990, "Please don't tell my wife. Then I'll have some money to spend myself." One wife refused her husband's requests for a hair permanent and for liposuction on his stomach, saying, "He wants to be beautiful, but this is too expensive." By controlling finances, women say they can reduce the chances of their husbands being unfaithful, since "girlfriends are expensive."

Family Resettlement Difficulties

After resettlement in the latter 1970s and early 1980s, Cambodians' memories of Cambodia and their difficulties with resettlement made them especially eager to be near family, but American placement policies often resulted in extended family units being separated and settled in different locations. Buildings and housing codes were ill-suited for large or extended families and often restricted "family" to those with biological or legal connections (Haines 1980). Despite these obstacles, Cambodian refugees devoted considerable energy to trying to live together in the same dwelling or near one another in the first decades after resettlement and found that low-income areas allowed greater freedom from regulations and scrutiny. Khmer households were flexible: relatives came and went, sometimes staying for years to attend school or work in a particular location or profession, or for companionship, for protection, or to share expenses.

The trend to live near extended family continues for many Cambodian Americans in the twenty-first century. In one survey conducted in southern California, 61 percent of the Khmer surveyed lived with extended family (Khmer Girls in Action 2011). In 1981, Pisey's family included his wife, three children, eight of the couple's siblings including five minors, an "uncle" adopted in the camp to be an additional male presence, and several Khmer foster children. A generation later, most live in the same neighborhood in several purchased homes and have been joined by wives, extended family from Cambodia, and numerous children. Khmer elders generally care for the household and children while parents work outside the home, and in-laws are often household occupants.

Cambodians say, however, that living together has not been easy. Particularly in the early years but still common in the twenty-first century, Khmer households have often been overcrowded, a situation that is especially stressful when family members feel used or do not get along. Cambodians find an irritating cousin, unstable grandmother, constantly complaining uncle, or mother confined to her bed by grief difficult to tolerate. In 1981, members of one family admitted the screams of their aunt frequently waking from nightmares disturbed their sleep and made it difficult to learn English and pay attention to their instructors at school and work. In 1987, a young couple said sharing an $800-a-month, three-bedroom apartment with a cousin and his wife was bearable, but they complained that the cousin's smoking irritated the wife's asthma and ventilation in the apartment was bad. Despite the difficulties of living with extended family members, most Cambodians are saddened when house size or restrictions do not allow them to live with a widowed sister or sick grandmother and her orphaned grandchildren. The presence or absence of both nuclear and extended family was often a factor in the success and ease with which Cambodians faced their new lives after resettlement. Through the decades of resettlement, Cambodians have continued to work at reconstituting their families, sponsoring spouses and kinfolk from Cambodia, and settling near one another.

Long before resettlement, Cambodians said their marriages were suffering from death, separation, and hardship. The death of a spouse from violence, starvation, or disease left a disproportionate number of families headed by widows and grandparents, and more women than men were resettled in the United States. Some Cambodians were forced into marriage by the Khmer Rouge, who arbitrarily paired couples and married them en masse. Others married in the camps for assistance with children or protection from assault or rape. Although Khmer survivors were anxious for peaceful lives, their experiences had consequences on their relationships. Many families struggled. Some men established a second household, acquired an additional wife, or left a first wife for a second. When divorce was followed by remarriage, conflict between children and stepparents often followed. Numerous couples remained together, however, raising children, reuniting family members, and learning to adjust to a new country. Although women-headed households frequently experienced financial difficulties and conflict, many Khmer women held their families together, sometimes taking low-paying jobs that separated them from home for long periods of time, reduced their ability to learn English and skills, and left children with little supervision.

Cambodians agree that women changed faster than men in the years after resettlement, with opportunities unavailable to them in Cambodia and better able to gain education and jobs than men if they learned English rapidly. Women also had more transferable skills, such as food preparation, childcare, and cleaning. With jobs, women were able to acquire funds, independence, and mobility and were able to move around without the permission or knowledge of husbands or families. Some women refused to marry. Kolab had her own job, car, and house, said she was happy being independent and able to devote her time to her siblings and their children, and asserted she would never marry.

Even women living traditional lives within extended families had new options. After failing to appear for work as a day-care aide, Jorani remained out of touch from eight in the morning until evening. Her husband retrieved their children from school and the babysitter's and was, in his words, "crazy" with worry the entire day. When Jorani finally returned home that evening, she said she "had run away" to the public library because her father, who lived with them, had spoken harshly to her. The cause for her distress was traditional, the abandonment of her responsibilities to family was new, and the library in which she took refuge was a new resource for her. Most women said they welcomed the changes they experienced in America and were happier working than staying home but said the changes in women's lives disturbed men, thus challenging traditional ideals and causing family tension (Tuyet-Lan Pho and Mulvey 2003).

In the early years of resettlement, many Khmer men expressed concern over the changes Khmer women were making in their lives. Men, especially elders, said they worried that women were changing too fast. "Families fall apart because women no longer do what is expected of them," one older man said, adding that many young women had forgotten Buddhist laws. Other men complained that women took jobs without their husbands' approval, were no longer "holding their culture" as was their duty, and were undermining their husbands' position as head of the family. Men complained that women were adopting American speech, movement, dress, and gestures, putting their own interests above their family's, not supervising their children, using birth control or having abortions, and being more vocal in the family, community, and temple. Men were particularly resentful when their own options narrowed and they experienced loss of face while their wives' opportunities increased. When wives earned more than their husbands or became the family's sole support, Khmer refugees said many husbands reacted by being depressed, some seeking solace in drink, gambling, or women, bringing further chaos to those around them.

Cambodians said they were most worried that women were abandoning traditional Khmer sexual mores, some men saying it was no longer possible for women to be virtuous. Women and girls, whose behavior most affected the family's reputation, spent days in the workplace or classroom where men were present, and for eight or more hours a day, the male members of their families were unable to supervise them. Some refugee parents arranged marriages for their daughters as soon as they legally left school, hoping to prevent premarital sex and pregnancy (Ledgerwood 1990a). Cambodians resented American sponsors, employers, and peers who urged women to assert their rights. One man said, "Even Christian Americans promote wrong behavior." He categorized wrong behavior for girls as attending college and waiting until they were older to marry and, for women, attending job training classes and working outside the house.

Women working outside the home brought up issues Cambodians said they had not had to deal with in Southeast Asia. Since women could not take children to work in America, as many who worked in the fields, village, or marketplace had been able to do in Cambodia, they had to find childcare. Cambodians said this was difficult when they lacked extended family members living nearby, were wary of entrusting their children to Khmer or American strangers, or worried that their children were not being raised as they considered proper. When both parents were working away from home, often being absent from home for long periods of time, Cambodians said their relationships with their spouses and children suffered. They described being too exhausted by jobs and household duties to pay attention to the family and said numerous spousal disputes resulted from fatigue alone. One woman said, "My husband comes home and flops in front of the TV and smokes a cigarette, even though I am tired, too." Another wife said she knew the codes of conduct that Cambodians have taught their children for generations, but "I don't have time to put the advice into practice. I am tired; so is my husband."

When spouses were at home together, they had to make decisions about finances and the myriad details of life and deal with their children's misdeeds. That left little time for companionship. One husband said, "I never talk to my wife about nice things." His wife added later, "I like him, but I don't know what he thinks." Some women added to the discomfort felt by the menfolk in their families and community by taking up new habits they said fit their new lives. One woman said that only one female in ten smoked in Cambodia, but in America many did, leading some elders to conclude they were "bad women." A male colleague told me one day that he had to go straight home after work to care for the children because his wife was going out with her friends after her day's work at a restaurant. "Never, never, did she do like that before," he said, adding, "My brother hit his wife when she didn't come home, but I don't want to do that. But I don't know what to do."

The greater the changes in spousal roles and the more husbands disapproved and attempted to reassert control over their wives, the more conflict couples experienced. Some men tried to assert their place as head of the family by forbidding, discouraging, or delaying wives from working or going to school, driving, or going out in public. Some did all the family shopping. One husband was angered when, without telling him, his wife purchased a car he was unable to return without losing money. Some husbands used their wives' ignorance of child support, custody laws, and court procedures to intimidate them by threatening to cut off support, abandon them, or take the children. One husband refused to allow his wife out of the house, telling her he could have her deported to "where the Khmer Rouge still rule" if she displeased him. Illiterate in Khmer and English and isolated, she stayed with him long after Cambodia had become stabilized in the early 1990s, and she was finally "freed," in her words, by her sister who lived in another state.

Some husbands reacted violently to women's increasing independence and nontraditional behavior (Bhuyan et al. 2005). A man in Long Beach killed his estranged wife, her boyfriend, and himself during a wedding at the same restaurant where he and his wife had celebrated their marriage several years before, unhappy that his wife had left him (Marosi and Ornstein 2002). Domestic violence came to be recognized as a serious problem among Khmer communities, even in families lacking an obvious male head of household, since most women were tied to a man in some way (Rasbridge and Marcucci 1992). Verbal abuse, forced marital relations, and physical abuse were common, and officials were often surprised by the brutality of Khmer family violence. In one infamous case, a young man locked his ex-girlfriend's children in the bathroom of her house and murdered her on her return home. His act was seen as particularly heinous because of the presence of the children, whom for years he had treated as his own. For his part, he considered her betrayal a threat to his integrity as a man.

When discussing specific incidents, Cambodians usually asked what the wife had done to cause her husband to hit her. When a Cambodian asked his American sponsor why another Khmer man had beaten his wife, the American replied, "Because he is a bastard." "But why did he beat her?" the man asked again. "Because he was drunk," the sponsor added. Again he asked her, "Yes, but why did he hit her?" Hearing the story, a Khmer woman asked, "And did you ever find out what she did to make him hit her?" When a woman pressed charges against her husband for hitting her in the face with his car keys, Cambodians became so upset with her that she canceled the court date, took her husband back, and moved with him to another state. One man beat his wife when he discovered she had not told him their daughter was living with her boyfriend. The Khmer women telling the story said a wife should never keep information from her husband, making clear they thought the wife was at fault, not the husband.

Many Cambodians were amazed at American views on domestic violence, saying men must be able to control women and children because men are responsible for the family's reputation, and husbands must ensure that women fulfill their duty to raise well-behaved children. Cambodians said violence is sometimes the only option for ensuring good behavior, and a husband's failure to properly discipline his wife and children may cause them to suffer spirit or karmic retribution for their misbehavior. Some Khmer said it was better to suffer the immediate physical harm inflicted by a husband on his wife than future bad karma by being reborn as a lower-status human being or an animal. Most Cambodians distinguished between physical violence and discipline, insisting that while violence is unacceptable, physical discipline is only inappropriate if it results in scars or permanent injury. A number of Khmer women said in the 1980s and continue to maintain in the twenty-first century that although Khmer men sometimes hit their wives and children, most are not excessively violent, and they resent Americans who think Cambodians are a violent people. "You've never even been to Cambodia," one woman told a social worker. "You don't know how Cambodians act there."

Cambodians who acknowledge that violence occurs in some Khmer families say the absence of traditional Khmer constraints has contributed to the problem of family violence. In Cambodia, an older relative, village leader, or monk was often asked to press a battering husband to change his behavior, and either spouse could stay with relatives during times of discord. Bona's grandmother stepped in when his father beat him by grabbing at her son's hands or falling on the floor and wailing loudly, which brought the attention of neighbors and stopped the beating. Children often went to live with relatives when family tensions grew high, and boys sometimes ran away, at least for a time, until parental anger subsided. Facing pressure from extended family members and the community to act calmer, husbands usually tried to repair the relationship with wife or child. In America, however, Khmer communities have consisted primarily of Cambodians who are strangers, with little knowledge of what occurs in one another's homes. It is much easier for Khmer families to conceal internal family conflicts in America than it was in Cambodia.

Cambodians who grant that excessive family violence exists among Khmer families nonetheless are critical of American solutions. Angered that some Khmer children were placed in foster care because of domestic violence in their families, Cambodians likened foster care personnel to the Khmer Rouge, saying they also removed children from their parents. Cambodians note that few American officials are trained to deal with refugee domestic violence, and most know little about Khmer customs or Cambodians' experiences. One man commented, "Maybe Americans wouldn't be so critical of us if they knew what we had endured." His sister countered, "Women suffered, too, and we don't want to be hit again in America."

A number of obstacles have prevented women from escaping violent situations. Linguistic and cultural barriers prevent many from accessing antiviolence services, even in the twenty-first century. Women with little education and English and few job skills or advisors to assist in calling the police, pressing charges, getting a restraining order, and going to court are especially vulnerable to violent husbands. In addition, women who press charges against their husbands fear they will return to continue their violence during usually lengthy legal proceedings.

Cambodian women have also hesitated using American solutions because they fear being blamed by other Cambodians for their husbands' increased anger. In addition, interpretation has often been a barrier to ending domestic violence, especially in the early years after resettlement. Khmer children often interpreted for their parents because they spoke more English, increasing the likelihood the family would downplay the violence, and that continues to be the case in some families. There were also numerous instances in the years after resettlement when perpetrators served as interpreters if they spoke more English than their wives. In such circumstances, few women were willing to describe their husband's abusive ways, and husbands were able to obscure their wives' accusations if they were sufficiently bold to express them.

Cambodian American reluctance to speak of private matters continues to be a deterrent to domestic violence prevention, and the consequences of fleeing an abusive husband are usually dire, with poverty almost certain. While excessive wife-battering among Cambodian American families remains a problem, more women are pursuing legal relief from the men who strike them by calling the police or going to women's shelters, and divorce, previously rare, has become common. A number of women have found that obtaining a job or public benefits allows them to support their children without the assistance of a man, and some Cambodian

American women say welfare workers are more sympathetic and benefits more easily obtained when an abusive husband or boyfriend is absent. Most women also continue to be submissive to their husbands, either reluctantly or willingly. Even women with considerable resources say they find it difficult to contradict their husbands, and several successful businesswomen told me they feared their husbands would leave them if they opposed them.

Many assertive and educated women with well-paying jobs and good English act "traditionally" submissive at home. A laughing "loud" woman becomes quiet and obedient, fetching the television remote, hushing the baby, and reacting to her husband's every demand. One woman said, "I want to be like my grandmother would be if she had to live here." Cambodians say many women are submissive in behavior and then do as they please overtly or covertly; others use persuasion or promises to sway husbands to their view. They act "bad" if displeased, "good" if pleased, always reacting cautiously to prevent their husbands' rage. Most Cambodians say a woman should stick by her husband in all circumstances, and if they cannot, they say they feel guilty about displeasing their husband. A well-paid social worker was a leader in her community but considered herself "a bad wife" because her husband frequently beat her. Even women who leave their husbands do not abandon their ideal of marriage. One woman, whose husband lives elsewhere, keeps his photograph above her bed although he continues to beat her on his rare visits home.

Since the 1990s, some young Khmer men who desire a traditional marriage married women who were born in Cambodia and came to America as immigrants. Some men said they did so because they could not find a wife in America because they lacked family to make marriage arrangements, or they wanted a "pure," traditional wife. Some men said they do not want wives who are "too pushy or loud," whether Khmer or non-Khmer, or who are more interested in partying than raising proper children. One 26-year-old man said, "American girls are spoiled, and Cambodians girls try to act like American girls. They want servants, their families want too much money, and young women do not respect their husbands as they should." Three years later, he sponsored a friend's cousin from Cambodia to be his wife. For their part, a number of women residing in Cambodia have been willing to marry Cambodian American citizens because it allows them to eventually serve as anchor relatives able to import close relatives to America. Such marriages have often been followed several years later by the immigration of the wives' parents.

Many men were in their late twenties or thirties before they had saved sufficient money to make the trip, take gifts to the bride's family, and pay for her paperwork and a journey that costs tens of thousands of dollars and includes money after the wedding to support the wife's family and their resettlement. These women have been particularly vulnerable to spousal violence. At least in the initial years after arrival, most were stay-at-home moms who speak less English than other Cambodians, are familiar with few people other than their husband's family and friends, and fear being deported, ostracized, or unable to find another husband if they return to Cambodia (Tuyet-Lan Pho and Mulvey 2003). Many families, however, have done well, with both husbands and wives pleased with the marriage arrangement they made. Since husbands had sufficient funds to bring wives and their families to America, most were able to support their families subsequently, and most wives attended school, learned English, and obtained jobs.

College-educated Laek visited Cambodia after working several years and met a woman named Kolab. He said she lacked education and came from a poor family, but was good looking and he felt sorry for her. Six years after her arrival, Kolab spoke English well, but her education was being delayed because they had two small children and another on the way. Laek said his wife would eventually study and work. Kolab has now completed an associate of arts degree and has a full-time job. Laek says he has been happily married for fifteen years and is glad he found his wife in Cambodia.

A number of Khmer men, especially second-generation Cambodian Americans, say they have adjusted their expectations about proper behavior, some concluding that women can remain virtuous if they are sexually inactive before marriage, faithful to their husbands after, and respectful to the men in their lives. Men say they are more willing to negotiate with their wives, some accepting their share of household chores. One woman returned home from work at midnight to find the sink full of dirty dishes. She woke her husband, saying, "If you don't do them, you tell your son to do them, but don't leave them like that." He had the dishes done in fifteen minutes, saying later, "I'm not stupid. She makes a lot of money." While some men have become househusbands unhappily because they cannot find work, others say they are content with their domestic situation. Some talk of being glad they can spend more time with their children or on their own interests, while others say they are happy to be away from workplace bosses, misunderstandings, and ridicule. One young man said that rather than marry a young uneducated woman he can "shape" himself, like other Khmer want, he prefers the equality of American spouses and is going to choose someone with whom he can share "all the projects of my life. I can work on the wall, and she can work on the roof."

Family Elders

In the United States, Cambodians learned that Americans correlate appearance and one's well-being with age and are more like to perceive a person as young if he or she is attractive and looks healthy and energetic. Americans also say a person is young if he or she feels young. Cambodians, in contrast, have traditionally defined age according to a person's stage in life, which is itself determined by family need, status, role, and circumstance, rather than by an individual's appearance and feelings. Thus, a person's obligations and privileges with the family shift as people age.

Cambodian individuals are provided for as children, provide for the family as adults, and are again provided for as elders. Young members are to be obedient as they learn the skills needed to support their family, become adults when they can display those skills, and remain adults until their children can support both young and old family members. Shifts are gradual, with people taking on more strenuous and demanding work as they grow into adulthood, and less as they age and their children take over. Shifts can also occur because of necessity: if a youth must care for his mother and siblings after the death of his father, he is considered an adult, and if a woman becomes invalided while still relatively young, she may be considered an old person.

Cambodians say old age is a time of leisure that follows a childhood of dependency and obedience and an adulthood of independence and nurturance. Several Cambodians told me that being old is the reward for having fulfilled one's obligations in life. People's responsibilities are less, their privileges are greater, and older people can spend their time as they wish: tending gardens or weaving, helping family, visiting friends, and being respected and appreciated for their experience, knowledge, and wisdom. They can also concentrate on earning merit to improve their next lives. Their position in the family ensures that they will be given care and security as they grow feebler. Traditionally, older couples often lived with an adult, married daughter, but living arrangements shifted according to family circumstances as reciprocal support flowed from parent to child and back to parent. This hierarchical ordering of exchanges between the generations provided both young and old Cambodians a place in society and a road map for understanding their identity in relation to others.

The first Khmer elders in America were those Cambodians considered elders on arrival. Most over fifty thought they were "old" if they had living or deceased adult children or grandchildren, and some widows considered themselves old even if they were raising small children. Others had ailments that made them feel "like old people." Years later, many resettled

Cambodians described forty as being old (Becker and Beyene 1999). A second group of older Cambodians are those who became elders in the following years. One woman who said she was old in the early 1980s said plaintively in 2012, "Now I am *too* old." A number of Cambodians said their experiences had made them old before their time, often then telling of the latest hospitalizations or deaths of other Khmer they knew. Other Cambodians said they felt old because Americans think they are old.

Cambodians frequently spoke of the love, respect, and care adult children and younger Cambodians extend to their parents and elders, many going to considerable trouble to provide shelter, food, respectful conversation, and a loving environment for their elders (Lewis 2008). Many older Cambodians, in turn, gracefully accept the shift in their own status, live as dependents, and try to find comfort in traditional activities and not think about the past. When possible, they go to weekday ceremonies at the temple and help prepare traditional foods for community celebrations. When they are not at the temple or with friends, they watch television and rent Khmer or Chinese movies.

Some elders expressed surprise at the difficulties they said they continue to endure, one saying, "I didn't know being old in America would be so hard. I thought I would die in comfort." Although some were comforted by Buddhism, many were frightened by aging. Some were pushed into being old by their inability to learn English and find work, and they lamented having too much leisure time. Many worried that they would end up with no one to support them. Others said that while grateful for government support that allows them to contribute to their families, they say it cannot substitute for the loss of status traditionally accorded Khmer elders. Men said they felt useless because they could not help their families; they said they did not know how things work in America, are not strong, and live in dangerous neighborhoods. Women often said they felt glad that they could continue caring for children, cooking, and cleaning for their family, even as they aged. When no longer able to provide childcare for their grandchildren because of physical incapacity or parents' preference for other childcare options, women also lost some of their traditional role in providing knowledge and advice.

Some Cambodians say Khmer elders in the twenty-first century face more difficulties than earlier elders who received considerable support. An illiterate grandmother resettled in the early 1980s with her four grandchildren, ages five to twelve, lived in a dangerous neighborhood, but was helped by a strong patron and caring Khmer neighbors who enjoyed her company, saying she was smart, charming, and kind. Her grandchildren graduated from college, with one always remaining at home with her. When the oldest granddaughter married, she and her husband lived with the grandmother until she died in her late seventies, after seeing her young-est grandchild graduate from high school. Having survived the Khmer Rouge, flight from her homeland, migration, and resettlement, this woman was admired by many for raising grandchildren who respect Khmer tradi-tion, are succeeding in America, and remember her with love and gratitude.

In the twenty-first century, Cambodians say they are alarmed at the rate their countrymen in their sixties and seventies are dying. Some talk of going to funerals "all the time." Virtually every week, an abbot said, there is a funeral ceremony at his temple. Since making that statement in 2014, the abbot himself has become incapacitated and is now cared for by temple participants. Cambodians say they are dying faster now than they would have if they had not experienced years of war and Pol Pot life. Yet Cambodians also point out that they do not age as they would have in Cambodia because of America's sanitation, good food and water, and health care. "If I still lived in Cambodia," Phal said, "I would not be alive." He went on to say that his siblings in Cambodia are dead, all from causes he ascribes to years of hardship. Some elders say they want to die in Cambodia, but few think they will do so. Some worried about the quality of health care they would receive in their homeland, and others expressed concern about returning permanently to a place where they had endured so much pain. "Maybe I would dream too much," one man said. Many Khmer elders say they cannot return permanently to Cambodia because they would miss their children or they would again risk experiencing a catastrophe such as occurred under the Khmer Rouge.

Yet many Cambodians in the United States say they worry about their own children's willingness to care for them. Saying they had cared for their own parents, parents-in-law, and other relatives, they wonder who will do the same for them. One man said, "I took care of my fiancée's grandmother during Pol Pot. I chewed food for her and put it in her mouth so she wouldn't die. But she died. Then I took care of my fiancée. And she died. I took care of my brother. He died." He looked at the floor, then said, "Now I have a wife and her parents and all my children to sup-port although I am feeling sick much of the time. But who will take care of me?" When Samy's welfare benefits were terminated and her son did not provide adequately for her, another woman commented, "I hope that doesn't happen to me."

Some elders were saving money in case their children did not follow Khmer tradition, one man saying, "My wife and I have saved enough money so if our children don't take care of us, we will survive." Looking at the ground, he continued, "I'm sorry to say this about our children, but Cambodians don't know if we can trust the children," then added, "Too American." Cambodians worry that Americans are influencing their youth to leave home when they are eighteen, have their own families, and abandon their parents, citing television programs as their evidence. Cambodians say their children's abandonment is especially threatening because so many kinfolk are deceased, remain in Cambodia, or are resettled in another state or country.

Other Cambodians fear that their children will care for their own children rather than their parents or that younger people raised in America and used to more space and privacy will exclude them from their households. One couple soon to retire were upset because their son and daughter-in-law decided to purchase a house for themselves and their own children, but the son did not ask his parents and siblings to move in with the couple. Cambodians speak of "hanging on" until their children have jobs, graduate from college, or get married, but many are eventually disappointed when they discover they must keep working because their children cannot support them: the children they raised drop out of school, cannot find jobs, get pregnant or get someone pregnant, or leave the household, leaving the parent without support.

One woman said, "I waited fifteen years for my children to finish college and come home to help me with the mortgage. Instead, they got married and bought their own houses. And they don't invite me to live with them." She was especially incensed that her son was spending funds to act as a financial sponsor to bring his parents-in-law from Cambodia. "He takes care of *those* parents, but not me," she said. For his part, the son thought he was acting honorably; his mother was going to receive a pension after she retired, and her house was almost paid off. He felt honor-bound to sponsor his wife's parents and tried to see his own mother as often as possible, although he tired of her constant complaining. "Anyway, she can live with me whenever she wants," he said. A number of parents paid for elaborate weddings for their children in spite of economic struggles, saying they did so in hopes their children would care for them later.

Many Khmer fear having to live in a nursing home. Even Cambodians with attentive, caring families harbor fears of abandonment in an American institution, away from their families and the Khmer community. One woman with especially devoted children had a well-paid job for twenty-five years but lost her pension when the company went bankrupt. Now she wonders, "Although my son and his wife and my daughter and her husband work, what will they do with me when I get too old to take care of myself? Will they send me away to one of those old people houses?" Another worried that her daughter might get rid of her because her family had money problems, saying, "They only keep me because of my social security."

A number of older Cambodians who live with family members say they experience considerable isolation. Elders who live with adult children in the suburbs are often left alone during the day and separated from other Cambodians by responsibilities at home, lack of transportation and language, or fear of discrimination or getting lost. They are often unable to operate sophisticated home equipment or understand descriptions of work, school, and play. How does a son explain his computer networking job to an illiterate grandmother? An older woman told me several months ago that her working daughter is gone from seven in the morning to seven at night, and her son-in-law is gone from six in the morning to eight in the evening. She said her daughter works with scissors, and she has no idea what her son-in-law does; in fact, her daughter works in a factory making scissors, and her son-in-law sells insurance. While most elders' abandonment fears do not materialize, others are left alone by divorce, death, and children involved in college, work, marriage, or the military.

Many older Cambodians express displeasure when their children do not exhibit the traditional respect their elders expect, one woman saying, "My daughter tells me how to cook and take care of children. Cambodians cannot talk like that. Did she forget I raised her?" With increasing age and diminishment, elders feel isolated from traditional relationships and the American-inspired lives of adult children and other Khmer around them. Older Cambodians feel they are growing "out of place," even when they have been in America for years, and find the stigma of being foreigners difficult to bear at a time they assumed they would be respected (Lewis 2009). Some complain that even television no longer provides them with comfort because they cannot hear or see it.

Yet young Cambodians continue to look after their elders. One woman lived alone for ten years while her children attended college, often receiving assistance from her siblings to pay her mortgage. She fought loneliness and stayed with relatives during the winter to avoid paying for heat. Ten years later, her son moved back to live with her, to the delight and financial relief of both. A young Khmer Cham man in Washington told me in the late 1990s that he and his Hawaiian European girlfriend loved one another, but he was not going to marry her because his parents had arranged for him to marry a Cham girl from New York. He had to follow his parents' wishes because "that's how Cham are." Two years after telling me that, he left his girlfriend and married the woman chosen by his parents. "I did what I had to do," he said. Years later, he and his wife are raising their children and caring for his widowed mother. He says he is happy with his wife and family because "I am acting in the right way."

Relationships between parents and children in America were of particular interest to Khmer refugees struggling with their memories and resettlement.

Chapter Six

Parents and Children

―――――

After arrival in the United States, Cambodian parents and their children described their worlds as very different and spoke of having different goals. While Khmer children wanted to please their parents, they also wanted to fit in with their peers. As they grew older, their desire to be like Americans increased, as did their realization that adjustment and success in America were dependent on learning English, becoming familiar with American customs, and gaining American job skills. Khmer parents, on the other side, said they wanted their children to respect the hierarchical nature of family relationships and behave accordingly, as they said Khmer children had done traditionally. Parents wanted children to respect their parents, grandparents, other older kinfolk, and older siblings by honoring and obeying them with the appropriate language and gestures.

Parents' Concerns

Khmer parents also wanted their children to learn the stories, proverbs, Buddhist texts, and sermons that embody Khmer values and emphasize acceptance of the social order but lamented that not many young people were hearing the tales their parents had learned in their childhood. Parents also regretted that their youth were not learning the "codes of conduct" (*chbap*) that Cambodians had been taught for generations, teaching girls, boys, and students how to act toward their superiors. Khmer parents were more concerned that their children's actions could bring shame to the family and retribution from the spirits. Yet Khmer parents said they also worried about disciplining their children in America.

After resettlement, Cambodian parents said they were confused by American child-rearing practices and felt deprived of their traditional means of discipline. If Americans consider adolescents to be children, Cambodians said, they should discipline them when necessary. However,

Cambodians said, it seemed that Americans view children as adults and thus allow them to do as they please. Cambodians said the lack of child discipline in America results from American parents putting their own interests before their children's, and they suggested that Americans do not know how to raise children because they lack a Buddhist framework for child-rearing and are themselves not raised well. They agree that Americans spoil their children, one man saying, I don't want to insult you, but Americans care about children more than old people, just like the Khmer Rouge did."

Cambodians think parental concern for children is best expressed by discipline rather than indulgence. Since the first years of resettlement, Cambodians have been puzzled by the numerous strictures American officials place on child discipline and have worried about violating them. One father said about his son, "I can't beat him or I'll go to jail. So he gets in trouble, and he goes to jail." One man was jailed for several days after hitting his daughter when she returned home late from a date. After attending parenting classes, he committed suicide, telling other family members that he was embarrassed by the shame he thought his daughter had caused the family. Cambodians were also confused by teachers who did not discipline students as teachers had traditionally disciplined students in Cambodia and said that children had to obey because they "belonged" to the teacher as much as to their parents. Teachers were so important, Cambodians said, parents did not intervene in their children's education (also Um Khatharya 1999).

In America, Cambodians complained, teachers instead expect parents to correct children's behavior. One woman said, "I don't know what they do over there at that school, so how can I punish my child?" Cambodian parents have been especially perturbed that schools hold corporal punishment in disrepute, saying it is sometimes necessary (also Kulig 1991). One woman said, "Americans have children, too. They must understand that sometimes you have to hit a child to turn him to the right way." When one fourth grader's parents were told they needed to deal with him because he cursed the teacher, neglected his homework, and caused trouble, the boy's mother asked me, "Why don't they just beat him?" She added, "If the teachers won't beat him, we must, but then we will be in trouble." Another mother grew impatient when her sponsor told her to use "time-outs," saying, "What really works with my child is my hand."

Khmer parents are initially indulgent with small children, who they consider incapable of rational behavior. Believing their children are born unique individuals who have been formed by their actions in previous lives, parents observe them carefully to detect their personality so they can treat them accordingly. Demonstrative toward small children, parents inhale as they press a nose against a child's cheek, coddling the child, and cooing endearments. Cambodians say they never leave their babies and toddlers alone. They sleep with parents, grandparents, or siblings, are never left to cry, and are almost always immediately picked up, comforted, or distracted. Small children are rarely rebuked, unless they are getting into something dangerous.

At around age four, however, Cambodian discipline begins quickly and harshly. Parents begin teaching proper behavior by reprimanding and striking children for their misbehavior. One man said, "If you love a child too much and let it do whatever it wishes, then you will have problems." As youth grow older, punishment increases in severity, and boys traditionally received beatings that occasionally left permanent scars. Punishment at home or school traditionally included withholding food or forcing youth to squat or stand for long periods of time in the sun, crawl on their knees, or hold heavy bags or bricks at arms' length. Although occasionally slapped or beaten, girls were treated more leniently than boys, their activities restricted or workload increased. Parents say children must be disciplined, but cautiously, so as not to crush their spirits. Many parents continue to consider physical punishment a demonstration of love and concern, not of abuse.

Khmer parents said they worried when their children were out of their home and out of their control. When the school bus took their children away on the first day of school, several parents said they had feared their children had been kidnapped and were relieved when they were returned by bus in the afternoon. Their worries that teachers were substituting American values for Cambodian, however, found no relief. Parents said they were appalled by their children's behavior and expressed dismay that teachers were encouraging their children to speak up before their elders, use first names with them, or exhibit ambition, aggressiveness, and selfishness that parents considered disrespectful and inappropriate. Parents disapproved of their children's willingness to challenge authority, which, they said, was antithetical to Buddhism ideals, saying that exhibiting proper behavior was more important than getting ahead. Parents also feared the influence of their children's American peers, who were usually in closer contact with young people than were their parents.

Sexual matters and activity were a particular concern for parents, who were determined their daughters not embrace American sexual values or behavior. As their parents taught them, many parents taught their girls to keep undergarments and menstruation a secret and to treat menstrual blood cautiously because of its power to deplete a man of potency and willpower. A number of Cambodian Americans said they no longer tell these "old ideas" to their children. Cambodian parents also told their daughters not to imitate the sexual behavior they saw on television. Determined to keep their daughters pure, parents forbade after-school activities, sleepovers, and dating, particularly in the first years after resettlement. Many opposed their children's involvement in sex education classes, saying they did not think it appropriate for youth to learn about sex. Others did not allow participation in sports, not wanting their girls to disrobe among strangers or wear shorts in gym classes that one father said "looked like underwear." Marriage became an avenue to keep girls pure, even if daughters had to sacrifice education for marriage, and arranged marriages, traditional in Cambodia, became a means for protecting daughters.

In the 1980s, resettled girls married at a younger age than girls in Cambodia, around sixteen rather than eighteen to twenty-one (Ledgerwood 1990a). Girls as young as twelve or thirteen were often given in marriage, although parents tried to conceal these marriages from Americans, and Khmer ceremonies were common, usually performed without filing legal documents. Decades later, cultural strictures on discussions about sex, sexuality, and sexual orientation continue to prevent youth from seeking birth control or to practice what they learn (Khmer Girls in Action 2011). Long Beach youth said their parents do not think young people should even talk about sex, one girl saying her parents call sex a "bad" thing to do.

Since resettlement, a number of American teachers and administrators have suggested that Cambodians do not value education, and some observers suggest Khmer parents place more importance on their children being obedient and respectful to elders and their family's reputation than they do on academic achievement (Tajima and Harachi 2010). Cambodians agree that they consider respect for elders very important. One man gave an example: "When you pass things to old people, you should pass them with two hands. When you pass something to someone your own age, you can pass it with only one hand, and when you pass something to children, you can hold it with your hand over the top of the glass."

However, while parents believe tradition is important and are reluctant to push their children in specific directions because their nature and future are predetermined, they want them to acquire a good education. They note that Buddhism emphasizes hard work, persistence, and excellence. In the Khmer Girls in Action 2011 survey of hundreds of youth, 93 percent said their parents expected them to get good grades and complete college. From the first months of resettlement, many parents told children they needed to study and think about careers (Theanvy Kuoch 2000). Those who had to defer their own dreams often shifted them to their children, one parent saying their eldest son applied to a prestigious academy because "we didn't have the opportunity to do it when we were his age" (Samkhann Khoeun, Thompson, and Strobel 2008).

Although parents want their children to become educated, some see educational achievement as an impossible goal, as impossible as it had been for them in Cambodia. Many others pressure their children to succeed and make enormous sacrifices to help them. Although they sometimes have difficulty understanding their children's progress or success, parents are proud of their scholastic achievements. Parents are disappointed when children drop out of school, as many who attend underfunded, low-achieving, and dangerous schools do. Dropouts are left with few economic options. Those with guidance, less disruptive environments, and caring and skilled teachers with high expectations of their students do much better than those without.

Children's Resettlement Struggles

Children faced resettlement challenges of their own. Each day took parents and children further from one another as young Cambodians saw opportunities increase with their improved English and knowledge (Portes and Rumbaut 2001). For most children, the younger they were on arrival, the stronger their interest in American rather than Khmer traditions. Children said their parents required them to act as Cambodians at home, but Americans expected them to act like Americans when they walked out their front doors. Classmates and friends pressed Khmer youth to act like Americans, laughing at their names, accents, and clothes.

In the first decades after resettlement, young Khmer said they felt uneasy when they participated in American activities and uncomfortable when they could not join in school sports or dances or after-school events. Some Khmer youth adopted the "street" talk and clothing of their peers. An eight-year-old who arrived in 1986 was nearly unrecognizable in 1994, with the crotch of his baggy jeans falling to his knees and bragging that "I talk 'black' now, Carol," as he talked about his life, friends, job at McDonalds, and the car he was going to buy. When I told him, "I can understand Khmer better than the way you talk!" he laughed, pleased at how "American" he had become. His parents were not pleased but were grateful he continued to respect them.

Children bearing the strain of dealing with traditional elders began realizing the difficulties of fitting in with Americans. They expressed hurt and anger at Americans' reactions to them. Some said they felt shamed by what Americans called their parents' superstitions, by American complaints about fish sauce, tamarind, and incense odors coming from

Khmer homes, or by insults relating to their own and their parents' experiences during the Khmer Rouge years and in the refugee camps or to their accented English. They cringed at Americans' negative comments about them being different. "They think we are terrorists," one boy said. Some blamed the Khmer Rouge for their situation, one girl saying, "Pol Pot killed millions of people in Cambodia, and he pretty much set us in our place for the rest of our life, to be poor." Others wondered if there was something wrong with Cambodians.

Most Khmer children experienced discrimination and hostility from American children, often hearing, "Go back to your country." Many said they hated school and talked of how alien they felt. A seven-year-old asked one day in 1985, "Why do boys call me 'Chink'?" When I said they probably thought he was Chinese, he said, "But I'm Cambodian!" "Well," I replied, "you know more than those boys," small consolation to a second grader. When his fifth grade classmates called another boy Vietnamese, he responded, "I'm Cambodian." They laughed and said, "No, you're Vietnamese!" Expressing his anger later, he said, "They don't even think I know what I am." High school students said they hated being repeatedly asked, "What are you?" and then referred to as Chinese or Vietnamese. They first answered in confusion, "A boy" or "A tenth grader," and then realized they were being asked about origin. Several boys said one day, "I guess we look different to them."

In the twentieth century, few American students or teachers knew why Cambodians were in their school, and many did not care. A high school freshman said one day, "I was so surprised today when a white girl asked me where I was from and then wanted to know all about my country." The situation is similar for many Cambodian Americans in the twenty-first century. Children say they resent being stereotyped either as high-achieving Asians or underachieving dropouts involved in gangs. Among respondents of a 2011 survey, almost half said they were disliked, unfairly disciplined, and graded lower at school than they deserved (Khmer Girls in Action 2011). Americans make little effort to provide bilingual classes to assist Cambodian American children caught between cultures and trying to cope with English. Throughout the twentieth century and into the twenty-first, many American teachers and administrators have viewed bilingualism as a handicap to learning English, despite evidence to the contrary, claiming that learning two languages hinders children from perfecting either one and leads to difficulties for them in achieving social mobility or success in the workplace.

Few schools have offered formal Khmer instruction because of competing demands on budgets and the lack of qualified teachers. Bilingual classes in Khmer and English have been sporadic at best, some ending when states passed anti-bilingual restrictions. Fresno, California, may have had the longest and best program in the country (Olsen 2001). Its Khmer Emerging Education Program began as a grassroots effort with support from some district teachers and administrators. Attendance was high at the after-school classes until the mid-2000s, when children dropped out to attend mandatory classes set up in response to new federal legislation (Wright 2007). In Lowell, Massachusetts, where a third of the students at Lowell High School were of Khmer origin, three full-time Khmer teachers taught Khmer language classes to between four hundred and five hundred students. In most of the country, however, antagonism toward bilingual education and shifting educational standards has replaced bilingual instruction with "sink-or-swim" English immersion (Wright 2003).

The academic reality for Khmer youth has been harsh. While many Khmer children have succeeded academically, the majority have not, instead exhibiting the lowest scores in English proficiency, grade point average, math scores, and career aspirations of Southeast Asians and Americans (Portes and Rumbaut 2006). In the mid-2000s, half of Cambodians twenty-five and older had less than a high school education, and only 6.9 percent had a college degree (Reeves and Bennett 2004). While Khmer children usually know more English than their parents, they experience language difficulties at school. Youngsters spoke of having tired tongues and, two and a half decades later, echo the words of an eleven-year-old who said she had a headache every day and "my ears hurt" from trying to speak and understand English (Horng Kouch 1989: 148). Decades later, almost 90 percent of young survey respondents said they read and write English (Khmer Girls in Action 2011), yet evidence does not support their claims. Schools have tended to categorize Cambodian American students as "limited English proficient" (Rumbaut and Cornelius 1995), and many in grades six through twelve study English as a foreign language (Vichet Chhuon and Hudley 2010).

A high percentage of Khmer children drop out of school. In 2000, 41 percent left high school without a diploma, compared to 15 percent of other students; Long Beach cited a 65 percent high school dropout rate (Chan 2003). Most Cambodian American students were not doing well; some felt their teachers considered them low achievers, and some left to help parents or siblings, marry, support a child, or earn money for cars and electronic devices. Most were supported by welfare benefits or found low-wage, unskilled jobs. Only a minority who graduated high school attended college, and in the mid-2000s, only 6 percent graduated (Niedzwiecki and Duong 2004). Some Cambodian American students spend years in community college rather than continuing at four-year schools. An obstacle to college admittance is a lack of mentors and the lack of information about accessing higher education through pre-college classes or scholarships and about the importance of school activities and community service in obtaining college entrance. Most students receive little help from teachers who are unfamiliar with Khmer lives (McGinnis 2009). In addition, community college personnel who benefit financially from their presence often do not encourage Cambodian Americans to transition to four-year schools (Chan 2003).

From the earliest days of resettlement, also, numerous Khmer secondary students have been tracked into vocational training programs because of the learning handicaps Americans assumed they had, including poor English, resettlement trauma, living in poverty or violent neighborhoods, or having illiterate parents unfamiliar with American schools. Many twenty-first-century educators make similar assumptions. One school devised a course to teach Khmer students the value of "hard work," unaware that most of the Cambodian American students had part-time jobs and helped at home, an obligation that sometimes interfered with completing their schoolwork (McGinnis 2009). American educators often do not take into account that Khmer families expect young people to place the needs of the family above their own wishes.

Research conducted with Khmer college students found that students in 1993 were comfortable with the behavior and speech of their parents and the Khmer community and missed being with other Cambodians when they were at school, while students in 2001, although they missed the expressions of family love, felt more attuned to American discourse and behaviors than those of their parents and Khmer community (Needham 2010). In California, students who attended University of California schools that are considered more rigorous in student admittance, more focused on scientific and academic research and theory, and more service-oriented than colleges in the state university system experienced guilt because of their parents' sacrifice in sending them to a prestigious school in an upper-class neighborhood. They also felt increased pressure to do well for their families and community and experienced more discrimination on campus (Kwan 2008). In contrast, state university students attended colleges close to their parents and hometowns and said they experienced less guilt about their families and less discrimination from their peers on campus.

A number of older Cambodians continue to describe some younger Khmer as being angry, saying they are uncomfortable with both Americans and Cambodians. One man said most of these "angry young men" hold low-paying jobs, know little about Cambodia, and are uncomfortable with being Khmer. Several men said they live in an "oyster" or "television" world and are unaware of the history of their family or their people. While some young people say being Khmer is embarrassing because everything Americans say about Cambodia or Cambodians is "bad, bad, bad," they also react strongly when Americans disparage Khmer identity. Prahm angrily reproached Vithy for saying he was American, not Cambodian: "You talk Cambodian! You eat Cambodian! I look at you, you hair, you eye, you nose. I see Cambodian! You Cambodian!" Even decades after their elders' arrival in America as refugees, many Cambodian American youth feel caught between two worlds, like the young woman described by Lin, Suyemoto, and Kiang (2009) who feels both "too Asian" and "not Asian enough" for her world.

Disconnected Worlds

As time passed and their interests deviated, both Khmer parents and children said they felt increasingly disconnected from one another. Parents were confused by the "inversion of authority" that occurred in what they saw as America's upside-down universe of values, with children interpreting the world for their parents and rapidly disregarding the customs of their "grandfathers and grandmothers." Parents expressed growing apprehension as young Cambodians increasingly incorporated American clothing, food, slang, and dating into their daily lives. Parents who expected children to follow their instructions but were dependent on them in negotiation with landlords and social workers felt humiliated. They said they were saddened that children were expressing increasing disdain for Cambodian ways. Some Khmer children and teenagers asked their mothers to prepare food "like at school," and when their mothers said they did not know how, children told them to buy it.

Family members often no longer shared the same language. Most children learned English more rapidly than their parents, and years after arrival, most parents spoke Khmer and struggled with English, while their children spoke English and barely understood Khmer. Parents worried that most young people saw no reason to learn Khmer; one man said emphatically, "If our children don't learn to talk to the monks properly, we will lose our culture." Four decades after the arrival of the first Khmer refugees, most young Cambodian Americans are able to converse in Khmer only with family members, and their conversations are usually limited to instructions and family logistics.

Some Cambodian Americans admit they have trouble talking to anyone but parents in Khmer and to anyone but peers in English. The shift from Khmer to English as the primary Cambodian household language has been dramatic. Of three hundred youth surveyed in 2011, 93 percent said their parents understand Khmer, but only 23 percent said Khmer is the main language used at home (Khmer Girls in Action 2011). A number of young people are exposed less to school English than street English, or what some youngsters call "ghetto talk," with its slang and expletives. In text messaging and online communication, young users combine abbreviations such as "143" and "AITR" ("I love you," and "adult in the room," respectively) with romanized Khmer.

Not only are youth changing primary languages, but their Khmer is changing. Playing a tag game on YouTube, young people described their Khmer as choppy, "kinda like Spanglish," and several called what they spoke "Camblish." A young girl of Khmer and African American descent began replying "Yes, Mom" (*chyea ma*) to her Khmer grandmother and then to other youth. Now *cha ma* is in use among a number of young Cambodian Americans and African Americans (*Urban Dictionary* 2012a), and its meaning is expanding. When a Cambodian American girl said, "I really want some fried rice," her African American friend replied, "Man, that is so *cha ma* of you to say." In reply to "I wore socks with my flip-flops to school today," another youth replied, "That's some *cha ma* shit."

Young people are relieved when they can follow their own traditions without offending Americans. Khmer teenagers in one town were proud when their high school celebrated Khmer New Year at a special assembly. Cambodian Muslim children in Fullerton, California, found it almost impossible to observe daily prayers during school hours but were grateful teacher aides warned them when the lunch menu contained pork (Efron 1990). Despite the efforts of the young to please both parents and Americans, they say they often fail. Although their American peers like Khmer teenagers' scanty clothing, heavy makeup, and gang symbols, their parents say they think their appearance demonstrates disrespect for Khmer traditions, and many American adults view their appearance as rebellious or disrespectful.

Problems that sprang up in the twentieth century continue in the twenty-first. While parents struggle to support their families and mourn their losses, children grow increasingly resentful of their parents' ignorance of American ways and inability to provide resources and say their parents are frequently overwrought and distant and always different from American parents. Children try to substitute for absent parents, cooking for depressed mothers or babysitting younger siblings in the absence of mothers and fathers. For their part, parents struggle to supervise children, transporting them to school, keeping them busy, entrusting them to relatives or neighbors, or keeping them at home much of the time, but many parents must leave children unsupervised because of jobs or lack the energy to deal with them.

Many parents fear their children are manipulating, stealing, and lying, as parents say they had learned to do from the Khmer Rouge, in the camps, or in more recent years, from American peers. A wife with a philandering husband said she had a difficult time listening to her children's concerns and had no idea what they were doing most of the time. Parents are exhausted, many spending their free time sleeping or sharing problems with one another rather than dealing with troublesome children. Most struggle to reconcile Khmer values with American realities.

For over twenty years, Vannak and his wife had a work schedule that allowed one of them to be home when their children were not at school. Vannak worked the early-morning shift as a hospital orderly, while his wife woke with the children and drove them to school. She worked the late-afternoon shift as a hospital technician, while he drove the children home and remained there until the next day's shift. When illness occurred, relatives living just houses away took over. Another man moved to suburbia to separate his boys from what he considered bad influences. "The outside atmosphere has more influence on kids' behavior than their parents," he said, lamenting that there was too much "violence, loose laws, and freedom" in America. In 2011 he said his children "go their own way, but they have turned out to be good sons." After college, they found high-paying jobs, their father concluding, "I'm just glad they didn't get sucked into too much American."

Cambodians say parental supervision is hampered by a lack of traditional community support from kinsmen, neighbors, and monks, not only in preventing domestic violence but in other aspects of family life. In Cambodia before the Khmer Rouge years, children were an integral presence at virtually every activity, and Cambodians took the proverb "It takes a village to raise a child" much to heart; monks oversaw religious upbringing, relatives and neighbors shared childcare, and neighbors rebuked rambunctious children. In America, family members and neighbors are few in number or often absent with their own family struggles. A colleague often took his infant daughter with him to meetings; on a two-day trip to a temple an eight-hour drive away, he was the primary caretaker of his tiny child.

Some parents said they feel guilt or responsibility for their children's hardships, one mother saying in the 1980s that she was unable to say no to her children, wanting to make up for their years of suffering. Another woman said much the same in 2013 about her children, saying they suffered because she had to work such long hours so, to compensate, she tried to buy them whatever clothes and electronics they wanted. Despite feelings of parental guilt, many work hard to control their children, one father saying it is more important to control his sons than anything he does. "If I lose control over them, they will abandon their responsibilities as Cambodian men to properly care for their families, honor their ancestors, and live proper lives." That, he said, "will make their lives worthless."

Family Conflict

After arrival in America, while parents regretted their lack of connection with their children, their children often concluded their parents did not love them, not realizing their parents considered instruction and admonishment stronger indications of love than overt displays of affection. Many claimed their parents paid no attention to them, were too occupied with their own struggles, could not help them with schoolwork, and had little awareness of being young in America. Children often expressed disdain for parental platitudes about proper behavior that seemed irrelevant in America.

Decades later, children continue to say they would prefer the hugs and kisses Americans give their children to their parents' sternness (Needham 2010). Some say their lack of respect for their parents and rebellion against them comes from a lack of freedom and parental attention. Other young people are disdainful of older Cambodians who "make us look bad," and they are disturbed by Cambodians' gossip, concern for image, and need to outdo one another (Sar 2010). Nevertheless, a number of young Cambodian Americans say the adults they truly admire are their parents, because of the struggles they endured and the efforts they make for their children.

The conflicting struggles and goals of parents and children have led to considerable conflict between them. They have clashed over dress, food, home decorations, homework, bedtime, entertainment, even traditions such as removing shoes at the doorway and bathing by bucket and scoop (Choi, He, and Harachi 2008). In attempting to control their children's behavior, particularly sexual behavior, parents have been unable to completely isolate their daughters from boys. The rift between parents and youth widens as children grow older and turn increasingly to peers for social support. Parental lack of English and ignorance of American ways is convenient for their children, who tell them, "This is the American way," without fear that parents will learn otherwise. Children say they often use the technique, boasting that their parents rarely catch on.

When they cannot get their way, young people frequently resort to subterfuge: leaving home in one set of clothes and switching to baggy pants, sports jersey, and cap or scanty dress for school; saying they are at work when they are with friends; or claiming to be doing well at school when the opposite is the case. Other youth said they cannot understand why spiked hair, punk clothing, or tattoos make them less Khmer, as their parents claim, but they conceal their behavior. One girl said, "My mom thinks I will turn into a slut if I wear makeup and go to a dance. So I tell her I'm staying with a friend, and do it anyway. But I don't sleep with boys, no way, but my mother wouldn't believe me, so I don't tell her." Many parents have no control over where their children go, what they do, or who their friends are. From the time youth leave in the morning until they return in the afternoon, parents have little authority to influence their behavior; there is little point in demanding children return home immediately after school if parents do not know when school ends or they are still at work. Parents whose children were compliant at home were often amazed to learn they were acting out at school or had been arrested.

One mother said she was happy her two sons were obeying her at home, but she wondered what they were doing elsewhere. Although she suspected her fourteen-year-old had dropped out of school, she was not sure. "I just ask the spirits to keep them out of trouble, because, really, I have no control over them." Virtually every child participates in activities they conceal from their parents, from engaging in harmless joking with youth of the opposite sex to committing criminal acts. Youth often run away from home, usually at adolescence but some as young as ten or eleven. Counselors estimated a third of refugee families in Seattle in the 1990s had at least one runaway child (Ingrassia 1994).

Some runaways are "couch surfers," staying with a series of friends until their welcome wears out or they find an alternate place to stay. Parents with few resources often said they felt unable to compete with their children's friends' offers of food and shelter and usually did not call police or other officials because they feared authority figures. Nevertheless, they say they are depressed and worried about their children. To prevent children from leaving home, some parents allow them to behave in nontraditional ways: curfews are expanded or dissolved, daughters are allowed to date, or boyfriends or girlfriends are permitted to live in the family home. After letting her son's girlfriend share his bedroom, one mother said, "I don't like it, but it's better than having my son go away."

Worry their children will join gangs is perennial among Khmer parents. Some young Khmer said they joined gangs to protect themselves, younger siblings, and other family members from other gangs rather than from any desire to cause trouble; others joined for a sense of belonging, to appear fearless or "cool," or because they wanted friendship, respect, purpose, and access to girls, money, and possessions. Many said they felt invisible or like outcasts or that their parents were not available for them, so they joined a gang (also Virak Khiev 1992). A number of young people said they found gang membership preferable to working low-wage jobs. One youngster said he joined a gang when he was ten because wearing fancy clothing and expensive jewelry and riding around in cars was more appealing than following his parents' directions. A fourteen-year-old growing up in an inner city neighborhood said his parents were trying to live as Cambodians, but he wanted to join a gang because it would give him comrades, status, and money. Some gang members live peacefully at home and hide their gang affiliation, which in itself reflects some parental ignorance of American culture and lack of communication with their children.

At first joining American or immigrant gangs, Cambodian youngsters were soon forming Khmer gangs. Over the years, Khmer gangs proliferated and included TRG (Tiny Rascals Gang), Cambodian Boyz, Lazy Boyz, and Cold Blooded Cambodians, also known as Crazy Brothers Clan (Chan 2003), and by the mid-1990s, Khmer gangs controlled several public housing neighborhoods (Mulick 2010). Some gangs had ties to other ethnic gangs; in one community, Khmer and Hispanic gang members shared ginseng extract drinks for energy and had children together (Hartocollis 2004). Gang violence usually results from fights over drug deals and territory. On Chicago's North Side, Khmer and Vietnamese gangs joined together to fight Filipino gangs (Salopek 1996). While Filipinos came from a country where gangs existed, had been in the America for generations, had better education and jobs than Khmer newcomers, and were greater in number, Cambodian youth came from a country with no history of gangs and no word for "gang" (Sody Lay 2010).

In 1995, four teenaged members of the Vietnamese-Cambodian Outlaw Loco Bloods mistook a Filipino for a gang member and kicked him to death in a Burger King parking lot. Police said the attack was payback for a fight the day before between Khmer and Filipino gangs at a mall, but a participant said it was initiated by fistfights between Cambodians and Filipinos at a local high school. A journalist suggested the conflict was driven by physical stature, quoting one participant who said, "The Cambodians want to be bad, but they're too small to pick on the blacks or the Spanish. So they attack Filipinos, who are kind of small" (Salopek 1996). On a cold February day after the fight, fifty people gathered in the fast-food parking lot, where Filipino dancers in colorful traditional cloth wrapped around their heavy coats performed a tribal reconciliation ceremony and Khmer Buddhist monks chanted.

Modeling themselves on the clothes, hand signs, and mannerisms of other gangs, Khmer gang members commonly wear "sagging," loose-fitting shirts over baggy pants hanging low on the hips. In Long Beach gang members shaved their heads, in Oakland they greased and slicked it back, and in Seattle many wore cornrows. Saying they wanted to show Khmer pride, many Khmer gang members use formal terms of respect with one another, such as "uncle" and "older sibling," and organize themselves as extended families, calling younger members "juniors" and older members OG for "original gangster" (Hart 1990). Gang members expect loyalty, respect, obedience, and confidentiality from one another, and younger members give their earnings to older members, just as Khmer youth traditionally gave their wages to their parents.

Khmer gang membership tends to be loose, with some members attending school or holding jobs. Some gangs are easy to leave and others are not; gangs also demonstrate varying interest in alcohol use, drug sales, or women. Many Khmer gang members consider themselves Buddhists; when two Khmer brothers committed suicide rather than face murder charges, one brother penned a note to his girlfriend just before he died, writing, "Baby I hope we could be husband and wife for the next life. I will wait for you." The other brother scribbled a note apologizing for committing suicide and telling his wife, "When you get my money pray to the Cambodian Temple for me."

Khmer girls quickly followed boys into gang life, some drawn by boyfriends, others joining on their own, and some forming their own gangs, such as Asia Girls in Long Beach (Rasbridge 1995). Their gang activity is often a revolt against parental discipline (Go and Le 2005). One father lamented that he did not know how to keep his daughter in school and out of the gang, and he worried that she would become pregnant, which she did. After her boyfriend was killed by gang violence, the father raised his grandchild, until his daughter finally left the gang. Girl gangs often follow the lead of boy gangs; a bloody street war in Long Beach between Khmer and Mexican male gangs led to fights between Khmer and Mexican girls (Needham and Quintiliani 2007).

When girls become pregnant, they tend to drop out of high school to be supported by their gang boyfriends, other family members, or public assistance. Their babies' fathers are often violent, non-supportive, or absent. One Khmer teenager belonged to a Hispanic street gang, and her "Spanish" boyfriend, as her family referred to him, lived with her family. Her best friend, also Khmer, who is not involved in a gang, urged her friend to leave the gang, saying, "She's smart. She'll leave one day soon." She was out within the year after breaking up with her boyfriend.

Over time, many Khmer gangs have turned from lesser crimes such as looting cars to more serious drive-by shootings and drug usage and sales, and guns have become more common (Ingrassia 1994). Some law enforcement personnel say Khmer gangs victimize their own people and participate in more spontaneous acts of violence and crime than do members of other gangs and were at one time considered among the most violent in America. Gangs in California have exhibited the highest murder rate of all Asian groups in the state (Ng 2001). In just two and a half months, Long Beach had thirty-two gang-related shootings: 43 percent of the victims were African Americans, 34 percent Hispanic, and 12 percent Asian Americans (Wride 2004).

In Tacoma, also, Khmer gangs were seen as particularly violent. In 1998, nine Southeast Asian members of the Loc'd Out Crips committed the city's worst-ever mass homicide, leaving five dead and five wounded (Mulick 2010). Khmer gang initiations are also known for their brutality. One young Khmer named Akara was beaten by six members of the gang he was trying to join; he ended up in the emergency room, but his stoic endurance of the beating gained him a place in the gang. Cambodians, including gang members, recognize parallels between Cambodia's violent history and gang violence (Isett 1994); both the Khmer Rouge and gangs put guns in the hands of children, giving them respect, status, and the power to kill others. However, Cambodians also say Americans have had a part in turning some of their youth into gang members.

The attraction of gangs for young people is often short-lived; when drinking, smoking marijuana, hanging out with gang members, and engaging in petty crime shift to armed robbery, assault, rape, even murder, many youth leave. One youth pawned his gold Buddhist amulet to pay court fines but, without the amulet's protection, left the gang because he felt vulnerable. Some reject gang life when they turn eighteen and realize gang involvement will likely result in prison. In the early 2000s, the deportation of noncitizen Cambodian refugees convicted of felonies to Cambodia became an inspiration for some to abandon gang life.

Gang violence subsided in many communities when law enforcement targeted the most violent gangs. After officers in Tacoma provided information to parents on detecting gang involvement, Khmer parents joined others in organizing block watches and painted over graffiti, which slowed gang activity (Mulick 2010). Some "original gangsters" helped other gang members leave, and many young people who remained in gangs were anxious that their own children not follow in their steps (Sody Lay 2010). A young hip-hop artist advised young people against gang membership because "we don't need it anymore" (Cambodian Alliance for the Arts 2011). Other Khmer teenagers chose less dangerous behavior, such as smoking blunts, hollowed-out cigars filled with marijuana, to distinguish themselves from drug users stigmatized by crack cocaine and methamphetamine use (Lee and Soller 2010).

Compromising with Children

In the 1980s, Cambodians said that family conflict was less when parents recognized the desirability of their children learning new ways
and younger people understood their parents' need to retain traditional
values, relationships, and behaviors. Decades later, they say the same is
true. A survey taken in Southern California by Khmer Girls in Action in
2011 found that many youth embrace American ways and respect their
parents' wishes, while their parents try to comprehend their children's
circumstances.

In the past few decades, families that retained some Khmer traditions
and accepted some American values were often the most harmonious and
had the most successful students. One father said he follows traditional
ways but does not have the same expectations for his sons, because they
need to follow American ways to "make it" in America. Another man
who was unable to learn English or find a job himself said he wants his
children to learn to work within the system. A number of parents purchased the clothes children said they needed and allowed them to play
sports although they considered the clothes and activity improper. "We
want her to be happy," one father said of his daughter, "and playing with
the other girls makes her happy." Even families experiencing considerable conflict often find peace with their changed circumstances. When
his foster son went to jail, Kiri refused to deal with him, saying he was
no longer "family." Years later, he accepted him back as a member of his
"real" family, saying, "Now he respects me and is taking care of his wife
and daughter."

For their part, many youngsters strive to get on with their parents and
succeed in school, saying they are aware of their parents' sacrifices on
their behalf. Others said they respect their parents, although their knowledge is of little value in America; one young man said knowing how to
drive an ox cart "does not help me in my high school studies." Others
stated repeatedly, "We're not in Cambodia now," and one youth said
speaking Khmer "had not done me any good. English is good because I
can get a good job." Youth are often confused about whether to act like
Cambodians or Americans. One young teenaged girl said she tries to
succeed in school and act as a proper Khmer girl. Contrasting herself at
the temple to girls in high heels and makeup, she said, "I wash dishes
with a garbage bag tied around my waist to protect my silk skirt while
they are parading around." Many older children care for younger siblings
and help support their families. After their father left, a teenaged brother
and sister attended school, worked full-time, and cared for their mentally

unstable mother, younger siblings, and the household. Ten years later, both had graduated from college, married, and had jobs and babies. Their mother and siblings lived with the daughter's family and were doing well, and the brother lived next door.

A number of young people have attempted to learn Khmer traditions and language. In the mid-1980s, a young Cambodian on scholarship at Cornell took Khmer classes, and over the years, numerous other Khmer youth enrolled in Khmer courses. At the University of Washington in the fall of 2012, eleven of the thirteen students in the beginning and intermediate classes were Cambodian Americans. Some bore traditional Khmer names, but most had names easier for non-Khmer to say, such as James and Jennifer. All spoke fluent English and ranged in their speaking and comprehension of Khmer from poor to excellent. The class was demanding, and the devotion to learning was obvious. Most Khmer students, however, speak little Khmer. Students in Long Beach had to ask Neou Kassie, human rights advocate and visiting lecturer, to switch to English because they could not understand his Khmer.

Khmer on many campuses belong to a Khmer college association, like students in Seattle who proudly wear sweatshirts bearing the legend "Khmer Student Association of the University of Washington." Association-sponsored events range from Khmer New Year celebrations to commemorations; University of Washington students in 2000 participated in a candlelight vigil to memorialize lives lost to the Khmer Rouge. Cambodians participate in online Khmer communities on the Internet, often expressing frustration at not speaking better English and Khmer. They write e-mails to pen pals, use text chat, and learn Khmer on YouTube. Although few young Cambodians listen to Khmer radio or cable programming, read Khmer newspapers, or participate in Khmer conversations at Cambodian gatherings, most young people attempt to speak Khmer with older family members. In a number of Christian churches, Sunday school classes are held in Khmer for adults and in English for young adults and children, reflecting the increasing divergence in language that is occurring among Cambodian Americans.

Close in importance to family, Khmer refugees said they found community vital to their survival in the United States.

Chapter Seven

Community

Cambodians reveal the importance of community to them in much of what they do and say. Cambodians spend much of their free time with those they consider community and talk often of what they have done and what they will be doing with those people. The older the Cambodian, the more likely the members of his or her community consist of other Khmer, but the majority of younger Cambodian Americans also spend a large proportion of their nonworking hours in the company of other Cambodian Americans.

Defining Community

Cambodians use difference in defining themselves in contrast to other groups of people. Although Cambodians recognized after resettlement that refugee status brought them resources and services they would not otherwise have received, such as initial stipends and refugee-specific benefits, and has contributed to their identity as Cambodians who had suffered pain, loss, survival, flight, camps, and resettlement, they resented being lumped with other refugees. Since resettlement, Cambodians have emphasized they are not Vietnamese or Thai and explain the Vietnamese or Thai by their differences, saying characteristics such as greed and duplicity make them different and dangerous, and the greater the difference, the greater their threat. Cambodians accuse both Vietnam and Thailand of stealing what is theirs: including the delta by the Vietnamese, and the thousand-year-old Preah Vihear temple by the Thai.

Cambodians are particularly hostile toward the Vietnamese, whom they often refer to as *yuon,* a term thought to date from the Angkor period (Headley 1977). Resettled Cambodians initially concealed their distrust of Vietnamese refugees, studying, working, volunteering, and socializing together often for years, but sooner or later and always in private,

Cambodians described them as aggressive, crude, loud, dishonest, greedy, or sneaky and warned Americans to be cautious because, as a Khmer refugee worker said, "They are all the same." An educated Cambodian said, "The Vietnamese hate us. They always want to abolish 'black people.' That's what they call us."

Cambodians accuse Vietnam of having wanted to "swallow" Cambodia for centuries and describe ancient events as if they occurred just years ago. They claim that Vietnam took their land and tried to turn Cambodians into Vietnamese and that Cambodia has been justified at various times in the past in attacking Vietnamese villages and forcing Vietnamese to leave Cambodia. "They have their own country," one man said. Khmer Rouge atrocities against the Vietnamese were legend, yet some Khmer refugees said the Vietnamese were responsible for the Khmer Rouge regime and described their atrocities against Cambodians following the overthrow of the Khmer Rouge. Many say they fled the country to avoid Vietnamese communist rule, what they call "the same car (truck, oxcart) driven by a different driver."

Several Cambodians said Buddha taught people to treat others equally, but they cannot be close friends with Vietnamese because they are untrustworthy, one man saying he can only exchange greetings with them. While "We are both refugees" was a common refrain among Cambodians in the early years of resettlement, the same people months or years later made disparaging comments about Vietnamese. One family tolerated their son's Vietnamese girlfriend for ten years, the mother several times rolling her eyes when the girlfriend's name came up, but saying nothing negative in all the years the son was dating her. When he turned thirty-five, however, the son and girlfriend broke up and the son moved in with his mother. "How do you say, good riddance?" his uncle said, and the family joined in with a barrage of critical comments against her.

Some Cambodians are appalled at the blame their countrymen direct toward Vietnamese, Oudom saying, "I'm at a loss at the paranoia they have about the Vietnamese. It's not logical." It was a topic he returned to often. After overhearing another antagonistic rant against the Vietnamese, he talked of Cambodians' obsession with Vietnam, describing with amused exasperation one man's wish to change the name of *banh chao,* a traditional Vietnamese food, to "Cambodian pancake." Other Cambodians are impatient with fellow Khmer who lambast Vietnamese but patronize Vietnamese doctors. When asked why she goes to a Vietnamese-owned store when her family often makes disparaging comments about the offerings, cleanliness, or greed of the owner, she mumbled, "It has what I need." Some Cambodians profit from the theme of Vietnamese exploitation, holding meetings across America to talk about how Vietnam continues to control Cambodia and seeking donations to overthrow them. In 2013, a Khmer from Rhode Island gave a professional-looking slide show of Vietnamese fishermen's houseboats they said demonstrated the Vietnamese colonization of Cambodia and raised $1,000 from forty donors.

Cambodians also use difference in identifying, explaining, and scapegoating one another. Cambodians remain vitally concerned with identity, a usual concern of diaspora survivors (Erikson 1976), and for Khmer, being Cambodian is central to their identity. Resettled Khmer competent at their jobs, with good English and middle-class possessions and manners, say they usually present themselves as Americans, but they define themselves as Cambodian. Vehicles are important for economic survival in America, but they also provide evidence of one's success as Cambodians in America to fellow Khmer in America and to relatives in Cambodia. Similarly, televisions and electronic devices are evidence of success but are valued also for viewing Khmer videos and DVDs and keeping in contact with the homeland. Cambodians participate in cultural activities not as something that would be "nice to do," as Americans often said, but as vital to life. "Being Khmer" continues to be central to the identity of most first- and second-generation Cambodians.

Cambodians speak of Khmer identity as a fixed, natural state stemming from ethnicity, nationality, religion, and appearance. For Cambodians, this includes looking Khmer, speaking Khmer, observing Buddhism, acting properly, and acknowledging the heritage of the "grandmothers and grandfathers" by following Khmer customs. Cambodians say possessing one or several of these characteristics does not make one Khmer: a European American can be fluent in Khmer and a practicing Buddhist, but that does not make her or him Khmer. Nor does the absence of one or more characteristics necessarily deny a person Khmer identity: numerous Khmer children are neither fluent in Khmer nor Buddhist but are considered Khmer, as are Chinese Cambodians with light skin, Cham who are not Buddhist, and Lao Khmer who do not speak Khmer.

Some Cambodians suggest being a Cambodian American requires being part of a Khmer American community, knowing one's history as both American and Cambodian, and remembering the killing fields (Lee 2010). Although most do not consider proficiency in Khmer a requirement for Khmer identity, many regret not speaking Khmer well and being unable to converse with monks. While Cambodians say a person's identity as a Cambodian does not rest on looking Khmer, speaking the language, acting appropriately, following Khmer customs, or being a Buddhist, they consider people who do not display several of these characteristics with suspicion. They occasionally describe a fellow countryman as "not really Khmer."

First-generation Cambodians view themselves as sharing an unchanging and continuous heritage and point to Angkor Wat as evidence. When two hundred Hawaii Cambodians were asked what it means to be Cambodian, all mentioned reverence for Angkor Wat. Yet Cambodians display a dynamic identity that shifts easily as Cambodians overlook inconsistencies from one display of themselves and others to an alternate display. Pros acted as a knowledgeable Cambodian American in the office, a dominant Khmer husband and father to his submissive family, a bossy Khmer patron with clients, and an illiterate refugee when seeking assistance from service providers. One woman was a devoted and knowledgeable believer at the temple and funny and irreverent in her American workplace. Companions in one setting are often startled by the behavior of a Khmer friend or colleague in another, as when supposedly quiet and passive Cambodians are loud and sassy.

Cambodians traditionally have had multiple roles with one another. An American may see a teacher only at school, while a Cambodian's teacher may also be the monk who leads temple ceremonies, counsels his mother, and is advisor or patron to other kinsmen. A nurturing father may also be his child's doctor, counselor, or employer. Americans shift roles and hold different status, privileges, and obligations—a prestigious professor can be a low-ranking volunteer fireman, and a student may be an influential supervisor at work—but Cambodians hold the same status, regardless of role or activity. A prominent businessman is shown respect in every part of his life, while a laborer is shown little in any of his. Only when a man of low status crosses the threshold of his own home can he demand from his wife and children the obedience and deference he must give superiors.

Cambodians shift their definition of community from situation to situation. Traditionally, community has meant contact with others who are Khmer, sometimes including all neighboring Cambodians and at other times including only a portion, such as family members, sponsor, donors to a temple, or those who share one's politics. In America, community for Cambodians has included Americans and new groupings of Khmer. Dismayed that Americans were clumping them with other refugees for service provision after arrival, Cambodians pointed out that not all their countrymen were victims of trauma, poor health, and little education. They pointed out that a number of Khmer in large cities such as Boston, Washington, DC, and Seattle were wealthier and higher class than their compatriots in cities such as New York, Chicago, and Long Beach. Status often outweighed enmity. When asked why she visited a woman she had long despised in the hospital, Thann said, "Our families were the same, and we were in the same school and neighborhood." She paused. "We are the same people."

In the early years after resettlement, Cambodians, particularly those of high status, tried to point out distinctions also among Cambodians, especially the sharp distinctions between urban and rural folk in Cambodia. They described their education and mentioned other marks of status, including their parents' wealth, occupation, residence, and ties to the royal family. Rural Cambodians, in contrast, spoke less about the importance of status in Cambodia and more about the importance of following tradition. Claiming that "community is where people act right," they said they judged other Cambodians on their adherence to the ways of the "grandmothers and grandfathers." Educated Cambodians also said they valued tradition more than other Cambodians, citing that as the reason they associated primarily with those of their own status.

Educated refugees often used Khmer accents and literary references to distinguish themselves from uneducated Cambodians. They also identified the geographic, ethnic, social, and educational background of fellow Cambodians by their accent. Some older Khmer refugees expressed pride at possessing a Battambang accent, saying it was evidence they had attended the same schools as many former Khmer officials and elite. Others were proud of their Phnom Penh accent. Cambodians frequently enhanced descriptions of their education and standing. I met numerous provincial governors, district chiefs, and military officers, more than seemed possible for Cambodia's size and the number killed. As arrivals increased and Cambodians learned English, their histories were corrected, usually by former neighbors; a man claiming to be a provincial governor had actually been his secretary, and a general was really a captain. When told he was going to meet the former chief of his district, a new arrival exclaimed, "He wasn't the chief. He was his bodyguard."

Although most Khmer refugees were ethnic Khmer, some were Chinese Cambodians, ethnic Khmer from southern Vietnam, Muslim Cambodians, or tribespeople. After resettlement, most Khmer-Chinese Cambodians who spoke Khmer and observed Khmer traditions identified with ethnic Cambodians. More recent immigrants from Hong Kong or China to Cambodia, who identified primarily with Chinese, spoke a Chinese language as their first language, and retained Chinese customs and language, were more likely to associate with other Chinese Americans after resettlement, encouraged not only by their Chinese affinity but by ethnic Khmer viewing them as different.

Cambodians argue over definitions, debating whether Khmer Surin refers to Cambodians living in Thailand or Cambodia, or emphasize their brotherhood with others, saying they hope someday for a reunion of Khmer from Cambodia, Vietnam, and Thailand (Kolbot Khmer 2008). More often, however, they do not recognize other Khmer groups as true

Khmer. Khmer refugees from Cambodia have consistently expressed reservations about the thirty thousand ethnic Khmer Krom refugees resettled in America from Vietnam. Khmer Krom who came in 1975 received more assistance and opportunities than was available to many Cambodians who arrived later, and a number of Khmer Krom who spoke Vietnamese, Khmer, and English were hired as resettlement workers and interpreters in the early 1980s, giving them opportunities and influence resented by many Khmer from Cambodia.

Because they spoke Khmer, shared religion and culture, and were familiar with English and Americans, Khmer Krom were often involved in resettlement activities with Khmer from Cambodia, such as setting up temples. Cambodians' traditional mistrust of anyone from Vietnam and anyone different soon intruded. Some said they found the American view that bilingual Khmer Krom were crucial to refugee service provision especially irritating. "Why do Americans think they are our leaders?" Vibol complained in 1983. Although Cambodians born in Cambodia sometimes admitted they were envious of Khmer Krom, many of whom had been educated in Vietnam, many claimed the Khmer Krom were not "real Khmer" because they were "too Vietnamese" and did not truly understand Khmer cultural mores and rituals. In addition, Cambodians said, they had not experienced the Khmer Rouge years, so could not comprehend the suffering and trauma of those who had. I heard similar complaints about the Khmer Krom thirty years later.

Cambodians have continued to refer to the Khmer Krom as Khmer when talking about the ills perpetrated by Vietnam on Khmer Krom but refer to them as Vietnamese when discussing characteristics they dislike. When a Khmer Krom told a client he would not lie for him on his work application, the client muttered to an American standing nearby, "He's not even a real Cambodian." Individuals who have both Khmer and Khmer Krom parentage usually identify with one group or the other. Cambodians warned one American about having a Khmer Krom teacher, saying the result would be a Khmer Krom accent and, thus, in one's woman's words, "You won't have a real accent."

Although Cambodians and Khmer Krom share a history of Vietnamese antipathy, Cambodians continue to define Khmer Krom as different from them, saying Khmer Krom brag too much. As evidence, several Cambodians explained that when Khmer Krom have the microphone at temple gatherings and Khmer festivals, they boast about themselves and their ancestors, achievements, income, and donations. Khmer Krom readily acknowledge their liminal status in Khmer communities and, over the years, have increasingly distanced themselves from non-Khmer Krom. Many moved out of leadership positions, established their own associations and temples, and turned their attention to increasing public awareness of the plight of Khmer Krom in Vietnam.

Claiming America owes much to the Khmer Krom for assisting them militarily, one man repeatedly said the Khmer Rouge killed fifty thousand Khmer Krom soldiers sent by America to fight in Cambodia after identifying them by their accent. Many are angered that America has not put pressure on Vietnam to return the delta area to Cambodia, and Khmer Krom demonstrated in front of the White House in 1987 and again in 2005 on behalf of Khmer Krom in Vietnam. Using media and political contacts, Khmer Krom continue to protest human rights violations in Vietnam and maintain a global identity by constructing their own websites and posting networks.

Re-establishing Community in America

Since resettlement, Khmer refugees have talked about feeling lost in the world; one man said he was carrying Cambodia with him because he was unsure where the "real Cambodia" was. They spoke also of their joy in again living among Cambodians. When resettled Cambodians were unable to form geographic Khmer communities because they were few in number and widely scattered, they formed non-geographic communities, talking to one another by telephone and sending messages through others. From their first days in America, however, Cambodians sought face-to-face contact with other Cambodians and as soon as possible obtained cars, often driving for hours to be with fellow countrymen. Living among other Khmer provided refugees with the company of fellow Cambodians and supplied vital survival information to arrivals, eased resettlement shock, and allowed Cambodians to live as Cambodians, acting toward others in familiar and predictable ways.

Cambodians began re-establishing communities as similar to those in Cambodia as possible, utilizing familiar decorations and colors and often leaving doors open to more easily welcome guests and chat with Khmer neighbors, even in cold weather and dangerous neighborhoods. Many Cambodians included non-Khmer in their communities. In Boston, young sneering and slouching African American and youth Cambodians called "Italy men" exchanged taunts with young Khmer, then respectfully greeted older Cambodians before escorting a visiting American to her car because, in one Cambodian's words, "It's a bad area, you know, but we are together with good neighbors." Cambodians say bad places to live are where there are no Cambodians, neighbors are hostile, and they cannot find what they need, while a good place is where Cambodians can gather, neighbors are friendly, and there are Asian shops and a Khmer temple. One family described their neighborhood as unsafe but said there were jobs and the temple was only three blocks away. In another city, Cambodians estimated that over one thousand Khmer lived within three square acres, because "Cambodians all want to live together."

Khmer communities crosscut American city, county, and state boundaries and are constantly expanding and contracting, and Cambodians travel often from one Khmer community to another. Khmer refugees initially named their communities according to the Khmer living there: Public housing was "public housing where Khmer live," and "Hilltop" in Tacoma referred to the area where Khmer resided and excluded Hilltop areas without Khmer. "Ithaca" referred to a neighborhood of Cambodians and excluded the town's renowned schools on neighboring hills. In some cities, Cambodians' "Main Road" was not the official Main Street but a side road running by more Khmer homes than any other in town. What to one Cambodian was a geography of opportunity was to another a geography of fear; twenty-year-old Sim saw a Boston street corner as a place to exchange information with friends, but Yon, also twenty, viewed it as the corner where five teenagers had attacked him. Cambodians often imagined they were elsewhere; one woman said she was living "in two places." A woman living in Boston spent her imagined time in Phnom Penh. Teachers said she did not listen in class, and her family said she was "not here."

Most first-generation Cambodians were unfamiliar with written maps, so they created mental maps of driving lanes, usually by following someone who knew the route to a destination, until they became familiar with an area. Cambodians often said, "I will follow you one time, and then I will know." Unfamiliar stretches, whether inner-city neighborhood, national park, or the breadth of Nebraska, remained areas to be crossed rapidly, uncharted and irrelevant. A mushroom picker did not know there were harvest areas other than where he worked and was not interested in learning of them because "I don't know how to go there." Khmer directions often included objects unnoticed by Americans: "Turn at the corner with the square on the top," or "Stop where there are many Cambodians." Many said they knew how to get places, but not street names.

When told he could reach a dentist's office by walking down Tucker Street in front of his house, one man said, "Oh, I don't know that street." "It's the street you live on," I said. "Oh, I don't know that street." I asked his address. "124 Tucker Street," he replied. "That's the street," I said. "I don't know about that," he said, turning away, so I drove him to his appointment three days later. His Tucker Street address had no connection to directions; he had never walked down his street, although he had walked miles through the town, and the dentist's office three blocks from his house was outside his territory, previously unneeded and thus unfamiliar.

His geography included areas important to him: the homes of friends, the temple, and a few stores. Over time, younger Cambodians quickly learned their way around, but older Cambodians continued to drive by the mental maps they had first constructed. In 2011, after a tedious drive on back roads busy with traffic and road construction, a group of women arrived at a temple in a nearby city. When asked why the driver took the back way rather than the interstate highway that would have cut the trip by half, she replied, "I always go that way." After admitting she did not know how to use the interstate, half a mile from her home, she said she did not want to learn because "that's too much for me." She then added, "And I don't care."

Cambodians continue to utilize technology to communicate with friends and relatives beyond their immediate community, using cell phones, e-mail, Facebook, MySpace, and other Internet sites as quickly as they appear. They chat in English, Khmer, and a mixture of both on the Internet, download and share music and movies, and sing karaoke on YouTube. Nonetheless, a geographic Khmer community remains vital to most Cambodians in both rural and urban America, as they periodically gather to immerse themselves in familiar sights, sounds, food, ceremonies, music, and dance, often inviting Americans to join them. At one Thanksgiving event, children performed Khmer dances and talked of becoming doctors, veterinarians, and marine biologists. An organizer told them their search for freedom was similar to that of the Pilgrims: "They were very much like you" (Kass 1997). The dancing was Khmer, the food nontraditional Khmer, and the decorations were both.

Cambodians have been prolific volunteers for their communities: sponsoring; donating; establishing temples and cultural centers; organizing events, art shows, and musical performances; and bringing performers, teachers, politicians, and religious leaders from Cambodia. The Lowell Water Festival recruits volunteers to serve on "Entertainment, Media and Public Relations, Fund-raising, Volunteer Recruitment, Booth and Vendors, Logistics, Branding, Boat Team, and Trash and Recycling" committees, and Cambodian Americans have served for years as volunteers in multiple communities in both America and Cambodia.

Khmer Communities in the United States

Statistics on the size of Khmer communities vary widely, with local population estimates consistently higher than official statistics. Leaders and agencies tend to have the best figures because they are in daily contact with refugees and immigrant communities, yet they sometimes inflate numbers to attract funding. Census surveys usually underestimate populations; Cambodians have been unfamiliar with censuses, are afraid of officials, and are often reluctant to respond. They have also moved frequently, making it difficult for officials to acquire accurate population counts.

Khmer communities developed rapidly as the Khmer population in America grew. Between 1975 and 1993, almost 150,000 Cambodian refugees entered the country, and by 2007, there were close to 250,000 people with Khmer ethnicity in America. The number of Cambodians grew from fewer than fifty in the state to thousands in Houston and Dallas alone. Despite considerable secondary migration, Cambodians remain dispersed in over 190 urban areas in all fifty states and the District of Columbia. Due primarily to secondary migration, however, over 80 percent live in just ten states, and about 75 percent reside in one of fifteen metropolitan areas, accounting for over three-fourths of the ethnic Khmer population in America. California remains home to most Khmer, with the largest Khmer community of many thousands located in Long Beach.

The Long Beach community began with the arrival of Khmer students in the 1960s and grew with the arrival of one to two thousand Cambodians in 1975 who were assisted by Khmer college alumni, American marines; refugee children remembered Camp Pendleton marines giving them their jackets. For many Cambodians in America, Long Beach has become a major center of Cambodians in the United States. Secondary migrants were drawn by a climate conducive to growing familiar vegetables, fruit, and herbs, the availability of Asian goods, generous welfare, refugee programs and services, temples, and proximity to the ocean. Khmer housing in Long Beach, as in other cities, ranges from low-income apartments to homes in gated communities. The heart of the community is Anaheim Street, where two hundred Khmer shops are located in the midst of Khmer residential areas. In 2007, the city designated a stretch of Anaheim Street as Cambodia Town.

Cambodian Americans say they travel to Long Beach to learn more about their culture, gather with Cambodians, or attend college. One young man said he and his girlfriend return to Long Beach at least once a week: "Each weekend we have to come down here. Long Beach just feels like home" (Knoll 2010). Cambodians in the Pacific Northwest speak of Long Beach as a mecca of Khmer culture, shops, and activities and say they regularly visit. Cambodians often put out wares purchased in Long Beach for sale at the temple or home back in the Northwest. Many thousands of Cambodians also live in San Diego, the larger Los Angeles region,

Stockton, Fresno, and the Oakland, San Francisco, and San Jose areas and maintain ties with Khmer in other Khmer communities.

The second largest Khmer population in the United States resides in Massachusetts, with between twenty thousand and thirty-five thousand residing in Boston and the neighboring cities of Lynn, Lowell, Chelsea, and Revere. Between ten thousand and thirteen thousand Khmer live in Providence, Cranston, Warwick, and Woonsocket, Rhode Island. The Khmer population of Lowell increased exponentially in the 1980s as Cambodians arrived to benefit from programs enabling them to get manufacturing jobs and become economically self-sufficient. Many Cambodians said that living in a city with a large Khmer population and a river similar to some in Cambodia comforted them. In reaction to the large influx of Khmer refugee children of school age and talk of setting up of bilingual classes for them, citizens passed a referendum in 1988 making English the official language of Lowell. In response, refugees filed a Title VI lawsuit against the city for denying educational opportunities to students with limited English proficiency.

After years of conflict in Lowell, Americans began recognizing that Khmer businesses were revitalizing downtown areas, elected the first Khmer city counselor in America, and began hiring Khmer policemen, teachers, nurses, and social workers. Lowell hopes to become known as "Little Cambodia" and has been working with the Massachusetts Institute of Technology to become a tourist destination by promoting its wealth of diversity. An annual Southeast Asian Water Festival held on the banks of the Merrimack River is modeled on the water festivals held for centuries on Cambodia's Mekong River and hosts fifty thousand visitors annually. Washington State also is home to thousands of Cambodians, most living in the Puget Sound region. Other Khmer are concentrated in Spokane, Vancouver, Centralia, and the Tri-Cities. Texas is fourth, then Minnesota, Pennsylvania, Virginia, New York, Rhode Island, Georgia, and approximately forty-five hundred in the Washington, DC, area.

Several groups of Khmer refugees across the country have purchased land and settled on lots surrounding a religious and cultural center. Resolved to find a refuge away from the difficulties attendant on living in urban areas, a group of Khmer families purchased 180 acres of forested land on Alabama's gulf coast, dividing it into three-acre lots. They set aside nine acres in the center for a Khmer Buddhist temple and cultural center and placed brick and mobile homes on the other lots, some new and others patched together with corrugated tin and heavy plastic (Lewis 2000). By the early 2000s, over two hundred Cambodians resided in the community. Many of the residents live as traditionally as possible, with elders caring for grandchildren, maintaining gardens, and devoting time to the temple. An elderly couple said that with relatives living close, their extended family can go from house to house without leaving their common yard. The wife added that her banana plants, although not all are fruitful, reduce their feelings of being out of place.

Although the majority of resettled Khmer were Buddhists, others were Cambodian Muslims from the largest minority in Cambodia. Expressing some confusion about their origins, most Khmer Muslims say they are either Cham descendants of the Champa polity in Southeast Asia or descendants of more recent Malay immigrants. Before the Vietnamese conquered Champa in 1471, the Cham converted from Hinduism to Islam. Some Cham then fled to Cambodia, where they continued their faith, culture, language, and dress. Friendly relations have prevailed between the Cham and Khmer for centuries, although intermarriage is rare because the Cham emphasize intragroup marriage and ethnic Khmer view the Cham somewhat suspiciously as skilled practitioners of the black arts, fortune-telling, and spells.

After suffering the loss of much of their population to the Khmer Rouge, between three thousand and five thousand Cham were resettled in America, where they have continued their religion and customs, many living near one another in California, Oregon, Washington, Colorado, and Pennsylvania. Over a hundred families clustered near mosques in Fullerton and Santa Ana once boasted they had not lost "a single child" to American ways: "No adultery, no robbery, no drugs, no gangs, no drunks" (Efron 1990). Three decades later, the community has shrunk, some youth have turned to gangs, and the mosque is often attended only by older people and small children. As difficult as Cham have found living in communities of other Khmer Muslims, those living in non-Cham communities sometimes said their lives were even more difficult.

The only Khmer Muslim in a community of two hundred Cambodians, Binn was resettled with his Khmer Buddhist wife, their children, and her extended family. The son of a prison guard and fish seller, Binn grew up in a Muslim village of three thousand. He quit school when he was fifteen after his father beat him, and worked as a fisherman on Tonle Sap Lake. Told they were going to see Sihanouk after the Khmer Rouge takeover, his family was killed by the Khmer Rouge; Binn was the only survivor. Married with cadre permission, Binn said he stays married because of his children. He is not happy in America but is glad to be resettled because being "in Cambodia and Thailand was very, very difficult." He said he told his "long story" to me because no one listened to him. "I am a Cham, alone." He once said being alone was worse than living with the Khmer Rouge, then added, "Almost as bad."

Cham who live in a community of other Cham often say they feel fortunate not to be alone. Such a community exists in Washington. The first
Cham arrived in the area in 1978. When a second family arrived in 1984
and a family member attended a Seattle mosque, he was told, "You look
like a man who came here last week." He was overjoyed to discover the
man was his cousin, and the two families began bringing other Cham to
join them at their mobile-home park. Within a few years, thirty-four families had joined the group. One trailer served as a mosque, and announcements to the Cham were made over the park's public-address system.
Finding the park too small for the community and wanting to live away
from Americans because "they don't understand us sometimes and lead
our children the wrong way," the Cham purchased ten acres nearby with
$300,000 earned by gathering and selling forest products. They cleared the
land, purchased inexpensive modular homes, and reserved the center lot
for the mosque.

Since Islamic law forbids collecting interest on loans, the Cham made
payments into a general fund. Each family received $20,000 in turn to
purchase a prefabricated home and continued making payments until
everyone was housed. By the early 2000s, Slamad Village, named for
the ancient Champa Empire and the Cham word for peace, had two
hundred residents. One of the few differences between residents in the
neat homes in the Champa Slamad cul-de-sac and those in neighboring
communities is the nearly completed mosque and the residents' head-
gear: female scarves and male hats. Although the mosque attracts other
Muslims, residents say it remains Cham-centered. The community faces
the challenges of all Khmer communities in keeping their youth interested
in the community, religion, and customs, but the Cham express more
determination to remain true to Islam and close to one another than do
most other Cambodian Americans. Residents emphasize the importance
of being together, one saying, "When you find Cham, you won't find just
one." When I said there was one Cham man living alone among Khmer
Buddhists, they expressed sympathy and told me to tell him he was welcome to join their community.

The Cham continue to observe three-day weddings, slaughtering meat
for the community according to Islamic law, heeding the call to prayer,
and observing Ramadan with fasting, prayer, giving alms, and listening to
Qur'an readings. Believers break their Ramadan fast at night with cream
cheese and dates before feasting on curried lamb, pickled vegetables, rice,
red chicken, and beef, often saying they are glad to be free in America
and Cham in their own community. One young woman in a gold-bead-
edged white head scarf said she had identified as Malay rather than
Cham for years, because Americans are more familiar with Malaysia than

Cambodia, but is now proud to tell people she is Cham. Some Cham say they have been treated poorly by Americans with anti-Muslim sentiments, but others say they continue to be respected by non-Cham neighbors.

Resettled Cambodians also include Thai Cambodians, most of whom lived in Cambodia near Thailand, and Lao Cambodians, who lived near Laos. Both groups were occasionally snubbed by other Cambodians because they were seen as different. A refugee born into a Lao family living on the Cambodia-Lao border was resettled with her Khmer husband. She did not speak Khmer, and Lao had trouble understanding her Lao accent; she lived for years in a community of resettled Lao who viewed her as Cambodian, and Cambodians who saw her as Lao. Several Lao or Thai women divorced their Khmer husbands and moved to be with those who spoke their first language. One associated with her ethnic group but stayed with her Khmer husband and studied English, saying if she did not do so, she was never going to have friends or be able to speak to her children.

Cambodian tribal people, whose ancestors lived in Cambodia long before the Angkorean period, were also resettled in America. One group of hunting and gathering subsistence farmers, called the Jarai, had been recruited in the 1960s by American troops, who called them "perhaps our bravest and most loyal ally in the Vietnam War" (Jazzar and Hamm 2007). A number of tribal folk fought the communists long after the 1975 end of the war, but in the early 1980s, United Nations peacekeeping forces convinced them to stop their resistance. In 1986, the first group of about two hundred tribal people, mostly men, was resettled in Raleigh, Greensboro, and Charlotte, North Carolina.

Soldiers at Fort Bragg and Special Forces veterans provided assistance, and supportive businesses provided entry-level job opportunities in an area the Jarai found similar to their homeland. In 1992, an additional 402 tribal people were resettled in North Carolina. By 2000, the tribal population of North Carolina had grown to three thousand; the population is now approximately ten thousand, one of the largest hill populations outside Southeast Asia. There are also one hundred Jarai living in the greater Dallas area, and as long as there are conflicts between them and their governments in Southeast Asia, said one Jarai, they will continue to seek refuge in America (Lap Minh Siu 2009).

Community Conflict

Despite their need for community and cooperation, conflict has accompanied Khmer struggles to re-establish community but has seldom been a reason for them *not* to live together. Conflict displays Cambodians' choices and power; whatever else they have lost, they have not lost the ability to like, dislike, please, and insult others as they wish, and factionalism is a major problem in many cities. To describe one Khmer community in 2006, a Khmer man quoted Winston Churchill's 1939 comment about Russia in 1939, calling it a "riddle, wrapped in a mystery, inside an enigma." Other Cambodians saw the same community as a boiling pot of fury and conflict, but Cambodians who knew of the community's discord said it was no worse than the conflict in their own community.

Cambodians said it was difficult after resettlement to trust the unfamiliar Cambodians around them. They lacked traditional means for judging other Cambodians who had come from many different villages and whose families and personal histories they did not know. Speaking of another man, one Khmer explained his caution with him by saying, "I don't know what he did during Pol Pot." They knew they themselves had been deceptive; Haing Ngor said of his acting in *The Killing Fields* movie, "I spent four years in the Khmer Rouge school of acting" (Donahue 1985), and some Khmer said they had lied to get into the camps and to America. While most did not judge their compatriots harshly for their actions, particularly ones they themselves had committed, they did wonder if Cambodians had lost their traditional morality and could be trusted.

Cambodians vacillate in their reactions to others, one day emphasizing the unity of their community, another day complaining they cannot tell who to trust for good advice. Although delighted to be reunited with family and friends, Cambodians are often distrustful of them and quick to disagree with them. Cambodians say they find it difficult to differentiate between victim and victimizer. They often view one another as threats, expressing doubts about their character and wondering if they are former Khmer Rouge. Cambodians acknowledge the conflict in their communities, often quoting a proverb that links the Chinese with fortune-telling, the Vietnamese with lying, and Cambodians with conflict. Several men said, "Cambodians never stop fighting with one another." Poet U Sam Oeur wrote, "Cambodians hate their fellow Cambodians / accuse each other, kill each other / offer their lovers, their children to crocodiles / for greed and foolishness daze their minds" (1998: 149).

Accusing others of not being Cambodian is common. One man said he disliked Sihanouk, saying he was one-third Chinese and his wife was "Siam," the historical term for the Thai (*KI Media* 2008). Glancing at another man at the temple, Phat said, "He doesn't look like a Cambodian. But he speaks Khmer. Maybe he is Chinese. I don't know." Cambodians say they are racially different from Chinese and Vietnamese: taller, darker, with larger noses, curlier hair, fuller mouths, and straighter eyes (McLellan

1995). They also say they have traditionally viewed lighter skin as preferable to dark skin, associating it with wealth, power, and beauty, and many
use skin-lightening cream because they say it will make them look more
attractive (Linna Teng 2012). For many, being American is being white
American.

Criticism of author Oni Vitandham has included attacks on her identity
and appearance, one anonymous writer saying, "Both her appearance and
name are not Khmer." A critic of her critics wrote, "You must be too short
and too ugly that is why you are too jealous with other Khmers who have
light skin and look better than you. May be you are a short Yiek Cong
with black teeth. Oni is truly Kaun Srey Khmer not an idiot and stupid
fool like you" (*KI Media* 2006). This single insult refers to appearance, skin
color, attractiveness, height, and intelligence and suggests that by practicing blackening of the teeth, the critic is Vietnamese, not Khmer. Personal
dislike, resentment, or crisis often causes one Cambodian to say another
is not a "real" Cambodian. When Sovan was angered by a neighbor's children walking through her garden, she said, "She's not really Cambodian.
She speaks Thai more than Khmer and never had to live in a refugee camp
like me." Her anger was short-lived, and the next day, she referred to her
as her Cambodian neighbor.

Cambodians explain their own conflict by pointing to Khmer leaders who want power, but "not to help people." One man said, "It's the
same in Stockton, with people fighting over power in the community,
even in the temples." He then added, "I think it's the same in Cambodian
communities all over America." Most Cambodians agree. Several
Cambodians said the conflict is caused by an unwillingness to forgive,
saying Cambodians hold grudges for life. One man said, "It's our nature.
It's in the genes. Cambodians never forget because they don't want to
lose face." Cambodians insist that face is vitally important to them and
say the Khmer cannot bear contradiction or humiliation. One Cambodian
said, "If you and I argue about global warming, I know we will remain
friends. But Cambodians never forget a disagreement because of face."
Cambodians also describe themselves as a people who cannot negotiate
or compromise, so they often irritate others and end up alienated from
one another. One man said, "Cambodians prefer death to negotiation."
Cambodians emphasize that they must protect their reputation and that
of their families and often Cambodians in general. When a contestant
blurted an obscene comment in Khmer on the television program *The
Bachelor,* several Cambodians asked American friends not to think poorly
of them.

Cambodians enjoy confrontation and conflict when it occurs between
others but avoid it themselves. They say Cambodians mask their anger,

shame, or revenge by choosing their words with care and speaking indirectly. They avoid contact with people with whom they are having problems, withdraw from dispute situations, or end relationships rather than express feelings or use third-party mediation. Cambodians avoid even listening to expressions of emotions; when Theary expressed anger about an old friend, her brother quickly left the room, saying she should not talk "like that." Cambodians say that when they argue, they want the other person to say he is wrong. They say they do not want to discuss disagreements or conflict and have been opposed to American forms of conflict resolution and therapy that depend on discussion for resolution. Saying it is always preferable to comply, Cambodians suggest following the proverb: "Don't reject the crooked road and don't take the straight one; instead, take the road traveled by the ancestors" (Fisher-Nguyen 1994: 97).

Cambodians substitute subtle insult for directness and confrontation. During a New Year celebration in 1982, a woman glanced at an American's Khmer-styled skirt and said in her hearing, "What a lovely cotton skirt!" The American's Khmer friends immediately took offense, knowing the comment meant the skirt should have been silk, since they were attending a festival; the comment also touched on the American's ignorance of Khmer custom and, more importantly at this Khmer gathering, her Khmer friends' inappropriateness in allowing her to wear it. The weight of the insult fell on one of the Khmer friends with whom the insulter had a volatile relationship. A polite "thank-you" was the only appropriate response and avoided confrontation, but the sting remained with the Khmer women. Other insults include wearing casual clothes on solemn occasions, leaving events early, bringing store-bought rather than Khmer food to an event (although this has become more acceptable over the years), sending a relative as a proxy to celebrations, or not visiting another's table in restaurants.

Civility and avoidance also allow Cambodians to maintain relationships with those they dislike or do not know how to treat, an important process in small communities where people regularly see one another. Sung revealed his disdain for Chann one morning by saying he knew Chann "left his wife for another woman, doesn't give her any money, and gambles and plays around," yet when he met Chann at the temple an hour later, Sung greeted him warmly, grabbing his arm and exchanging pleasantries. Only a week later, Chann expressed a similar dislike for Sung but later greeted him as enthusiastically as Sung greeted him. Sung later described his intense dislike for Chann, saying he was "always trying to be big." While Cambodians were puzzled by gays, saying there are no gay people in Cambodia and Cambodians "don't have a word for that," they were as polite to them in public as to other Cambodians. When one man saw a young gay man and his partner arriving at the temple for morning prayers, he said to others sitting nearby, "Here comes Soth's son-in-law," speaking of the partners as spouses. None of the men showed any sign of amusement or disgust.

Cambodians utilize gossip and slander to enhance their own standing and encourage traditional behavior from others. Some said gossip disgusts them because it is harmful to others and can result in karmic punishment. The consequences are often severe; after becoming the target of vicious gossip, several Cambodians fled their community to settle elsewhere, a traditional way to deal with the loss of one's reputation. Sorpheny's family had been negotiating her marriage for some time, and when the fiancé suddenly married another woman, her family moved to a city a thousand miles away. When Sam was fired from his interpreter position at a local agency, he moved his family from California to Washington to avoid embarrassment, and when Peng said his family became the subject of "too much gossip," he moved from Washington to California.

Cambodians occasionally respond aggressively against those who spread gossip about them. When gossip began spreading through one community that a Khmer Christian pastor was leaving his family to return to Cambodia, he e-mailed his supporters, writing, "Please do not be stupid, my family is going together," and threatened legal action if the misleading information did not stop. Although the rumors continued, he did not respond legally, but he gained sympathy for his defense even among those who disliked him. Most Cambodians are less resilient after becoming gossip victims, and a few who did not leave the community reacted with violent retaliation or suicide.

Self-Help Groups

Soon after arrival, Khmer refugees formed mutual aid associations (MAAs), or self-help groups, to provide services to refugees, establish temples, hold cultural events, or advance political agendas in Cambodia (Mortland 1993). Although they used an American model, with boards of directors and American consultants, many MAAs operated through patronage, with a patron gathering family and clients to form his group, then asking Americans to help make the association official. While clients wanted organizations to establish a temple or dance troupe or hold celebrations, many leaders were interested primarily in enhancing their prestige. Invisible to most Americans, MAAs made evident to fellow Cambodians a patron's ability to acquire and distribute resources and services.

As the number of Cambodian refugees increased, so too did the number of Khmer MAAs, and those offering employment services received the most government funding. By the middle 1990s, with falling refugee numbers, funding declined and refugee-specific services shifted to mainstream facilities. By 2008, the one thousand self-help groups existing in 1988 had dwindled to less than two hundred. Some remaining MAAs have broadened their reach to other refugees and immigrants; in 2003, the International Refugee Center of Oregon, founded by Southeast Asia refugees to serve their countrymen in 1976, had staff representing over thirty ethnic groups and speaking fifty different languages in 2016, and it offered one hundred social service programs.

Prominent MAAs in California, such as the Cambodian Family of Santa Ana, the Cambodian Association of America in Long Beach, and the United Cambodian Community also in Long Beach, had considerable impact with refugees, serving them for decades; as a result, they have gained considerable community recognition. Some patron-run MAAs, on the other hand, had little impact on Cambodians. Americans described one MAA as a humanitarian agency working tirelessly for refugees, but Cambodians in the area said they were unaware of the organization. In the early 1980s, typical of Khmer refugees in a number of other cities, most Rochester, New York, refugees said they were not active in MAAs, although they had attended events they thought were sponsored by one Khmer family.

Hay S. Meas said an MAA was organized in Tacoma in 1979 to help refugees, yet few Cambodians lived there in 1979, and refugees and refugee staff said the organization did not exist in the early 1980s. Meas's history of Tacoma MAAs makes no mention of organizations that were actually assisting refugees, including Tacoma Community House, Catholic Community Services, and the Indochinese Cultural and Service Center. Asked about factionalism in Tacoma, Meas said it may have existed in the past "but not at this time, because what I tried to bring to their attention is that you cannot get together on the issues of politics or religion or anything like that" (Chan 2003: 237). Yet Khmer factionalism in Tacoma is legendary, and his comment that coming to Tacoma was like walking "into a hornet's nest" was his only statement about Tacoma that resonated with Khmer residents.

Community Leaders

Since many of the first Khmer refugees had more education and contacts than later arrivals, some became Khmer community leaders. Leaders included those who spoke English and were familiar with Americans.

Among new arrivals, a number of recognized leaders were older men who were knowledgeable about Khmer tradition but lacked the language or knowledge to help others with resettlement. Soon, however, younger men able to learn English and make contacts with Americans became leaders, often in jobs or positions far beyond their training or experience. In one city in the mid-1980s, two leaders were in their early thirties, and Samkhann Khoeun became the executive director of a Lowell MAA in his late twenties.

A number of community leaders also held bilingual positions in refugee agencies due to their knowledge of English and American ways. By the time many of these positions disappeared in the later 1980s, numerous bilingual workers had founded cultural organizations, temples, dance troupes, and orchestras. Some moved on to permanent employment as hospital or community liaisons, interpreters, or social workers; others used their English abilities to work as insurance agents, realtors, car salesmen, or retail clerks or opened retail stores, restaurants, or laundromats. Bilinguals working in government agencies were more likely to keep their positions, many until retirement in the 2010s.

Cambodians were often unhappy with their agency-chosen or self-appointed leaders, saying they were ineffective, selfish, or unqualified and spent more time competing with one another than aiding Cambodians. Early leaders often falsified their resumes; one man said he had a master's degree and had fought the Khmer Rouge and Vietnamese, but Cambodians familiar with him knew him as a bandit robbing people on the Cambodian-Thai border. For years, his admirers were furious at the criticism; by the time the criticism was confirmed, the community had lost respect for him because of his greed as a leader. Another leader in the community claimed he was secretary general of the Cambodian Network Council, a position he never held, and said he had founded a women's health organization in Cambodia, although critics said his "nonprofit" enriched him rather than the women it was purported to serve.

Cambodians lamented that many economically successful countrymen turned from their communities to be "more like Americans," caring only for their families. Some Khmer leaders began encountering legal difficulties; several were accused by the government of accepting fees for salaried work and lying to officials. The Federal Bureau of Investigation (FBI) began questioning Cambodians about illegally applying for benefits, falsifying information, and paying fees for their services and, in the 1980s and 1990s, charged several bilingual workers and welfare recipients with tax, mail, and welfare fraud. Cambodians described frightened illiterate Khmer being handcuffed and taken away "almost every night" and lying to agents to avoid punishment.

In the mid-1990s, federal officers alleged a man named Veha was the center of a conspiracy to steal from the federal disability program. The local newspaper called his work a "sophisticated scam" run by immigrant groups and foreign nationals (Paige 1998) and described the groups as "well-organized, high-tech, border-crossing con artists." Another description portrayed immigrant scammers as third-party facilitators who pose as translators helping immigrants through the disability process and skimming a portion of the benefits for themselves in the process. Many Cambodians thought the description should not be applied to uneducated refugees, and although Veha insisted he had not engaged in corruption, he spent five years in prison. The local Khmer community continues to be divided over his guilt, many respecting him for the assistance he gave other Cambodians for years. Some claimed the primary FBI informant was a rival patron who intimidated Cambodians being interviewed and inaccurately interpreted their words.

Other Cambodians said they do not know if Veha acted illegally because they do not know the laws; one man said, "I can't speak English. How can I know?" Many said he did nothing wrong, and others said he may have but claimed his possible misdeeds did not detract from his good work. One man said he never heard of Veha requesting money for assistance, saying, "Cambodians sometimes give money to those who help them out of gratitude." He added, "Maybe what he was doing was breaking the law, but it doesn't merit prison." Khmer often expressed frustration when Americans did not respond to Cambodians' charges of corruption against Khmer bilingual workers. American supervisors sometimes ignored accusations from disgruntled Khmer clients saying they had been treated unfairly; some Americans refused to believe "their" Khmer employee would participate in illegal or unethical behavior, saying "their" refugee was "too nice" or would not do that (Ledgerwood 1990b). Cambodians also expressed surprise that corrupt Khmer were not being punished by their karmic inheritance.

Despite the conflict or in part because of it, Cambodians said they were eager to re-establish the religious ceremonies they had observed in Southeast Asia. Immediately after resettlement, they began discussing ways they could do so.

Chapter Eight

Religion

After resettlement, Cambodians began seeking ways to celebrate religious ceremonies that had been practiced for centuries in Cambodia until interrupted by the Khmer Rouge, because, Cambodians say, "to be Cambodian is to be Buddhist." In Cambodia before 1974, Theravada Buddhism was practiced by almost 90 percent of Cambodia's population in twenty-eight hundred monasteries with 53,400 monks (Whitaker et al. 1973). The remainder of the population included Chinese and Vietnamese Mahayana Buddhists, Cham and Malay Muslims, hill tribe people observing traditional religions, and a tiny minority of Christians.

Khmer Buddhism

Khmer Buddhism is based on the teachings of Buddha, born in India in the sixth century BC. When Buddhism was carried to Cambodia around two thousand years ago, the region's rice cultivators already practiced rituals to appease a pantheon of spirits (Porée-Maspero 1962–69), and most Cambodians see little separation between Khmer Buddhism and spirit beliefs. From 1975 to 1979, the Khmer Rouge tried to replace religion with new values and behaviors, "like a new god" (Picq 1989: 3), disrobing monks, dismantling temples or using them as pigsties, prisons, or charnel houses, and forbidding rituals. Cambodians again practiced their rituals after flight to refugee camps in Thailand, praying for forgiveness for previous actions and pleading for resettlement. In America where there were no Khmer temples and anxious to earn merit for deceased relatives, Cambodians went to Theravada temples if available or invited surviving monks to hold funeral ceremonies in homes, gymnasiums, community centers, granges, or fraternal halls.

Cambodians said, however, that they needed their own Khmer temples and monks. Frequently they said the temple was "everything to them": the locus of rituals, monks, and services, providing education, counseling, guest facilities, and emergency help. The center of village and neighborhood, a temple compound was surrounded by a fence and included a sanctuary with altar, meeting hall, classrooms, monks' quarters, kitchen, crematorium, trees, paths, vegetable gardens, and often a pond. Cambodians say that without temples, there can be no monks, and without monks, who are Buddha's representatives, "the people go astray." They also say a temple without monks is a meaningless shell, and a monk without a temple is homeless; believers cannot earn merit to improve their next lives and will eventually lose their religion and identity.

To establish a temple, some Khmer communities began with space, some with monks. Cambodians quickly realized that American buildings and lots were inappropriate or too expensive, and re-establishing a temple would require serious adjustments to property, laws, and codes. With few resources, Cambodians located sanctuaries and monks' quarters in rented apartments or houses, usually in low-rent, rundown areas where they were resettled. The first temples were in Washington, DC, New England, and California, and by 1983, there were also Khmer temples in New York, Boston, Chicago, Minneapolis, Nashville, Houston, Portland, and Seattle, often identifiable by a modest sign in Khmer and English and numerous crowds and cars on festival days.

Saying their temples were adequate but inferior to what they envisioned, Cambodians continued their efforts to turn profane American space into sacred Khmer space. As their knowledge of American construction procedures and resources increased, Cambodians moved temples from rentals to houses, churches, stores, factories, warehouses, union halls, even an Odd Fellows Hall, and remodeled temples to closer fit traditional temples. They enlarged rooms and added structures to the grounds, such as statues, stages, canopies, and stupas holding ashes of the dead. They decorated fences with Khmer motifs and roofs with cornices and borders. To build their own temples, Cambodians typically purchased property in rural or suburban areas with lower costs and fewer regulations than in central urban areas.

The first Khmer temple built from the ground up was an elaborate, traditionally styled complex located near the nation's capital. The sermon hall was built first at a cost of between one and two million dollars, with upswept edged, sloping roofs, and three decorative towers; a sanctuary was then added. In Hampton, Minnesota; Jacksonville, Florida; Stockton, California; Denver, Colorado; and Dallas and Houston, Texas, Cambodians erected buildings in traditional Khmer style and compounds full of stupa and statues, often at considerable expense and over many years. By 2014, there were over one hundred Khmer temples in America established by Khmer from Cambodia, most undergoing constant revision. Khmer Krom from southern Vietnam established at least seven temples in America (Khmers Kampuchea-Krom Federation 2009).

Cambodians learned about zoning and nonprofit regulations, raised money for construction, and dealt with neighbors confused over unfamiliar sights and sounds. They remodeled apartments and homes into temple space: removing furniture and adding an altar with statues, flowers, incense, candles, and decorations; Buddhist posters on the wall; a dais and low tables for the monks; and mats and rugs on the floor. Living rooms became sanctuaries, dining rooms turned into food preparation areas, and bedrooms were monks' quarters or storage areas. Finding it difficult to obtain appropriate materials, Cambodians borrowed statues, cloth, sacred oils, paper, and wax from non-Khmer temples and substituted Christmas bulbs for lighted candles and Indian for Khmer fabric. In New York, mountain laurel from the backyard served a visiting monk as a brush to flick blessed water over participants; the monks also used candles he brought from his temple and incense from a "new age" shop. In the following years, Cambodians acquired items from France, from Thai camps or temples, and, as contact with Cambodia increased, from the homeland.

At one temple, the altar held candles, lights, and plates from Fred Meyer, molded statues from a garden shop, gold trees from Michael's, orange fabric from JoAnn's, flowers from Safeway, decorations made from banana leaves (*baysey*) from the Philippines, and parasols sheltering a Buddha statue made of construction paper. Walls were decorated with National Geographic maps of Southeast Asia, photographs and paintings of Angkor Wat, illustrations of Buddha and events from his former lives, and posters of Hanuman the monkey, Shiva the bull, and other Hindu mythological figures.

One temple displayed a drawing of Mary with baby Jesus and photographs of the Dalai Lama, Mahatma Gandhi, and Chuon Nat, a Khmer monk famous for his knowledge of Buddhism and "everything about Khmer culture" who died in 1969. There was a photograph of Maha Ghosananda, a well-known Khmer monk, hugging Pope John Paul II. Temples exhibited photographs of Sihanouk and other members of the royal family, politicians, monks, and nuns. There were grocery calendars printed in Khmer, Thai, English, Vietnamese, Lao, or a Chinese language; handwritten or computer-produced announcements in Khmer and English; literature sent from Protestant and Unification churches; and hexagonal Bakelite clocks, beadwork, and telephone numbers written on faded scraps of paper.

Cambodians first washed linen and dishes in the temple bathtub and wrote out invitations and announcements in longhand, but they soon acquired household and outdoor appliances and electronics for their temples. Telephones and cell phones in the 1990s became ubiquitous, and discussions about whether monks should avail themselves of such conveniences were quickly quieted. Radios, televisions, video recording equipment, CD players, VCRs, digital cameras, and smartphones are often in use, and most temples own vehicles for errands and transporting monks to religious ceremonies outside the temple. Cambodians say American technology does not violate Vinaya rules and allows them more time for spiritual concerns.

Cambodians say the very sight of saffron-robed monks, white-dressed elders, and Cambodians gathered around an altar comforts them. The ground floor of most temples serves as the public area and includes a sanctuary and an area for classes and food preparation and consumption. A lower floor usually has a room for sermons, classes, and occasional "feeding the monks" rituals; storage areas; and accommodations for overnight guests. The floor above the main floor generally serves as monks' quarters; if there is no second floor, monks' rooms lie adjacent to the public area. In the most important room of the temple, the sanctuary, monks sit beside the altar, often on a mat-covered dais with pillows to support them. A low table before them holds ritual items and donated food and gifts. The kitchen and public restrooms usually adjoin the sanctuary, with pantry, several refrigerators, a coffeemaker, and a row of rice cookers on a narrow table commonly present. Areas adjacent to the sanctuary usually hold an elaborate sermon chair, rugs, tables, chairs, and electronic devices, and a television often sits in a neighboring meeting room, also used by praying and resting elderly women during the day.

Obtaining Monks

Resettled Cambodians say they have found it difficult to obtain monks for their fledging temples; most communities solicited the first monks from the refugee camps or were assigned them by Oung Mean in Washington, DC, or Maha Ghosananda in New England, both known for their knowledge of Buddhism and Western ways, education, and leadership. The followers of both claimed each was the head Khmer monk in America and had helped bring monks and establish temples in many communities. Both were influential until their deaths, Oung Mean in 1993 and Maha Ghosananda in 2007. Both men were studying abroad when the Khmer Rouge took over, surviving when most monks were killed and all were disrobed.

Despite the efforts of these prominent monks, Khmer temples had difficulty obtaining monks. Surviving monks were few in number, and most men did not want to put on robes, even temporarily, to gain religious knowledge or fulfill a parent's wish. Cambodians consider former monks worthy marriage partners who have demonstrated the obedience, patience, and discipline important for family life and potential as a temple leader. From early resettlement years, however, refugees were tempted by American ways, and despite the benefits of serving as a monk, few men did so. Temples were left to sponsor monks from the refugee camps and from Cambodia after contact opened up. Most monks continue to come from Cambodia, and leaders expend considerable efforts to ensure that monks remain with the temple. In 2016, many temple leaders wish they had more than the one to four monks residing at their temple.

Monks in Cambodia were regulated hierarchically by their order, but monks in America had no formal organization and little scrutiny. They comprised instead an informal network of monks with seniority based as much on length of residence as length of service and were separated from one another by distances that made organizing difficult. Their greatest obligation was to the local Khmer community, which insisted monks act as they had in Cambodia. Monks can withdraw from the clergy at any time, but they must be separated from the secular world by act, residence, and appearance while they are monks. Monks pray, study, and observe 227 precepts, including 10 major ones: not to kill living beings, steal, engage in sexual intercourse, drink, be deceitful, eat after noon, sleep on a raised bed or sit on a raised seat, touch gold or money, or engage in sensual activities such as drama, dance, and song. They must live in the temple and wear distinctive robes, and they cannot touch women.

When a Khmer monk arrived at a small American airport, he wore orange robes with his right shoulder bared, head shaved, and carrying a bag over his shoulder. Only his plastic sandals distinguished him from monks seven hundred years before, and his square, white plastic bag containing refugee documents was the only item shared with other refugees. Considering monks separate and special, Cambodians accord them great respect, kneeling as they greet them and bowing three times to the ground with joining palms and using special terms to speak with them. Monks try to maintain a traditional schedule, rising, reciting prayers, and eating early and taking their second and final meal before noon. Their days are spent in prayer, counseling, tutoring, meetings, private ceremonies, and participation at other temples. Many travel extensively, adding clothing under or over their robes in cold weather, risking contact with women, and enduring strangers staring and often mocking them. "It's not comfortable," one monk told me, "but it is my duty."

Re-establishing Ceremonies

Cambodians believe humans can affect the balance of good and evil in
their lives. While they say events can be caused by natural forces, astro-
logical circumstances, an imbalance of elements, or spirits, underlying all
their explanations is the notion that a person's actions in this life affect
how he or she lives in the next. One reaps what one sows, and just as
humans prosper from the good they do, so they suffer from their evil. The
doctrine of dharma, the laws that govern birth, death, and rebirth, consists
of four noble truths: there is suffering, the cause of suffering is attachment,
suffering can end by removing attachment, and the way to end attachment
is by following the Eightfold Path—exhibiting right knowledge, attitude,
speech, action, occupation, effort, mindfulness, and composure.

Cambodians believe merit-building activities provide insurance against
future misfortune and demonstrate virtue and power in the present. In
addition to following the Eightfold Path, Cambodians say they earn merit
for themselves and others by obeying Buddhist precepts for behavior,
participating in ceremonies, observing holy days, making food or gift
contributions to the temple, and sponsoring fund-raising ceremonies, and
males can earn merit by being monks. Prohibited by their vows from earning a living, monks in Cambodia go on daily alms rounds to collect food
from laypeople. In America, Cambodians bring food to the monks at the
temple, and "Feeding the monks" is a primary way of earning merit in
America.

Khmer Buddhist ceremonies follow a lunar schedule that fits religious
observances during periods of less work, such as after harvesting crops.
The major celebrations of New Year and Festival of the Dead (*pchum ben*)
occur in April and September, and the ceremony for Offering Gifts to the
Monks (*kathen*) follows. Rites for predicting the future and requesting
good fortune usually occur during the "waxing fifteen days" following
the new moon and before the full moon, with expulsion and funeral rites
usually occurring during the "dark fourteen or fifteen days" following the
full moon and before the new moon. Holy days occur on the eighth and
fifteenth days of the waxing moon and the first and eighth days of the
waning moon. Work is prohibited during the transition rites that mark the
change of seasons, and violators risk attracting misfortune.

Resettled Cambodians observe the traditional Buddhist schedule as
closely as possible but have adjusted it to American work and school
schedules, since the five-day workweek does not correspond to the lunar
calendar and festival days seldom coincide with American weekends and
holidays. Cambodians often celebrate festivals together, such as the Gift

Offering ceremony with the Festival of the Dead, and shorten ceremonies to fit American timetables. The important three-day New Year celebration has been reduced to one, with religious ceremonies and feeding the monks in the morning and games, music, and dancing in the afternoon and evening.

Whatever reductions to rituals are made, vital elements such as feeding the monks continue. Weddings, temple dedications, memorial services, ritual purifications, and blessing ceremonies have continued in importance. Although most weddings occur on weekends, families seek a propitious day for the event, as their ancestors did before them. Funerals have been adjusted to accord with American laws but follow tradition as much as possible, with days of praying, feeding the monks, and cremation. Non-Buddhist Cambodians often attend temple events because they are *Khmer* events. Driving up to the entrance of a temple in 1986, one young man who had never seen a Khmer temple in America exclaimed, "Ah, here we are! Look at all these other Cambodians. See, Carol, these are our monks!"

Cambodians enjoy their celebrations. Khmer festivals are colorful, loud, and busy, with temple compounds featuring music, banners, and flowers, and vendors selling food and items. During ceremonies, Cambodians sit close together facing the monks, wearing their best clothes. Before and after prayers, women prepare food in the side room and wash dishes in the kitchen, men tend to temple business or chat, and children run in and out. After chanting and announcements, people feed the monks, placing bowls and plates before them and sometimes lining up to put a spoonful of rice into each monk's bowl. As the monks complete their meal, food is served to everyone else.

Difficulties Practicing Khmer Buddhism

Cambodians often find it difficult to participate in temple activities. Many live at some distance from the temple or lack transportation. Community conflict creates discord in temples and prevents some from participating in activities. Homeland politics have often been discussed at temples, one of the few Khmer gathering places, and advocacy and fund-raising events for politicians and parties in Cambodia frequently caused disagreements and led to open conflict. Rivalries between community leaders occasionally led to the establishment of multiple temples in a city and created disruptions within temple communities that have endured for decades.

Monks and temple leaders have also varied in their attitudes toward folk beliefs, some allowing spirit practices, while others try to eliminate them by forbidding magical rituals, exorcisms, astrology, and numerology.

Without a central religious authority, political and doctrinal disagreements have been difficult to resolve, as are disputes between monks and accusations by temple participants against them. Several temples were set up by believers who preferred establishing their own temple to participating at a temple with a monk they thought was violating monastic rules.

For a number of years, a Khmer monastic organization in Massachusetts has been trying to place monks in temples throughout the country, shifting temple ownership to their group, and insisting they want to build a unified order that ensures conformity, unity, and legitimacy for Khmer Buddhists in America. Their efforts have resulted in considerable conflict in communities, however, even violence. A number of lawsuits have been filed by local Cambodians accusing the Massachusetts organization of illegally seizing property purchased by the community and installing monks against their will, and some disputes have lasted for years.

Funding the temple and its monks remains an ongoing problem for most temple communities, since Cambodians with limited resources are temples' primary source of funds. Cambodians have accused some monks of being too interested in attracting non-Khmer to their temples for donations or of being "like Americans" to demonstrate that Buddhism is compatible with science and modern American life. Some Cambodians worry that the progressive ideas some monks are developing will lead to the weakening and eventual collapse of Khmer Buddhism in America. They say their temple is neglecting to provide the traditional services they desire.

Cambodians also worried about threats to the legitimacy of Khmer Buddhism in America. In the early years of resettlement, Cambodians wondered if ritual materials having different appearances, textures, and smells than in Cambodia carried less potency, and they were uneasy with substitutions. Later events confirmed people's confidence or doubt about substitutions. "See Carol!" one young man exclaimed at the hospital where his little sister had just come by ambulance. "She's sick because that monk didn't use the right candles." This was rare; Cambodians more commonly accepted that their substitutions were efficacious and blamed misfortune on misbehaving monks or neglected prayers.

Some participants also disapprove of Khmer monks holding ceremonies with non-Khmer temples or devoting time to ecumenical activities, because, they say, they worked hard to construct Khmer Buddhist temples and support Khmer monks for their own needs. While some Cambodians were displeased when ceremonies took on an American cast such as adjusting rituals to fall on Sunday morning or acquiring an American appearance by adding a foyer, other Cambodians were pleased, saying such moves would help preserve Khmer Buddhism in America. Cambodians had the same reactions to printing bulletins of an event's schedule, increasing the use of English during ceremonies, adding Christmas or Mother's Day decorations to the temple, or adding Sunday schools, vacation schools, and family evenings to a temple's activities; some Cambodians worried the adjustments would harm Khmer Buddhism in America, while others were certain they would help.

Since monks owe their support to temple participants rather than a religious organization or authority, they are less inclined to rebuke them, and without a formal structure, there are fewer constraints on monk behavior or ways to deal with complaints against them. Cambodians have criticized monks for improper sexual behavior, smoking cigarettes, swearing, listening to music, attending festivals, or incorporating American items or clothes into their everyday lives. A few monks who in Cambodia would have been ejected or eased out of the clergy have been allowed to remain because of the scarcity of monks or because they have powerful lay supporters. A tolerance by some believers for misbehaving monks shakes the faith of others, thus some Cambodians said they did not want monks answering the telephone during a ceremony, handling money, or being active in temple planning, while others were not bothered.

Cambodians also criticize monks for lacking proper knowledge of Pali, Khmer, and Buddhist doctrine and making it difficult to maintain temple legitimacy or for neglecting their duties in order to travel to other temples or Cambodia. As temple leadership has shifted from older, more knowledgeable men to young men able to speak English and handle finances and logistics, some Cambodians worried that lay and monastic discipline would weaken. Other Cambodians worry about the lack of sacred texts, saying temple legitimacy is threatened when there are few sacred texts to consult and console. Cambodians said legitimacy resides not only in the ideas expressed by sacred texts, but in the medium itself, with pages from old manuscripts used for good fortune or healing potions. Temples initially struggled to obtain Khmer texts, even photocopied materials. Although most now have libraries of books gathered from various sources, some Cambodians say they worry that the technology used in temples has become more important to many young Cambodian Americans than their traditional texts.

Cambodians' dimming memories also concern them. With few temples or opportunities to hear recitations, songs, stories, and sermons and little time to observe ceremonies, Cambodians say their cultural knowledge has faded. Even in the first decade after resettlement, Cambodians had little to stimulate their memories and said their memories consisted only of fragments of chants, stories, songs, and sermons. In addition, Cambodians say second-generation Cambodian Americans were learning American language, history, and values rather than traditional Khmer traditions and Buddhist values. Each passing year has brought fewer opportunities for Cambodian Americans to learn about Khmer Buddhism. Even when a Khmer temple is nearby, most Cambodian Americans do not spend much time there. Cambodians also lament that the number of lay leaders is decreasing, since many men have forgotten or never learned chants and doctrine and thus cannot serve as *achar,* or temple leaders.

Because most Khmer Buddhist temples in America have been consecrated and enlarged, most Cambodians no longer worry about holding rituals in unconsecrated temples, monks and women sleeping under the same roof, or monks eating in the sanctuary rather than an adjacent hall, but some Cambodians continue to be concerned about the inappropriate use of temple space. Some dislike allowing dance classes to be held in the sanctuary or anywhere in the temple, others think monks spend too much time visiting rather than praying, and still others think too much time is spent by both monks and laypeople at the temple watching television and movies and creating videos of festivals and rituals. Most Cambodians dismiss such concerns, saying they could not have done anything in their temples if they had to obey all traditional rules.

Since early resettlement years, Cambodians struggled over the truth and potency of their beliefs. Some said they were believers before but have doubts now, particularly about karmic law, asking how anyone deserved the devastation and loss of country they experienced. The absence of Khmer Buddhist institutions, overwhelming number of American believers, and American arrogance in their beliefs and eagerness to proselytize eroded Cambodians' own certainty, and many felt less pressured to observe their traditional rituals. The availability of alternative religions also caused some to question Khmer Buddhism (Mortland 1994). A few months after arrival in 1981, a young woman jotted in her notebook, "I don't know if maybe American Christian God is stronger than Buddha." In 2016, she continues to participate at the temple regularly but occasionally expresses disdain for others' devotion.

Some Cambodians said their basic cosmological ideas were threatened when they heard scientific ideas about the creation of the universe. Bong, a monk before the Pol Pot years, was shocked to hear that men had walked on the moon. He said ancient Buddhist texts stated that men would never go to the moon, so how could this be? He slowly accepted it as fact only after a professor he respected assured him it was true and recounted watching it on television. Many Cambodians remain undisturbed by contrary ideas and practices, convinced the ways of their ancestors are the only truth for them if they continue to believe. One man pointed to the good luck strings on the altar, saying, "If you don't believe in the power of the strings, it doesn't work to protect you. But I believe, so it is true."

Spirits

Cambodians equate belief in spirits with being Khmer, many saying spirits have a more direct influence on their daily lives than does karma; while karma works slowly, spirits work fast. Cambodians integrate Buddhist and spirit rituals in America, communicating with spirits through Buddhist incantations and exorcisms performed by Buddhist monks or lay leaders (*achar*). After a monk conducted an exorcism to erase thoughts of a man's 22-year-old American girlfriend from his mind, at his wife's request, he stopped seeing her; he and his wife said the spirit who caused the behavior was forced to stop. Cambodians say spirits reside in the pedestal of Buddhist statues, and at some temples, feeding the monks includes feeding the spirits.

Initially confused about the existence of Khmer spirits in America and hesitant to talk about them, Cambodians were soon describing them at length. One man said, "The spirits came to America when we came, but they don't bother Americans because Americans don't believe in them." Cambodians speak about several categories of supernatural beings: the most discussed are guardian or territorial (*neak ta*), ancestor (*meba*), and evil, benevolent celestial, individual, or teacher spirits. When displeased, spirits may retaliate by causing mischievousness or serious trouble to people or their families. Cambodians try to avoid offending them by acting properly, inviting them to family rituals such as marriages or childbirth, and giving offerings. Darany said, "I respect them, just in case." One woman said she decided to stay in her apartment because spirits bothered her so much when she went to a movie that her hair fell out in the car on the way home and she became ill.

Christians, Muslims, and Mahayana Buddhists

Not all Khmer from Cambodia are Buddhists. Cambodians are also Christians, Cham or Malay Muslims, or Chinese Mahayana Buddhists. In addition to Chinese Cambodians who are integrated into Khmer culture and practice Theravada Buddhism, there are Chinese Cambodians who practice Mahayana Buddhism and honor their ancestors and household gods. Many Mahayana Chinese have identified with the Chinese American community, restricting their ties to other Cambodians primarily to business; their children see themselves as Chinese Americans rather than Cambodian Americans.

The largest number of non-Buddhist Cambodians are Christians and Muslims. Few in number in Cambodia, a number of Cambodians converted to Christianity in Thailand's camps, some to obtain more services, others thinking they had a better chance at resettlement. Many more Khmer refugees became Christians after resettlement, either identifying themselves exclusively as Christian or attending Christian churches but also participating in Buddhist rituals. Most were introduced to Christianity by church and individual sponsors. Protestant, Catholic, and Mormon individuals and churches across America who sponsored Khmer families, assisted communities, and offered English classes. Numerous American pastors and missionaries learned Khmer and established refugee ministries.

Some Cambodians said they converted to Christianity out of gratitude for what Christians had done for them; others said they were pressured into attending church and proclaiming themselves Christians. Members of some churches, such as Presbyterians and Catholics, sponsored refugees as part of their tradition of social service; most did not have high expectations that refugees would become members. Members of fundamentalist and evangelical churches, on the other hand, pressured refugees to become Christians from a belief that not doing so condemned nonbelievers to permanent damnation. They often gave considerable material assistance to refugees, and some insisted on total commitment, demanding that Cambodians abandon Buddhist or spirit rituals they considered "superstitions" and "pagan." Some churches held idol-burning services to destroy Khmer converts' home altars, statues, amulets, necklaces, magical inscriptions, and talismans.

A number of Khmer Christians stopped participating in Buddhist rituals and joined wholeheartedly in Christian beliefs and rituals. Some said they accepted Christianity as an alternative to Buddhism because the Christian God, not Buddha, had protected them. Some said they thought Christianity was more powerful than Buddhism because there were so many Christians in America and America is so powerful. Other Khmer converts said they were attracted to Christianity by Christians' emphasis on family. Several said they found the Christians in their church a welcome family after the loss of their own. Some said they turned to Christianity for relief from their memories, grief, and distress.

Numerous Cambodian Christians said they had been attracted to a Christian church by its emphasis on social respectability and economic advancement. They said they saw conversion as an avenue for entering the American middle class and found estrangement from other Khmer the price they had to pay to be accepted by Americans. Cambodians spoke explicitly of attending church as an effort to form ties with congregational members who could connect them to educational opportunities and resources. They said they were also happy that their children could more rapidly learn English and American customs and make valuable contacts for the future. Both Cambodian Buddhists and Christians claimed that Khmer children active in Christian churches and schools were less likely to drop out of school than those attending public schools, and many attended Christian colleges on scholarship.

While some Cambodians became exclusively Christian, many more practiced Christianity while continuing to participate in Buddhist activities. They were Christians, they said, from gratitude and to acquire patrons, jobs, shelter, resources, services, and advice. A faithful church attendee said he always felt uncomfortable around Americans and dreaded going to church, "Even though they like me very much and think I like them. But I go because I want to get my English better and get a better job." One family contributed regularly to the collection plate because "our family needs as much protection as possible." In 2007, a family said that while they were still uncomfortable with Americans after two and a half decades, they needed the exposure and assistance that association with an American church congregation brought them. They said what Cambodians had been saying for years: they were able to practice English, and even more importantly, the church provided guidance for their children. They also said they needed to attend the Khmer temple because they are Cambodian.

Typical of many Cambodian Buddhists, the wives of two temple leaders faithfully attended a Presbyterian church and saw no contradiction in doing so. Some Cambodian Americans said both religions teach a message of love and reverence and, as Christians, they feel more like Americans, while being Buddhist reinforces their Khmer identity. While some Cambodians criticize Cambodians who participate in both Buddhist and Christian ceremonies, most say they understand other Cambodians' need to fit in with Americans while remaining Khmer. Over the years, the division between Khmer Buddhists and Christians has deepened as Cambodian converts have either returned to Khmer Buddhism or become strongly identified with Christianity. There is little contact between the two groups, and while there is little explicit animosity, Buddhists say Khmer Christians have abandoned their traditions, while Khmer Christians lament that Buddhists are going to hell, and both express sadness that the other has abandoned truth and salvation.

The number of Khmer Christians in America is difficult to determine, for both Christians and Buddhists exaggerate their numbers. Early estimates suggested that from 5 to 40 percent of Cambodians had converted, with most Khmer communities hovering between 10 and 15 percent despite the intense proselytization and assistance aimed at them in the camps and after resettlement. Observers and Cambodians agree that most Cambodians who initially became Christians reverted to Buddhism as they acquired income through work or welfare and located Khmer communities and temples where assistance was available. Cambodians with more Christian sponsors, more American Christians contacts, no Khmer temples nearby, and Khmer Christian leaders are more likely to convert to Christianity. An additional group of Christian converts are tribal people who traditionally relied on spirit mediums and animal sacrifices to placate benevolent and malevolent local and ancestral spirits, but who converted to Christianity after contact with Americans.

Resettled Cham or Malay Muslim Cambodians have expended great effort to maintain their religious beliefs and cultural values in America, following the five Islamic pillars: acknowledging Allah as the only god and Muhammad as his messenger, praying five times a day, giving alms, fasting during the month of Ramadan from sunup to sundown, and making a pilgrimage to Mecca if able to do so. Resettled Cham began attending mosques soon after arrival, saying association with other Muslims was more important than with other Cambodians, not surprising since most had lived in side-by-side but in separate Buddhist villages in Cambodia before the 1975 Khmer Rouge takeover. One man said, "I don't visit Cambodians. I just speak the language. Now I talk to people from Iran and Africa and America," and a woman said, "Religion is everything to us. We live it. We eat it. We breathe it."

As soon as they found one another, Cambodian Muslims clustered in communities and established Khmer mosques, saying the decimation of their people during the Khmer Rouge years gave them increased impetus to live together and observe their beliefs. For those living near Khmer mosques in Southern California in the early 1990s, marriages were arranged, marriage with non-Muslims was forbidden, children were told to avoid violent and sexually explicit television programs, and teenagers prayed during school breaks and studied the Qur'an after school. To keep their children in the faith and close to them, parents continue to prohibit dating, enforce strict clothing standards, and encourage children to continue their language and heritage. Although children and youth find it difficult to appear Muslim among Americans in the twenty-first century, many continue to respect their beliefs and communities.

Much of Khmer refugees' religious concerns focused on their health, an issue all survivors of the Khmer Rouge faced.

Chapter Nine

Health

Khmer refugees said health was their greatest concern. "Number one, I'm worried I will die," one man said, "and then who will take care of my children?" He died several years later at thirty-nine years of age. In a 1987 survey, less than 6 percent of 589 Cambodians in Oakland described themselves as healthy (Gong-Guy 1987). Virtually every Cambodian at one time or another complained of stomach distress, headaches, insomnia, weakness, vertigo, and exhaustion. Some described difficulty with walking, faulty memory, and impaired vision, and many suffered from chronic ailments caused by poor sanitation and living conditions, such as malaria, hepatitis B, diabetes, infection, anemia, and intestinal parasites.

Health professionals supported Cambodians' complaints that they had arrived in the United States with a wide array of health problems, most significantly tuberculosis, hepatitis, and dental problems (United States Department of Agriculture 1982). One study found that, while 15 percent of Americans had moderate to severe needs for medical services, almost 50 percent of Khmer reported such a need (Krich 1989). Years later, Marshall and others (2006) found that 70 percent of Cambodians were receiving medical care, and 46 percent mental health services.

Causes of Health Problems

Cambodians say illness can be the result of natural, psychological, supernatural, or situational causes. If a man is lazy in caring for his fields, the rains come late, or locusts descend in hordes, his crops may fail and his children suffer malnutrition and disease. They say a person who does not maintain a balance among the elemental forces of his or her body, which include earth, water, fire, and wind, damages the functioning of major organs; thus, excessive excitement can harm the heart, anger threaten the liver, anxiety the lungs, shock the kidneys, and a pondering mind the spleen. Cambodians also say an imbalance in the earth element can cause rigidity, thus arthritis, and water affects fluidity, thus digestion problems and diarrhea. According to one Cambodian, each element can cause 101 diseases.

A lack of balance or harmony in a person's life may allow noxious winds to invade the body as a person's breathes, causing "wind illness" (*krun khyol*), with symptoms of vomiting, diarrhea, and "feeling bad," and can lead to the common cold, diabetes, and hypertension (also Pickwell 1999). If not treated properly, wind illness can become "ripe," resulting in stroke or heart attack. The "devil's wind," which Khmer say originates from buried bodies and appears as large balls of fire, causes diseases that are curable only by specialized healers. Several Cambodians said that is the reason most Cambodians are cremated. A lack of equilibrium can also result in mental stress, thinking too much, or concentrating too much on the past. Diagnosing my headache, one woman or another would tell me sternly, shaking her head and patting my arm, "You think too much, Carol." A study of 120 Khmer women found that "thinking too much" was Cambodians' most common symptom (Frye and D'Avanzo 1994).

Cambodians say excessive thinking can lead to excessive emotion, and many agree with the Thai who claim women are not meant to think (Muecke 1991). Cambodians say it is important for equilibrium to consume a balance of hot and cold substances; being too cold can cause diarrhea and menstrual pain, while being too hot can result in fever, high blood pressure, or severe emotional distress. People in a cold state should eat hot foods, including pepper, ginger, sugar, meat, lobster, and shrimp, and in a hot state should eat cold foods such as raw vegetables, coconut, pineapples, bananas, shellfish, and crabs. Hot foods given to people in a hot state worsen their condition; similarly with cold foods to cold people. Cambodians also say excessive emotions, such as "the three poisons" of greed, ignorance, and anger, can lead to disease. Greed for food may lead to overeating, bloat, and obesity, which can lead to diabetes and heart problems. Ignorance can cause people to ignore factors that prevent disease, and anger can lead to stress, hypertension, and poor circulation and then heart disease and stroke.

Supernatural forces can also cause illness. If offended, ancestor spirits may cause those who offend them to become ill, usually because they have neglected to inform the spirits of events such as birth or marriage, or if Cambodians do not keep their promises, such as offering food to the spirits if saved from the Khmer Rouge or granted resettlement. Cambodians blame guardian spirits for headaches, dizziness, stomach distress, joint aches, exhaustion, nightmares, emotional instability, and sudden and unexplained death. Cambodians also say that a person can become susceptible to spirit possession or witchcraft if weakened by death or separation from family members. A Khmer healer, or *kru khmer,* told a couple in one American city that the wife kept walking into walls in her sleep because she missed her family and might be possessed by the spirits of her grandparents. After the couple offered food to the ancestor spirits, the wife stopped sleepwalking.

Cambodians often turn to karmic explanations of illness, saying improper behavior in a person's previous life can lead to disease and pain in the present life; in Dara's words, "Maybe you did something bad in a life before, and now you pay for it." Cambodians also worry that others may place curses on them. Some suspected one man's wife poisoned him, knowing his liver cancer would conceal the cause of his death, but not all were convinced it was poison that killed him. One man said, "I think she just put a curse on him." Another man blamed a friend's heart attack on someone magically sending water into his heart and was outraged that some would use such magic. "They really shouldn't do that here in America," he said. "Don't they know not to do that here?"

Resettled Cambodians also attributed some health difficulties to situational causes. Most Cambodians saw the violence, destruction, uncertainty, and whole-scale disruption of the Khmer Rouge years as devastating to their health, leaving them with a legacy of injury, disease, starvation, and stress (Kinzie et al. 1984). Numerous studies revealed the extent of their suffering. Out of 586 Khmer adults between thirty-five and seventy-five years of age, 99 percent came close to starving to death, and 90 percent had family or friends murdered during the Khmer Rouge years (Marshall et al. 2005). The effects of malnutrition on small children left them smaller and weaker than their siblings. Ninety-five percent of the respondents in one survey said they had been sexually abused or raped (Mollica 1986), and in another, 80 to 90 percent of women said they were raped by Thai bandits, a fate some escaped by wearing white and shaving their heads to appear as nuns (Chan 2003). Viewed as especially distressing, Cambodians described rape as the worst crime (Ledgerwood 1990a) and said their suffering endured for years rather than minutes or days. In addition, flight and refugee camp life resulted for many in intestinal parasites, sexually transmitted diseases, hunger, and stress (Keller 1975).

Resettlement itself was hazardous to Cambodians' health, and people who had remained strong for years said they began to fall apart after coming to America. Cambodians often said if they had not come to America, they probably would not be as sick as they were, saying that life among strangers who had different values, behaviors, and attitudes drained them of energy. Some said they could not sleep because bedrooms were not situated to allow them to rest with their heads to the south to imitate the sun setting in the west. They said the loss of tradition, family, and home left Cambodians depressed, anxious, and frightened, and many exhibited mental problems somatically as generalized pain, lethargy, headaches, amnesia, fatigue, and breathing difficulties.

Aging naturally complicated Cambodians' health problems, with heart attacks, strokes, and cancer common. Many said it was difficult to eat certain food as they aged because they had lost teeth to injury, malnutrition, and inadequate dental care. As health problems intensified over the years, the diet of most became more problematic. Cambodians were able to afford more meat and prepared food and were attracted to inexpensive, immediately available, and easily consumed American food. Having experienced food deprivation, some Cambodians developed unhealthful eating practices in reaction, and limited English kept many from learning about healthy diets and weight control or learning the nutritional value of processed foods. Parents were often guided in their food choices by children, themselves influenced by television commercials and school food choices. Several Khmer mothers said Reese's Puffs was their children's favorite cereal, unaware of a Yale University study that concluded Reese's Puffs was the most aggressively marketed directly to children but had the highest concentrations of sugar and sodium and the least fiber of all cereals (*CBC News* 2009). Khmer parents were also unfamiliar with marketing techniques that placed sugary foods on child-level store shelves, processed foods closer to the front, and meats, fruits and vegetables farther away.

A woman in the Bronx thought being a good mother meant feeding her children junk food so they grew up round and healthy (Chira 1993). She told a reporter, "I saw a lot of children look a little chubby. I said, 'Maybe that's good food.'" Another mother said, "When I had money, I fed my children McDonalds because it is healthy food." Several mothers said they knew the chicken nuggets, pizza, and chocolate milk being served to their children were healthy for them because the government would only provide good food. Cambodians also said they hoped American food would help their children grow up healthy and strong like big American children, and "not like children in Cambodia," one woman said. "Our food was good, but we didn't have enough." As a consequence, a richer diet replaced the traditional diet of fish, rice, vegetables, and a spoonful of meat sauce for the members of many Khmer refugee families, who were more likely to report being overweight or obese.

Cambodians have also said substance abuse has become a problem for many first- and second-generation Cambodians. Alcohol was traditionally associated in Cambodia with wealth and was thus available to most Cambodians only on important occasions. In America, on the other hand, alcohol is available to virtually everyone regardless of economic means, and Buddhist prohibitions have lost some of their influence on Cambodian Americans whose reliance on community opinion has faded. Many Cambodians say families who can provide expensive alcohol to their guests gain considerable status. Cambodians say most Khmer drink to excess only at weddings and other celebrations. An older man said, "If we really want to get drunk, we drink our herbs." Hard liquor and beer are most common among older Khmer, with Remy Martin and Hennessy especially valued. Khmer refugees say they often substitute "white" liquors such as vodka and gin for the home-brewed rice wine of Cambodia. Younger people favor beer and wine, particularly brands consumed by their American peers.

Some studies have found Cambodians at high risk for alcoholism (D'Avanzo, Frye, and Froman 1994; Yee and Thu 1987), while other studies conclude Cambodians are not at high risk for alcoholism (Marshall et al. 2005). A number of Cambodians worry about alcohol, tobacco, and drug consumption, lament that the traditional social controls on excessive drinking have been more difficult to maintain in America, and worry that alcohol and drugs are major threats to Khmer traditions and proper behavior. Other Cambodians see substance abuse as a logical outcome of the memories and loss they have endured, some suggesting that a number of Cambodians use alcohol, tobacco, and other drugs to ease their feelings of depression and anxiety.

Traditional Khmer Healing Solutions

In response to their experiences, some Cambodians reacted with startle reactions, hallucinations, or withdrawal, refusing to leave their homes or hiding in corners. Cambodians said the shame they felt over their own actions, from being unclothed, forced to defecate in public, betraying loved ones, or contributing to others' death, caused their greatest pain. Referred to as "Cambodian sickness" or having "broken" or "ruined heads," Cambodians said, "Our brains don't work anymore." They found it difficult to remember, memorize, think, or talk, thus to learn English, find a job, or deal with unruly children. One young man said he could memorize whole books before, but now when someone spoke to him in English, the words vanished. He added, "My hand shakes when I try to eat or sign my name."

A number of women suffered psychosomatic blindness, ranging from total vision loss to seeing only shadows. In the 1980s, brain wave tests revealed that 150 women with unexplained vision loss had 20/20 eyesight

(A. Smith 1989). They said they gradually lost their vision after resettlement or could not see after witnessing their husband's murder. Some could not care for themselves, others would not leave their homes, and all claimed to be "constantly depressed," spending hours weeping, staring into space, or lying in a fetal position. Convinced her soul had been beaten out of her, one woman wondered if she was alive or dead. Some medical personnel said the women were inventing or exaggerating their affliction to obtain sympathy or money or became hysterically blind in response to repressed childhood dilemmas, and others advised them to stop worrying and be happy.

A few medical personnel took their symptoms seriously, however, concluding the women's blindness resulted from an inability to deal with their memories (Wilkinson 1994). The women said they were "pursued by memories" and drained of energy and serenity. When therapists, medical personnel, or social workers listened to their distress and taught them skills, such as use of the telephone, the sight and well-being of some women improved (Van Boemel and Rozee 1992).

Some Cambodians dealt with their experiences by developing a "dummy personality" (*tiing moong*) similar to that exhibited by concentration camp survivors (Mollica and Jalbert 1989). Having acted deaf and dumb, foolish, confused, or stupid with the Khmer Rouge, many continued the behavior in the camps and after resettlement; some Cambodians claimed to be without motive or enthusiasm. A high schooler described himself as "leftover from a dead man." Others reacted by exhibiting the opposite reaction, seeking sensation and emotion by watching violent movies, although unable to explain their enjoyment beyond saying, "They are funny" or "They make me feel real." As the years passed, some young Cambodians who had earlier talked of feeling numb began saying they felt angry; most turned their attention to improving their economic standing.

Finding that resettlement brought only temporary relief to their pain and that withdrawal and numbness brought only temporary relief, most Cambodians turned to traditional healing techniques (Pickwell 1999). Contrary to Yang Sam's (1985) claim that few Cambodians believed in traditional healing, most Khmer said they had faith in traditional healing methods; Yang Sam was the only Cambodian I ever met who said he did not believe in the efficacy of Khmer medicine. Even after learning that many Americans saw traditional healing techniques as contrary to biblical teachings, uncivilized, or unscientific, Cambodians persisted in practicing their traditional healing methods and seeing Khmer healers (Marcucci 1986).

In addition to eating, drinking, and acting moderately and remaining serene, Cambodians said observing religious rituals aids one's health:

bowing to the monks and altar increases bodily flexibility and strength, aids circulation, and helps believers focus on spiritual matters, and meditation helps believers avoid evil thoughts and selfishness. Believers also sought monks' assistance in determining causes and cures of illness. Cambodians consider amulets and tattoos important in protecting them from misfortune. When Sann fled Cambodia, he took "my wife, son, teaching certificate, and remaining amulets." One of his most valued amulets is an elephant tusk his grandfather found embedded in a tree while cutting wood and collecting medicinal plants in the forest.

Sann said the amulet saved his family one night while they were sleeping by yelling, "Fire! Fire!" Sann's amulets include a solid pig tusk and bison horn, an interwoven piece of bamboo, a lake sponge containing a piece of hardwood, and a frizzy ball of hair that causes people who touch it to fall ill. "Only one man in a million has that," Sann said, adding that he offers incense and annually sprays the hair ball with perfume to ensure its protective value. Cambodians said bison horn shavings mixed with rice and water or wine can cure a child's fever and heal a snakebite and a bug or bee sting. Amulets can be gems or made of gold and ivory, chicken spurs, pig, tiger, or human teeth, inscribed copper or silver leaves, or a simple thread that has been blessed by a monk or healer.

Cambodians say a bead dabbed with pork fat; rolled copper, lead, silver, or gold cylinders containing Pali inscriptions on a string around the neck or waist; and small Buddha necklaces offer protection, and amulets inserted just beneath arm or chest skin prevent injury from knives or bullets. A former soldier said a bullet grazed his head in 1973, but an amulet implanted in his shoulder saved him, and Cambodians spoke admiringly of a healer who, when shot in the mouth, spit out the bullet. They attributed his lack of injury to his amulets. Some Cambodians said they no longer wear visible amulets, to avoid American mockery. One man admitting he felt unsafe driving without his amulets, but he did so to avoid being jeered at by work colleagues, but most wear their amulets under their clothing. One man said a Khmer friend who has a doctorate has a number of amulets because "science cannot explain the whys of everything, so it is best to believe."

Protective tattoos include Pali and Khmer alphabetic characters and images of the Buddha, Hindu gods, mythical beings, and animals. Men were often shy about revealing their tattoos in front of Americans; one man with face tattoos seldom ventured outside his house, but he credited them for protecting him from bullets and the Khmer Rouge. While men have the most tattoos, women may wear tattoos near their hairline or on neck, shoulders, back, or chest. Cambodians said some people are born with protection: a person born with a birthmark on the tongue cannot be killed by a poisonous snake, and others have birthmarks indicating they are blessed. One man said being born with his umbilical cord wrapped around his neck protected him from machine gun fire in the early 1970s. Former soldiers also reported wearing neckerchiefs or garments imprinted with their parents' hand and foot prints, incantations, or designs, most in the protective color of red.

Cambodians use a wide array of herbal medicines to treat illness and injury, preparing them from plant and animal parts and minerals. Cambodians utilize wet medicines made from boiled substances and medicinal powders stirred into water or rice alcohol or made into pills, or they spray chewed vegetable substances on wounds. Cambodians take medicine internally for fevers, coughs, and serious diseases such as smallpox and beriberi and use liquids, ointments, and pastes for external use. Cambodians believe that vapor inhaled from burning medicine prevents headaches and fever and beautifies the skin and that bitter root "attracts" evil spirits inhabiting a person. The Khmer use opium mixed with marijuana to cure severe cases of diarrhea and fresh opium with tamarind powder for back pain, headaches, and menstrual and leg cramps. Women sometimes drank ginseng pickled in liquor when ill or to prevent illness.

Cambodians also said food could prevent and cure illness, claiming vegetables and fresh fruit can prevent cancer and boiled ginger root water helps blood circulation and hangovers by softening and cleansing the blood. For colds, one couple instructed, "Boil fresh lemongrass, orange peel, sliced ginger, a teaspoon of rock salt, and a few drops of mineral oil in water. Breathe in the steam until you sweat, and then you will get relief." Resettled Cambodians have used over-the-counter medicines extensively. Rather than the traditional cold bath, they commonly take Tylenol and warm rice soup or orange juice and use a wet cloth on the forehead to treat a child's fever. Many speak of taking one or two Tylenol for fever, dizziness, or headache, waiting a few hours, and then seeking medical care if they do not feel better. Some said they do not read the instructions on medicine bottles. "I only use Tylenol," one woman told me "because the television says it's safe."

Cambodians use various manipulative techniques, including rubbing mentholated monkey or tiger balm, available in virtually every Khmer home, on affected areas to relieve muscular pain, headaches, stomachaches, itching, and congestion. Cambodians apply medicated tape to sore muscles and broken bones, to the forehead for headache relief, and the neck for sore throats, and they apply massage to veins that are thought to be the source of pain rather than muscles. In addition to acupuncture, Cambodians also use coining (*choup kchall*), or "rubbing the wind," which

Cambodians say rids the body of noxious carbon dioxide, the cause of numerous ailments such as dizziness, headache, or fever.

Cambodians usually coin with a quarter or a coin attached to a handle after lubricating the skin with tiger balm, herbal liquid, skin lotion, or water to increase effectiveness. The scraping friction creates heat, which Khmer believe makes the carbon dioxide, known as bad wind or black blood, leave the body. Cambodians say the darker the bruises left by the coin, the greater the amount of wind causing the problem. Yam said, "You can spend the whole day scraping." After coining, a patient often consumes hot water or rice soup, wraps up in warm clothing or bedding, and avoids taking a cold bath. Cambodians say the cure generally comes in one or two days, and if the patient's symptoms do not improve, the illness has another cause. Coin rubbing was met with intense American disapproval. Medical and school personnel were shocked by the long red strips they saw on children and reported parents for child abuse, and parents were warned to cease scraping, advice they usually ignored. In the twenty-first century, Cambodians continue the practice and continue to be reported for suspected child abuse when they scrape their children. They acknowledge that coining is painful and most do not enjoy having it done. "Children cry, and some women, too," said one Cambodian.

Many Cambodians continue the practice. In 1992, while working at Weyerhaeuser, a Khmer man became faint; instead of going home, he took a quarter and some water and coined himself on the chest and arms, much to the astonishment of his colleagues. Ten minutes later, he said he returned to work feeling fine. Twenty years later, he forgot to stretch his muscles before going out to trim his trees. Feeling a deep pain in his back and unable to straighten up, he dropped the trimmer and went inside to his wife, who coined him. Within fifteen minutes he was able to return to his gardening. "Why should I go see a chiropractor and wait so long?" he said. "I know how to cure my family the fast way."

Another popular Khmer technique is pinching, or "pinching the wind," pulling on the skin between the eyebrows sufficiently hard to cause bruising. Pinching is used for headaches, dizziness, coughing, and sinus discomfort, and for years, it was unusual to go to a Khmer gathering without seeing someone with a red mark between the eyebrows caused by the practice. Cambodians also practice moxibustion, also called cupping or "sucking the wind," to cure headaches and prevent mental illness. The healer lights a candle and a small ball of vegetable fiber or bit of pitch (moxa) inside a small bottle or series of bottles, cups, or jars and places them on the patient's forehead, back, upper chest, or stomach.

The heat creates a vacuum inside the bottle that "sucks" out the wind, leaving red or dark circular marks on the skin. One healer said moxibustion is like an electric shock to the nerves, and burning the moxa reconnects the nerve ends. Sareth explained that unlike other people, Cambodians cannot get sufficient oxygen when they breathe, so they supplement their respiration by breathing through the skin. Some Cambodians prefer cupping to coining, saying it is less painful, but they said it requires experience and the proper equipment, and the bottles can overheat and burn the skin (Graham and Chitnarong 1997). Americans are also often upset by cupping marks.

Blowing (*plum balai*) is another technique used by Khmer healers for sores, bites, and swelling. Cambodians said blowing is most effective if done early in the morning before the healer has brushed his teeth or eaten. The technique was performed on a colleague when she woke one morning with a swollen cheek that was hard and painful by evening. A friend took her to a healer. After lighting a stick of incense, he sat next to her and began praying, running his fingers along her cheek and over her jaw. He suddenly blew three quick puffs. As he repeated the stroking, prayers, and blowing, she felt her cheek grow warm. The healer asked if she had gone into the forest and touched a tree or any kind of poison, and when she said she did not think so, he said a ghost may have caused the swelling. The swelling had gone down by the time she reached home, and her cheek was back to normal in two days. She later discovered the healer had been generous in working with her; Cambodians said healers can become ill if their patients do not improve, and Americans are difficult to treat, so healers must be careful with them.

Although resettled Khmer were unable to observe childbirth rituals in American hospitals, they continued to recite invocations, spit betel leaf juice on infants, and purify mothers by cleansing their breasts to prevent breast cancer. While no longer able to be warmed by a fire tended under their beds, mothers observed dietary restrictions to restore heat lost during the cold postpartum period that Cambodians say follows the hot months of pregnancy. Decades after their families left Cambodia, some Cambodian American mothers continue to drink for at least thirty days postpartum a concoction of steeped leaves, bark, and tuber roots or animal bones in wine that they say restores their blood, pelvic organs, and strength. Often prepared by husbands, one man said the reason for his wife's rapid recovery from childbirth was ensuring his wife consumed the drink he prepared daily. After birth, some also continue to avoid foods that "make their bodies hot," such as meat and strongly spiced food, and steam themselves in a lemon concoction rather than bathing.

While Cambodians took care of many of their family's health needs after resettlement, they called on Khmer healers when they thought they were needed, although through the 1980s they often concealed the extent to which they utilized them (Sargent, Marcucci, and Elliston 1983). Cambodians continue in the twenty-first century to deny to most Americans that they consult traditional Khmer healers, although the number of healers is smaller, as fewer people are being taught Khmer healing techniques, and some older healers say they have forgotten what they learned. Some Cambodians returned to Cambodia to consult with healers and utilize traditional medicines, and although Cambodians lamented the loss of traditional medical knowledge since the 1960s, several healers said they were able to learn more about their craft from healers there.

Cambodians say some people have the ability to be healers, while others do not. Chhaya told me his fiancée's grandmother was a good healer with healing hands "like fire," but she told Chhaya he did not have healing abilities. One young man said he did not want to become a healer because bad spirits would eventually lead him to do evil things, and another said he declined the role because "it is like the Mafia. Once you start, you can't stop." Cambodians said people with disabilities are often powerful healers because of their handicaps, as are monks and former monks because of their purity. In Southern California, an older blind woman was considered an especially powerful healer, and Cambodians from as far away as Oregon and Washington sought her services. Cambodians also described people who spoke different languages, lived in other regions, or practiced different religions or customs, such as tribal people, Cham, Vietnamese, and Khmer Krom, as formidable healers able to cause and heal disease.

Before instructing students in the spirits' complex rules, Cambodians say healers inform their teacher spirits of the students' desire to learn healing by offering candles, incense, paper money, flowers, cigarettes, betel leaves, and two meters of white fabric to the spirits. Healers must observe certain rules to retain their power, and those who lose their power are "not salty." A healer must not eat certain vegetables and fruits or some species of animals, such as cats or dogs. A healer may have relations with his wife, but only in a room separate from his own; the Khmer say most healers avoid sexual activity. No one except clients may enter a healer's bedroom, sleep in his bed, or use his pillow or blanket.

Healers are most valued for their ability to appease angered spirits. When people give proper respect to the spirits, offering incense, candles, and food in a small shrine and notifying them of family events, they are generally harmless. When someone falls ill and Cambodians suspect spirit involvement, they seek help from a healer. If a healer concludes a guardian spirit is the cause, he compares the time of the illness and the patient's heartbeat and birthdate and urges the family to make an offering of the best food they can afford. Some Khmer say healers are not paid for their work; others say they accept donations. In the mid-1980s, blowing treatments cost about $20, and spirit ceremonies around $2,000.

A typical healing begins with a water blessing: the healer holds a lit candle over a pot of water, adds Pali-inscribed paper, and sprinkles the water on the patient. Love healers (*kru snae*) are especially valued because they can use love spells, potions, or magical incantations and objects, such as wax figurines, photographs, or pieces of paper or fabric inscribed with the beloved's name to influence love. A healer might bury a wax figure in the backyard of the intended in hopes the loved one will be influenced and fall in love. A colleague was certain his wife left him because love magic had been practiced on her, saying, "I know she was stolen by a love doctor." Deciding he could not find as powerful a love healer as the one who had swayed his wife, he found another wife.

Cambodians said evil doctors practice their craft for profit and assert that an unusual number of evil men who practice magic are Thai, several saying AIDS may have originated as the work of one of these men. In turn, many Thai consider Cambodians especially skilled at dealing with spirits and casting out spells. Some Khmer healers serve non-Khmer clients, and Cambodians often use non-Khmer healers, including Mexican *curendaros* (Rasbridge 1995). Usually working in secret, a practitioner such as a sorcerer (*kru tmup*) places a hex or propels a needle, knife blade, rice grain, bit of ox skin, thorn, or other object into a person's body to cause misfortune, such as illness. Khmer say evil doctors gain their power by eating the flesh of a human corpse or bathing annually in liquids from a rotting corpse.

Some monks and healers are stronger than sorcerers and know, sometimes just by touch, whether a person is trying to cause harm. After making an offering to good spirits to identify an offending sorcerer, a good healer recites a Pali incantation, extracts the projected object from the victim's body, and throws it away or propels it back to whomever sent it. Cambodians say they most fear powerful demon spirits (*kon krak*) who help people kill, rob, and control others (Marcucci 1986), and some suggested Pol Pot may have been a demon spirit, which would explain his power to harm so many people.

Cambodians say some in America have used evil power to harm or kill people they know. A healer gains demon power by asking his wife if he can take her fetus; if she "truly loves" her husband, she agrees. After cutting the fetus from the womb late in the pregnancy, he marks a sacred circle in the forest, smokes the fetus over a fire, and asks the demon spirit to come. The fetus, smoked down to the size of a thumb, holds the demon power. If the owner fails to offer food, candles, and incense to the spirit, serious misfortune comes to him, but if he offers the appropriate ceremonies to his evil power, it becomes a powerful magical tool. When used for evil, however, such doctors can lose their power, particularly against good people. A number of Cambodians said these evildoers do not operate in America; others assured me they do. Cambodians say all healers can lose their power by revealing secret words, identifying their teachers, exhibiting improper behavior toward women, or allowing a woman to touch their shrines, walk through their ritual areas, or put menstrual blood in their food.

Cambodians say "heart and spirit medicine" is vital to a patient's healing. Sick people heal more rapidly when they are surrounded by loving and solicitous relatives who relieve them of responsibilities, prepare special food for them, prevent arguments or unfortunate news from disturbing them, and give them positive messages. Patients' attitudes are also important in healing, and those who want to get better, know their family is supportive, and are willing to cooperate and do whatever is necessary improve more quickly than patients who lack such desire, support, and willingness. The darkened bruises of coining, red circles from cupping, and scent of tiger balm indicate a state of crisis, identify the bearer as a follower of Khmer tradition, and invite others to sympathize. When one woman said to a classmate, "Oh, you have been coined, you are sick, and still you come to English class," the classmate nodded her head, said her husband had coined her, and returned to her books smiling. She was Cambodian, sick in a Khmer way, and able to be cured and comforted in a familiar way.

Western Medicine

Western medical attention became available to many Cambodians for the first time in the refugee camps, where they were treated for malnutrition, ailments, and injuries and given health, sanitation, and reproductive information (Rowat 2006). Refugees with conditions thought to threaten public health, such as active communicable diseases, mental illnesses accompanied by violent behavior, or drug addiction, were denied resettlement. Before leaving the refugee camps and processing centers, refugees received health screenings, inoculations, and medical treatment. Carrying their health records with them, Khmer refugees were again given health screenings soon after arrival, usually at the local county public health center, which tested for tuberculosis, inoculated school-age children, and treated obvious health problems, such as medicating refugees who tested positive for tuberculosis. Officials assured Americans that, although contagious, tuberculosis was not a threat to them and advised Americans in contact with refugees to go for annual testing.

American health providers encouraged Cambodians to see a doctor for ongoing services and helped them find treatment for immediate, chronic, and emergencies conditions. Many were able to have their physical health needs met quickly. Cambodians came with more documented illnesses than other Southeast Asians (Baughan et al. 1990). In a mid-1980s survey, 84 percent of Khmer households in California reported a member under a physician's care, compared to 45 percent of Vietnamese and 24 percent of Hmong and Lao households (Ebihara 1985). One Khmer leader stated unequivocally, "Cambodians are mentally and physically sicker than other refugees" (Theanvy Kuoch 2000: 431), and in 2001, her agency, Health Advocates, estimated that at least twenty-five thousand Cambodians were disabled, more than four times the rate of the general population (Ng 2001).

Resettled Cambodians were opportunistic in obtaining both traditional and nontraditional medical care. Most responded gratefully to Western medicine and quickly became familiar with terms such as CT scan, ibuprofen, and the antidepressant imipramine. Cambodians' distaste for invasive procedures, such as immunizations, laboratory tests, biopsies, pap smears, and surgeries, was well documented (Muecke 1983), and they often avoided laboratory or clinic procedures that involved needles or other insertions. Cambodians also said they were dismayed at Americans' lack of shyness and shocked at commercials for sanitary napkins, impotency medicine, and personal cleaning products. They said they hated disrobing and being examined by doctors of the opposite sex. Khmer healers do not have patients disrobe and usually do not touch the bodies of female patients; instead, they point at a body part or figurine to indicate a patient's problem area.

Many women refused to use tampons because they "didn't seem right" or self-inserted birth control devices because "they look scary, and it is strange to put one inside." Some did not want to use birth control pills because "they make you weak." Despite disliking invasive treatments, many women preferred getting birth control shots every three months to taking pills, but most did not have access to the shots until the early 2000s. Women were especially distressed by gynecological examinations and childbirth practices, including induced labor, episiotomies, and manipulation of the baby in the birth canal, especially when performed by men (also Hansen 1988). Most did not want tubal ligations, fearing that if they divorced, a second husband would want his own children. Many men would not use condoms or consider vasectomies because they believed they would lose strength and potency. It was only after Cambodians became aware of the economic advantages of having fewer children that many became interested in birth control.

Cambodians are reluctant to reveal personal information to medical personnel, particularly in the presence of interpreters with whom they have personal ties or when the information can affect their welfare or legal status. One young man was reluctant to discuss his HIV symptoms with his doctor because the interpreter was a friend of his mother's and he did not want her to know he was gay. However, he did so, the interpreter soon spread his information throughout the community, and the family felt forced to move to another city. Cambodians have also worried that health care providers are ignorant of basic health facts and do not really understand what Cambodians had experienced, how poor their health is, or how they should be treated.

Cambodians themselves were often surprised at the damage their bodies had sustained. Vithana expected recurrent pain in a knee struck by a Khmer Rouge soldier, but he was startled when he learned malnutrition had compromised his cardiovascular system and tainted water had damaged his liver. As he aged, he was increasingly despondent over his failing body and angry that doctors could not help him. Some Cambodians operated on misconceptions that led to health crises, as when a young man refused to follow a life-altering course of medication because his parents told him he could not possibly have AIDS. A number of women said they were not worried about getting AIDS because their husbands were free of the disease, and they disagreed when told AIDS can remain inside a person for years, saying they can tell if someone has AIDS by looking at them. Other Cambodians said men can get syphilis from a prostitute, but not AIDS, and thought AIDS can be treated like other venereal diseases.

Cambodians usually knew little about their bodies anatomically and were reluctant to talk about them. Women knew little of menstruation or the processes of reproduction. Many consumed pills immediately on the theory that if a little is good, a lot is better. Impatient with the idea of taking her tuberculosis prescription for a year, one woman swallowed the 365 pills at one sitting. The emergency room staff assumed she was trying to commit suicide until she explained she did not want to wait a year to be cured of tuberculosis. She survived but continued to wonder why she could not take all the medicine at once and immediately become tuberculosis-free. Some Cambodians did not understand that prescriptions were not to be shared. I was frequently offered someone's prescription drugs when complaining of a cold or allergies and told, "Since we have the same problem, the same pills will work for us." Some neglected prescription instructions they felt did not solve their problem. Several men did not take their hypertension medicine, saying they had no symptoms of being sick and the pills made them dizzy.

Yet most Cambodians believe in the superiority of Western medicine for all but some illnesses and trusted injections, bottles, white coats, and paperwork. Despite their dislike of them, most Cambodians view injections as superior to all other medication and are particularly grateful for shots. When Seyha went to a doctor about a sore jaw, the doctor said it was stress-related and gave her an injection. Pleased, she has been to the same doctor many times in the years since because "he knows how to take care of me." Now over seventy years of age, she is treated by injection for stomach and bowel problems, headaches, sore muscles, and exhaustion.

However much Cambodians appreciate Western medicine, many know little about it and are often disappointed. They express surprise when American medicine does not eliminate their health problems and wonder if Americans are "holding something back from us." In the mid-1980s, a man asked the doctors who were treating him for blindness, "Can't you give me some medicine so there is more light in my eyes?" Cambodians say Western medicine is impersonal, expensive, and never-ending, and most view follow-up visits as excessive and pointless (also Pickwell 1999). Some say they are treated rudely by Americans and their traditional healing methods are ignored. Many are unhappy with the "cold" ice water, ice cream, milk, fruits, vegetables, and meat given them after childbirth, saying they need hot foods like steamed rice and boiled chicken to restore heat to their bodies.

Cambodians often access multiple offices for prescriptions and in Southern California purchase prescriptions in Tijuana, Mexico, that are prohibited in America. Cambodians also order pills from France, Southeast Asia, or on the Internet and self-administer antibiotics, steroids, tranquilizers, and analgesics. Most resettled Cambodians switched from breast-feeding to formula after resettlement, with working women and students especially appreciative of the convenience of bottles. Some switched because Americans stared at them in public, and several said they quit when they realized breast-feeding is not "civilized." The trend away from breast-feeding to using formula and bottles has continued (Straub, Melvin, and Labbok 2008), and when told many doctors now encourage breast-feeding, several women laughed, one saying, "Oh, it's too hard. All the Americans tell me bottles are good."

In the first years of resettlement, Cambodians often expressed dismay that Americans cared more about Cambodians getting jobs than they did about their health. While Americans saw jobs as bringing health care to refugees by providing them with health benefits, Cambodians saw that employment seldom gained them health insurance and instead led many to be ineligible for public assistance and Medicaid. Over the years, many Cambodians insisted their physical and mental difficulties precluded employment, and numerous Americans and health care providers agreed, one Khmer health provider saying, "With the kind of problems [Cambodians] have, there is no way they could work" (Theanvy Kuoch 2000). County health department personnel stated at an interagency meeting in 1982 that older Cambodians had a "minimal potential" for employment due to mental instability.

Despite the traditional enmity between Cambodians and Vietnamese, Cambodians have been grateful for the care of resettled Vietnamese doctors, saying their offices are in the neighborhood, appointments are unnecessary, waits are short, interpreters and transportation are provided, medical personnel give shots rather than pills, and the treatments work. American medical personnel were critical of giving intravenous dextrose to pregnant women or Depo-Provera injections for birth control before it was legally sanctioned, using more injectable antibiotics than American doctors customary use, spending five minutes on an appointment rather than the usual fifteen, and not involving patients in diagnosis and treatment. Cambodians, however, continue to patronize Vietnamese doctors who listen to their complaints and give them what they want. They also use hospital emergency rooms for routine care and to avoid payments and long waits, and they commonly call 911 to get friendly paramedic assistance for minor problems.

Many Western providers grew frustrated with Cambodians' lack of compliance and have developed time-saving explanations to obtain their cooperation; based on half-truths, exaggeration, and falsehoods, the explanations give Cambodians misleading ideas about their health and possible solutions. Some Cambodians say American health care providers are quick to define Cambodians' problems but seldom listen to their stories, value their pain, or support them in finding their own healers, medicines, and religious leaders. American doctors occasionally express their frustration with Khmer patients by not treating them, encouraging them to go elsewhere, or losing their tempers.

Mental Health

Researchers found that Khmer refugees also suffered more psychological trauma than other Southeast Asian groups (Mollica, Wyshak, and Lavelle 1987). Rates of depression were 10 to 20 percent higher among Khmer refugees in the Boston area after resettlement than the general population (Mollica et al. 1990). In Long Beach, Cambodians were found to be suffering mental illness six to seventeen times higher than the national adult average and accessing mental health services at a higher rate than other Asian groups (Marshall et al. 2006). Multiple studies conclude that Cambodians remain at higher risk for schizophrenia and traumatic stress-related diseases than other Asian groups (Leakhena Nou 2006).

In the early 1980s, several mental health agencies, such as Seattle's Asian Counseling and Referral Service and the Bronx's Montefiore Family Health Center, set up programs for Southeast Asians or incorporated them into existing programs. In other areas, mental health facilities were slow to comprehend refugee needs but quick to apply the phrase "post-traumatic stress disorder" (PTSD) or "post-traumatic stress" (PTS) to Khmer refugees who had experienced the loss of family members (Carlson and Rosser-Hogan 1991). Some Cambodians with severe symptoms of mental disturbance were sent to state mental institutions, where doctors wondered why they did not respond to treatment, despite speaking little or no English.

Some observers claimed mental health practitioners associated Cambodians with mental and affective disorders, causing health providers to consider them incompetent, superstitious, uneducated, and disturbed victims rather than competent survivors, and tried to fit their suffering into "little boxes on the psychiatrists' charts" (Ong 1995: 5). Some American health providers continue to categorize Cambodians as inferiors who are likely to suffer from affective and mental health disorders because of their experiences (Douglas 2004). Over time, evidence of Khmer distress was mounting. The more "negative life events" Cambodians experienced, the greater their incidence of PTS (Leakhena Nou 2007). Khmer Health Advocates concluded that about 90 percent of Cambodians suffered from PTS or depression (Theanvy Kuoch 2000) and noted that the number of patients with symptoms of PTS was not decreasing and symptoms could increase in severity (Cambodian Health Network 2012).

A study of 46 children found 40 percent suffering from PTS, 21 percent from depression, and 10 percent from anxiety (Kinzie et al. 1990). Three years later, levels remained high, with 48 percent exhibiting PTS and 41 percent suffering from depression; after six years, PTS was still prominent among the youth. Cambodians have continued to have high rates of psychiatric disorders associated with trauma, particularly those with little English-speaking proficiency and who are unemployed, retired, disabled, living in poverty, or without physical and mental health care. Marshall et al. (2005) found that more than half of those surveyed suffered from PTS and depression. Some Khmer research associates say Americans continue to focus on Khmer pathology and rarely take seriously the suggestions of Khmer contributors (Leakhena Nou 2008). One, Porthira Chhim, said America has "never created a place" for the refugees. "They never received holistic service. They never received psychological treatment.

Now we're seeing the degenerate effects of that in juvenile crime and gangs" (Ng 2001).

Cambodians traditionally viewed mentally ill people as being crazy, out of balance, possessed by spirits, or having acted inappropriately and saw the malady as incurable. A sole psychiatric hospital and psychiatrist existed in Cambodia before 1975, with tranquilizers and electroconvulsive therapy common treatments and even medical personnel thinking mental illness was incurable. After resettlement, Cambodians handled family mental health problems as they had traditionally, by taking them to healers or monks. If Cambodians concluded a person could not be cured, the illness or the person was concealed in order to avoid causing shame to the family. Because they associated being mentally ill with being crazy, Khmer refugees evaded any mention of mental illness, expressed their distress as physical symptoms, and sought relief through a variety of traditional healing techniques (Pickwell 1999).

Many remain hesitant to talk about mental problems, fearing Cambodians' reactions and worried about what Americans will do. Cambodians said they are appalled by American therapeutic techniques, especially those that focus on talk, saying therapy is not a Khmer tradition, it hurts as much as it helps, and social workers cannot help them because they do not understand them. Offered therapy, Cambodians often refused it (Moon and Tashima 1982), saying they did not see the value in dredging up painful memories. The parents of children shot in a Stockton schoolyard were disturbed by the scores of news reporters, victim advocates, social workers, psychologists, and public health nurses offering to talk with them.

The bereaved parents saw no point in talking, sought privacy from comments and questions they could not understand, and wanted only the comfort of friends and fellows who shared their language and culture. When asked why Americans came to his house, one father "drew a blank" and then pulled out dozens of business cards (Kam 1989). He said they came four or five times day, sometimes as late as midnight. "I wanted to be left alone. I felt sick when they came." Cambodians were appalled to hear Americans weeping in public and giving out personal information on television, "like on the Oprah show," one woman said, claiming some things are better left unsaid (Chung 2001).

Khmer refugees used the term "crazy" in one of two ways: "crazy" as in unable to function, and "crazy" as in often feeling overwhelmed but continuing to deal with one's responsibilities. In the first category were those who had "lost control," like the man who was in a mental institution for many years. Severely beaten on the street just after his arrival in America in 1982, he was diagnosed as paranoid because he thought everyone wanted to hurt him. He spoke virtually no English and communicated with no one except the agency workers who occasionally visited him. He had no other visitors. If he was not paranoid before being attacked, he had cause to be after being beaten for no reason he could ascertain, and if he was not "crazy" before entering the institution, he certainly had cause to be after.

Other Cambodians said they were so mentally distraught they were unable to engage in fundamental activities, from getting a job to caring for children. Many became passive: sitting at home, staying in bed, and not speaking. Men spent years buying groceries, medicine, and children's clothes because their wives were afraid to leave their apartment. One wife in 2002 had not left her home since arrival in 1983, and another who went to the temple on quiet days was unable to attend ceremonies on crowded festival days. Other Cambodians said they drank and gambled so they would not feel crazy, although they said they then neglected their responsibilities, and a woman who had a driver's license said she could not drive because it made her feel "almost crazy."

The second category of "crazy consisted of Cambodians who said they often felt crazy, but they tried to hide their emotions as they went to work, talked with family and colleagues, cooked dinner and cared for children, and laughed with friends. Always, though, they said they struggled with feelings of anxiety, inadequacy, loss, and grief. When asked how many Cambodians in one city had mental health problems, one woman said most did. These Cambodians stoutly resisted any description of themselves as crazy or mentally ill, for they saw the struggles they were overcoming, and they were often critical of Cambodians who could not maintain as they were or of Americans who had no idea of their struggles. Saying therapists and counselors underestimated their ability to recover from trauma, they asserted they could deal with problems themselves. They not only lived their lives, they asked others for advice, tried to make life better, or focused on the future, saying they just had to wait for time to pass, although often, they said, that did not help.

When one young woman feared her husband was sleeping with other women, she became depressed, developed headaches, and lost weight until she was down to ninety pounds. She said she thought she was going to go crazy, but "there was nothing I could do," adding that she had to stay with her husband because she loved her children, so she just "sits at home and waits for him to return." He eventually returned to her, and she said she was no longer crazy. She and other Cambodians told me that was the proper way for a woman to solve a problem. She was distraught, yes, but she concealed her emotions, fulfilled her obligations to her family, and made her husband see the error of his ways.

One man said he went to a psychiatrist about his depression and temporarily felt better, but it was not until he saw a monk that he was permanently healed. He concluded, "Only a religious man can really heal you." Since Cambodians also thought mental illness could result from spirit activity, imbalance in their lives and bodies, or neglect of proper rituals, monks or healers frequently advised people to present food to Buddha or the spirits or to hold a balance restoration or protection ceremony that included praying and sprinkling holy water over participants. One man said psychologists help people with their lives, but monks give them spiritual strength relevant to their past, present, and future lives.

Cambodians also turn to healers for help with depression. To restore the patient's spirit, a healer has the patient drink holy water and sprinkles the rest over the patient while chanting incantations. The healer may make an amulet for the patient to wear or play music for the spirit. Some healers claim they can heal anyone, but others say healers are only occasionally successful. If monks or healers cannot help a patient, the entire family is sometimes considered crazy, family members have difficulty finding marriage partners, and the family can lose status in the community (Theanvy Kuoch and Scully 1984).

Cambodians are more tolerant of strange behavior when they think it is caused by spirits because, they said, the rules for dealing with spirits are difficult to follow, so it is easy to offend them. Several healers said they know mental illness is caused by an *arak* spirit after a patient eats unusual food such as an unpeeled banana or a piece of chicken with its bone, because "the *arak* eat everything." To effect a cure, the healer summons the *arak* spirit, asks the spirit to tell him what he wants, burns incense and candles, and relays the spirit's request for an offering to the patient's family.

While language and culture continue to be major obstacles to Cambodians in obtaining help with mental problems, cost, lack of transportation, and ignorance about available services also influence the help they get. From the first days of arrival, many Cambodians sought assistance only when desperate, such as when women heard voices coming from furniture and walls or men thought they were still in combat. While many suffering from mental health problems continue to seek help for physical ailments, more Cambodians are also receiving help from mental health clinics. In a twenty-first-century survey of 339 Cambodians in Long Beach with a probable diagnosis of PTS, major depression, or excessive alcohol use, 70 percent were in contact with medical care providers and 46 percent with mental health care providers (Marshall et al. 2006).

Both Cambodians and observers have noted that in labeling Cambodians "highly likely" to suffer from mental health disorders, Americans must be careful not to categorize them as passive and helpless victims, thus ignoring their resilience, compassion, and innovativeness (also Douglas 2004). What Americans see as weaknesses, Cambodians have viewed as their strengths: surviving, practicing their values and traditions, helping one another and strangers, and improving their lives. Parents raise their children despite their own mental struggles, and children gain education and employment despite theirs. Cambodians see their resilience as vital to their survival and say they are proud they have endured what they think Americans could not have survived; their pride has been important in their struggles.

Accessing Both Western and Traditional Medicine

Most Khmer refugees have utilized both Western and traditional medicine. They initially turned to traditional medicines and healers first. Over the years, they have tended to use Khmer healers and strategies when accessing Western providers is difficult and to use Western providers when traditional methods are unavailable or ineffective. Many Cambodians have come to trust American providers, some even claiming that talking therapy can be effective (Silove, Chang, and Manicavasagar 1995). While some Cambodians say they heal themselves by listening to others, some agree that telling stories can help them achieve balance in their lives (Detzner 2004). One monk said Cambodians should seek balance, but those suffering from mental illness should also use medicine and therapy (Mellen 2011). First-generation Cambodians have been increasingly willing to do so, and those most likely to seek assistance are those who had little education in Cambodia, lack English, and are retired or disabled. Cambodian Americans also are more likely to access services in ways similar to other Americans.

Some Americans have developed a new perspective on Khmer distress, seeing it not as disease or post-traumatic stress but as a normal response to horrid circumstances and a form of psychological resilience (Eisenbruch 1991; Davis 2000). One physician had success in dealing with a middle-age woman's type 2 diabetes after discovering her children had starved to death, her husband had been violently taken away, she had been sexually violated by the Khmer Rouge, and her remaining daughter was stabbed by a gang burglarizing her home (Mollica 2004). September 11, 2001, had so traumatized her that she left home only to see her doctor. With this awareness, the doctor treated both her diabetes and depression with medication and counseling. Some health providers have developed new ways to assist Cambodians. Providers in Lowell look at Cambodians' previous experiences and seek solutions and cooperation with Khmer and community organizations (Grigg-Saito et al. 2010). A few providers make home visits to patients, one saying, "Even if they don't come to the center, we still go and talk to them" (Ng 2001).

Many say providers must understand Khmer culture, use sensitive interpreters as cultural guides, avoid drawing assumptions, listen to patients' explanations, explain symptoms and possible treatments, and be aware that many Cambodians use traditional as well as Western medicine. While some observers have suggested that many problems caused by the Khmer Rouge years can be overcome by immunization, improved nutrition, and sanitation, they do not begin to touch the depths of Khmer despair. Listening to their stories, respecting their solutions for their own lives, and meeting their needs as they express them honor Khmer refugees and their children as survivors, Cambodians, and new Americans.

Whatever their health concerns and other resettlement struggles, Khmer refugees expressed an interest in Cambodia, an interest that did not lessen over the years.

Chapter Ten

Homeland

After resettlement, as Khmer refugees struggled to find their way in the United States, thoughts of their homeland were never far away. Their first concern was for relatives left behind. In the 1980s, with villages, roads, and postal system in ruins and direct communication with people in Cambodia virtually impossible, Cambodians were uncertain about what was happening with their kinfolk, even of the country itself. Many refugees were uncertain of their family's location, even their existence. Most of the information Khmer refugees received about relatives and the homeland came from newly resettled refugees coming from the Thai camps. Despite their own survival struggles and scarce resources, resettled Khmer sent money, packages, and information to relatives in the camps and eagerly awaited replies and word on the possible resettlement of family and friends.

Back in Cambodia

In the 1980s, although the new Cambodian government, the People's Republic of Kampuchea, established by Vietnam began restoring some order in Cambodia, there remained considerable violence in the country. Vietnam, backed by the Soviet Union, maintained hundreds of thousands of soldiers in Cambodia to counter the activities of the Khmer Rouge who continued to fight from their bases in eastern Thailand. The Khmer Rouge were supported by the Chinese, who supplied them with military hardware and financial assistance, seeing them as a buffer against the Vietnamese. Despite increased awareness of Khmer Rouge atrocities, the United States and its allies also saw the Khmer Rouge as a counterbalance to the Vietnamese occupation. As a result, the United States donated millions to the Khmer Rouge for their rehabilitation and rearmament while, at the same time, it was resettling the regime's survivors.

Khmer refugees in America were aware that relatives in Cambodia were struggling. While American and international support granted the Khmer Rouge time and money to rebuild their strength, the United States designated Cambodia an enemy, imposed an embargo on trade and development assistance, and prevented nongovernmental organizations from sending relief supplies or equipment to repair the infrastructure (Charny and Spragens 1984). When the Khmer Rouge were overturned, Cambodia was in shambles, and Cambodians who tried to reach home villages and search for relatives were hampered by destruction and confusion. A shortage of manpower and seeds and an undependable water supply left food shortages throughout the country, and thousands died of starvation and illness (Chandler 1991). Ongoing violence by Vietnamese, resistance, and Khmer Rouge soldiers made conditions grim.

Despite Cambodia's political situation and the hostility between Cambodia and the United States, Khmer refugees began sending money and packages to kinfolk in Cambodia. Because letters and packers were frequently stolen and checks and money orders were nearly impossible for relatives to process, resettled Cambodians sent small amounts of cash, usually between twenty and fifty dollars. By the late 1980s, most resettled Khmer sent their packages through companies that assured their arrival for a percentage of the cost and often provided videos of relatives receiving letters and packages from America as proof the packages were being delivered. Cambodians eagerly shared photographs and videos just arrived from Cambodia of their relatives and expressed their relief at no longer feeling so isolated from family members and home.

The end of the 1980s brought an end to the Cold War, increased global interest in ending the violence in Cambodia, and an opening of the country to the world that allowed overseas Cambodians to more freely communicate with relatives. Although travel to Cambodia remained limited, a nongovernmental agency brought two high-ranking monks to America for a visit in 1990 (Teteak 1992), and leaders of resistance armies on the Thai border came to America to raise money from Khmer refugees and seek support from American politicians. When Americans were able to travel to Cambodia, Cambodians utilized them to carry money and packages back to their kinfolk.

By the early 1990s, a growing number of Cambodians were in direct contact with family and friends in Cambodia, and travel to the homeland was becoming increasingly frequent. As refugees' resources and contact with the homeland by mail, telephone, and travel increased, so too did remittances, and millions of dollars flowed from Khmer in America to kinfolk in Cambodia. Occasionally, requests for assistance exceeded refugees' resources and generosity. For years, Than complained about his cousin's requests for money. He sent the cousin more than $5,000 over the years, along with money to other relatives. When I met the cousin in Phnom Penh, my funds also quickly vanished, spent on school uniforms, a bike for him, and a sewing machine for his wife. Than eventually stopped writing to him, saying that although he felt guilt over his cousin's needs, he could no long bear the financial drain on his own family in America.

Another man sent $1,000 to his brother in 1986, telling him to "start a business that will support your family," and telling me, "My wife doesn't know I sent that money." In 1997, his wife still had no idea of the amounts he sent over the years, nor did he know the amount she sent her relatives. The combined amount in 1997 was close to $100,000, and in 2010 the sum was far larger. In 2008, overseas Cambodians sent over $350 million to Cambodia in private transfers (Economic Institute of Cambodia 2009). As more Cambodians traveled to Cambodia carrying money and goods, many returned with little, one man saying, "I even left my suitcase." Remittances to Cambodia continue to drain families' resources. Arguments are frequent as families struggle to balance their own needs with pleas from homeland relatives for funds for houses, oxen, businesses, and pumps. Over the years, requests from Cambodia have shifted from immediate survival assistance to requests for funds to purchase a motorbike, build a house, pay school bribes, or begin a business. Even the supreme patriarch of Khmer Buddhism in Cambodia turns to Minnesota Khmer when he wants to build a temple or school (McGill 2006).

When Vietnamese troops withdrew from Cambodia in 1989, resettled Cambodians expressed great delight, but many continued to fear Vietnam was running Cambodia. Oudom illustrated how he thought Vietnam was controlling Cambodia by sketching a floor of government offices, with each Khmer office backed by an office occupied by a Vietnamese official who entered his office from a private hallway. He said the arrangement allowed the Vietnamese to review every Khmer decision and is the reason things take so long to happen in Cambodia. Sotha claimed in 2010 that Vietnamese advisors used "an actual tunnel" from Vietnam to Phnom Penh in the 1980s to oversee the government of Cambodia and said the tunnel has since been removed because Cambodia now willingly does what Vietnam wants.

In the 1980s, some Cambodians claimed that Vietnam's occupation troops were taking Cambodia's rice and fish to Vietnam, and Vietnamese settlers were moving into Cambodia; their evidence included a photo in *National Geographic* of young dancers wearing Vietnamese dresses (White 1982). Refugees said Vietnamese were killing as many Cambodians as Pol Pot had killed. After the announced withdrawal of Vietnamese troops from Cambodia in 1989, Cambodians feared Americans would believe

Vietnamese propaganda, and despite the country's changing its name to the "State of Cambodia" and adopting a new flag restoring the colors of the Sihanouk period, many Khmer refugees said the withdrawal had not occurred. When the United Nations reported finding only three remaining Vietnamese soldiers in Cambodia, all married to Khmer women (Boutrous Boutrous-Gahli 1993), a number of Cambodians echoed one Khmer refugee who said, "Foreigners do not know how to look for Vietnamese. Only Cambodians know how to do that."

In 1991, the State of Cambodia, the Khmer Rouge and resistance groups, and numerous nations signed a peace agreement agreeing to an immediate cease-fire and the placement of a UN peacekeeping force in Cambodia to oversee the demobilization of 70 percent of all Khmer Rouge and resistance soldiers. The United Nations Transitional Authority in Cambodia (UNTAC) was also to repatriate refugees from the refugee and border camps in Thailand and temporarily administer key ministries before turning them over to elected officials. The UNTAC mission from March 1992 to September 1993 involved one hundred countries and twenty-two thousand soldiers and civilians at a cost of between $2 billion and $11.7 billion (Heininger 1994).

Even after the Vietnamese withdrawal of troops from Cambodia, many Cambodians in America were convinced Vietnam was rewriting Khmer history, settling Vietnamese in Cambodia and encouraging them to marry and raise Vietnamese children. Cambodians said they would turn the country into a province of Vietnam by 2000. In 2016, Cambodians said the process might take longer, but the Vietnamese would never give up trying to "eat" Cambodia. Stories about Vietnamese cruelty are common, and the tale "Do not spill the tea of the master" is popular. The story relates how the Vietnamese buried three Khmer prisoners up the neck and built a fire to boil tea in a pot placed on their heads, killing the "pot-holders."

Observers claimed the United Nations mission in the early 1990s did not produce peace and prosperity; the gap between urban wealthy and rural poor deepened, the Khmer Rouge remained a threat, and Cambodia had the same government it had before (Findlay 1995). Resettled Cambodians complained that the mission left Cambodia with little democracy, considerable corruption, and a prime minister who was an ex-Khmer Rouge dictator. Despite fair elections in which millions of Cambodians and several hundred resettled Cambodians voted, candidate Hun Sen lost but refused to give up his power. The winner, Prince Norodom Ranariddh, and Hun Sen agreed to share power by double-staffing each ministry, and Sihanouk was reinstated as king and head of state without political power. Despite its problems, Cambodia had opened up to trade, diplomats, nongovernmental agencies, and overseas Cambodians.

Numerous first- and second-generation Cambodians in the twenty-first century claim Vietnam's attempts to control, even murder, Cambodians are ongoing. A former John Hopkins professor who is Khmer wrote, "Vietnam has been committing genocidal against the Cambodian people" [*sic*] (NaranhKiri Tith 2001). After a Phnom Penh bridge stampede that killed at least 345 people in 2010, Cambodians speculated the stampede was caused by the Vietnamese, since they had constructed the bridge. One resettled Khmer said an employee of Phnom Penh's power company told him many of the victims were electrocuted because the bridge was poorly built and claimed the police present at the time were Vietnamese dressed in Khmer uniforms.

During a 2011 summer barbeque, several Cambodians said angrily that seventy thousand Vietnamese boats had fished the country's "king of fish" into extinction and were dumping their excrement into Cambodia's largest lake. They agreed that "Hun Sen is a Vietnamese puppet," and claimed Hun Sen's family had been robbers for four generations, stealing water buffalo from Cambodians to sell in Vietnam. At a separate event in 2011, Cambodians had other charges: that Cambodia has lost over thirty thousand square kilometers to Vietnam, seven million Vietnamese militia disguised as colonists reside in Cambodia, and most who rule Cambodia under Hun Sen are Vietnamese. Presented with contrary evidence, they urged Americans not to be naïve, "like other people who don't really know what's going on in Cambodia." They claimed also that a son of King Sihanouk works in Cambodia's Interior Ministry to help "Vietnamize" Cambodia.

Returning Home

From the early days of resettlement, Cambodians wondered if they would ever return to Southeast Asia, and many found it unbearable to think they would spend the rest of their days in exile. The theme of exile and return echoes throughout Khmer literature: with a banished person who travels westward into exile entering a realm that requires him to face danger, tests, and transformations, before eventually making a triumphant return eastward. For modern Cambodians fleeing their land, the path had led west to resettlement. Now they wanted to return to their homes, and as contact with Cambodia increased, so too did their desire to return. Many wanted to return permanently, particularly as they realized the difficulties of resettlement. "I want to go back," one man said, "because my life here is so empty." Sorya often lamented, "If only I could live in Cambodia again, I would be so happy." A few Khmer refugees delayed applying for citizenship, hoping America was merely a temporary "detour" before going home, the last leg of their migration.

Most Cambodians said permanent return was unlikely, but they wanted to see relatives and home or just be reassured the Khmer Rouge were out of power. Some resettled Cambodians said they wanted to see Angkor Wat or Phnom Penh. Some worried about the amount of freedom they would have and whether they would be targets of hostility because they had escaped hardship endured by those left behind or had fought with the resistance. They also wondered if kinfolk would resent them because they could leave if there was trouble (Reed 2002). Some refugees feared a return of the Khmer Rouge or Vietnamese (Mong 1994), and many worried that peace would not last. Some Cambodians said peace could only be achieved if UN soldiers stayed permanently; otherwise, said one man, "the killing will just erupt again." Despite their worries, increasing numbers of Cambodian returned to the homeland. Resettled Cambodians took money and gifts to kinfolk, conducted rituals for deceased relatives, sought out old friends and neighbors, or checked on homes and possessions stashed when they evacuated towns and villages in 1975. Many said they wanted most of all to experience the sights and smells of Cambodia again.

Even before travel to Cambodia was possible, Cambodians expressed their desire to return to help countrymen "left behind" (Mellen 2007), hopefully by using skills they had gained in America to fill the leadership and expertise lacuna they said had been left after the Khmer Rouge years. The government invited overseas Khmer to return, the prime minister saying, "Please, I ask the overseas Khmers to come and help" (Chou Meng Tarr 1990: 9), and Prince Sihanouk traveled the world, reassuring overseas Cambodians they would be able to return home, adding that it was fine if they did not return because Cambodia lacked employment for them. The United Nations and Khmer newspapers also encouraged Cambodians to return to help rebuild the country (Poethig 2001). Resettled Cambodians responded. Through the 1980s, one refugee postponed marriage and a permanent job to devote his energies to working for Prince Sihanouk, hoping eventually to return to Cambodia. Although his dream seemed ludicrous to many Cambodians and Americans in the 1980s, he returned with Sihanouk in 1993 to a high-ranking job and an air-conditioned office next to the National Assembly building in Cambodia's capital.

Some of the first returnees took seats in parliament, several became cabinet members, and many became advisors to various high-ranking officials; with two prime ministers and two staffs manning each ministry, there were numerous openings. Those most eager to return were elite Cambodians who had high-level contacts in Cambodia, many of whom held entry or mid-level jobs in America and were glad to return to their previous status. They were grateful to America, sometimes noting that they were leaving a country that had put them back on their feet to devote themselves to a country that had nearly destroyed them. Some were desperate to return, but not all did well. One man borrowed $30,000 from family and friends and left his wife to join Sihanouk's entourage; three years later he died, leaving his debt unpaid.

Many of the returnees were from the Pacific Northwest, where they faced fewer obstacles and had greater opportunities to gain middle-class success than many Khmer resettled elsewhere (Bock 1999). Among them was Ananda Yath Noranarith, who left his job, sold his house, cashed in his IRA, and moved his family to Phnom Penh in 1996 to serve as public information officer for Prince Ranariddh. The 1997 coup that felled his patron and made Hun Sen the sole prime minister brought threats to his own life, and he returned to his home north of Seattle. Less than a year later, however, he returned to Cambodia and continued to be involved in Khmer politics through the 2000s, although his patron and political party declined in power. In 2006, when director of a Phnom Penh radio station, he was threatened with violence when he refused to denounce the prince and accused a government official of being involved in an illegal drug production (*KI Media* 2007).

Politicians from Cambodia continued to visit the United States to elicit support and money. At a political rally in Seattle in 1999 with deposed Prince Ranariddh, attendees included a refugee doughnut shop manager who had served as Cambodia's undersecretary of defense, a subcontractor who had been a senator, and a housing development manager who had been a consultant. They had different ideas about what was best for Cambodia but said they were attending in order to help their homeland. One resettled Khmer, Chhang Song, fled Cambodia with the prime minister in 1975. He returned to Cambodia in 1989 to witness the Vietnamese withdrawal, joined the Cambodian People's Party, and acted as a liaison between Cambodians and Western nations. Ted Ngoy, who made a fortune opening doughnut shops, also returned to Cambodia. He did not win a parliament seat, but Prime Minister Hun Sen made him an advisor on commerce and agriculture. He successfully lobbied the American government for most-favored-nation trade status in 1995, helping to establish thousands of garment industry jobs in Cambodia.

In the 1990s, a number of young Cambodians returned to "help their people" by working for the United Nations, the American government, or nongovernmental organizations. Often in their thirties, these young refugees remembered Cambodia but had been young enough when resettled to learn fluent English and become engineers, counselors, teachers, and middle managers. They went to Cambodia, in one returnee's words, because "Cambodians need a chance" (Bock 1999: 24). Often ridiculed for their idealism by other Cambodians, some were well compensated for their efforts by governments, organizations, and temples, but others worked for little reward. Among these were approximately one hundred graduating college student volunteers with the Cambodian-American National Development Organization (CANDO), based on the Peace Corps model and funded by the United States Agency for International Development. CANDO placed volunteers with nongovernmental organizations or government ministries to teach English, computers, accounting, and business management and help rebuild schools, temples, and clinics (Reed 2002).

Other returnees included philanthropists, explorers, and exploiters trying to reclaim status, find their identity, get rich, gain recognition, encourage peace for Cambodia, or find peace for themselves. Some returned to establish a business, hoping to profit from their knowledge of both America and Cambodia's languages and customs (Nien-chu Kiang 1994). Some Cambodians, including a number of pastors, returned as Protestant missionaries. The Reverend Sam Duong, pastor of churches in the Carolinas, led a team that spent fourteen days visiting congregations, leading services, baptizing believers, and helping villagers. Resettled Cambodians also promoted human rights; advocated against corruption; provided safe water, irrigation pumps, and improved seeds; and cleared land mines. Medical personnel provided inoculations, medical supplies, dental and eye care, prosthetic limbs, and information and resources about sanitation, basic health, nutrition, and AIDS.

In the early 2000s, a Cambodian chef at a Japanese steakhouse nicknamed Cook took baseball to Cambodia (Baxter 2008). The game spread in five years from one rural diamond to fifty teams in three provinces involving approximately one hundred schools, five thousand children, and two thousand adults. The first game in November 2002 had twenty players and revised rules: a ball lost in the rice paddy was out of play, while a ball hit off a water buffalo was in play. Cook built a shelter for abandoned children, supplied meals and schoolbooks, hired former teenage prostitutes he taught to read and write to work as scorekeepers and administrative assistants, and started Bible study classes. Major League Baseball sent coaches and donated more than $50,000 to his efforts. In December 2007, Cambodians wearing revised Dodgers uniforms played for the first time in the Southeast Asian Games, but were outscored 67 to 1. Cook continues to coach and solicit donations by video, e-mail, and Internet, despite numerous critics. One Cambodian noted, "In the States he is nobody, but in Cambodia he is powerful." He has been accused of insurance fraud, misusing donations, to build an extravagant house, neglecting his family in America to support another in Cambodia, and using American sympathy and money to promote himself (Hruby 2009).

While some resettled Cambodians admired returnees for their concern for Cambodia and were willing to financially assist their efforts, others mocked them for their naiveté or desire to be "big shots." Young returnees spoke of parents grateful for their children's interest in Cambodia but bewildered by their willingness to work for little reward. Cambodians told stories about returnees to Cambodia who left their homeland sooner than they had expected after not finding the prestigious job or financial wealth they sought, or they became ill, or they found life in Cambodia too difficult. Stories were not always accurate: returnees rumored to be unhappy, destitute, or living in disgrace were often doing fine after their return to the United States.

Makara told me excitedly in 1992 that Vannak, his former patron with whom he been engaged in a bitter rivalry through the 1980s, returned to Cambodia as a provincial vice-governor but was soon fired from his position. For the next four years, I heard about Vannak every time I was in town. Some said he had been charged with corruption and was hiding in Phnom Penh; others said he was in America. Cambodians said his wife was destitute and had mental problems, his children dropped out of school or were in gangs, and his two wives in Cambodia, one just sixteen, were penniless. The story changed repeatedly, but always the emphasis was on how poorly he was doing. At the end of 2011, it was confirmed that his wife and children were doing well, but he had recently died, broke and alone. "Well," said one woman turning back to her soup, "he got what he deserved."

Money was often an issue for both returnees and their benefactors. Not all returnees or their supporters prospered. Loans to returnees were frequently not repaid when businesses or political dreams failed, angering family, lenders, and investors, and families were left without resources in America or Cambodia. Several men invested money with a man who left a good-paying job in Dallas to purchase cars to sell in Cambodia. While there, he married a second wife, who spent his money gambling. When he returned to America, his passport expired, and his first wife would not allow him back in the house. He was forced to declare bankruptcy, and his investors lost their money.

Cambodia's reception of overseas Cambodians was selective and restricted, although financial contributions to temples, organizations, and individuals were welcomed, and Cambodian media coverage often showed a resettled Cambodian standing in front of a temple built with donated funds or handing over a check or goods. While there was no formal government support for those wishing to establish a nongovernmental organization, project, or business, the government occasionally gave overseas Cambodians the right to multiple visa entries with no entry fees (Mehmet, Tahiroglu, and Eric 2002). Although Cambodian Americans can regain citizenship status if they request new passports in Cambodia, most use Western passports and are treated as aliens requiring residency visas (Poethig 2001).

While some Cambodian government officials encouraged the recruitment of overseas Cambodians in the mid-1990s, the controlling Cambodian People's Party began criticizing officials with dual nationalities. Some said they worried that returnees would take their jobs, and party officials began suggesting that people with more than one passport should not stand for elections. Many native-born Khmer disliked criticism from overseas Cambodians about corruption, illegal logging, and judicial misconduct. Some officials claimed the ruling party no longer benefited from the presence of overseas Cambodians, and after the 1998 election, one leader stated that senators from overseas were "a spent force" (Reed 2002).

Resettled Cambodians were often shocked by homeland Cambodians saying Khmer from America no longer walked, talked, or acted Khmer, accusing them of driving around in chauffeured cars and carrying bottles of water into restaurants. Tension between Cambodia's residents and overseas Cambodians continues in the twenty-first century, although most returnees now acknowledge their differences and are less concerned with them. Many Cambodians call overseas Cambodians *anikachun*, translated variously as "immigrant," "foreigner," "minority," or "ethnic Khmer" to contrast them with "true Khmer" (*khmer angkor*) who never left Cambodia (Poethig 2001: 192).

While overseas Cambodians clearly distinguish themselves from Cambodians who reside in Cambodia, they are disturbed that *anikachun* are likened to Vietnamese settlers, noting that Cambodians call overseas Cambodians "Americans" when they do not need them, but "Cambodians" when they do. Christian Cambodians are even further alienated from those Cambodians consider true Khmer, although Cambodian Christians themselves say they are citizens of both Cambodia's constitutional monarchy and the kingdom of heaven and say a transnational, non-Buddhist identity is possible. Buddhist Cambodians strongly resist this Christian concept of identity, saying it has caused additional hostility toward missionaries from America.

In the 1990s, returnees were also discouraged to find a country they said remained devastated, with a ruined infrastructure, malnourished people, and considerable violence. One returnee said Cambodia was descending into a chaotic and lawless place of extreme wealth and poverty, noise, and traffic jams. Others described greedy officials and broken Cambodians. One returnee said, "The strong feed on the weak," and another, "Cambodia is full of grief and ruin and greed, and that is all." Cambodia's inequality, injustice, and corruption became major concerns of returning Cambodians.

Some Cambodians returned to America with their ideals and goals in tatters, saying their idealism about helping Cambodia had faded on seeing a corrupt government and meeting other returnees greedy for wealth and prestige. One man returned to America before finishing his volunteer tour, saying, "Everything was like it was before." For many, commitment to helping Cambodia faded after Hun Sen's full assumption of power following the 1997 coup and political participation became more dangerous. Some returnees were appalled by the country's system of patronage, one saying soon after going to Cambodia, "To be successful, you must have the governor as a partner in your business." In late 2012 after returning to America, he said, "Not much has changed."

Some refugees thought money spent on communities in Cambodia was better spent in America. Other returnees were able to reconcile their dreams to Khmer realities and stayed for years, often after adjusting their views on issues like corruption. Some defined bribes as "voluntary" contributions that reflect Khmer values of sharing and support. One returnee who continued his periodic service in Cambodia for years as a high official said he allowed his staff to collect fees because their salaries were too low for survival and said he had had to pay for his position, but "not too much."

A few refugees took more radical steps to effect change in Cambodia. A group of refugees founded Cambodian Freedom Fighters, intending to overthrow Cambodia's government. In 2000, eight men were killed and several more wounded when the group attacked Phnom Penh karaoke bars and fuel depots. After the Freedom Fighters president, a resettled tax accountant, boasted of participating in the attacks, he and two other Americans were sentenced to life without parole in Cambodia. Sentenced in absentia, he received the same sentence in the United States in 2010. Cambodians said they supported the group's goals, but not its actions. Defined as a terrorist group by the United States, some Cambodians claim the group remains active. While many first-generation Cambodians continue to see Vietnam as a threat to Cambodia's survival and to hold strong feelings of prejudice toward Vietnamese, the attitudes of many Cambodian Americans are changing to be more inclusive.

Routine Travel

Despite their worries about Cambodia, their fears about returning, or the costs of the trip, travel by resettled Cambodians to Cambodia has become routine. By the mid-1990s, Cambodians estimated that as many as 20 percent of resettled Khmer had visited the homeland. By 1999, Cambodians on the West Coast had access to inexpensive flights and phone cards for eighty-one cents a minute. More recently, the recession and high cost of air travel has been restrictive, and cost remains the major deterrent to travel to Cambodia. Not only are travel and gifts expensive, most resettled Cambodians cannot afford to pay American rents or mortgages in their absence. Cambodians also remain concerned for their safety. Having feared Khmer Rouge attacks through the 1980s and 1990s, many continue to worry about a Khmer Rouge revival. Others fear the government itself. One man's sister wanted him to visit her, but he was afraid officials would kill him if he "said something they disagree with." Some refuse to return because they fear being overcome by grief. Others who went found unexpected difficulties, such as the weather, one shortening his trip by weeks, saying, "It's too hot there. I couldn't stand it."

Those who move back to Cambodia permanently are few in number. Many say they would miss the amenities, political freedom, and health care of America, often commenting that Cambodia is "too poor." Some said they can no longer carry water and build their own homes. Most say they cannot return to live in Cambodia because their children, who "are American now," will not go with them; their children never knew Cambodia, do not speak Khmer or know Khmer etiquette, and are unfamiliar with monsoon rhythms or ritual cycles. Many do not even wish to visit. As I waited for an arrival at the Phnom Penh airport in June 1995, I was approached by a nineteen-year-old Cambodian returnee, who immediately began complaining. He had lived in America since he was five and said Cambodia was dirty and hot and nobody spoke English. "I don't know these people," he said, adding that he was there only because "my parents made me come. But I can't wait to go home."

A number of young Cambodian Americans revealed on YouTube sites that they did not know where their parents had lived in Cambodia, had not been to Cambodia, and did not particularly want to go because the country is poor or "bad" or dangerous and the food "disgusting," "crazy," and weird. Many consider Cambodia a third-world despot-ruled disaster that has nothing to do with them. Some struggle to remember the names of Khmer food they like. Their parents say, however, that visits home are the highlight of their lives, although many find visits difficult. "Everyone thinks Cambodians in America are rich, and they all want something," said one man.

Relatives beg to be sponsored or to visit America, and resettled Cambodians occasionally seek visa and travel information for their visits, saying it would be less expensive to bring one or two relatives to America than to take their own family to Cambodia. "Then maybe they'll see we're not rich!" one woman exclaimed. Both governments restrict Khmer travel to America, however, fearing visitors will not return to Cambodia. One resettled Khmer woman became stuck in Cambodia when her money and identification were stolen by her new "boyfriend," and she was isolated, without funds, and anxious for months before being able to establish she was a resettled Cambodian. Despite their experiences in Cambodia and their families and integration into Khmer communities in America, most resettled Cambodians have remained devoted to the homeland and have never abandoned their Khmer frame of reference. Van said the morning of the Festival for the Ancestors in September 2011, "Cambodia is always in our minds and our hearts."

Increasing numbers of Cambodians who said they would never return to Cambodia have done so. Some who returned permanently also maintain a house in America so they can return in the event of trouble in Cambodia (Chan 2003). Some Cambodians alternate periods of work in the United States with work or leisure in Cambodia, saying they have no idea where they will end up, and some continue to dream of returning to serve Cambodia. One man speaks often of the guilt he feels for not having "helped his people," despite twenty-five years of working in humanitarian aid and four years serving resettled Cambodians. He vows he will someday help Cambodia.

Many first- and many second-generation Cambodians who cannot afford to return to Cambodia remain vitally interested in their homeland. Cambodians discuss Khmer issues and watch videos by the hour, disturbed that politicians and journalists are routinely murdered, and Cambodians complain that corruption is rife and the government has made obvious its first concern is for its own continuation rather than the future of its people. They are increasingly expressing their concerns about Cambodia politically in America. Resettled Cambodians called on President Obama to intervene on Cambodia's behalf in its dispute with Thailand over an ancient temple on the border, and demonstrators at the White House in 2014 protested Cambodia's human rights violations.

Many Cambodians say they are disturbed that Hun Sen continues to rule with dictatorial power. They mistrust his government and blame him for everything from their flight in the early 1980s to his despotism in the twenty-first century. Khmer refugees tend to be avidly anticommunist, many noting that Hun Sen was once a Khmer Rouge cadre. They also worry about the homeland's relationships with its neighbors, calling Cambodia a small stone between big stones. Conversation among resettled Cambodians sooner or later turns to worry that corruption will ruin the country. In 2010, several men said bribery is also a problem, but since it is not a Khmer concept, it must have come from elsewhere, "probably the Chinese," in one man's opinion. A disagreeing bystander shook his head and said, "In Khmer politics, left is right, and right is wrong," adding "Cambodians can lie and be corrupt. They don't need to be taught how."

After the 2011 "Arab spring," resettled Cambodians discussed the possibility that an "Asian spring" or "jasmine movement" would come to Cambodia. Most agreed it would not happen, but several said it will eventually occur because Cambodian oppression cannot last forever. Monks and laypeople at one temple hoped the uprising against Hun Sen would happen in 2012. When Bunroeun asked who would start the uprising, they answered, "America." He contradicted them, saying that Hun Sen is no threat to America and Cambodians' human rights are not "that big a deal" to American politicians. He pointed out that Hun Sen had just warned that his government would not tolerate a jasmine movement and, if it arose, he would put it down. Not impressed, they repeated that a coup was likely and would probably be led by the United States. Many Cambodians see American intervention as the solution to Cambodia's problems, "like in Iraq," and think Cambodia needs to become more like America.

Cambodians continued to wonder why Khmer Rouge leaders have not been brought to trial. In 1979, Cambodia yielded to foreign pressure and held a show trial, condemning Pol Pot and Ieng Sary to death in absentia. In the late 1990s, Khmer Rouge leaders Khieu Samphan and Nuon Chea defected to the government and said they were sorry, Khieu Samphan adding that Cambodians should "let bygones be bygones." Some Cambodians agreed, as did Hun Sen, who proposed that Cambodia "dig a hole and bury the past." Others said not holding leaders accountable had an unfortunate impact on survivors and said they wanted justice by whatever means. Cambodians celebrated Pol Pot's 1998 death but continued to doubt that attempts to put Khmer Rouge leaders on trial would succeed. "See how long it's been," Munney said, "and still nothing happens. Soon, they'll all be dead!"

Most resettled Cambodians thought Cambodia's rulers, themselves former Khmer Rouge, would allow only show trials. Appalled at how slow the wheels of justice were turning, Cambodians were surprised when actual trials began three decades after the Khmer Rouge were forced from Cambodia. The Khmer government charged top leaders with crimes against humanity, war crimes, and genocide. Although five were indicted and one was convicted, Cambodians were angered at the light sentence. Cambodians continue to follow the trials but debate their value, most saying they will have little lasting value and most of the trial money will go to officials (Galto 2010). Many Cambodians think the trials are a way for the Khmer government to keep the international community at bay while receiving international aid and engaging in trade, several again noting that surviving Khmer Rouge leaders "will all soon be dead."

Many Cambodians think the damage currently being caused to their homeland is permanent, noting the country's poverty: an international economic ranking of 211 countries in the mid-1980s ranked Cambodia last (Rumbaut 1995). In 2009, the purchasing power of individuals in Cambodia was estimated to be $2,000, compared to $46,000 for the United States. Overseas Cambodians claim that businessmen from countries like China and Malaysia are buying land in Cambodia, displacing rural Cambodians, and investing in businesses that make foreigners and a few elite Cambodians rich but do not benefit most residents. Several said the Chinese government is also "buying up the country" to send one to two million "invaders" to Cambodia. Several Cambodian Americans said the last statement is ludicrous but emphasized that greed of a few business-men is not benefiting most Cambodians.

American Interest in Cambodia

Interest in resettled Cambodians has drawn Americans to Cambodia. In the late 1980s, when resettled Cambodians had not yet returned to Cambodia, Americans began visiting, some taking charter flights from Ho Chi Minh City on tours advertised for "thrill-seekers and the jaded" (Frommer 1987). By the 2000s, two million tourists had visited the country (MacSwan 2010). Other non-Khmer Americans worked with nongovern-mental organizations or visited to study Buddhism or work with Buddhists or Christians, and politicians went to strengthen ties between America and Cambodia. Cambodia also became a prime target of American "vol-untourism." Typical is a Seattle educator and his wife who worked for a month at a rehabilitation program for land mine and polio victims and an orphanage for orphaned or AIDS-affected children; they returned the fol-lowing year to spend a longer period of time teaching English and clerical skills (Large 2003).

Other foreigners are exploiters. A freelance writer fabricated a story for the *New York Times Magazine* about meeting Khmer Rouge guerril-las, basing his story on previous trips, his imagination, and a passage from an Andre Malraux's 1982 novel *The Royal Way* (Markham 1992). Sex tourists saw Cambodia as "the world's ground zero for child sex tour-ists" (Abdulrahim 2009), and charges of sex crimes were brought against Americans in both Cambodia and the United States. An American was convicted of sexually abusing as many as fifty boys whom the judge said he paid less money than "you pay for a latte here in Seattle" (Associated Press 2004).

Marriage is also a business. Twenty-five Cambodians were indicted for recruiting Americans to marry Khmer nationals with all-expenses paid "vacations" that included airfare, lodging, meals, drinks, entertainment, sex, and cash. Recruiters provided photographs of engagement and marriage ceremonies and documentary support to help Khmer nationals obtain lawful permanent residence in the United States (Immigration and Customs Enforcement 2010; Department of Justice 2015). Adoption is another business. Americans adopted hundreds of Khmer children before 1999 and over twenty-three hundred between 1999 and 2002. The number of orphanages in Cambodia doubled in response to the global adoption industry, but most "orphans" in Cambodia had a living parent (Ruhfus 2012), and while organizations and orphanages were receiving significant donations, volunteers and Cambodians were receiving virtually nothing for their children. The United States ended its adoption agreement with Cambodia after discovering Khmer recruiters were paying parents to release their children for adoption (Cambodia Adoption Connection 2012).

Among the agencies that paid recruiters to buy and abduct babies and small children from Cambodian orphanages and rural parents for adoptive parents in America was Seattle International Adoptions, owned by two sisters. A 1997 *Seattle Times* article lauded the sisters for helping Americans adopt abandoned and starving Khmer babies and gave their contact information (Reang 1997). On December 19, 2003, however, one sister pled guilty to "conspiracy to commit visa fraud and conspiracy to launder money in relation to adoptions arranged in Cambodia." The other sister was sentenced to eighteen months in prison and ordered to forfeit more than $1.4 million in property. Investigators do not know how many of the more than seven hundred agency-placed children were orphans.

Concerns about the Khmer Rouge

Despite their escape from the destruction of the Khmer Rouge to America, Khmer refugees continued to be concerned about the Khmer Rouge. Some refugees said they did not understand how the United States could recognize the Khmer Rouge diplomatically and support them financially or how the United Nations could also recognize the Khmer Rouge as Cambodia's government-in-exile. While a top Khmer Rouge leader chatted in French with diplomats at a United Nations reception in New York (Allman 1990) a few years after the Khmer Rouge killed people for speaking French, my

Khmer colleague collected used clothes for their survivors a few hundred miles north. A Khmer refugee at the New York reception later said he could not believe his eyes at "seeing rich European women flirting with Khmer Rouge representatives."

The flag of the Khmer Rouge–founded Democratic Kampuchean government-in-exile continued to fly at the United Nations complex in New York until February 1990, and Thiounn Prasit, Pol Pot's associate, was granted political asylum in the United States at a time when many Khmer refugees were being rejected. Accredited by the UN secretary-general as Cambodia's permanent representative, Thiounn Prasit resided in an upscale house in a New York suburb until May 1992 (Fifield 1998), while Khmer refugees lived in low-cost housing a few miles away and refugees who had arrived as toddlers were high school age, although many were too traumatized to graduate. Still, they were alive, while many overseas Cambodians Thiounn Prasit had been instrumental in convincing to return to Cambodia had been killed. He consistently downplayed the deaths of the Khmer Rouge years, saying that between ten thousand and twenty thousand persons had been killed, most by Vietnamese agents.

Khmer refugees also said they worried that resettled Khmer Rouge still committed to their ideology would attempt to convert resettled Cambodians to communism. In the 1980s, Cambodians said they found the idea that the Khmer Rouge were using the isolation and poverty of Khmer communities to promote their ideas terrorizing. In the 1990s, some Cambodians claimed a number of resettled Cambodians supported the Khmer Rouge, while others said only a small number of Khmer refugees were Khmer Rouge supporters. Cambodians said that even in communities in which Cambodians, resettlement agencies, and law enforcement personnel were unaware of Khmer Rouge activity, the Khmer Rouge were "everywhere," engaging in propaganda and recruitment and claiming to control entire communities. The president of the Cambodian Business Association in Southern California said, "We always watch what we say. People told me, 'Be careful. They are here, even in Long Beach'" (Brandon 1996).

In Massachusetts, Cambodians said Khmer Rouge recruiters were soliciting donations and political support and publishing a bimonthly Khmer newspaper distributed in Khmer markets and restaurants around the country (Dunn 1995). Some Cambodians said they believed the newspaper's content, but most said they ignored it. The publisher said, however, that he supported national unity, not the Khmer Rouge. Over the years at various community events, Cambodians furtively pointed to certain individuals as being Khmer Rouge. Khmer refugees in one city repeatedly claimed a bilingual state employee was Khmer Rouge, saying they had seen a photograph of Ing Sary, a Khmer Rouge leader, on his wall; their accusations continued until his death years later. Craig Etcheson of the Cambodian Genocide Project at Yale University said in late 1997 that he was often harassed by Khmer Rouge who dropped by his home in New Haven, Connecticut, and in 2009, one Khmer said Khmer Rouge cadre even controlled the local temple. When I noted that he had talked about this several decades earlier, he said, "Yes, and it's still true." Several others also claimed Khmer Rouge controlled the temples in their cities.

When a grandmother killed members of her family in Seattle in 2010, one newspaper reported that she had taken a self-defense class, knew how to use a gun, and may have been mentally disturbed (Thompson and Clarridge 2010). Dumbfounded at the shooting, several Cambodians wondered if she knew about guns because she was Khmer Rouge, one man saying, "She was a young adult when the Khmer Rouge took control of Cambodia. Maybe she learned from them." Some were convinced that the Khmer Rouge murdered actor Haing Ngor in 1998 in revenge for his portrayal of Khmer Rouge cruelty in the movie *The Killing Fields*. Haing Ngor himself told an official in Cambodia just before his death that resettled Khmer Rouge were unhappy with his activities against them (Brandon 1996). Los Angeles police concluded, however, that Haing Ngor was killed during a robbery, and three Oriental Lazy Boyz gang members were convicted of his murder. Doubts about his death were again sparked during Khmer Rouge trials in 2009 when a torture prison warden claimed Haing Ngor was killed because he appeared in the 1984 *The Killing Fields* film.

Cambodians continue to wonder about his death. Cambodians frequently accused one another of being Khmer Rouge, usually behind their backs, claiming they attended conferences and collected money to resist the Khmer government. Cambodians often accuse fellow refugees who criticize Sihanouk or the Vietnamese for contributing to the atrocities committed against Cambodia of being Khmer Rouge. The accusations are often vicious. One anonymous resettled Khmer accused another of joining the Khmer Rouge in 1968 and having a "Siam wife" who was related to Khmer Rouge leader Nuon Chea (*KI Media* 2008). A year later, the critic called the supposed Khmer Rouge "one of the most dumbest EX-former school teacher in Lycée Battambang," and one of the most "extremist Anti-Sihanouk" opponents (*KI Media* 2009). After a dispute divided Trairatanaram Temple in North Chelmsford, Massachusetts, into two congregations, the head monk of one faction said the other group compared him to the Khmer Rouge (Rice 2004). Other resettled Cambodians say the Khmer Rouge were never in America, and they had never heard such rumors.

Most Cambodians said the presence of the Khmer Rouge was most evident in their daily memories. Over the years, the memories remained strong although discussions about the Khmer Rouge years faded, one reason being that most Cambodians were not discussing the topic with their children because they did not want to disturb them. Many said they did not want to dwell on their memories but were dismayed their children did not know their parents' history (Etcheson 2005). When an American asked a 25-year-old when she came to the United States, she said, "Oh, in 1977 or '78." Her father was ashamed she could not remember the important dates of her life: the end of the Khmer Rouge regime, flight to Thailand, and resettlement. Young people said they did not know why their parents were distressed when they were young because their parents were silent or told only portions of their stories (Ng 2001). Academic Jonathan Lee said his parents had not mentioned Cambodia or spoken a word of Khmer during his childhood, instead speaking to one another in their "secret" Khmer language (Lee 2002: 1). It was not until he was an adult that he realized many of his kinfolk had died during the Khmer Rouge years.

Children often did not believe the stories their parents told them, saying the tales sounded too incredible to be true, and they could not imagine people acting so cruelly or understand why there was no uprising by the people (Galto 2010). A college counselor in Massachusetts found half of the twenty-five students he surveyed supporting the Khmer Rouge because they "just couldn't believe that Cambodians could kill their own people" (Dunn 1995: A1). Parents said they were upset that their words fell on deaf ears or that their children said they cared only about what was going to happen to them in America. When his friend brought up the topic, one youth said, to the laughter of his friends, "Yeah, I just want to get a girlfriend and a car."

Cambodians were distressed to hear the Khmer Rouge were gaining supporters among the young. In the 1990s, increasing numbers of young people said they preferred the Khmer Rouge to the current government of Cambodia, seeing corruption as a larger threat to the people. Others hated the Khmer Rouge, dreaded their return, and talked of revenge. They wanted to know their history and worried about their parents (Dith Pran 1997). Some said their parents referred to the Khmer Rouge when children misbehaved; when they refused to eat certain foods, parents told them of surviving on leaves and rotten fish heads. Some said they first heard about the Khmer Rouge when they were ten or eleven years old, when they may have triggered parents' memories of their own lives at that age (Uehara 2001). Many children of survivors insisted it is important for future generations to know the past so they can help prevent such acts in the future.

Resettled Cambodians continue to dwell on the causes of Khmer Rouge violence. Some blame the violence on ignorance, saying most Cambodians were not educated, did not know much Buddhist doctrine, and were easily swayed by the Khmer Rouge, luring youngsters as young as eight and nine. Many blame the Khmer Rouge on Cambodia's previous leaders. Although some Khmer refugees revered Norodom Sihanouk, others wondered if he was partially responsible for Cambodia's turmoil. A college student wrote, "Could it be possible that my beloved sister Tvedara and millions of others were victims of Sihanouk as well as victims of the Khmer Rouge?" (Vaddhana Kchao 1989: 13). He concluded that Sihanouk was a "puppet ruler who went into exile for fear of his own life," leaving his fellow Cambodians to suffer. Khmer writer Polin Soth said the cause of the Khmer Rouge cataclysm belonged to all Cambodians, but "we were manipulated by our king" (Wiscombe 1998).

Some Cambodians point to Sihanouk's arrogance and greed and say his susceptibility to flattery and aggrandizement blinded him to people's needs and the world's dangers (Hansen and Phath 1987). One man cited a photograph of Sihanouk praying before a table holding a portrait of Ho Chi Minh as evidence of Sihanouk's betrayal of Cambodia. Few Cambodians discussed Sihanouk's death in October 2012; a class of Khmer college students made no mention of him, and when asked for their reactions, one said, "He was nothing to us." Addressing Sihanouk, Hin Sithan wrote, "Cambodia will not survive by my view. She will be a second Champa because of you and you alone, the main actor in Khmer killing Fields" (*KI Media* 2009). Some Cambodians accuse foreigners of having helped the Khmer Rouge, while others say it is probably easier to blame outsiders because Cambodians are ashamed that the instigators of their horror were Cambodians.

As Cambodians have gained schooling in America, they have become increasingly critical also of American actions in Cambodia, asking why America bombed Cambodia but did not move against the Khmer Rouge and regretting that America was not going to force Cambodia to become more democratic or less corrupt. They indicated confusion over Americans' vacillating interest in Cambodia, from intense focus on refugees in the later 1970s to disinterest in the later 1980s, intense interest again in the peace agreement of the early 1990s and again fading as Cambodia stabilized and Bosnia and Rwanda filled the headlines in the mid-1990s. One young Cambodian wrote, "It is sad to realize that many Westerners are not offering much concern," adding, "Many Cambodians of the new generation and I will never fully understand" why Americans did not care about them (Vaddhana Kchao 1989: 13). Another Khmer concluded, "I guess only Cambodians can care about us."

When trials began in the 2000s for Khmer Rouge leaders, several men said, "Now Americans can understand." Within weeks, however, as news items declined, they were saying, "Americans are not interested in us." However important Cambodia was to first-generation refugees, it was an invisible world to most Americans, including many Khmer children. When non-Khmer did notice Cambodia, Cambodians often expressed resentment, saying Americans see Cambodia as unimportant or do not understand the situation there. In 1985, Yang Sam criticized a non-Khmer scholar, Michael Vickery, for talking about Cambodia with "sarcastic comments," and accused him of calling Cambodia "a very bad land." He also criticized historian David Chandler for viewing Cambodians as "rude and violent." According to Yang Sam, Chandler claimed that "Cambodians have had many wars, did a lot of killing, kept grudges, were savages, and probably barbarians, especially against the Vietnamese" (1985: 14). Few thought Chandler held those views, but Yang Sam was not persuaded.

While some Cambodians say America is partly to blame for Cambodia's travail, others say the Vietnamese are responsible or point to China as the model for the Khmer Rouge "experiment," claiming the Khmer Rouge kept half the harvested rice and sent the rest to China as repayment for weapons and military advisors. They also say Khmer Rouge clothes were "just like Chinese," including Maoist peaked caps they claimed were previously unknown in Cambodia. Others say some Khmer Rouge leaders were actual Chinese (F. Smith 1989). If not foreigners, say Cambodians, the Khmer Rouge were different from other Cambodians, more evil and with darker skin that many claim indicated rural origins, poverty, lack of education, and poor character. Some Cambodians say, however, that Cambodia carried the seeds of her own destruction and claim the Khmer Rouge were rooted in Khmer traditions of violence, echoing Chandler (1991) and Becker (1986), who assert the roots of Pol Pot can be found in Khmer history and say the Khmer Rouge regime was imposed on Cambodia by Cambodians themselves.

Other Cambodians see Cambodia's misfortunes as the latest in a long line of misfortunes that have occurred since Angkorean days (Chandler 1982a), and some view the Khmer Rouge as heir to a Khmer warrior heritage that has promoted violence in Cambodia (Seanglim Bit 1991). Some Khmer say they have always been reluctant to discuss such issues with other Cambodians with little knowledge of history and overwhelmed with resettlement difficulties. Others say Cambodians' inability to reconcile opposing conflict and xenophobic urges contributed to Khmer Rouge excesses, and numerous Khmer Christians say God allowed the Khmer Rouge period as punishment for corruption and greed, one saying God was angry at Cambodians for not turning from their evil ways. In one pastor's words, "But Cambodians didn't listen, and He was patient for some time, but eventually He had to do something."

Some Cambodians claim they and their countrymen endured a collective karmic experience that threatened their survival or say the suffering caused by the Khmer Rouge was a continuation of bad karma that began with the Lon Nol coup in 1970 when Cambodia stopped following its policies of neutrality toward Vietnam. Tep Vong, supreme patriarch of Buddhism in Cambodia, also intimated that victims of the Khmer Rouge may have died in part as a result of bad karma (McGill 2006). Cambodians agree that Pol Pot earned merit in his previous lives that allowed him to gain great power in Cambodia but say he subsequently earned hundreds of years in hell because of his deeds. Other Cambodians blame their own lack of merit for their suffering or attribute their survival to the good karma they earned in previous lives. Other Cambodians doubt that karma was the cause for such an enormous tragedy, asking how a whole country of people could have bad karma at the same time. Many say they are confused, making a statement about karma and contradicting it moments later. Such discussions often end with someone saying, "It wasn't karma that caused our suffering. It was the Khmer Rouge!"

For many Cambodians, suffering is part of the inescapable and inexplicable suffering Cambodians have experienced through time. A young man said in 2005 that Pol Pot happened because "things happen," and his wife suggested the existence of the Khmer Rouge was forecast, pointing to Puth, a nineteenth-century Khmer who predicted the social order would be turned upside down in the future: demons or members of the lowest rungs of society would rule, people would suffer horribly, and the enemies of religion would triumph over the religious. Many Cambodians agree and view the Khmer Rouge period as a stage in the Buddhist cycle. Cambodians who previously derided Puth's predictions (*buddh damnay*) changed their minds after their experiences of the Khmer Rouge years, saying senseless and inexplicable events are inevitable in the cyclic flow of Buddhist history.

Some Cambodians see the Khmer Rouge period as the period that lies midpoint between the death of the last Buddha and the birth of the next. If so, they say, the Khmer Rouge period will be followed by a time of peace, morality, and prosperity under a righteous ruler. Whatever their explanations for the Khmer Rouge, many have said they felt tainted by the Khmer Rouge years: doing what they were told, being afraid, surviving, or collaborating to stay alive. One Khmer man said of his neighbor, "I know about him. He obeyed the Khmer Rouge. He can't hide it." Many Cambodians in the twenty-first century say it is easier to avoid discussion of the Khmer Rouge years altogether.

In addition to their concern for the homeland, Khmer refugees have been intensely interested in the preservation of their culture.

Chapter Eleven

Preserving Culture

Khmer heritage and culture have been central to resettled Cambodians' cultural identity. From the first days of resettlement, Cambodians worried their culture had been destroyed, having witnessed and heard of damage, dead artists, destroyed instruments, ruined buildings, burned books, temple walls specked with bullet holes, thousand-year-old statues vandalized, and art vanished. The damage seemed irreversible to Cambodians even decades later. In the 1980s, they spoke of the extensive damage being caused to Cambodia's cultural patrimony by remaining Khmer Rouge soldiers in the country and others, and in the 1990s, Cambodians said Cambodian statues were being stolen by Cambodians and foreigners for financial gain. Saying their homeland was worse off than it had been centuries before, Cambodians said they were devastated that they could do nothing about the ongoing exploitation of their country.

Preservation Efforts

Because of the damage in Cambodia, Khmer refugees said they had to preserve Khmer culture in America. In the years following, Cambodians expressed relief that Khmer culture in Cambodia was surviving, but they continued their efforts to observe traditions practiced by their "grandmothers and grandfathers." They contributed to a temple before buying a home and purchased Khmer silk to make a new blouse rather than buying ready-made clothes. They tried not to compromise rituals when making adjustments and argued about goals and how to achieve them. In the 1980s, refugees criticized students for pursuing advanced degrees rather than contributing money to soldiers fighting the Hun Sen government, as well as criticizing several men who concentrated on their immediate family to the neglect of extended family members.

Most Cambodians engaged in "a balancing act" between surviving economically and honoring their culture; the president of one temple board still finds it difficult to attend major celebrations at his temple because of his work obligations.

Cambodians adjusted their traditions to American concepts, space, schedules, and culture through reductions and substitutions in repertoire, personnel, and accoutrements. Activities once embedded in daily life, such as art and work (carving scythe handles into serpent heads) and entertainment and work (workers singing while transplanting rice seedlings and dancing after the harvest), became separated into daily jobs and public and occasional stage performances. Although Cambodians speak of their culture as ancient and consistent, they have been creative in preserving it, and the importance of ceremonies and performances in displaying Khmer culture has influenced their acceptance of re-created rituals as authentic. To define and adjust cultural activities that best fit their lives, they have had numerous discussions about their options, often trying first one, then another. Cambodians usually chose activities they could most easily afford and incorporate, such as listening to recorded Khmer music or cooking traditional meals, and they continue to observe cultural activities primarily during private times and in more private places, such as temples, homes, and vehicles.

Some Cambodians say elders are more interested in preservation, because they have more knowledge of Khmer culture; other Cambodians say women are more interested, because it is their duty to pass on tradition to the next generation. Through the years, Cambodians have said also that Khmer refugees and their children are more likely to be interested in preserving Khmer culture if they live among other Khmer and less likely if they are isolated from one another. Cambodians have tended to ascribe preservation efforts to others like them, urban Cambodians saying they are more likely than rural farmers to retain their culture, while rural folk view themselves as more likely than "rich people from the cities" to do so. First-generation refugees have often said they are more interested in maintaining tradition than their children, while younger people's interest usually correlates with the age they fled Cambodia. Those who came as teenagers were more likely to observe Khmer traditions and spend their time with Khmer friends, while younger siblings spent their time in American activities. Second-generation Cambodians, unfamiliar with much of their heritage, are then unable to pass traditions on to their own children.

Cambodians often express the hope that their descendants will rediscover their roots, and some younger people are seeking to learn what was lost to their parents. Any evidence of the young following traditional ways was welcomed by their elders. At one New Year celebration, hundreds of young people were playing traditional games, to the delight of their elders. Young Khmer toughs wearing leather jackets and carrying ghetto blasters stood by watching, but most of the youth were enthusiastic participants. Cambodians spoke proudly of children who did not question adults, avoided eye contact, and tried to learn their parents' traditions. Local Khmer communities play a critical role in preserving culture; young Cambodian Americans in Long Beach said they are more likely to be proud of their culture and interested in learning about it when with other Cambodians (Khmer Girls in Action 2011).

Listening to a Khmer CD, one youth said, "I don't really understand the words. But there is something about the music, the sound. Outside I am American, but the music, it speaks to my Khmer soul." Young Cambodian Americans poke fun at themselves in YouTube videos and various Internet forums. A "How to Tell If You Are Cambodian" video listed such characteristics as loving fermented sauce (*prahok*), having at least one luxury car for pulling up to Khmer parties, a furry blanket with five more stored in the closet, and parents who use bucket and scoop rather than the shower. A Massachusetts student made a video for his Khmer language class on "How to Be Cambodian," and by 2010, it had been viewed 256,461 times (Wright 2010).

Food

Food provides constant opportunities to "perform" tradition, and Cambodians do so with daily meals involving just one person to community celebrations involving thousands. The years of starvation made Cambodians hungry, in every sense of the word, and from the earliest days of arrival, Cambodians have prepared traditional Khmer dishes. Many said American food was unsatisfactory: the packaging was confusing, and the food made them ill. Cambodians sometimes referred to cheese as "French *prahok*" and found it as inedible as most Americans find *prahok*. They did not understand American attempts to help them prepare food; several mentioned being appalled when given brown rice, as they considered it fit only for prisoners and birds. They were relieved when they were able to purchase rice and fish, start their own gardens, and go fishing.

Rice and fish are to Cambodians what bread and potatoes are to European Americans, and many Cambodians said a meal without rice is not a proper meal. While American speak of "breaking bread together," Cambodians talk of rice being the center of every meal. Cambodians ask, "Are you hungry?" (*ñam bay day*, literally, "Have you eaten rice?"), and say they are "hungry for rice" (*klean bay*) or are "eating rice" (*ñam bay*). A traditional meal consists of rice, soup or sauce, and a bit of *prahok*, followed by fruit and water or tea. Resettled Cambodians said rice and fish are not as varied, fresh, or delicious as in Cambodia, where rice is heavy, light, or medium; sticky, fluffy, or regular; rainy, dry, or transitional; but they said they were grateful for its abundance. Evidence that one has enough food to eat is important, and many Khmer refugees preferred being stout to slender, which they equated with hunger.

Preparing traditional dishes is a primary activity in many families, with an older woman preparing food full-time if possible. In many homes, rice and a main dish are available throughout the day. Weekend trips to Asian markets are outings that often involve the entire family as they shop for Asian vegetables, dried fish, soy sauce, lemon grass, curry, mint, hot peppers, ginger, tamarind, fish sauce, and rice and noodles in bulk. In many areas, Asian foods have become available at A&P and Safeway stores. Many resettled Cambodians have adopted American food but prefer Khmer dishes, and many Cambodian Americans also say they favor the Khmer food they ate as children.

Cambodians have often expressed surprise that Americans do not treasure eating together, as Cambodians say they do. They lament that work and school schedules interrupt family meals, with women and children serving men and their guests, laughing and tossing comments to one another as they carry dishes to and from the table or mats spread on the floor before partaking of the meal themselves. Christian Cambodians say one of the reasons they like going to church is eating with others. "I love the potlucks and coffee hours!" exclaimed an older woman as she filled my plate with doughnuts and rice cakes one Sunday after services. Another woman often rushes to the temple for a quick meal during her late morning work break, and a man works an extra hour a day in order to return home to eat lunch with his wife.

Possessions

Cambodians' homes in America are very different from the rural stilted houses built of wood and thatched palm leaves or urban cement block buildings they inhabited in Cambodia before 1975, the tiny shacks or open air of the Khmer Rouge years, or the huts of the refugee camps. In America, their substantial apartments were usually larger and more tightly enclosed. To feel more comfortable in homes with an unfamiliar bathroom, electricity, secondhand furniture, and appliances, Cambodians added elaborately decorated clocks and knickknacks; silk or plastic flowers; posters of Angkor Wat; cushions, blankets, curtains, and hangings in brilliant colors of red, pink, purple, and orange; and woven plastic mats purchased from Asian stores.

Common in early resettlement years were lists of telephone numbers on the wall, metallic tinsel garlands, blinking Christmas lights, crepe paper streamers, images of Krishna, and carvings of dancing girls. Most homes had a television and stereo set. A wok, rice steamer, mortar and pestle, and large cleaver were usual in the kitchen, and in other rooms, rolled-up bedding, mats, large bags of rice, chairs lined up against the wall, and ancestor photographs hung high on the walls. As resources increased, families added art and crafts from Cambodia and state-of-the-art electronics: flat-screen televisions, video recorders, and karaoke machines. Calendar photographs and sketches were replaced by handmade carvings, paintings, and sculptures, with elephants, tigers, ibis, monkeys, temple ruins, and pastoral scenes of Cambodia dominating, such as a wooden house on stilts surrounded by rice fields and sugar palms or water buffalo or fishing boats before a backdrop of banana and coconut trees.

Worried they would never see another Cambodian in such a large country after their arrival in 1982, Chea's family walked the streets of New York looking for countrymen. Chea and his sister finally passed a house they knew was Khmer because, Chea said, "I saw shoes outside the front door. So I looked in the window and saw a *krama* (a traditional long scarf about one foot wide and four feet long, usually checkered in white and red or blue) hanging there. Then I knew," he remembered. "Oh how happy we were!" Cambodians continue to identify Khmer homes by curtains tied at the bottom in a loop, a *krama* scarf thrown over a railing, the scent of garlic and fish, Khmer music, and a spirit house in the yard, but most Khmer passersby already know the location of every Cambodian in the area.

Many Cambodians were especially interested in cars, unavailable to most in Cambodia, but they took some "getting used to," one man said. The spiraling exits of the Seattle-Tacoma International Airport parking garage were rough on newly arrived refugees, and their first ride in America was usually done with open windows to provide relief for unsteady stomachs. Driving was also a strain; Visoth had to rest on his thirty-mile drive from his home to a community college and twice on the return, saying, "I am too tired to go all at once." Nothing, however, stopped Cambodians from acquiring what they saw as tangible marks of success, and temple parking lots are full of BMWs and Mercedes. Funeral corteges from temple to crematorium are often lengthy because, several men explained, each Cambodian drives his or her own car to demonstrate status.

Cambodians say their cars are protected space into which they can withdraw from American contact while being surrounded by the sounds of Khmer language and music. They embellish their cars with stencils of the Khmer flag, Angkor Wat, or "I love Cambodia" stickers on windows and bumpers. Asian lanterns hang from the rearview mirror, and dried jasmine flowers, images of birds and elephants, feathers, a Buddhist image, or a photograph of a deceased parent decorate the dashboard. A bobblehead celestial female (*apsara*) danced on one young man's dashboard, and on another, a Hawaiian dancer wrapped in a bit of Khmer fabric. "Well," said the driver laughing, "I had to make do."

Particularly in the first years of resettlement, Cambodians said they used their cars to carry them from one island of Khmer space to another, providing them with control they experienced in few other areas of their lives. Several Cambodians said they were happiest when driving. One man proudly took his family to see the Washington and Oregon coastline and said Multnomah Falls and Deception Pass were their favorite destinations. One woman was delighted she could drive to the beach when she was hot and go shopping for food and clothes whenever she felt like it. "I don't have to tell anyone. I just go." Speed became a metaphor for their changed lives, one man saying, "Now I drive my car like an American—fast! Just like American life."

Crafts, Clothing, and Bokator

Unable to acquire goods from Cambodia after resettlement, Cambodians made musical instruments, dancers' costumes and masks, amulets, carvings, and paintings for performance and personal use. They made paper clips into fishing hooks, ties, and locks; used tin cans for cutting, piercing, and scooping; made traditional carts, toys, instruments, and costumes; and put toy wheels on boats, bicycles, and carts of every size. Saying they were inspired by Cambodia's landscape, religion, and epic legends, they made items not attempted before, using materials at hand, with little fanfare or notice. They also learned Western-style painting to record their experiences (Arabas 2012).

After arrival, many Cambodians wore a traditional cotton wraparound skirt, falling to the calves on men and lower on women with a blouse or shirt above, and a traditional sarong for weddings and performances, its ends coming up between the legs and tucked into the waist, with a belt. Realizing that most Americans viewed skirts as unmanly, a number of men shifted to wearing their sarongs only at home. Cambodians used the traditional *krama* as a scarf, shawl, bandage, baby sling, towel, bag, lunch box, and umbrella; when unavailable, it could be substituted by a towel. When I invited Nov to accompany me to Wegmans to pick up soda drinks for a Khmer festival, he headed for my pickup, then dashed back to his apartment, grabbed a towel, wrapped it around his neck, and with a big smile jumped in. I seldom saw him in public without a *karma*. A number of women and some men continue wearing traditional clothing at home, such as a cotton *krama* for everyday use or silk for festive occasions.

Some Khmer women are committed to preserving traditional weaving, including tie-dyed *ikat* fabric with patterns resembling those in Angkorean bas-reliefs and described by thirteenth-century Chinese traveler Chou Ta-Kuan (1992). Weavers talk of weaving their experiences into their work and describe the comfort weaving brings them. Weaving exhibits and demonstrations are popular, and fabric illustrations grace the cover of several books about Cambodians. Women also sew elaborate dancers' costumes and the multiple outfits desired by brides and grooms.

Resettled Cambodians have also taken up *bokator*, a Khmer martial art of hand-to-hand combat. Using bamboo staffs and short sticks, competitors attack one another with head, jaw, shoulders, elbows, hips, knees, and fingers. Bas-reliefs on Angkorean ruins portray *bokator* techniques; in one scene, two men fight with their elbows, and in another, they appear to be grappling with one another. Modern-day opponents wear the uniform of ancient troops, tying blue and red silk cords around their heads and biceps and a *krama* scarf around their waists to reflect their level of expertise. Each training session begins with fighters paying respect to a Hindu deity.

The art of *bokator* was nearly exterminated during the Khmer Rouge regime, when many practitioners died, and since the art was not taught for years, older fighters worry that the young are using not the flowing movements of true *bokator*, but a mutated hybrid that includes elements of tae kwon do and judo. One trainer complained, "Some of these kids look like crabs walking" (Kimsong and Maloy 2006). Many Cambodians are glad the form is being revived; at the annual Khmer New Year parade in Long Beach in 2010, a teacher dressed in a bright red uniform with a green scarf around his head led his students in a demonstration of the ancient art, proud of this exhibition of Khmer art in America.

Literature

Cambodians describe the beauty and power of the Khmer language with reverence, saying it is poetic, vivid, insightful, and romantic, with "decorative" words that can be added for humor or beauty. They frequently say their language must be expressive in order to convey Khmer emotions, which many claim are deeper and more genuine than those of non-Khmer. Educated Cambodians explain that their language borrowed administrative, military, and literary vocabulary from Sanskrit and religious terms from Pali, and many Cambodians say Khmer is complex and difficult to speak, write, and comprehend.

Cambodians point to the ritual vocabularies used with monks and royalty and the poetic and musical dialogues between men and women as evidence of Khmer's superiority to other tongues. Appreciating both written and oral language, Cambodians express delight in folktales about spirits and humans that explain natural occurrences, provide lessons on life and morality and harsh warnings to children about the evil of the world, and promote and reflect cultural values. In Khmer folktales, injustice often prevails, cruelty is not uncommon, and naivety is met with amusement. There are few militant or powerful heroes, but numerous clever monkeys and hares who outwit slower, more powerful elephants and crocodiles, and peasants who outsmart spouses, relatives, merchants, and authority figures. Many Khmer refugees were also familiar with over five hundred Jataka tales in Buddhist literature about the previous lives of Buddha.

Resettled Khmer often recited proverbs that were used traditionally to educate children at temple, school, and home. Proverbs teach trust: "Scales must not be larger than what they weigh"; and accountability: "Don't try to hide a dead elephant with a winnowing basket." They also teach discretion: "Drag a boat without leaving a trace; catch a fish without muddying the waters" and "Better to close your mouth than open it; better to be quiet than to speak"; and advise adaptiveness: "Enter a river where it bends; enter a country by its customs" (Fisher-Nguyen 1994). Proverbs warn against pride: "Don't take the sky to make a seat for yourself" and "Don't try to shit like the elephant"; tell Cambodians how to treat superiors: "Don't hit a stone with an egg, because you will lose" and "When elephants dance, the ants die"; and suggest wariness: "Don't sit on rotten wood." Proverbs are also practical: "If you have a long eel, don't look for a long pot in which to cook it."

Most Khmer literature was traditionally passed orally from generation to generation; memorized, narrated, sung, and danced, it remains popular among many resettled Cambodians. Cambodians say they worry that as first-generation Cambodians pass away, Khmer oral literature is dying. In the years after resettlement, if the television was off and a good storyteller was on hand, adults and children listened intently. Cambodians say now, however, that only older Cambodians and younger Cambodian Americans with a special interest in their heritage listen to the traditional stories (Kuong Chhang Ly 2010).

Much of Khmer literature is in verse, including scriptures, fables, dance manuals, and epic stories (Sam-Ang Sam 1994). Much of it, such as funeral laments, is chanted, with the poet accompanying himself on a two-stringed guitar (*chabey*) or wooden flute (*kloy*) (McCullough 1994).

Poetry is valued for being sweet and melodious and is recited in a variety of styles; it can also be performed as dance and theater. Cambodians express special delight in humorous or sarcastic stories, such as "The Wise Hare" (*Thmenh Cheyy*), who makes fools of authority figures. Hare Judge is selfless in fighting against social inequity and dispensing common sense, but he also engages in mischievous, comic, and buffoonish acts (Chor Chanthyda 2004).

Before the twentieth century, most literate Cambodians were monks interested in religious manuscripts, but Cambodia's literary tradition goes back to seventh-century Sanskrit inscriptions on stone columns that speak of conquests, lineages, and religious edicts (Vickery 1990a). The first inscription in old Khmer, the precursor of modern Khmer, appeared in 612, and more than twelve hundred Angkorean inscriptions record administration details, temple assets, land transfers, royal orders, and royal salutations. Buddhist religious texts in Sanskrit were inscribed on palm leaf manuscripts as long ago as six thousand years (Ross 2008).

Leaf manuscripts are made of flattened, trimmed, and smoothed leaves inscribed with a needle-pointed stylus, rubbed with pigment or soot, and cleaned, leaving the incised letters legible. The leaves are strung on string to make a book or fan and covered with wood or ivory panels. Extremely fragile and stored in organic cabinets and buildings, leaf manuscripts in Cambodia's tropical climate do not long endure. Cambodians view leaf manuscripts as sacred, magical, or medicinal and sometimes burn them on the pyres of beloved monks to earn merit (Ang Chouléan 1997) or store them in funerary monuments (Harris 2005).

Most classical literature, including commentaries on Buddhism's Tripitaka, was produced between the sixteenth and nineteenth centuries at court or temples (Nepote and Khing Hoc Dy 1981). Nineteenth-century French scholars wrote about Khmer history, architecture, art, and oral literature and recorded Khmer versed moral codes (*chbap*) written from the fourteenth to eighteenth centuries and copied and memorized since. The codes give advice on daily life and instruct children on religion, tradition, literacy skills, good manners, and language appreciation (Thierry 1978). Cambodians say the rules for females are of greatest importance, cautioning them not to take a seat in the wrong place or walk in other people's houses, and women not to forget their husbands, cause them dissatisfaction, or chatter in their absence; instead, they are to do what their husbands say. While most Cambodian Americans speak of the codes as old-fashioned and irrelevant to modern American life, many know them.

After independence in 1953, Khmer novels and short stories grew in number. Soth Polin's risqué novels shocked readers with their political messages, suggesting in an article entitled "Pol Pot's Diabolical

Sweetness" that his former teacher had learned the beauty of words from Buddhist poetry and French poet Paul Vertaine before leading Cambodia to its downfall. During the Khmer Rouge years, "literature" became propaganda, with a focus on heroes, revolution, and the transformation they claimed the agricultural and hydrological systems were having in the countryside "in a way so miraculous that it has not been seen in two thousand years of history" (Khing Hoc Dy 1994: 27).

So many books disappeared during the Khmer Rouge years that Cornell University was the major repository of Khmer books in the early 1980s. After the overthrow of the Khmer Rouge, a number of books were reprinted, but the lack of funding hindered the publication of new works; authors had to pay their own publishing costs, and most Cambodians lacked literacy, time, or money for leisure reading. Along with renewed publications in Cambodia, Cambodian writings have increased in America, primarily survivors' memoirs and poetry (Im Sothearith 2010). Cambodians expressed joy at hearing of the poems of abbot Akaktipo Ly Van describing the plight of Khmer refugees fleeing Cambodia, found on the day of his death. Educated Cambodians speak of their excitement at finding Khmer publications, some saying literature is an escape from their memories. In the 1980s, a Cornell graduate student spent hours copying manuscripts to send to friends, and numerous young Cambodian Americans three decades later are themselves disseminating works they discover, written in either English or Khmer.

Newspapers in America have included *Big Country News* (*Nokor Thom*), a fifty-two-page general interest weekly; *Angkor Borei*, focused on politics; and *Serey Pheap*, focused on social issues. A number of Cambodians said they lacked time to do the writing they wanted to do. Luoth Yin told me of his desire to write in 1983, and in 1998, he published, in Khmer and English, *The Land of Tears: Poems: The Garland of Sentiment toward Motherland; Deep Wistfulness;* and *The Heart's Legacy* and, in Khmer only, *Lives in This World; The Drifting Cloud;* and *The Rainy Day*. Many Cambodians wrote poems, essays, and novels without concern for publication. Among published work, Soth Polin's writings continue to arouse respect or criticism (Wiscombe 1998). In 2011, a middle-aged Khmer described Soth Polin as a brilliant Khmer who has "inspired my generation for so many years."

Poet U Sam Oeur survived the Khmer Rouge by destroying his manuscripts and pretending he was illiterate. He now writes poetry in America, chanting his narratives in a flat recitative manner and singing the emotional passages (McCullough 1994). His *Sacred Vows* (1998), written in the Khmer "crow-hopping" form with seven-line, four-word stanzas and a tightly-woven rhyme scheme, describes the Khmer Rouge as "red eyes" whose color changed, Cambodians say, when they ate human livers and swallowed human bile, especially from "freshly-killed virgins" (McCullough 1994). U Sam Oeur claims he can still identify these men, including top leaders in Cambodia, because their eyes remain the same color. Cambodians frequently say Khmer poetry is complex; when I worked with Hin Sithan translating a nineteenth-century poem (Tauch Chhuong 1994), he often insisted that English lacks words to adequately translate Khmer words.

In 1993, resettled college students published poems and essays focusing on their identity, family, and nostalgia for the homeland and, in 2001, published writings revealing that many students were growing less secure over the years in their identity as Cambodians, exhibiting more American behavior, and feeling marginalized by both cultures (Needham 2010). Navy Phim (2007) wrote about having a name Americans found difficult to pronounce and skin color other Cambodians considered too dark. She expressed also her love for Cambodia and confusion over her life. She puzzled about blaming the Khmer Rouge, looked for similarities with other Cambodians, and wondered about differences in her own family: her curiosity in contrast to her mother's reserve, and her attachment to Khmer ways in contrast to her younger siblings' attraction to American ways.

Although many Cambodian American children and youth are competent with computers, a number of educated Cambodians deplore that few Khmer homes have more than a handful of books. Several Cambodians noted that older Khmer continue to revere their language for its magical potency; they want the temples to have Khmer books and religious writings, and they treasure sacred pages for their value in providing protection and good fortune. One woman took a few flaking page edges off a palm leaf manuscript purchased in Cambodia, mixed them in hot water, and gave the mixture to her family to drink. Younger Cambodian Americans have frequently been tattooing their bodies with Khmer characters for protection and decoration. After acknowledging Cambodians' reverence for the written page, one man said, "Still, it makes me sad that my people do not read very much. They don't read Khmer, and they don't read English."

Music and Dance

After resettlement, Cambodians put major efforts into reviving traditional Khmer music and dance, calling them enduring symbols of their culture. Angkorean temple bas-reliefs portray four-reed oboes (*sralai khlang khaek*), gong circles (*kong vuang*), and suspended barrel drums (*skor thum*) similar to those still in use (Sam-Ang Sam 1994). Traditional Khmer music includes a *pin peat* orchestra that accompanies court and ceremonial occa-sions; *lkhaon kbach* for court dance and *lkhaon khaol* music for masked dances, shadow plays (*sbaek*), and religious ceremonies; secular *mohôri* for folk dance; *areak ka* music for weddings; a *yike* folk ensemble; and *basăk* music for folk theater.

Between 80 and 90 percent of all musicians and dancers died during the Khmer Rouge years, the rest were forced to work in the fields, and orchestral ensembles, instruments, costumes, masks, dances, pho-tographs and films, and historical records were destroyed (*Kampuchea Review* 1982). The loss of most of the performers of Cambodia's oral tradition meant the erasure of much of one thousand years of tradition, an almost irredeemable loss (Beers 1990). Abhorring religious or folkloric songs and dances, the Khmer Rouge allowed only performances focused on work and war. The dancers dressed in black, and survivors said the first dance was always "Hammer and Sickle." Revolutionary songs were played often and loudly, particularly "Glorious April 17!" and "The Red Flag of the Revolution," both with an emphasis on blood. The first song begins, "Ruby blood that sprinkles the towns and plains," and the second, "Our red flag is born from the blood of workers, peasants, intel-lectuals, monks, youth, and women who have sacrificed themselves to free our people."

Cambodians described their revulsion at having to hear, and occasion-ally sing, Khmer Rouge songs. After resettlement, they said unwelcome refrains about working and revolution popped into their heads. "Blood, blood, blood," one man told me. "I hear the words, I hear the sounds. I hate it." Others said they liked the music because singing was a relief from work and a distraction from hunger and grief. One young woman said, "I just like the music." She was twelve when she was chosen to sing for the Khmer Rouge, and despite her hatred for them, she could not erase the joy music brought to her in a terrible time. Some musicians, including Arn Chorn-Pond, were forced to play music for the Khmer Rouge and survived *because of* their musical talents.

After resettlement, Cambodians collected libraries of traditional and popular Khmer music, usually tapes imported or copied from Thailand and Hong Kong, and although often static-filled and raspy, they were greatly treasured. In the early 1980s, groups of Cambodians immediately surrounded anyone just arrived from California with tapes to sell. As compact discs became popular, a number of men said they purchased a new car so they could play them. Many Cambodians own hundreds of videotapes, compact discs, digital video discs, and Blu-ray discs of tradi-tional and popular Khmer dances and songs and download them from the Internet. Live music is usual at Khmer celebrations and weddings, and at home, television programs are often muted as Khmer music plays in the background.

Many resettled Cambodians say Khmer music is the "sweetest sound" on earth, reminding them of childhood joys and of family and village life. "Oh, that reminds me of my grandmother!" Sonith exclaimed one day. "She loved that song and played it when she was happy. So it makes me happy, too." At weddings, guests inevitably described how a particular song reminded them of their own wedding or another treasured moment. Many, however, also commented that it was not always easy to listen to Khmer music, as it brought memories of suffering and loss, and some appreciated instead the strong beat and noise of American music.

After resettlement, Cambodians began performing Khmer music, some learning songs from cassette tapes brought from the refugee camps to perform for New Year and other celebrations and crafting Khmer musical instruments. In 1985, former farmer Rithy, who had never made an instrument before, made a three-stringed fiddle from a coconut shell found in an Asian market, an animal-skin covering, and three silk strings. He said it was "not good," but he had a pleased smile on his face as he strummed a few notes, and acclaimed master musician Sam-Ang Sam called him a skilled musician. Wedding music that is short, simple, and easy to remember has been popular with resettled Cambodians and their descendants, providing an incentive for many to learn to play Khmer music and instruments.

In the early 1980s, a few surviving professional musicians gathered with amateurs to form traditional orchestras with three-stringed fiddles (*tro khmae*), long-necked lutes (*chabey dang vaeng*), double-reed instruments (*pey brahos*), a monochord bow (*khsae muoy*), and handmade goblet drums (*skor areak*) with sculpted or inlaid decorations (Sam-Ang Sam 1994). Before performing, musicians make offerings of incense, candles, and food to their teacher spirits, usually in front of the small barrel drum believed to house the spirits of the arts. Over the years as Cambodians' resources increased, more musicians were able to perform for Khmer ceremonies and festivals and at concerts at universities, community centers, and multicultural fairs and events. Musicians Chinary Ung and Sam-Ang Sam performed at the White House, Carnegie Hall, and the Lincoln Center and won prestigious awards; Sam-Ang Sam was a MacArthur fellow in 1994.

However, Cambodians have found it difficult to keep Khmer music alive; communities can support only an occasional visit by traveling groups, and most musicians must work for a living. The lack of knowledgeable performers and musicians has caused numerous changes in Khmer musical ensembles: music is shortened and simplified, and the instrumentation is reduced (Sam-Ang Sam 1994). *Mohôri* instruments are often replaced by electronic organs, accordions, and saxophones. The Raksmey Khemera group used a Western recorder for the traditional flute and Northumbrian small pipes for the double-reed instrument (Light from Heaven 2006), and a *pin peat* ensemble included additional Khmer instruments and a recorder rather than a Khmer flute. Some ensembles substitute a banjo for a long-necked lute (Sam-Ang Sam 2010).

With most weddings reduced to an evening and a day or just part of a day, the repertoire of forty-two pieces, each associated with a particular ritual, has been shortened, and amateurs often take the place of professionals. Since many amateur musicians learn from family members or are self-taught from videos, compact discs, and occasional traveling performers, their play can be inconsistent and inaccurate (McKinley 2003); they often play the cymbals in a reversed manner. One professional musician said he allows amateurs to perform with him, and although their skills are rudimentary, they are at least present. Although practices are irregular and performances unrefined, Khmer audiences say they appreciate them.

Older Cambodians express sadness that their children prefer American and Asian pop to Khmer music. Finding traditional music boring, many young people prefer guitar, keyboard, and drums to traditional instruments. A few children are attracted to traditional music and hum and dance to it, and a student at Stanford studied the Khmer dharma song tradition that combines liturgical texts with complex melodies, recording nearly fifty hours of songs and photographing over one hundred manuscripts of dharma song masters (Humanities at Stanford 2010).

The more time young people spend with fellow Cambodians, the greater the likelihood they enjoy Khmer music. Some are interested in both Khmer and American music. During breaks in one traditional music class, a group rapped and danced the "electric slide" and "Macarena" in the 1990s during breaks, and in the 2010s, they dance hip-hop. A number of musicians combine Khmer and American music. Some say the improvisatory style of the Khmer two-stringed fiddle is good for playing American jazz, particularly Gershwin and early jazz. Kong Nay's "Mekong Delta Blues" can be downloaded from iTunes, and the songs of Cambodia's famous singer Meng Keo Pichenda can be heard on YouTube, as can the music of Sin Sisamuth, Pan Ron, and Ros Sereysothea, musicians who did not survive the Khmer Rouge, and Arn Chorn-Pond and Sam-Ang Sam, who did.

Cambodian Americans share music and videos through YouTube and online virtual communities. Cambodian Americans often want American-style music at their celebrations, and it is common to begin an evening

with Khmer music and dancing for older people, followed about nine or
ten o'clock by a band playing rock and roll while young people dance
American-style dances, adjusting their behavior to avoid offending their
elders, with boys dancing with boys and girls with girls or everyone dancing separately. Karaoke singing is popular, as are videos and CDs featuring lip-synching actors in lovely settings with the Khmer lyrics rendered
phonetically in English. Elaborate karaoke microphones are prominent
in many homes, and impromptu concerts are frequent. One woman said
of her husband, "Once he gets started, he'll sing all night if I let him."
I listened one evening as her husband sang karaoke for hours with his
brothers in Phnom Penh, laughing and weeping together, eight thousand
miles apart.

Other Cambodian Americans devote themselves to performance.
Several young men in Massachusetts who were more interested in
American than Khmer music grew interested in becoming musicians after
hearing a Latin group perform and deciding they could do the same.
Although discouraged by friends who told them, "You're short, you're
Cambodian. You're never going to make it," they formed a group, named
themselves Seasia, and asked renowned flute player Arn Chorn-Pond
advice on producing a compact disc. Their contact with the older musician
brought traditional music into their rap repertoire, and they contributed a
song to one of his recordings. The local community raised money to send
the band and Arn Chorn-Pond to Cambodia, where they performed with
music masters and appeared on television. After visiting Khmer Rouge
killing sites, one member wrote in a rap song, "As I reflect in the glass, in
the back of skull fractures . . . who could give me answers to all this killing?" (Rimer 2002).

A Cambodian American rapper in Long Beach named Prach Ly, or
praCh, produced a hip-hop album in his parents' garage in 2000; unable
to get it published, he handed it out to friends. A Phnom Penh radio and
television music host heard it in a local nightclub and realized it was the
first time he heard rap music that referred to the Khmer Rouge killings
(*AsiaWeek* 2001). After "The Khmer Rouge, Khmer Rap" was played on
the radio, praCh became the number one music artist in Cambodia. His
first album, *Dalama: The End'n Is Just the Beginnin'*, includes Khmer Rouge
propaganda speeches and family stories of Khmer Rouge survival. Telling
his story because "no one else was going to tell it for me," praCh raps a
survivor's plea: "All you can do is remind people what happened so it
doesn't happen again" (Schlung-Vials 2008: 207). Speaking to the tragedy
of resettlement, he wants to "knock down the walls / between me and my
parents," adding a hopeful "but since I'm bilingual / I'ma use communication as a bridge."

In his second album, *The Lost Chapter*, praCh included traditional *pin peat* music with Khmer instruments and used Khmer alternate singing (*apai*) as "sort of like rap music" (Schlung-Vials 2008). The Dengue Fever band of six American musicians and renowned Khmer singer Chhom Nimol reworked Khmer music of the 1960s and 1970s using Khmer and American styles and instruments, including an instrument that combines an electric guitar with a Khmer long-necked lute (Jenkins 2011). They have been well received in Cambodia, where they studied with master musicians, and their album, *Venus on Earth*, was selected by iTunes Store as one of the best world music records of 2008.

Since Cambodians' first years in America, they have spoken of Khmer dance as quintessentially Khmer, the pinnacle of their arts and the epitome of gentle, demure women, strong viral men, and adoring lovers. Dancers performed for Jackie Kennedy in Phnom Penh in 1967 and at the Kennedy Center in Washington, DC, in 1971. Khmer dance is inspired by themes of the *Reamker*, the Khmer version of the Indian *Ramayana*, episodes of Buddha's lives, Khmer myths, legends, and tales, and daily life. Cambodians say dancers are intermediaries between the ordinary and sacred worlds and see an "intrinsic bond" between the two thousand stone dancers carved at Angkor centuries ago and dancers today. In the nineteenth century, dance costumes, gestures, and movements were codified according to interpretations of Angkorean celestial dancers (Shapiro-Phim 2007). Dancers present offerings to the spirits before performances, asking guidance, and if pleased by the dancing, the deities respond with blessings.

Classical dance requires highly skilled and extensively trained dancers with extensive training to execute the formally composed and stylized positions, gestures, and expressions (Gardner 1999). Cambodians are proud of the stamina, flexibility, and discipline required by both male and female dancers, whose fingers and wrists are flexible from years of long and painful bending exercises. Costumes for classical dance are usually made of silk and brocade. They are gilded, encrusted with sequins and gems, and worn with tiaras, ornate headpieces, and elaborate masks (Wheelock 1990). In contrast, folk dances portray local legend and everyday life, and the costumes are simpler. Spontaneous and emotional rather than formal and prescribed, folk dance was traditionally performed in village squares or on crude stages by amateurs (Sam-Ang Sam and Chan Moly Sam 1987).

Cambodians began dancing their communal dances as soon as they were free of the Khmer Rouge, sometimes until dawn (Haing Nhor 1987). In the refugee camps, professional and amateur dancers with even the least bit of knowledge performed and taught dances hoping to dance their way to American resettlement (Stein 1981). After resettlement, Cambodians worried about how the loss in dancers and dance knowledge and Western influences would affect traditional Khmer dance. In Cambodia, a handful of artists re-established the School of Fine Arts and documented the work of older artists, and across America, dancers taught others and performed. Communities lacking dance troupes begged dancers to come to them. When Sam-Ang Sam visited Ithaca, New York, in 1986, he said Cambodians constantly invited him to dance in towns across the country. Repertoires were retrieved from memory, and costumes were adapted from whatever materials were available. Quality varied considerably, but that mattered little to most Khmer refugees; at performance after performance, Cambodians nudged me and exclaimed in wonder and delight, "This is Cambodian!"

Khmer leaders competed to expand their power and legitimacy by establishing dance troupes, and rivals often established several troupes in the same community. Professional dancers tried to improve dancing, forming troupes and teaching classes. Kong Theap, who danced at the Royal Palace before the war, taught classical and folk dance in San Francisco after resettlement and formed a professional troupe in Stockton, California. Local Cambodians assisted in teaching and sewing costumes and were so hungry for dance they attended not just performances but dance rehearsals (Catlin 1987). For years, professionals Sam-Ang Sam and Chan Moly Sam performed, recorded, and taught Khmer music and dance, and their professionalism and attention to detail was legendary. I helped a Khmer woman sew Sam-Ang Sam into his costume for a 1985 performance at Cornell University as he stood silently, meticulously directing and checking our work and encouraging the other dancers. Cambodians said that day they never thought during the terrible Pol Pot days they would be as happy again as they were watching his performance.

Since resettlement, Khmer dancers have frequently performed at both Khmer and American celebrations across the country: at the Smithsonian Institution, National Gallery of Art, Freer Gallery of Art, American Red Cross, schools, colleges, community centers, and art and heritage festivals and in the movies. The Angkor Dance Troupe of Lowell, Massachusetts, performed at the Clinton White House, visited Cambodia, and participated in a 2006 documentary about Khmer dance called *Monkey Dance*. Master dancers have participated in workshops at colleges and prestigious art venues, and more recently, artists and performers from Cambodia have become popular at casinos.

Over the years, performers have also come from Cambodia to perform. In 1990, the first cultural exchange between America and Cambodia since the Vietnam War occurred when Cambodia's National Dance Troupe visited, although there were problems with visas and unwelcoming refugees who resented visitors coming from their Vietnamese-dominated homeland (Haithman 1990). Dancers were distressed when they were threatened with kidnapping and knife attacks, but a preview performance was warmly received by the Long Beach community, some saying they were happy to learn that dance was alive in Cambodia. Additional trouble ensued when the star performer and four other dancers defected, causing considerable turmoil in Cambodia and among resettled Khmer (Butterfield 1990). Only a year later, however, dancers visited from a border camp and encountered no problems or encouragement to defect (Johnson 1991), and the 1990 defectors taught and performed in America in the following years with no apparent hostility, even when they performed for the visiting Cambodian minister of culture (Shapiro 1994). Dancers from Cambodia and America performed together in 1996 in Honolulu, including several who had defected in 1990.

Although some defections have occurred, tours have continued (Sam-Ang Sam 2010), and dancers say the interactions between artists in America and Cambodia have improved the quality of dance in both countries. Although dance classes have continued to be popular, Cambodians acknowledge that dance revitalization has been a challenge. Khmer dance is difficult, with forty-five hundred basic gestures and movements for some dances (Angkor Dance Troupe 2011). In temples, community centers, and homes on any given weekend, children of all ages practice the difficult and subtle steps. Teachers and students vary in quality, but the more renowned the teacher, the harder they press students to perform.

Numerous substitutions and abbreviations have been made to dances: court dance has yielded to folk dance, simple pieces substitute for difficult ones, shorter dances take the place of longer, regional variations are abandoned, and familiar portions are repeated (Sam-Ang Sam 2010). The New Year "Blessing Dance" that traditionally has seven dancers now usually has fewer. Cambodians say Khmer dance in America has been democratized, "open to anyone willing to learn" (Sam-Ang Sam 2010: 187). Some substitutions are not welcome, as when one troupe used ashtrays instead of coconuts for the "Coconut Shell Dance," insulting many older people. The number of young Cambodian Americans who consider traditional dance old-fashioned or quaint led to a shortage of dancing students in many communities. "I ain't dancing that sissy stuff," one young teenager said in the late 1980s, and another repeated the sentiment in 2014. Other youth who are interested are prevented from participating by family obligations. The vitality of dance in particular community usually depends on the personality and strength of teachers, popular student dancers, local leaders, and family encouragement.

Among other young Cambodian Americans, however, dance is important. In the early years of resettlement, a sixteen-year-old attending a folk opera performance at a New Year celebration in Long Beach said the event was a chance to "memorize my culture" (Holley and Kendall 1987). Since then, some students have said they studied dance so they could learn about their culture. Several dancers have gained considerable status as trained performers and role models for children. Cambodians say learning to dance helps maintain their heritage, and parents who have difficulty telling their children about their experiences can talk about what dancing represents and means to them. The first Cambodian American to compete in the Miss USA Pageant proudly stated that she was the principal dancer for the Cambodian Classical Ballet. Another teenager said, "I dance to show how beautiful Cambodians are. There has been so much ugly stuff about Cambodia, but dance is only beautiful."

Typical Khmer dances include the "Blessing Dance," performed at New Year celebrations to bestow blessings for the coming year. The "Dance Peacock" represents tribal people of northwest Cambodia, and the "Fishing Dance" portrays playful and energetic lovers fishing with rattan baskets and scoops. The women are shy but flirtatious, while the men are assertive and mischievous. In the "Fishing Dance," one couple becomes separated from the others, and as the young man grows assertive, the woman retreats. His attempts to placate her fail until he apologizes on bended knee. His renewed attentions are interrupted by the return of the group, and all return to their activities. Forced to exit on opposite sides, the young couple put index fingers to their mouths, subtly hinting they will meet again.

In a striking display of international recognition of Khmer dance, Sophiline Cheam Shapiro was invited to perform in Vienna on the 250th anniversary of Mozart's birth. On December 8, 2006, she performed "Pamina Devi: A Cambodian Magic Flute" at Schönbrunn Castle in Europe's oldest continually operating theater (Kourlas 2007). Sophiline Cheam Shapiro choreographed, directed, and danced a classic Khmer dance drama influenced by Mozart with a traditional dance troupe, four singers, and a *pin peat* ensemble of drums, marimba, gongs, reed instruments, and small brass cymbals, to which she added a bamboo flute as the "magic flute." The celestial beings of Cambodia appeared in the gold-gilded, jewel-box theater of Europe dressed in elaborate crowns, silks, and bejeweled fingers and ankles to tell a story of family struggle and a search for balance between tradition and individual choice. The art and beauty of Cambodians had spread far beyond small Cambodia, carried by Cambodian American citizens from a large and powerful nation who were driven to preserve and present their ancestral arts.

As Schlund-Vials (2012) has discussed in detail, Cambodian American artists have been prolific in "reimaging" the Cambodian cataclysm and the effects its losses have had on resettled Cambodians. Through music, dance, film, art, and memoirs, Cambodians are remembering their heritage in ways that challenge long-held political stances and solutions that continue the consequences of American activities on Southeast Asians, particularly Cambodians. As the years pass, the imaginings of Cambodian American writers, performers, and artists are expanding in size and impact.

The entry of Khmer refugees into the United States has been difficult, traumatic, and rewarding for both Cambodians and Americans. It also raises questions about meeting the challenge of refugees, both before and after they enter the country.

Chapter Twelve

Beyond Refugees

Americans often described Cambodians as a victimized group of Khmer Rouge survivors whose experiences of violence were the result of their own and their leaders' actions, characteristics, and national character. Daniel (1996: 7) suggests that ascribing violence to a particular people or place tranquilizes "those of us who live self-congratulatory lives in times and countries apparently free" of massive violence and leads us to think we are above such brutalities.

Dissolution: Creating Cambodian Refugees

To call Cambodians a violent people or to blame their suffering on their nature or incompetent leaders is to miss a broader reality: that Cambodia's devastation was less the result of refugee actions than it was of the actions of Cambodia's leaders, Vietnam's civil war, and the intervention of powerful countries trying to contain communism in the region. America's responsibilities to Cambodian refugees must be seen in light of America's role in creating them in the first place through military involvement in Southeast Asia and the withdrawal of support from neutralist Sihanouk to an anticommunist but incompetent general, which drew Cambodia further into the war and strengthened Cambodia's communists also (Hein 2006). America's military support and carpet bombing played a crucial role in bringing the Khmer Rouge regime to victory and the country to ruin. One young Cambodian said of those years, "America landed on us" (Sear 2004).

America's acceptance of Southeast Asian refugees was less a commendable act than an obligation. Cambodia was a country "whose peace we had shattered, whose balance we had tipped toward an unimaginable catastrophe" (Haines 2010: 461), and Cambodians would not have fled their country if not for its destabilization. This was not the stated intention of Americans, either citizens or leaders, who intended to help, not harm, Southeast Asians. Most people "most of the time, think they are doing good" (Davis 1992: 159), but Americans also tended to see other groups of people as different from them. Many said what had happened to Cambodians could not happen to Americans because "we are not like that." Most Americans remained blind to the actions of their leaders. An American pilot involved in the secret air war over Cambodia said he and his fellow airmen valued friendships with Khmer interpreters, but he does not discuss the consequences of his bombs on people, villages, fields, and stock (Wood 2002).

America's intentions, however noble or benevolent, had generational consequences. Khmer civilians suffered or died, and their descendants continue to suffer. American political, business, and military elites gained profit, advancement, and accolades, while their fellow Americans bore the burden of dealing with the consequences of resettling and financially supporting refugees (Nordstrom 2004; Maier 1996). When a young Cambodian learned in the early 1980s that professors and students throughout America shut down their universities in the spring of 1970 to protest the war in Southeast Asia, he was shocked, wondered if they were communists, and asked why Americans had not cared about Cambodians then. Years later, after America invaded Iraq, he said he then understood why Americans demonstrated against expanding the war in Cambodia, but he wished the United States had done more to help his country, saying, "Then I wouldn't be a refugee. I'd be home."

Cambodian Americans have increasingly recognized America's role in Cambodia's tragedy. Him Chanrithy (2000) includes B-52 targets on her map in *When Broken Glass Floats* to illustrate America's illegal bombing. A 45-year old man, who was only a year old when the Americans began bombing Cambodia, said indignantly in 2009, "I have the right to be here because the United States ruined my country." When asked if someone had questioned his right to be in America, he replied, "Oh, at work they always ask me why I am here." In accent-free English, he continued, "The bombs killed our culture and our self-esteem. Then the Khmer Rouge killed us."

Broken Promise: Evaporated and Faded Resettlement Services

The amount of assistance given to refugees from Vietnam, Laos, and Cambodia is difficult to overstate. Millions of Southeast Asian refugees were resettled by hundreds of thousands of Americans working for thousands of agencies in hundreds of cities and towns across America.

Americans who disagreed vehemently over politics and religion cooperated to assist people who came with the shirts on their backs and little
else, spoke no English, and seemed unprepared to enter the American
workplace or society. After acknowledging that refugee workers operated
on little foreknowledge of refugee arrivals, inadequate preparation, and
confusion over funding and resources, both Americans and Cambodians
had suggestions on how resettlement could be improved but these were
often ignored. Despite massive levels of assistance, several negative patterns in its administration were evident across the country.

American refugee workers and health providers did not adequately
recognize or understand Cambodians' lingering psychological trauma,
thus compounding their resettlement difficulties (McLellan 1995).
Although research was conducted on refugee needs and behaviors, most
resettlement agencies and workers did not utilize research conclusions
and had little knowledge or training on how to deal with refugees,
Cambodians, or torture survivors. Research on Southeast Asian refugee
mental health reveals that prevention and treatment programs have continued to have difficulties such as developing appropriate and effective
services, obtaining or retaining clients, and meeting client compliance
and satisfaction.

While some researchers realized Cambodians would benefit from their
practices, few programs accepted or were even aware of their advice, to
the detriment of Khmer refugees (Leakhena Nou 2008). Programs that
attempted to meet refugee needs but lacked cultural sensitivity often
had unanticipated consequences (Rasbridge and Marcucci 1992): some
Cambodians became permanent clients of physical or mental health facilities, developed unrealistic expectations of what providers could do for
them, or avoided services altogether. Many Americans saw Cambodians'
problems "as temporary, isolated, deviant, unique, atypical, [and] non-
recurring" (Stein 1981: 64), and Cambodians agreed, saying Americans
viewed refugees as poor, helpless victims rather than strong resilient
people.

Such a view led some Americans to ignore refugee capabilities to overcome their experiences. Such a view also led some Americans to fail to learn
the lessons of the past, leading to programs being constantly "invented"
to solve newly perceived problems (Stein 1981). Some Cambodians suggested their countrymen should be using their resiliency to solve their
problems rather than complain; others said they hoped their experiences
would be a cautionary tale to policymakers about the need for appropriate mental health services for refugees arriving in the future (Theanvy
Kuoch et al. 1996). Vireth said resettlement services could have been better
but added, "The world is not a fair place. Would young men who had it

rough in poor neighborhoods in America rather have been killed under the Khmer Rouge or still be living in refugee camps?"

While America honored its obligation to resettle Khmer refugees, the burden was carried by a minority of Americans. Initially welcoming, many Americans shifted from interest to disinterest in a remarkably short time (Truong 2007). Cambodians' usefulness in helping the country recover from the discord of the Vietnam "conflict" proved ephemeral, and most Americans perceived refugees to be more foreign and problem-causing than they had anticipated. No longer useful or interesting, Americans tired of Khmer refugees and turned their attentions elsewhere. Even policymakers and refugee workers did not realize the level of services needed by illiterate and rural rice farmers, widows, poorly educated laborers, and soldiers who had endured years of torture and hardship and were poorly equipped to deal with learning a new language and developing skills appropriate in a Western context.

For people who had lived in simple houses without electricity, running water, or modern appliances, the complexities of life in their new country were often overwhelming. Because Americans never understood the level of assistance required, provisions were never made to provide the quantities of assistance and support needed by many. The expectation of self-sufficiency for many Cambodians was also unreasonable, and educational plans failed largely because of American inattention to the social and cultural realities of refugee lives.

In addition, the arrival of Khmer refugees was followed by a recession that led to rising economic concerns for many Americans (Ryono 2010). Refugee services were reduced and then halted; as a consequence, benefits granted by the Refugee Act of 1980 were not accompanied by adequate financial reimbursements to the states, and as initial grants faded, states were left unable to fund programs. In addition, funding to private agencies and nongovernmental organizations had been drastically reduced by the early 1990s.

Particularly egregious for Khmer refugees was welfare reform instigated in the mid-1990s. The anti-immigrant provisions of welfare reform threatened Khmer recipients with the withdrawal of support the American government had given them since rescuing them from the refugee camps. Cambodians had experienced governmental betrayal before, most atrociously by Khmer Rouge leaders, but they said it was especially shocking to face abandonment by the government that rescued them. Many were seized with fears of homelessness and the return of the disorder and chaos they had experienced two decades before. By failing to provide the resources and support necessary to enable refugees to gain the education and jobs they needed to secure income adequate to support their families and deal with their memories, coupled with the later reduction in refugee health and social services, the United States broke the commitment made to Khmer refugees.

Broken Resettlement Promise Par Excellence: Deportation

Cambodians consider that the major broken promise made to them has been permanent residency in America. Congressional Acts in 1975 and 1980 mandated permanent resettlement to eligible Southeast Asian refugees in the aftermath of the Second Indochina War, including Khmer refugees resettled in the United States. Although America has historically refused entry to immigrants who have criminal records and deported immigrants who commit crimes after arrival, Cambodians differed from other immigrants by being given permanent refuge.

In response to terrorist threats and increased illegal immigration, however, Congress passed the Illegal Immigration Reform and Immigration Responsibility Act in 1996, which expanded the types of crimes resulting in permanent exile for noncitizens. The category of crimes making immigrants eligible for deportation was expanded from aggravated felony crimes such as gang violence, drug offenses, welfare fraud, and possession of illegal weapons to include petty crimes such as driving while intoxicated, shoplifting, and marijuana possession. Cambodians were not immediately deported, however, because of the absence of official relations between the United States and Cambodia and Cambodia's refusal to accept returned Cambodians (Watanabe 2003).

Amid the heightened anti-immigration sentiments that followed attacks on the east coast on September 11, 2001, the federal government authorized the arrest, detainment, and deportation of hundreds of thousands of refugees and immigrants. Representative Lamar Smith, coauthor of the 1996 deportation law, claimed that strict adherence to the law would make the country safer, and other officials said the agreement would make deportation fairer, claiming non-Americans convicted of crimes are routinely required to leave the country and Cambodians who are convicted lose their protected status as refugees (Watanabe 2003).

After the American government increased pressure on Cambodia to accept deportees, the two countries signed a repatriation agreement in 2002, with Cambodia agreeing to accept fifteen hundred deportees (Hing 2005). Khmer refugees who committed crimes and had not become citizens were subject to deportation after completing their prison terms in the United States. Effective retroactively, convicted noncitizens sentenced to at least one year of prison regardless of how long they had been in the

United States could be deported. Provisions for fairness hearings were eliminated, denying deportees the right of due process and making it more difficult to obtain waivers from deportation (Heim 2007). Deportation laws also removed the ability of immigration judges to consider discretionary factors, such as length of residency in America and family ties.

The first group of six Khmer refugees was deported to Cambodia in June 2002 (Borann Heam 2003). A seventeen-year-old, after being tried as an adult for his first offense on a felony charge, spent seven and a half years in state penitentiary and, on his release, was immediately turned over to immigration officials (Hanifah 2002). One man was ordered deported after being convicted of urinating in public, and a woman, whose children were born in the United States and are thus citizens, faced deportation after serving three years in jail for disciplining her offspring with unlit incense sticks. Several thousand Cambodians were deported in the 2000s (Ryono 2010), and in 2011, one out of three young Cambodians knew someone who had been deported or was facing deportation (Khmer Girls in Action 2011).

Deportation shocked the Khmer community; many were unaware that acceptance as refugees did not bestow citizenship on them. Having been reassured for years they could not be deported, Cambodians now discovered that was not the case. Unlike siblings born in the United States and unless their parents had applied for citizenship on their behalf, young refugees remained permanent residents until majority, at which time they could apply for citizenship (Isett 2009). Most, however, were unaware of their legal options, and those least aware of the legal subtleties of citizenship and immigrant status were the most likely to live in families struggling with resettlement in disadvantaged neighborhoods where criminal activity was common. Cambodians asked if they could be deported if they did something Americans disliked. One woman said her American neighbor hates the smells of Khmer cooking and threatened daily to call the landlord. "The landlord is okay. He's Vietnamese, so he likes my cooking. But if she goes to the government, will they send me back to Cambodia?" she asked. Cambodians were never fully persuaded they could not be deported by angry neighbors, bosses, husbands, or "the government."

Cambodians and their families were devastated when threatened by deportation. Deportation meant a life sentence "of the strangest sort" (Isett 2009): shipped to a country to live with strangers. Deportees had no idea how they were going to survive in a country whose ways were as foreign to them as they would be to any American. After struggling to adjust to a new life in America, they were now to undergo the experience again, this time alone and with little hope, compassion, family, or help and little prospect of escaping poverty. Most deportees had little or no memory of Cambodia, since they had left as small children or were born in Thailand (Bennion 2011). Many did not know Cambodia had a king, could not pick out its location on a map, and did not know the name of the prime minister.

Most had lived in the United States an average of twenty years, could not read or write Khmer or even speak it fluently, had done poorly in school, and experienced considerable family conflict (Toness 2010). Many worried they would not be accepted or would be attacked in Cambodia because, several said, "there is no rule or law there." One man told Sear (2004), "If someone kills you, no one is going to investigate why." The Cambodian Embassy in Washington, DC, stated that deportees have the same rights as other Cambodians and have not been mistreated, but there were reports that deportees were victims of extortion and other serious crimes and, when imprisoned, were subjected to torture, including electric shock, near-asphyxiation with plastic bags, and mock executions (Chak Sopheap 2009). Deportees found adjustment to life in Cambodia difficult, in part because native-born Cambodians viewed deportees as different from them. One deportee said that after two and a half years, his neighbors still called him "the American."

Some deportees said they were glad to have access to television, radio, or other electronic devices. A dropout from the Puget Sound area was deported after a drunken fight with his girlfriend and, in Cambodia, has learned to plow, transplant rice, and cast fishing nets from his father-in-law (Heim 2007). He wears clothes he brought with him but has lost thirty pounds, survives on money he receives from his family in Seattle, and carries a mobile phone to talk weekly with his mother and follow Washington sports. His worries about the Cougars of Washington State University beating the University of Washington's Huskies have been replaced by worries about whether he will have enough rice and fish to eat or will ever see his children again. He plays his American CDs on a stereo powered by clamping cables to a car battery but says he does not play them often because they depress him.

A number of deportees have developed bonds with other deportees, some before deportation, some after. Fifty Cambodians in a Bakersfield penitentiary awaiting deportation connected "like brothers because most of them have families that can't afford to go visit them in Cambodia" (Hanifah 2002). Saying no one understands their situation as well as those who share it, deportees gathered on weekends in Phnom Penh, often at the Sweet Home bar on Street 51, bearing tattoos and dressed in hip-hop clothing. One deportee said that when he is with returnees, "I'm back in the States," no longer missing the culture, lifestyle, hanging out, and handshakes he knew before.

Deportee adjustments to Cambodia included introducing American music and dance to Cambodians (Melamed 2005). Other deportees work with social agencies to provide services to other deportees. One man returned to Cambodia in 2002 after spending a third of his resettled life in juvenile detention and prison. He earns three dollars a day doing maintenance, plumbing, and painting for a nonprofit agency and dreams of going back to school and becoming an elementary school teacher. His earnings and those of his wife, who sews piecework to pay for food for their small family, barely keep them alive, but he says his life has turned around.

Critics of the deportation of Khmer refugees describe deportation policies as part of a larger program of expulsion introduced during periodic episodes of anti-immigrant hysteria in America (Chak Sopheap 2009). Immigration has often become a political issue during presidential election campaigns, and the 1996 deportation law was signed in September as Clinton was struggling for re-election. Fear was also a factor in deportation policies, beginning with the September 11, 2001, terrorist attacks. Although Khmer deportees are not American citizens in the legal sense, they are not illegal, and their experience in America calls into question definitions of citizenship (Sear 2004). Neither are many Khmer refugees technically citizens of Cambodia, particularly those born in Thailand's refugee camps. Critics said deportees experienced legal double jeopardy because their offenses occurred long before deportation policies were announced and they had served out their sentences. One man fighting deportation in the Bay area noted, "This is a double punishment" (Mangaliman 2002).

Critics claimed many deportees were poorly represented at their trials or pressured by immigration officials to accept "final orders of removal" in exchange for temporary release from indefinite detention, without understanding the implication of doing so (Southeast Asia Resource Action Center 2002). Critics also called deportation policies cold and antiseptic (Hing 2006), noting that "the War on Terrorism" "normalized violations of immigrants' civil, constitutional, and human rights" (Borann Heam 2003). The House of Representatives approved a federal resolution honoring the victims of the Cambodian genocide and pledging the pursuit of justice for them, while simultaneously deporting their children (Lefferts 2003). Deportation was also expensive. While Americans were suffering from an economic recession, the government was spending millions to deport fathers and husbands back to Cambodia (Bennion 2011) and spending more to support families they left behind.

Deportation has had enormous consequences for deportees. The world's most powerful country accepted them, many when they were children, and then rejected them, expelling youngsters the country produced itself, one deportee saying, "We're the product of the American system" (Cowan 2010: 456). Refugees who came to America as children and never knew Cambodia are certainly more the children of America than of Cambodia. America then returned them to one of the world's poorest countries—the one that had slaughtered their families—with no provisions for rehabilitation or resettlement. These youth had no part in their flight, resettlement, or placement and were doing in their environment what their parents had done in Cambodia: trying to survive. While the American resettlement program was built on good intentions and expended enormous resources on behalf of Cambodians, it failed to provide many with a safe environment or resources for integrating into American society. From the violence of the Khmer Rouge, many young Cambodians grew up on America's violent streets where shelter, education, and knowledge were inferior or scarce.

Living in poor, splintered, and struggling families, many turned to gang membership for protection and crime for survival (Chak Sopheap 2009). The consequences for deportees' families left behind were also severe, not only removing the main support of many, but leaving them grieving the possibility of permanent loss of a family member (Hanifah 2002). Some observers saw the deportation of Cambodian refugees as a quiet campaign to break up refugee families (Ryono 2010), but of more import in explaining American immigrant policy decisions has been American ignorance about Cambodians' experiences during the Khmer Rouge years and the consequences of deportation. Protests against deportation occurred across the country. In late 2002, families gathered for a "Day of Action against Deportation" in various American cities, and a protest held in Long Beach was attended by Cambodian, Latino, and other civil rights groups. On Martin Luther King Jr. Day in 2011, three hundred people of varying ethnicities and religions gathered at immigration offices in Philadelphia to protest Khmer deportation (Bennion 2011).

While protests and rallies attracted attention to the Khmer deportation issue, of greater import to declining Khmer deportation has been the aging out of refugees who arrived as youth and never attained citizenship. Young people of Khmer ethnicity now in the United States were born in America and are thus American citizens. As Cambodians who came as young refugees near their forties, the number of Cambodians subject to deportation is falling, but those deported continue to suffer (Large 2015).

Improving Refugee Resettlement

Refugee resettlement in the United States has not been a qualified success for Cambodians. The acts perpetrated by the Khmer Rouge endured long past their relatively brief reign. The first consequence of the Khmer Rouge regime has been the separation of Cambodians from their homeland and one another: Cambodians who thought they had won the resettlement lottery rethought that idea as they increasingly realized their losses and estrangement from the homeland, their new country, and their own children. The best way to improve refugee resettlement is to render it unnecessary. After fifteen years of Southeast Asian resettlement, many UNHCR officials questioned the appropriateness of resettlement as a durable solution, seeing it as a pull factor that drew numerous people for economic and social reasons (Robinson 1998). Many other observers wondered the same, one noting that the decision of refugees in refugee camps to seek resettlement was "more the taking of a plunge than an enthusiastic reaction to a pull" (Kunz 1973: 134). As an Hungarian military officer familiar with displaced people noted over 150 years ago, "There is no greater curse in the world for any cause than a demoralized emigration and the handling of its affairs is the most thankless task on this earth" (Kunz 1973:133, from Janossy 1851-1852:688).

American leaders who made the decisions to drop bombs on Cambodia have never taken responsibility for their decisions and actions and have not been held sufficiently accountable for the harm they rendered to millions of people in multiple countries, nor have the refugees they helped create benefited from their concern or assistance (Hruby 2009). Instead, the refugee burden was taken up by hundreds of thousands of American citizens and millions of American taxpayers who had little to do with making decisions about war, many of whom demonstrated against American military involvement in Southeast Asia. Since the decisions to take America into war are made by a small number of leaders, it is difficult to know how citizens can resist them; despite American resistance to past wars, leaders have often pressed on with their own plans. It is regrettable that the political, social, and financial efforts expended on behalf of Cambodian refugees over the decades could not have prevented the conflict that resulted in their displacement.

When resettlement becomes the best option for refugees, its consequences need to be dealt with more caution, planning, and resources than was given Khmer refugees. Cambodians placed in poor, violent neighborhoods and ineffective schools have had the least success in adjusting to American life and the least economic success, which has hurt Americans as well as refugees. Many resettled Cambodians have been hardworking but say they have had marginal results. Kuong Chhang Ly describes her father as growing old with resettlement, saying her father "had worked beyond his limits" (2010: 341). One voluntary agency resettling refugees recognized as early as 1983 that "meaningful resettlement requires a few years, not a few months" (Church World Service 1983: 75), saying it is unrealistic to think that ninety days of support can prepare refugees for full-time employment. Resettling survivors of torture may take even more time, services, and resources.

When public and private funds, resources, and people cooperated to assist refugees, Cambodian refugees fared best. Most Cambodians and Americans concluded early on that intensive English and vocational training courses were more appropriate than early employment for both illiterate farmers and laborers and those who came with advanced skills or professional training (Church World Service 1983). Whatever their previous economic and social situation or the suffering they had endured, Cambodians who received intensive language and employment training for as long as several years did better than those who did not. Church World Service found that refugees' mastery of English "strongly correlates" with higher rates of employment and lower rates of public assistance (1983: 77). The organization also found that providing English training for women at home helped prevent family tensions, culture shock, and general adjustment problems and helped women gain employment when their children were older.

A clinical psychologist with the Center for Victims of Torture in Minneapolis, Minnesota, says the trauma and subsequent effects described by Khmer refugees are markedly similar to the experiences of other refugees (Brown 2003), whether they come from Bosnia, Liberia, West Africa, or the Middle East. Her claim that refugees are best able to work through their trauma when they are resettled in an "enriched environment" that pays close attention to emotional as well as physical needs is supported by other researchers (Theanvy Kuoch 2015; Watters 2001). She says also that initial investments in language and vocation training and cultural orientation are advantageous for both Khmer refugees and American taxpayers because they transform refugees into taxpayers themselves rather than welfare recipients, and their families consequently do better in resettlement.

American refugee decision-makers and workers frequently neglected previous research on providing effective services for refugees and tended to treat specific refugee situations as unique, atypical, individual historical events rather than behaviors, problems, and situations that recur in multiple contexts, times, and regions. Communities are more successful with refugees when government, education, religious, and social services agencies cooperate; when one agency is befuddled by a problem, another may be successfully coping with it. As the United States becomes increasingly diverse, with immigrants and refugees from throughout the world becoming American citizens, many communities are finding that adjustment by both Americans and migrants is facilitated when Americans listen to others describe their lives; learn formally and informally about other groups and customs; participate in educational, civic, social, political, and recreational activities with them; and cooperate with them in finding solutions for resettlement problems (Tajima and Harachi 2010).

If Americans are going to invite others to share citizenship with them, the burden of adjustment falls on both migrants and Americans. When people of different cultures, including Cambodian refugees and their children, are our neighbors and play with our children, we have reason to get to know them (Eck 2001). After conducting a sophisticated survey of their peers, young Cambodian Americans in Long Beach came up with a list of recommendations for future work with Cambodians (Khmer Girls in Action 2011). Because so many speak poor English, although born in America and educated in American schools, the group suggests that Cambodian Americans with little or poor English proficiency be provided with programs that develop English language skills and translation and interpretation assistance when needed.

The Khmer Girls in Action group encourages the provision of information about college preparation and application processes to Khmer students and their parents and active interaction with high school students to prevent them from dropping out. They also suggest that curriculum for elementary and secondary school grades include information on Cambodians' experiences and history and that educators develop cultural competency training for school counselors, provide information on contraception options other than abstinence, and have knowledge about available mental health services. The perceptive suggestions of these young people provide encouragement for the continuing interest and ability of all Americans to live with one another.

Resettled Cambodians in the United States are resilient. They have experienced and survived extremely difficult circumstances. They have navigated uncertainty, learned a new language and incorporated new practices, and adapted Khmer ways to maintain their identity. Although Cambodians often talk about how life continues to be a struggle, many remain optimistic about the future. A man who arrived when he was thirty-one said recently, "I am sixty-five and I have survived. My children will survive, too, and we Cambodians will be Americans for a long time." Just weeks after that, a woman said, "We Cambodians lived with the Khmer Rouge. We survived. We came to America and survived. And our children will survive. I know they are American. I hope they will be Khmer."

Bibliography

Abdulrahim, Raja. 2009. "US Charges Three Men with Having Sex with Children in Cambodia," *Los Angeles Times*, 1 September.

Affonço, Denise. 2009. *To the End of Hell: One Woman's Struggle to Survive Cambodia's Khmer Rouge*. London: Reportage Press.

Ahuja, Sarita, and Robert Chlala. 2013. *Widening the Lens on Boys and Men of Color*. San Francisco: Asian Americans/Pacific Islanders in Philanthropy.

Allman, TD. 1990. "Sihanouk's Sideshow," *Vanity Fair*, April.

American Community Survey. 2007. "American Community Survey." Retrieved 3 August 2013 from http://www.census.gov/acs/ www/ guidance_for_data_users/comparing_2007/.

Andrist, Steve. 1983. "Refugees Encounter Some Bias," *Rochester Post-Bulletin* (Rochester, MN), 14 November.

Ang Chouléan. 1997. "Les manuscrits Khmers: Survol thématique," *Kambodschanische Kultur* 5: 53–62.

Angkor Dance Troupe. 2011. "Troupe History," Angkor Dance Troupe, Inc. Retrieved 28 July 2011 from http://www.angkordance. org/history.html.

Applied Research Center. 2001. *Welfare Reform as WE Know It*. Oakland, CA: Applied Research Center.

Arabas, Jan. 2012. "Cambodian Diaspora Artists in the US," Cambodia Studies Conference, Northern Illinois University, DeKalb, 13–16 September.

Ardery, J. 2008. "Cambodian Settlers Glaze a Donut Trail," *Daily Yonder*, 18 February. Retrieved 1 July 2010 from http://www.dailyyonder.com/ cambodian-settlers-glaze-donuttrail/2008/02/18/1062.

AsiaWeek. 2001. "Hard Rap on the Rouge: A Pirated CD Stuns Young Cambodians with Their History," *AsiaWeek*, April 19. Retrieved 1 April 2011 from http://khmer.cc/community/t.c?b=12&t=490.

Associated Press. 2004. "Man Sentenced for Sex with Cambodian Boys," *Spokesman Review (Spokane, WA)*, 26 June.

Baker, RP, and DS North. 1984. *The 1975 Refugees: Their First Five Years in America*. Washington, DC: New TransCentury Foundation.

BaoChannara. 2012. "My Donut Shop Is to Open Later This Month," *Khmerlife*, 13 March. Retrieved 29 March 2012 from http:// www. khmerlife.com/show thread.php/1813-My-donut-shop-is-to-open-later-this-month.

Baughan, David M, et al. 1990. "Primary Care Needs of Cambodian Refugees," *Journal of Family Practice* 30(5): 565–68.

Baxter, Kevin. 2008. "A Real Diamond in the Rough," *Los Angeles Times,* 18 February, A1.

Becker, Elizabeth. 1986. *When the War Was Over: Cambodia's Revolution and the Voices of Its People.* New York: Simon and Schuster.

Becker, Gay, and Yewobdar Beyene. 1999. "Narratives of Age and Uprootedness among Older Cambodian Refugees," *Journal of Aging Studies* 13(3): 295–314.

Beers, Carole. 1990. "Cambodian Dancers' Visit Has Historical Significance," *Seattle Times,* 20 September. Retrieved 29 July 2011 from http://community. seattletimes.nwsource.com/archive/?date=19900920&slug=1094092.

Bennion, David. 2011. "On MLK Day, Philadelphians Protest Ice's Deportation of Cambodian Refugees," *Citizen Orange,* Philadelphia, 17 January. Retrieved 10 January 2012 from http://www.citizenorange.com/orange/2011/01/on-mlk-day-philadelphians-prot.html.

Beydoun, Lina. 2004. "Review, Ideology and Cultural Production: Buddha Is Hiding: Refugees, Citizenship, the New America," *Contemporary Sociology: A Journal of Reviews* 33: 684–85.

Bhuyan, R, et al. 2005. "Women Must Endure according to their Karma"— Cambodian Immigrant Women Talk about Domestic Violence," *Journal of Interpersonal Violence* 20(8): 902–921.

Bock, Paula. 1999. "Phnom Penh Connections—A Generation of Former Refugees Balance Lives in Two Worlds—the Cambodia They Once Fled and the Northwest that Gave Them the Determination to Go Back and Help," *Seattle Times,* 11 July, 20–30.

Borann Heam. 2003. "History Sleeps for No One: War, Militerrorization and Southeast Asians," *Objector,* San Francisco.

Boreth Sun. 1989. "My Personal Experience." In *The Far East Comes Near. Autobiographical Accounts of Southeast Asian Students in America,* ed. Lucy Nguyen-Hong-Nhiem and Joel Martin Halpern, 115–20. Amherst: University of Massachusetts Press.

Boutrous Boutrous-Gahli. 1993. *Fourth Progress Report of the Secretary General on the United Nations Transitional Authority in Cambodia.* New York: UN Security Council, April.

Brandon, Karen. 1996. "Actor's Murder Rekindles Fears of Cambodians," *Sunday Oregonian* (Portland, OR), 10 March, A21.

Briggs, Lawrence P. 1951. *The Ancient Khmer Empire.* Philadelphia: American Philosophical Society.

Brown, Karen. 2003. "Voices of Experiences: Cambodian Trauma in America," WFCR radio, Amherst, MA, 5 March. Retrieved 10 May 2011 from http://www.theinfinitemind.com/mind260. htm.

Bruno, Ellen. 1984. *Acculturation Difficulties of the Khmer in New York City.* New York: Cambodian Women's Program, American Friends Service Committee.

Bruno, Ellen, and Ellen Kuras, directors. 1984. *House of the Spirit: Perspectives on Cambodian Health Care.* American Friends Service Committee, 42 min., videocassette.

Buckley, Brendan M, et al. 2010. "Climate as a Contributing Factor in the Demise of Angkor, Cambodia, *Proceedings of the National Academy of Sciences* 107(15): 6748–52.

Bunkong Tuon. 2013. "Inaccuracy and Testimonial Literature: The Case of Loung Ung's *First They Killed My Father: A Daughter of Cambodia Remembers*," *MELUS: Multi-Ethnic Literature of the US* 38(3): 107–25.

Butterfield, Fox. 1990. "Cambodia Troupe's Star Dancer Stays in US," *New York Times,* 18 October, A10.

Cafazzo, Debbie. 2008. "Tacoma Couple Serves up Cambodian Khmer Cuisine," *Herald Business Journal,* 3 September. Retrieved on 4 September 2010 from http://www.theheraldbusinessjournal.com/apps/pbcs.dll/article?aid=/20080908/BIZ/709089974&template=bizmobileart.

Cambodia Adoption Connection. 2012. "Cambodia Adoption Connection," Cambodia Adoption Connection. Retrieved 18 September 2012 from http://www.cambodiaadoptionconnection.com.

Cambodian Alliance for the Arts. 2011. "Emerging Hip Hop Artist/Producer—Phinale," Cambodian Alliance for the Arts, 11 March. Retrieved 2 February 2012 from http://www. cambodianallianceforthearts.com/emerging-hip-hop-artistproducer-/.

Cambodian Association of Illinois. 2000. *Campaign for Hope and Renewal.* Chicago: Cambodian Association of Illinois.

Cambodian Health Network. 2012. "About Khmer Health Advocates," Cambodian Health Network. Retrieved 10 March 2012 from http://www.cambodianhealth.org/.

Campbell, P. 1983. "Dispersal or Concentration? Placement Strategies and Secondary Migration," *Refugees* 18: 6.

Carlson, Eve B, and Rhonda Rosser-Hogan. 1991. "Trauma Experiences, Posttraumatic Stress, Dissociation, and Depression in Cambodian Refugees," *American Journal of Psychiatry* 148: 1548–51.

Carter, Richard. 1992. *The Gentle Legions: National Voluntary Health Organizations in America.* New Brunswick, NJ: Transaction Publishers.

Catlin, Amy (ed.). 1987. *Apsara: The Feminine in Cambodian Art.* Los Angeles: The Woman's Building.

CBC News. 2009. "Marketing of Unhealthy Cereals to Kids 'Staggering': Yale Study," *CBC News,* 27 October. Retrieved 25 February 2012 from http://www.cbc.ca/news/story/2009/10/27/consumer-unhealthy-kids-cereals-yale.html.

Chak Sopheap. 2009. "Agony of Repatriated Khmer Rouge Refugees," *UPI Asia,* 29 April. Retrieved 10 January 2011 from http://www.upiasia.com//04/29/agony_of_repatriated_ Khmer_ rouge_ Human_Rights/2009 refugees/5361/.

Chan, Sucheng. 2003. *Not Just Victims: Conversations with Cambodian Community Leaders in the United States.* Chicago: University of Illinois Press.

———. 2004. *Survivors: Cambodian Refugees in the United States.* Chicago: University of Illinois Press.

Chandakhan Nuon. 1983. "My Story—by Chandakhan Nuon." Unpublished paper distributed locally by literacy volunteer, Debbie Bender, Ithaca, NY.

Chandler, David P. 1982a. "Seeing Red: Perceptions of Cambodian History in Democratic Kampuchea." In *Revolution and Its Aftermath in Kampuchea: Eight*

Essays, ed. David Chandler and Ben Kiernan, 34–56. New Haven, CT: Yale University Southeast Asia Studies.

———. 1982b. "Songs at the Edge of the Forest: Perceptions of Order in Three Cambodian Texts." In *Moral Order and the Question of Change: Essays on Southeast Asian Thought,* ed. DK Wyatt and A Woodside, 53–77. New Haven, CT: Yale University Southeast Asia Studies.

———. 1983. *A History of Cambodia.* Boulder, CO: Westview Press.

———. 1991. *The Tragedy of Cambodian History: Politics, War, and Revolution.* New Haven, CT: Yale University Press.

———. 1994. Preface to *Cambodian Culture Since 1975: Homeland and Exile,* ed. May M Ebihara, Carol A Mortland, and Judy Ledgerwood, xi–xiii. Ithaca, NY: Cornell University Press.

———. 2010. "Looking Back at US-Cambodian Relations: A Personal View," Embassy of the United States," Phnom Penh, July 21. Retrieved 16 December 2012 from http://www. cambodia.usembassy. gov/academic_ symposium_ david_chandler.html.

Chareundi, Van-Si. 1992. *Understanding Southeast Asian Cultures: Their Cultural Traits and Implications in Casework Practice.* Oak Grove, OR: Asian American United Press.

Charny, Joel, and John Spragens. 1984. *Obstacles to Recovery in Vietnam and Kampuchea: US Embargo of Humanitarian Aid.* Boston: Oxfam America.

Chileng Pa and Carol A Mortland. 2005. *Escaping the Khmer Rouge: A Cambodian Memoir.* Jefferson, NC: McFarland.

Chira, Susan. 1993. "For Refugees, Help with Double Burden of Child-Rearing," *New York Times,* 9 December.

Choi, Yoonun, Michael He, and Tracy W Harachi. 2008. "Intergenerational Cultural Dissonance, Parent-Child Conflict and Bonding, and Youth Problem Behaviors among Vietnamese and Cambodian Immigrant Families," *Journal of Youth and Adolescence* 37(1): 85–96.

Chor Chanthyda. 2004. "An Analysis of the Trickster Archetype as Represented by the Rabbit Character in Khmer Folktales," MA thesis. Buddhist Institute of Cambodia, Phnom Penh.CAMBO SASTRA. Retrieved 27 March 2012 from http://www.cambosastra. org/?p=1158.

Chou Meng Tarr. 1990. "A Talk with Prime Minister Hun Sen," *Cambodia 1990, Cultural Survival Quarterly* 14(3): 6–10.

Chou Ta-Kuan [Zhou Daguan]. 1992. *The Customs of Cambodia,* 2nd edn, trans. from French version of Paul Pelliot by J. Gilman D'Arcy Paul. Bangkok: Social Science Association Press.

Chung, Rita Chi-Ying. 2001. "Psychosocial Adjustment of Cambodian Refugee Women: Implications for Mental Health Counseling," *Journal of Mental Health Counseling* 23(2): 115–26.

Church World Service. 1983. *Making It on Their Own: From Refugee Sponsorship to Self-Sufficiency.* New York: Church World Service.

———. 2001. *Manual for Refugee Sponsorship.* New York: Church World Service, Immigration and Refugee Program.

Cockle, Richard. 1995. "E. Oregon Harvest of Morels Mushrooms," *Oregonian* (Portland, OR), 23 May, B1, B4.

Coedès, George. 1968. *The Indianization of Southeast Asia*. Honolulu: University of Hawaii Press.

Coleman, Cynthia M. 1987. "Cambodians in the United States." In *The Cambodian Agony*, ed. DA Ablin and M Hood, 354–74. Armonk, NY: ME Sharpe.

Consortium. 1982. "Intensive English Language and Cultural Orientation," The Consortium of Experiment in International Living, World Education, Save the Children, Panat Nikhom Refugee Camp, Chonburi, Thailand.

Cowan, Sylvia R. 2010. "Forced Return: The Deportation of Former Cambodian Refugees from the US." In *Cambodian American Experiences: Histories, Communities, Cultures and Identities*, ed. Jonathan HX Lee, 454–58. Dubuque, IA: Kendall Hunt Publishing.

Criddle, Joan D. 1992. *Bamboo and Butterflies: From Refugee to Citizen*. Dixon, CA: East/West Bridge.

Criddle, Joan D, and Mam Teeda Butt. 1987. *To Destroy You Is No Loss: The Odyssey of a Cambodian Family*. New York: Atlantic Monthly Press.

Croke, Vicki. 1994. "Miami's Tiger: An Innocent Killer," *Boston Globe*, 11 June, 25.

Cultural Orientation Resource Center. 2012. "About COR Center: Our History," Cultural Orientation Resource Center. Retrieved 4 March 2012 from http://www.cal.org/co/about/history. html.

Daggett, Stephen. 2010. "Cost of Major US Wars," Congressional Research Service, 29 June. Retrieved 15 August 2012 from http://www.fas.org/sgp/crs/natsec/RS22926.pdf 2010.

Daniel, E Valentine. 1996. *Charred Lullabies: Chapters in an Anthropography of Violence*. Princeton, NJ: Princeton University Press.

Darina Siv. 2000. *Never Come Back: A Cambodian Woman's Journey*. St Paul, MN: Writer Press.

D'Avanzo, CE, Barbara Frye, and R Froman. 1994. "Culture, Stress and Substance Use in Cambodian Refugee Women," *Quarterly Journal of Studies on Alcohol* 55: 420–26.

Davis, J. 1992. "The Anthropology of Suffering," *Journal of Refugee Studies* 5(2): 149–61.

Davis, RE. 2000. "Refugee Experiences and Southeast Asian Women's Mental Health," *Western Journal of Nursing Research* 22(2): 144–68.

Department of Justice. 2015. "Cambodian Man Sentenced to Six Months for Marriage Fraud," United States Attorney's Office, District of Maine, July 16. Retrieved 9 August 2015 from http://www.justice.gov/usao-me/pr/cambodian-man-sentenced-six-months-marriage-fraud.

Detzner, Daniel F. 2004. *Elder Voices: Southeast Asian Families in the United States*. Walnut Creek, CA: AltaMira Press.

Dillingham Commission. 1911. *Dillingham Commission: Statistical Review of Immigration 1820–1910; Distribution of Immigrants 1850–1900*. Harvard University Library Collections Program. Retrieved 27 July 2012 from http://ocp.hul.harvard.edu/immigration/vcsearch. ?any=3.2002.1654.2.

Dith Pran, ed. 1997. *Children of Cambodia's Killing Fields*. New Haven, CT: Yale University Press.

Donahue, Deirdre. 1985. "Cambodian Doctor Haing Ngor Turns Actor in the Killing Fields, and Relives His Grisly Past," *People* 23(5), 4 February. Retrieved

28 March 2012 from http://www.people.com/people/archive/ article/0,20089843,00.html.

Douglas, Thomas James. 2004. "Crossing the Lotus: Race, Religion and Rationality among Cambodian Immigrants in Long Beach and Seattle," PhD dissertation. University of California, Irvine.

Dunn, Ashley. 1995. "Shadows of the Khmer Rouge Haunts Cambodians in US," *New York Times*, 14 August, A1, 9.

Ebihara, May M. 1971. "Svay, A Khmer Village in Cambodia," PhD dissertation. Columbia University, New York. Ann Arbor, MI: University Microfilms.

———. 1985. "Khmer." In *Refugees in the United States: A Reference Handbook*, ed. David W. Haines, 127–47. Westport, CT: Greenwood Press.

Eck, Diana. 2001. *A New Religious America: How a "Christian Country" Has Now Become the World's Most Religiously Diverse Nation*. San Francisco: Harper San Francisco.

Economic Institute of Cambodia. 2009. "Cambodia Economic Watch," Economic Institute of Cambodia, April. Retrieved 15 October 2012 from http://www. wds.worldbank.orgt.

Efron, Sonni. 1990. "Column One: A Culture Struggles to Survive: The Cham, a Group of Indochinese Muslims, Maintain a Strict Regimen in the Face of Southland Lifestyle. But Try as They May to Prevent It, Some Practices Are Fading," *Los Angeles Times*, 25 November, 1.

Eisenbruch, Maurice. 1991. "From Post-Traumatic Stress Disorder to Cultural Bereavement: Diagnosis of Southeast Asian Refugees," *Social Science and Medicine* 33(6): 673–80.

Ellis, Tony. 2006. "Oni Vitandham's Cambodian Legacy: On the Wings of Hope," *Iowa Source: Iowa's Enlightening Magazine*, July. Retrieved 31 July 2011 from http://www.iowa source.com/books/oni_0706.html.

Erikson, Kai T. 1976. *Everything in Its Path: Destruction of a Community in the Buffalo Creek Flood*. New York: Simon and Schuster.

Etcheson, Craig. 2005. *After the Killing Fields: Lessons from the Cambodian Genocide*. Westport, CT: Praeger Publishers.

Federale. 2011. "Who I Became: Violent, Dangerous, and Welfare Dependant," Federale, 16 May. Retrieved 12 January 2013 from http://federaleagent86. blogspot.com/2011/05/who-i-became-violent-dangerous-and.html.

Fein, Helen. 1987. *Congregational Sponsors of Indochinese Refugees in the United States, 1979–1981: Helping beyond Borders*. Cranbury, NJ: Associated University Presses.

Fiffer, Sharon S. 1991. *Imagining America: Paul Thai's Journey from the Killing Fields of Cambodia to Freedom in the USA*. New York: Paragon House.

Fifield, Adam. 1998. "The Apologist in Suburbia: Pol Pot's Comrade Enjoys the Quiet Life in Westchester," *Village Voice*, New York, 5 May. Retrieved 21 October 2013 from https://www. google.com/#q=Thiounn+Prasith.

Findlay, Trevor. 1995. *Cambodia: The Legacy and Lessons of UNTAC*. SIPRI Research Report 9. Oxford: Oxford University Press.

Finot, Louis. 1916. *Notes d'épigraphie indochinoise*. Hanoi: Imprimerie d'Extrême-Orient, 4.

Fisher-Nguyen, Karen. 1994. "Khmer Proverbs: Images and Rules." In *Cambodian Culture Since 1975, Homeland and Exile,* ed. MM Ebihara, CA Mortland, and Judy Ledgerwood, 91–104. Ithaca, NY: Cornell University Press.

Fletcher, Roland, et al. 2006. "The Greater Angkor Project 2005–2009: Issues and Program." In *Uncovering Southeast Asia's Past: Selected Papers from the 10th International Conference of the European Association of Southeast Asian Archaeologists,* ed. EA Bacus, IC Glover, and VC Pigott, 347–54. Singapore: National University of Singapore Press.

Flinn, John. 1995. "Success the Old-Fashioned Way: Cambodians Making Dough before the Sun Shines," *San Francisco Chronicle,* 30 April.

Fox-Martin, Stuart, and Bunheang Ung. 1986. *The Murderous Revolution.* Bangkok: Tamarind Press.

Froese, Brian. 2006. "Compassion and Culture: Southeast Asian Refugees and California Mennonites," *Journal of Mennonite Studies Research Papers* 24: 129–48.

Frommer, Arthur. 1987. "Tours for the Jaded: Cambodia to Red Sox Baseball Camp," *Chicago Sun-Times,* 30 August. Retrieved 10 April 2012 from http://www.highbeam.com/doc/1PP2-3842717.html.

Frye, Barbara A, and Carolyn D D'Avanzo. 1994. "Cultural Themes in Family Stress and Violence among Cambodian Refugee Women in the Inner City," *Advances in Nursing Science* 16(3): 64–77.

Fujiwara, Lynn. 2010. "Cambodian American Women and the Politics of Welfare Reform." In *Cambodian American Experiences: Histories, Communities, Cultures and Identities,* ed. Jonathan HX Lee, 312–29. Dubuque, IA: Kendall Hunt Publishing.

Galto, Shay. 2010. "Oral History in Cambodia after the Khmer Rouge," Report on Research Supported by the USOAR and EYE Grant, History of Genocide-Cambodia. Northern Illinois University, DeKalb.

Gardner, Janet. 1999. *Dancing through Death: The Monkey, Magic and Madness.* Janet Gardner Filmmakers Library, 56 min.

Go, Charles G, and Thao N Le. 2005. "Gender Differences in Cambodian Delinquency: The Role of Ethnic Identity, Parental Discipline, and Peer Delinquency," *Crime & Delinquency* 51(2): 220–27.

Gong-Guy, E. 1987. *The California Southeast Asian Mental Health Needs Assessment.* Oakland, CA: Asian Community Mental Health Services.

Gordon, Linda. 1987. *Southeast Asian Refugee Migration to the United States.* Washington, DC: Office of Refugee Resettlement, US Department of Health and Human Services, September.

Gorer, Geoffrey. 1936. *Bali and Angkor or Looking at Life and Death.* London: Michael Joseph Ltd.

Graff, EJ. 2009. "Out of Cambodia," *Washington Post,* January 9. Retrieved 9 April 2012. http://www.washingtonpost.com/wpdyn/content/article/2009/01/09/AR2009010903118.html.

Graham, EA, and Jip Chitnarong. 1997. "Ethnographic Study among Seattle Cambodians: Wind Illness," *Ethnomed,* November 1. Retrieved 10 March 2012 from http://ethnomed.org/ clinical/culture-bound-syndromes/ethnographic-study-among-cambodians-in-seattle.

Grigg-Saito, Dorcas, et al. 2010. "Long-Term Development of a 'Whole Community' Best Practice Model to Address Health Disparities in the Cambodian Refugee and Immigrant Community of Lowell, Massachusetts," *American Journal of Public Health* 100(11): 2026–29.

Grognet, Allene Guss. 1981. "Refugees and the English Language: A Crucial Interface," *Journal of Refugee Resettlement* 1(4): 43–50.

Haines, David W. 1980. "Mismatch in the Resettlement Process: The Vietnamese Family versus the American Housing Market," *Journal of Refugee Resettlement* 1(4): 15–21.

———. 2010. "Epilogue." In *Cambodian American Experiences: Histories, Communities, Cultures and Identities*, ed. Jonathan HX Lee, 460–74. Dubuque, IA: Kendall Hunt Publishing.

Haing Ngor, with Roger Warner. 1987. *A Cambodian Odyssey*. New York: Macmillan.

———. 2003. *Survival in the Killing Fields*. New York: Basic Books.

Haithman, Diane. 1990. "Applause, Not Protests, Greets Cambodian Troupe," *Los Angeles Times*, 12 September. Retrieved 3 February 2012 from http://articles.latimes.com/1990-09-12/entertainment/ca-294_1_cultural-exchange.

Hanifah, Sophia. 2002. "A New Nightmare: Cambodian American Deportation Carries History's Weight," *Asian Week*. Retrieved 4 October 2010 from http://asianweek.com/2002_11_ 22/ feature.html.

Hansen, Anne R. 1988. *Crossing the River: The Secularization of the Khmer Religious Worldview*, MA thesis. Harvard Divinity School, Cambridge, MA.

Hansen, Anne R, and Bounthay Phath. 1987. "Understanding Suffering in the Context of Khmer Buddhism: Preliminary Research Observations," unpublished paper, Harvard University, Cambridge, MA.

Hardin, Garrett. 1995. *The Immigration Dilemma: Avoiding the Tragedy of the Commons*. Washington, DC: Federation for American Immigration Reform.

Hardy, Rodger L. 2006. "Please Help Soben Huon, First Cambodian-American to Go to Miss USA Pageant," *Deseret Morning News, KI Media*, 21 March. Retrieved March 27, 2012 from http://ki-media.blogspot.com/2006/03/please-help-soben-huon-first-cambodian.html.

Harper, Lee. 1960. *To Kill a Mockingbird*. Philadelphia: JB Lippincott.

Harris, Ian. 2005. *Cambodian Buddhism: History and Practice*. Honolulu: University of Hawaii.

Hart, Jordana. 1990. "Cambodian Refugees Preyed on by Gangs," *Boston Sunday Globe*, 15 July.

Hartocollis, Anemona. 2004. "Fleeing the Killing Fields, But Not Escaping," *New York Times*, 17 October. Retrieved 11 December 2005 from http://www.nytimes.com/2004/10/17/nyregion/thecity/fleeing-the-killing-fields-but-not-escaping.html.

Headley, Robert K, Jr. 1977. *Cambodian-English Dictionary*, vols 1 and 2. Washington, DC: Catholic University of America Press.

Heim, Kristi. 2007. "Banished to the Land His Family Once Fled," *Seattle Times*, 4 February, 1, 12, 13.

Hein, Jeremy. 2006. *Ethnic Origins: The Adaptation of Cambodian and Hmong Refugees in Four American Cities*. New York: Russell Sage Foundation.

Heininger, Janet E. 1994. *Peacekeeping in Transition: The United Nations in Cambodia; A Twentieth Century Fund Report.* New York: Twentieth Century Fund Press.

Higham, Charles. 1989. *The Archaeology of Mainland Southeast Asia: From 10,000 BC to the Fall of Angkor.* Cambridge: Cambridge University Press.

Him, Chanrithy. 2000. *When Broken Glass Floats.* New York: WW Norton.

Hin Sithan. 1992. "Democratic Kampuchea: Cause for Its Fall, Reasons for the Vietnamese Invasion, and Possible Solutions," unpublished.

Hing, Bill Ong. 2005. "Detention to Deportation—Rethinking the Removal of Cambodian Refugees," *UC Davis Law Review* 38(3): 891–971.

———. 2006. *Deporting Our Souls . . . Values, Morality, and Immigration Policy.* Cambridge: Cambridge University Press.

Hoffman, Nathaniel. 2008. "Stalking the Morel Carpet: Global Mushroom Culture Hits the Idaho Forest," *Boise Weekly,* 18 June. Retrieved 19 November 2012 from http://www. boiseweekly.com/boise/stalking-the-morel-carpet/ Content?oid=937052.

Holley, David, and John Kendall. 1987. "Folk Opera: Cambodians' 'Memory and Yearning' Satisfied by Long Beach Performance," *Los Angeles Times,* 12 April. Retrieved 16 February 2011 from http://articles.latimes.com/1987-04-12/news/ mn-1192_1_folk-opera.

Hopkins, MaryCarol. 1996. *Braving a New World: Cambodian (Khmer) Refugees in an American City.* Westport, CT: Bergin and Garvey.

Horng Kouch. 1989. "My Bloody Nightmare." In *The Far East Comes Near: Autobiographical Accounts of Southeast Asian Students in America,* ed. Lucy Nguyen-Hong-Nhiem and Joel Martin Halpern, 142–49. Amherst: University of Massachusetts Press.

Hruby, Patrick. 2009. "Field of Schemes?" *Outside the Lines,* ESPN, 19 November. Retrieved 1 March 2012 from http://sports.espn.go.com/espn/eticket/ story?page=JoeCook.

Huffman, Franklin. 1970. *Cambodian System of Writing and Beginning Reader.* New Haven, CT: Yale University Press.

Immigration and Customs Enforcement. 2010. "12 More Indicted in Large-Scale Cambodian Marriage Fraud Conspiracy," Immigration and Customs Enforcement, 30 September. Retrieved 14 September 2013 from https://www. ice.gov/news/releases/12-more-indicted-large-scale-cambodian-marriage-fraud-conspiracy#wcm-survey-target-id.

Im Sothearith. 2010. "Monk's Poetry Describes Grim Refugee Camps," *Voice of America Khmer,* 5 April. Retrieved 28 March 2012 from http://www.voanews. com/khmer-english/news/a-40-2010-04-05-voa2-90235112.html.

Ingrassia, Michele. 1994. "America's New Wave of Runaways," *Newsweek,* 4 April, 64–65.

Isett, Stuart H. 1994. "From Killing Fields to Mean Streets (Gang Activity among Young Cambodians in the US)," *World Press Review,* 1 December. Retrieved 1 April 2011 from http://business.highbeam.com/136920/ article-1G1-15966091/ killing-fields-mean-streets.

———. 2009. "Cambodian Gangs in America: Then and Now," *Norococo,* 15 April. Retrieved 18 March 2010 from http://norococo.blogspot.com/2009/04/ featured-story-cambodian-gangs-in.html.

Jánossy, Dennis Anthony. A Kossuth-Emigráció angliában és amerikában, 1851-1852. Budapest, Hungary: Magyar Történelmi Társulat.

Jazzar, Michael, and Carl Hamm. 2007. "A School Leader's Guide to Improving the Achievement, Assimilation, and Improvement of Montagnard Children," National Council of Professors of Educational Administration, 2 April. Retrieved 23 February 2012 from http://cnx.org/content/m14423/latest/.

Jenkins, Mark. 2011. "Dengue Fever: Turning Up the Heat at Black Cat," *Washington Post*, 9 June. Retrieved 3 February 2012 from http://www. washingtonpost.com/lifestyle /style/dengue-fever-turning-up-the-heat-at-black-cat/2011/06/09/AGmqh2 NH_story.html.

Johnson, Kevin. 1991. "Cambodian Dancers' US Tour Collapse," *Los Angeles Times*, 5 October, A22.

Johnson, Kevin R. 2003. *The Huddled Masses Myth: Immigration and Civil Rights.* Philadelphia: Temple University Press.

Kam, Katherine. 1989. "A False and Shattered Peace," *California Tomorrow*, Summer, 8–21.

Kampuchea Review. 1982. "Chheng Phon [and] Others Address Drama Day Ceremony," *Kampuchea Review*, March 31, H1.

Kass, Jeff. 1997. "Harvesting Old and New: Group Serves American Feast with Dash of Cambodian Culture," *Los Angeles Times*, 23 November. Retrieved 16 February 2000 from http://articles.latimes.com/1997/nov/23/local/me-56867.

Keller, Stephen L. 1975. *Uprooting and Social Change: The Role of Refugees in Development.* Delhi: Manohar Book Service.

Khing Hoc Dy. 1994. "Khmer Literature Since 1975." In *Cambodian Culture Since 1975: Homeland and Exile*, ed. May M Ebihara, Carol A Mortland, and Judy Ledgerwood, 27–38. Ithaca, NY: Cornell University Press.

Khmer Girls in Action. 2011. "Khmer Girls in Action Case Report on the Progress of Cambodian Resettlement in Long Beach," A Report by Khmer Girls in Action, November 2011. Long Beach, CA. Retrieved March 7, 2012 from http://www.kgalb.org/images/misc/PAR%20Survey.Report/KGA_Full%20 Report. pdf.

Khmer Institute. 2000. "Review of *First They Killed My Father: A Daughter of Cambodia Remembers*, Loung Ung." Retrieved 9 October 2011 from http://www. khmerinstitute. org/ung.html.

Khmers Kampuchea-Krom Federation. 2009. "Khmer Krom People Statistics." Retrieved 22 September 2011 from http://www.khmer krom.org/node/31. 2.

Khuon Kiv. 1997. "The Darkness of My Experience." In *Children of Cambodia's Killing Fields: Memoirs by Survivors*, ed. Dith Pran, 100–3. New Haven, CT: Yale University Press.

Kiernan, Ben. 1990. "The Genocide in Cambodia, 1975–1979," *Bulletin of Concerned Asian Scholars* 22(2): 35–40.

———. 1996. *The Pol Pot Regime: Race, Power and Genocide in Cambodia under the Khmer Rouge, 1975–79.* New Haven, CT: Yale University Press.

———. 2003. "The Demography of Genocide in Southeast Asia," *Critical Asian Studies* 35(4): 587–88.

Kiernan, Ben, and Chanthou Boua. 1982. *Peasants and Politics in Kampuchea 1942–1981.* London: Zed Press.

Kiljunen, Kimmo. 1983. "The Tragedy of Kampuchea," *Disasters* 7(2): 129–41.

Kilong Ung. 2009. *Golden Leaf, a Khmer Rouge Genocide Survivor.* KU Publishing LLC, self-published.

Kimball, Nancy. 2008. "Mushroom Pickers Clear Out After Fight," *Daily InterLake.com,* 15 July. Retrieved 12 January 2012 from http://www.daily interlake.com/news/local_montana/article_a5745d16-92de-5632-bcc0-74f6615 c1d38.

KI Media. 2006. "Upcoming Book: *On the Wings of a White Horse* by Oni Vitandham," *KI Media,* 24 March. Retrieved 31 July 2011 from http://kimedia. blogspot.com/2006/03/ upcoming-book-on-wings-of-white-horse.html.

———. 2007. "Nhiek Bun Chhay Proposes the Closing of NRP Radio Program," *KI Media,* 31 August. Retrieved 18 April 2011 from http://ki-media.blogspot. com/2007/08/nhiek-bun-chhay-proposes-closing-of-nrp.html.

———. 2008. "Ex-Cambodian King Fighting Cancer," *KI Media,* 27 December. Retrieved 31 July 2011 from http://ki-media.blogspot.com /2008/12/ex-cambo dian-king-fighting-cancer.html.

———. 2009. "King-Father in His Own Words: He Receives Funds from the CPP and Its Leaders to Maintain an Honorable Life . . . NOT from the State of Cambodia?" *KI Media,* 9 February. Retrieved 31 July 2011 from http://ki-media.blogspot.com/2009 /02/king-father-in-his-own-words-he.html.

Kimsong, Kay, and John Maloy. 2006. "Tournament Sets Stage to Pass On Fighting Tradition," *Cambodia Daily,* 6 October. Retrieved 18 February 2011 from http://www.camnet.com.kh/ cambodia.daily/selected_features/cd-oct-6-2006.htm.

Kinzie, J David, et al. 1984. "Post-traumatic Stress Disorder among Survivors of Cambodian Concentration Camps," *American Journal of Psychiatry* 141: 645–50.

———. 1990. "The Prevalence of Posttraumatic Stress Disorder and Its Clinical Significance among Southeast Asian Refugees," *American Journal of Psychiatry* 147: 913–17.

Knoll, Corina. 2010. "A New Year for Cambodian Americans," *Los Angeles Times,* 5 April. Retrieved 16 February 2011 from http://articles.latimes.com/2010/ apr/05/local/la-me-cambodian-new-year5-2010apr05.

Kolbot Khmer. 2008. "To Khmers in Thailand," *The Son of the Khmer Empire,* 18 October. Retrieved 29 May 2012 from http://sokheounpang.wordpress.com/ tag/khmer-khmer-kandal/.

Kourlas, Gia. 2007. "Mozart Tale With Accent of Cambodia." *New York Times,* 11 October.

Krich, John. 1989. "Culture Crash," *Mother Jones,* 24–26 October, 52–53.

Kulig, Judith C. 1991. "Role, Status Changes and Family Planning Use among Cambodian Refugee Women," PhD dissertation. University of California, San Francisco.

Kunz, EF. 1973. The Refugee in Flight: Kinetic Models and Forms of Displacement," *International Migration Review* 7(2): 125–46.

Kuong Chhang Ly. 2010. "Between Two Lives." In *Cambodian American Experiences: Histories, Communities, Cultures and Identities,* ed. Jonathan HX Lee, 332–42. Dubuque IA: Kendall Hunt Publishing.

Kwan, Yvonne. 2008. "Antidote to the Poison Tree: Ways Khmer American Youth Negotiate the Ghosts of the Past, Present, and Future," *San Diego Ethnic Studies,* University of California, 2007–2008 Honors Program, June 9.

LaFreniere, Bree, and Daran Kravanh. 2000. *Music through the Dark: A Tale of Survival in Cambodia.* Honolulu: University of Hawaii Press.

Lap Minh Siu. 2009. "Developing the First Preliminary Dictionary of North American Jarai," MA thesis. Texas Tech University, Lubbock.

Large, Jerry. 2003. "Service in Cambodia Feeds the Souls of Seattle Couple," *Seattle Times,* 29 June, M2.

———. 2015. "End This Pattern: Stop Deporting People to Places They Never Lived," *Seattle Times,* April 26.

Leakhena Nou. 2006. *A Qualitative Examination of the Psychosocial Adjustment of Khmer Refugees in Three Massachusetts Communities.* Boston: Institute for Asian American Studies, University of Massachusetts.

———. 2007. "Exploring the Psychosocial Adjustment of Khmer Refugees in Massachusetts from an Insider's Perspective." In *Southeast Asian Refugees and Immigrants in the Mill City: Changing Families, Communities, Institutions—Thirty Years Afterward,* ed. Tuyet-Lan Pho, Jeffrey N Gerson, and Sylvia R Cowan, 173–91. Burlington: University of Vermont Press.

———. 2008. "A Sociological Analysis of the Psychosocial Adaptation of Khmer Refugees in Massachusetts." In *Strengths and Challenges of New Immigrant Families: Implications for Research, Theory, Education, and Service,* ed. RL Dalla, John Defrain, and Julie M Johnson, 33–51. Lexington, MA: Lexington Press.

Leclère, Adhémard. *Histoire du Cambodge.* Paris: Euthner, 1914.

Ledgerwood, Judy. 1990a. "Changing Khmer Conceptions of Gender: Women, Stories, and the Social Order," PhD dissertation. Department of Anthropology and Southeast Asia Program, Cornell University, Ithaca.

———. 1990b. "Portrait of a Conflict: Exploring Changing Khmer-American Social and Political Relationships," *Journal of Refugee Studies* 3(2): 135–54.

Lee, Jonathan HX. 2002. "Pilgrimage of the Spirit: Connecting with My Ancestors," *Review of Vietnamese Studies* 2(1). http:// Retrieved 5 October 2009 from hmongstudies.com/Lee2002.pdf.

———. 2010. "Cambodian American Ethics of Identity Formation." In *Cambodian American Experiences: Histories, Communities, Cultures, and Identities,* ed. Jonathan HX Lee, 343–53. Dubuque, IA: Kendall Hunt Publishing.

Lee, Juliet P, and B Soller. 2010. "Drug-Intake Methods and Social Identity: The Use of Marijuana in Blunts among Southeast Asian Adolescents and Emerging Adults," *Journal of Adolescent Research* 25: 783–806.

Lefferts, Jason. 2003. "Honoring Victims of Cambodia Genocide," *Lowell Sun,* 20 November. Retrieved 1 April 2011 from http://khmer.cc/community/t.c?b=1&t=1258.

Lester, Robert C. 1973. *Theravada Buddhism in Southeast Asia.* Ann Arbor: University of Michigan Press.

Levin, Claudia and Lawrence Hott. 1991. *Rebuilding the Temple: Cambodians in America,* Florentine Films. Retrieved 8 April 2012 from http://www.folk-streams.net/context, 235.

Lewis, Denise Clark. 2000. "From Cambodia to the United States: The Disassembly, Reconstruction, and Redefinition of Khmer Identity," MA thesis. University of Kentucky.

———. 2008. "Types, Meanings and Ambivalence in Intergenerational Exchanges among Cambodian Refugee Families in the United States," *Ageing & Society* 28: 693–715.

———. 2009. "Aging Out of Place: Cambodian Refugee Elders in the United States," *Family and Consumer Sciences Research Journal* 37(3): 376–93.

Light from Heaven. 2006. "Music of Cambodia," Light from Heaven. Retrieved 24 January 2012 from http://www.lightfromheaven.org/cambodia.html.

Lin, Nancy J, Karen L Suyemoto, and Peter Nien-chu Kiang. 2009. "Education as Catalyst for Intergenerational Refugee Family Communication about War and Trauma," *Communication Disorders Quarterly* 30(4): 195–207.

Linna Teng. 2012. "*Khmao Euy Khmao*: Colorism among Cambodian Americans," Cambodia Studies Conference, Northern Illinois University, 13–16 September.

Loung Ung. 2000a. *First They Killed My Father: A Daughter of Cambodia Remembers.* New York: HarperCollins.

———. 2000b. "Hello Fellow Khmers." Khmer Institute, 13 December. Retrieved 31 October 2011 from http://www.khmerinstitute.org/comments/comr6.html.

Lowell Sun. 2007. "Martin J. McNulty . . . Lowell Attorney, Activist in Cambodia; 56," *Lowell Sun* (Lowell, MA), 28 February, 1.

Ly Y. 2000. *Heaven Becomes Hell: A Survivor's Story of Life under the Khmer Rouge,* ed. John S. Driscoll. New Haven, CT: Yale University Southeast Asian Studies.

MacSwan, Angus. 2010. "Cocktails with Khmer Rouge Killers," *Global News Journal,* 30 July. Retrieved 18 February 2011 from http://blogs.reuters.com/global/2010/07/30/cocktails-with-khmer-rouge-killers/.

Maher, Daniel. 2010. "Indochinese Resettlement Program. aka: Operation New Life," *Encyclopedia of Arkansas History and Culture.* Retrieved 8 November 2010 from http://encyclopediaofarkansas.net/encyclopedia /entry-detail. aspx?entryID=5562.

Mai Bunla. 2013. *Shoulders to Freedom: A Cambodian Diaspora Memoir.* North Charleston, SC: CreatSpace Independent Publishing Platform.

Maier, Karl. 1996. *Angola: Promises and Lies.* Rivonia, UK: William Waterman.

Mangaliman, Jessie. 2002. "INS Deports 11 Cambodian Refugees Convicted of Various Crimes," *San Jose Mercury News,* 18 October.

Marcucci, John L. 1986. "Khmer Refugees in Dallas: Medical Decisions in the Context of Pluralism," PhD dissertation. Southern Methodist University, Dallas, TX.

Markham, James M. 1992. "Writer Admits He Fabricated an Article in *Times Magazine*," *New York Times,* 22 February, A:1.

Marosi, Richard, and Charles Ornstein. 2002. "Man Kills 2, Then Self at Wedding Party," *Los Angeles Times,* January 7. Retrieved 10 November 2012 from http://articles.latimes. com/2002/jan/07/local/me-20856.

Marshall, Grant N, et al. 2005. "Mental Health of Cambodian Refugees 2 Decades after Resettlement in the United States," *Journal of the American Medical Association* 294(5): 571–79.

———. 2006. "Rates and Correlates of Seeking Mental Health Services among Cambodian Refugees," *American Journal of Public Health* 96(10): 1829–35.

Marston, John. 1997. "Cambodia 1991–94: Hierarchy, Neutrality and Etiquettes of Discourse," PhD dissertation. University of Washington, Seattle.

Mason, Linda, and Roger Brown. 1983. *Rice, Rivalry, and Politics. Managing Cambodian Relief.* Notre Dame IN: University of Notre Dame Press.

Massey, Douglas S, and Magaly Sanchez R. 2010. *Brokered Boundaries: Immigrant Identity in Anti-Immigrant Times.* New York: Russell Sage Foundation.

May-lee Chai. 1994. "Rockwall, Texas," *Seventeen* 53(11): 136–41.

May, Sharon. 2004. "Beyond Words: An Interview with Soth Polin." In *In the Shadow of Angkor: Contemporary Writing from Cambodia,* ed. Frank Stewart and Sharon May, 9–20. Honolulu: University of Hawaii Press.

McCullough, Ken. 1994. "Translating U Sam Oeur," *Artful Dodge,* Iowa City, 20 June. Retrieved 27 March 2012 from http://www3.wooster.edu/artfuldodge/introductions/2627/ mccullough.htm.

McGill, Doug. 2006. "A Supreme Patriarch of Cambodian Minnesotans," *McGill Report,* 24 February. Retrieved 27 October 2008 from http://www.mcgillreport.org/tepvong06.htm.

McGinnis, Theresa Ann. 2009. "Seeing Possible Futures: Khmer Youth and the Discourse of the American Dream," *Anthropology & Education Quarterly* 40(1): 62–81.

McKinley, Kathy. 2003. "Cambodian Music and Dance in the Diaspora: Social Cohesion and Transnationalism through the Performing Arts," Canadian Ethnic Studies Conference, 2–5 October.

McLellan, Janet. 1995. *Cambodian Refugees in Ontario (Canada): An Evaluation of Resettlement and Adaptation.* Toronto: York Lanes Press.

McMillian, Meta. 1981. "Sponsors Sought for Cambodian Refugees," *Pittsburg Press,* 21 September, A2.

Mehmet, Ozay, M Tahiroglu, and AL Eric. 2002. "Social Capital Formation in Large-Scale Development Projects," *Canadian Journal of Development Studies* 23: 335–37.

Melamed, Samantha. 2005. "Stranger in Their Homeland: Cambodians Deported from the US Build New Lives on Fragile Foundations," *Cambodia Daily,* 30–31 July. Retrieved 28 April 2011 from http://www.camnet.com .kh/cambodia. daily/-7-selected_features/cd-30a05.htm.

Mellen, Greg. 2007. "Helping 'The People Left Behind,'" *Tate Publishing,* 7 June. Retrieved 4 September 2011 from http://www.tatepublishingnews.com/tag/on-the-wings-of-a-white-horse/.

———. 2011. "Obituary: Wat Khemara Buddhikaram's Abbot Ven. Dr. Kong Chhean," *Long Beach Press Telegram,* 11 January.

Mollica, Richard F. 1986. "The Trauma Store: The Psychiatric Care of Refugee Survivors of Violence and Torture." In *Post Traumatic Therapy and Victims of Violence,* ed. Frank M. Ochberg, 295–314. New York: Brunner/Mazel.

———. 2004. "Surviving Torture," *New England Journal of Medicine* 351(1): 5–7.

Mollica, Richard F, and Russell R Jalbert. 1989. *Community of Confinement: The Mental Health Crisis in Site Two (Displaced Persons Camps) on the*

Thai-Kampuchean Border. Alexandria, VA: Committee on Refugees and Immigrants, World Federation for Mental Health.

Mollica, Richard F, G Wyshak, and J Lavelle. 1987. "The Psychosocial Impact of War Trauma and Torture on Southeast Asian Refugees in American," *Journal of Psychiatry* 144(22): 1567–72.

Mollica, Richard F, et al. 1990. "Assessing Symptom Change in Southeast Asian Refugee Survivors of Mass Violence and Terror," *American Journal of Psychiatry* 147: 83–88.

Mong, Adrienne. 1994. "A Home in the Bronx," *Far Eastern Economic Review* 157: 38–39.

Moon, Anson, and Nathaniel Tashima. 1982. *Help Seeking Behavior and Attitudes of Southeast Asian Refugees.* San Francisco: Pacific Asian Mental Health Project.

Moore, Elizabeth. 1992. "Cambodian Refugees: Troubled Past, Troubled Present Trap," *News Tribune* (Tacoma, WA), 31 May, A1, 13.

Mortland, Carol A. 1987. "Transforming Refugees in Refugee Camps," *Urban Anthropology* 16(3–4): 375–404.

———. 1993. "Patron-Client Relations and the Evolution of Mutual Assistance Associations." In *Refugee Empowerment and Organizational Change: A Systems Perspective,* ed. Peter W. Van Arsdale, 15–36. Arlington, VA: American Anthropological Association.

———. 1994. "Khmer Buddhists in the United States: Ultimate Questions." In *Cambodian Culture since 1975: Homeland and Exile,* ed. May M Ebihara, Carol A Mortland, and Judy Ledgerwood, 72–90. Ithaca, NY: Cornell University Press.

Mortland, Carol A, and Judy Ledgerwood. 1987a. "Refugee Resource Acquisition—The Invisible Communication System." In *Cross-Cultural Adaptation Current Approaches,* ed. YY Kim and WB Gudykunst, 286–306. International and Intercultural Communication Annual 11. Newbury Park, CA: Sage Publications.

———. 1987b. "Secondary Migration among Southeast Asian Refugees in the United States." *Urban Anthropology* 16: 291–326.

Muecke, Marjorie A. 1983. "Caring for Southeast Asian Refugee Patients in the USA," *American Journal of Public Health* 73(4): 431–38.

———. 1991. "Trust, Abuse of Trust, and Mistrust among Refugee Women from Cambodia: A Cultural Interpretation," UN-WIDER Workshop on Trust and the Refugee Experience, Bergen, Norway.

Mulick, Stacey. 2010. "Gangs Sprang Up When LA Groups Saw Untapped Drug Market Here," *News Tribune* (Tacoma, WA), 28 February.

Murakami, Kery. 1993. "Bridging Culture Gap for Cambodians," *Seattle Times,* 16 March, B2.

NaranhKiri Tith. 2001. "Letter Exchange between Pen Sovann and NaranhKiri Tith," Cambodian Information Center, 2 February. Retrieved 15 April 2012 from http://editorials.cambodia.

National Security Education Program. 2015. "Analysis of Federal Language Needs." Retrieved 2 August 2015 from http://www.fas.org/irp/congress/2001_cr/s032201.html.

Navy Phim. 2007. *Reflections of a Khmer Soul.* Tucson, AZ: Wheatmark.

Nawuth, Keat, and Martha Kendall. 2009. *Alive in the Killing Fields: Surviving the Khmer Rouge Genocide*. Washington, DC: National Geographic.

Nealon, Dennis. 2001. "Buddhist Monk Tells Gathering of the 'True' America He Has Adopted," *Brandeis Reporter*, 20 November–17 December. Retrieved 5 December 2011 from http://my.brandeis.edu/ news/reporter/ 19.3.pdf.

Needham, Susan. 2010. "Reports from the Edge: Cambodian American College Students' Narratives of Experience." In *Cambodian American Experiences: Histories, Communities, Cultures and Identities*, ed. Jonathan HX Lee, 264–71. Dubuque, IA: Kendall Hunt Publishing.

Needham, Susan, and Karen Quintiliani. 2007. "Cambodians in Long Beach, California," *Journal of Immigrant and Refugee Studies* 5(1): 29–53.

———. 2008. *Images of America: Cambodians in Long Beach*. Charleston, SC: Arcadia Publishing.

Nepote, Jacques, and Khing Hoc Dy. 1981. "Literature and Society in Modern Cambodia." In *Literature and Society in Southeast Asia*, ed. Tham Seung Chee, 56–81. Singapore: Singapore University Press.

Ng, Janet. 2001. "Silent Survivors," *Asian Week*, 3–9 August. Retrieved 2 June 2004 from http://asian week.com/2001_08_03/feature_cambodian.html.

Nguyen-Hong-Nhiem, Lucy, and Joel Martin Halpern, eds. 1989. *The Far East Comes Near: Autobiographical Accounts of Southeast Asian Students in America*. Amherst: University of Massachusetts Press.

Niedzwiecki, M, and T Duong. 2004. *Southeast Asian American Statistical Profile*. Washington, DC: Southeast Asia Resource Action Center.

Nien-Chu Kiang, Peter. 1994. "When Know-Nothings Speak English Only." In *The State of Asian America: Activism and Resistance in the 1990*, ed. Karin Aguilar-San Juan, 125–46. New York: South End Press.

———. 2007. Foreword to *Southeast Asian Refugees and Immigrants in the Mill City: Changing Families, Communities, Institutions—Thirty Years Afterward*, ed. Tuyet-Lan Pho, Jeffrey N Gerson, and Sylvia R Cowan, vii–x. Burlington: University of Vermont Press.

Nordstrom, Carolyn. 2004. *Shadows of War: Violence, Power, and International Profiteering in the Twenty-First Century*. Berkeley: University of California Press.

North, David S, Lawrence S Lewin, and Jennifer R Wagner. 1982. *Kaleidoscope: The Resettlement of Refugees in the US by the Voluntary Agencies*. Report prepared for the Bureau for Refugee Programs, US Department of State.

Olsen, Laurie. 2001. *And Still We Speak: Stories of Communities Sustaining and Reclaiming Language and Culture*. Oakland, CA: California Tomorrow.

Ong, Aihwa. 1995. "Making the Biopolitical Subject: Cambodian Immigrants, Refugee Medicine and Cultural Citizenship in California," *Social Science & Medicine* 40(9): 1243–57.

———. 2003. *Buddha in Hiding: Refugees, Citizenship, and the New America*. Berkeley: University of California Press.

Oni Vitandham. 2005. *On the Wings of a White Horse: A Cambodian Princess's Story of Surviving the Khmer Rouge Genocide*. Mustang, OK: Tate Publishing.

Osborne, Milton E. 1980. *The Kampuchean Refugee Situation: A Survey and Commentary*. Report prepared for the United Nations High Commissioner for Refugees (UNHCR), Bangkok, 23 April.

Owen, Taylor, and Ben Kiernan. 2006. "Bombs over Cambodia," *Walrus*, October. Retrieved 26 October 2010 from http://www.yale.edu/cgp/Walrus_CambodiaBombing_OCT06. pdf.

Paige, Sean. 1998. "Social Security—Fighting Fraud from Abroad," *Insight on the News*, 29 June. Retrieved 2 April 2011 from http://www.insightmag.com.

Paludan, Anne. 1974. *The New Refugees in Europe*. Geneva: University Exchange Fund.

Perkins, Gary. 1981. "An International View of a Human Problem: The Refugee as Universal Citizen," *Journal of Refugee Resettlement* 1(4): 6–8.

Pickwell, Sheila M. 1999. "Multilevel Healing Pursuits of Cambodian Refugees," *Journal of Immigrant Health* 1(3): 165–79.

Picq, Laurence. 1989. *Beyond the Horizon: Five Years with the Khmer Rouge*. New York: St Martin's Press. Originally published as *Au-delà du ciel: Cinq ans chez les Khmers Rouges* (Paris: Barrault, 1984).

Pin Yathay with John Man. 1987. *Stay Alive, My Son*. New York: Simon and Schuster, 1987.

Poethig, Kathryn. 2001. "Visa Trouble: Cambodian American Christians and Their Defense of Multiple Citizenships." In *Religions/Globalizations. Theories and Cases*, ed. Eduardo Mendieta and David Batstone, 187–202. Durham, NC: Duke University Press.

Porée-Maspero, Eveline. 1962–1969. *Etude sur les rites agraires des cambodgiens*, 3 vols. The Hague: Mouton.

Portes, Alejandro, and Ruben G Rumbaut. 2001. *Legacies: The Story of the Immigrant Second Generation*. Berkeley: University of California Press.

———. 2006. *Immigrant America: A Portrait*, 3rd edn. Berkeley: University of California Press.

Quinones, Sam. 2005. "From Sweet Success to Bitter Tears," *Los Angeles Times*, 19 January. Retrieved 16 February 2011 from http://articles.latimes.com/2005/jan/19/local/me-donutking19.

Rasbridge, Lance A. 1995. "Cambodians in Dallas/Ft. Worth," American Anthropological Association Meeting, Washington, DC.

Rasbridge, Lance A, and John L Marcucci. 1992. "Reactions to Coupon Coercion: Dallas Cambodian Women's Autonomy in the Acculturative Process." In *Selected Papers on Refugee Issues*, ed. Pamela A. DeVoe, 81–88. Washington, DC: American Anthropological Association.

Reang, Putsata. 1997. "Cambodian Orphans Find New Homes," *Seattle Times*, September 1. Retrieved 1 August 2011 from http://community.seattletimes.nwsource. com/archive/?date=19970901&slug=2557870.

Reasey Poch. 1989. "Pol Pot: The Rise to Power," *Changing East Asia* 1(2): 17–20.

Reed, Matt. 2002. "Coming Home a Foreigner: Life Full of Contradictions for Overseas Cambodians Returning Home," *Cambodian Daily*, 16–17 March.

Reeves, TJ, and CE Bennett. 2004. *We the People: Asians in the United States, Census 2000 Special Reports*. Washington, DC: US Census Bureau.

Rice, Lewis I. 2004. "The Battling Buddhists: A Bitter Feud between Two Monks Divides a Community and Its Temple. Literally," *Boston Magazine*, 15 May.

Rimer, Sara. 2002. "Journeys: The Sound of Home: An 8,690-Mile Echo,"
    New York Times, 23 August. Retrieved 1 May 2011 from http://www.nytimes.
    com/2002/08/23/travel/journeys-the-sound-of-home-an-8690-mile-echo.
    html.

Rithy Panh. 2014. *The Elimination: A Survivor of the Khmer Rouge Confronts His Past
    and the Commandant of the Killing Fields*. New York: Other Press.

Robbins, Katie. 2010. "Chinese and Doughnuts: A California Mystery," *Atlantic*,
    11 March. Retrieved 26 March 2012 from http://www.theatlantic.com/health/
    archive/2010/03 /chinese-and-doughnuts-a-california-mystery/37319/.

Robinson, W Courtland. 1996. *Double Vision: A History of Cambodian Refugees in
    Thailand*. Bangkok: Institute of Asian Studies.

———. 1998. *Terms of Refuge: The Indochinese Exodus and the International Response*.
    London: Zed Books.

Rochester Post-Bulletin. 1986. "Durenberger: Refugees a Hardship," *Rochester Post-
    Bulletin* (Rocheser, MN), 24 April.

Roeun Chea. 1989. "My Unforgettable Experiences." In *The Far East Comes
    Near: Autobiographical Accounts of Southeast Asian Students in America*, ed.
    Lucy Nguyen-Hong-Nhiem and Joel Martin Halpern, 105–14. Amherst, MA:
    University of Massachusetts Press.

Roosevelt, Margot. 2010. "Gulf Oil Spill: Cambodian Cleanup Workers Speak
    Out," *Los Angeles Times*, 8 June. Retrieved 7 March 2012 from http://latimes-
    blogs.latimes.com /greenspace/2010/06/gulf-oil-spill-cambodian-cleanup-
    workers-speak-out.html.

Ross, Diane DeCesare. 2008. "Palm Leaf Manuscripts." University of Southern
    Mississippi Libraries, Special Collections, November. Retrieved 6 September
    2012 from http://www.lib.usm.edu/spcol/exhibitions/item_ of_the_month/
    iotm_nov_08.html.

Ross, Russell R, ed. 1987. *Cambodia: A Country Study*. Area Handbook Series.
    Federal Research Division, Library of Congress. Washington, DC: US
    Government.

Rowat, Richard. 2006. "International Rescue Committee Thailand." International
    Rescue Committee, New York. Retrieved 2 April 2012 from http://www.web-
    sitesrcg.com/border/NGO/IRC-1985.html.

Ruhfus, Juliana. 2012. "Cambodia's Orphanage Business," *Huff Post World*, 21
    June. Retrieved 15 October 2012 from http://www. huffingtonpost.com/juli-
    ana-ruhfus/cambodias-orphanage-busin_b_1616255.html.

Rumbaut, Ruben G. 1995. "Vietnamese, Laotian, and Cambodian Americans." In
    Asian Americans: Contemporary Trends and Issues, ed. Pyong Gap Min, 232–70.
    Thousand Oaks, CA: Sage Publications.

Rumbaut, Ruben G, and Wayne A Cornelius. 1995. *California's Immigrant
    Children*. La Jolla, CA: Center for US-Mexican Studies, University of
    California, San Diego.

Rumbaut, Ruben G, et al. 2006. "Debunking the Myth of Immigrant Criminality:
    Imprisonment among First- and Second-Generation Young Men." Migration
    Policy Institute. Retrieved 6 January 2016 from http://www.migrationpolicy.
    org/article/debunking-myth-immigrant-criminality-imprisonment-among-
    first-and-second-generation-young.

Russell, Matt. 2010. "Christian Volunteers Help Out Buddhist Temple in Rochester," *Post-Bulletin* (Rochester, MN), June 26. Retrieved October 26, 2010 from http://www.postbulletin.com/newsmanager/templates/localnews_story. asp?z=2&a=458783.

Ry Kea. 2010. "President's Message," Modesto Cambodian Temple Society, Inc. Retrieved December 10, 2010 from http://www.watkhmermodesto.org/ PresMessage.aspx.

Ryono, Angel. 2010. "The Quiet Campaign to Break Up Cambodian Refugee Families," *Media Democracy in Action*, Project Censored, 26 March. Retrieved 3 March 2012 from http://www.projectcensored.org/top-stories/articles/ the-quiet-campaign-to-break-up-cambodian-refugee-families/.

Sakamoto, Arthur, and Hyeyoung Woo. 2007. "The Socioeconomic Attainments of Second-Generation Cambodian, Hmong, Laotian, and Vietnamese Americans," *Sociological Inquiry* 77(1): 44–75.

Salopek, Paul. 1996. "Deadly Clash of Cultures on the Streets. Cambodian, Filipino Gangs War in Chicago," *Chicago Tribune*, 3 March, 1.

Sam-Ang Sam. 1994. "Khmer Traditional Music Today." In *Cambodian Culture since 1975: Homeland and Exile*, ed. MM Ebihara, Carol A Mortland, and Judy Ledgerwood, 39–47. Ithaca, NY: Cornell University Press.

———. 2010. "Cambodian Music and Dance in North America." In *Cambodian American Experiences: Histories, Communities, Cultures and Identities*, ed. Jonathan HX Lee, 182–94. Dubuque, IA: Kendall Hunt Publishing.

Sam-Ang Sam and Chan Moly Sam. 1987. *Khmer Folk Dance*. Newington, CT: Khmer Studies Institute.

Samkhann Khoeun, Susan Thompson, and Christoph Strobel. 2008. "Ethnographic Study of Lowell, MA: Making, Remaking, and Remaking Again," Lowell National Historical Park, University of Massachusetts, Lowell, Oral History Collection, 8 January.

Sar, Michael S. 2010. "Out of the Killing Fields, Out of the Closet: A Personal Narrative on Finding Identity as a Gay Cambodian American." In *Cambodian American Experiences: Histories, Communities, Cultures, and Identities*, ed. Jonathan HX Lee, 381–91. Dubuque, IA: Kendall Hunt Publishing.

Sargent, Carolyn, John Marcucci, and Ellen Elliston. 1983. "Tiger Bones, Fire and Wine: Maternity Care in a Kampuchean Refugee Community," *Medical Anthropology* 7(4): 67–79.

Savuth Penn. 1997. "The Dark Years of My Life." In *Children of Cambodia's Killing Fields: Memoirs by Survivors*, ed. Dith Pran, 42–49. New Haven, CT: Yale University Press.

Schanberg, Sydney. 1985. *The Death and Life of Dith Pran*. New York: Penguin Books.

Schlung-Vials, Cathy J. 2008. "A Transnational Hip Hop Nation: praCh, Cambodia, and Memorialising the Killing Fields," in *Life Writing* 5(1): 11-27.

———. 2012. *War, Genocide, and Justice: Cambodian American Memory Work*. Minneapolis: University of Minnesota Pres.

Scott, James C. 1985. *Weapons of the Weak: Everyday Forms of Peasant Resistance*. New Haven, CT: Yale University Press.

Seanglim Bit. 1991. *The Warrior Heritage: A Psychological Perspective of Cambodian Trauma.* Self-published.

Sear, Katherine. 2004. "Raised on American Streets, Cambodian Youths Face Deportation." Pacific News Service, August 11. Retrieved 28 April 2011 from http://infowire.bae3ccnewamericamedia.org/news/view_article. html?article_id=e79ba9d5990b56616740d75d45.

Seng Ty. 2014. *The Years of Zero: Coming of Age under the Khmer Rouge.* CreatSpace, self-published.

Shapiro, Toni. 1994. "Dance and the Spirit of Cambodia," PhD dissertation. Cornell University, Ithaca, NY.

Shapiro-Phim, Toni. 2007. "The Dancer and Cambodian History," Dance Advance, Pew Center for Arts & Heritage. Retrieved 16 January 2012 from http://www.pcah.us/m/ dance/dance-and-cambodian-history.pdf.

Shawcross, Willam. 1979. *Side-show: Kissinger, Nixon, and the Destruction of Cambodia.* New York: Pocket Books.

———. 1984. *The Quality of Mercy. Cambodia, Holocaust and Modern Conscience.* New York: Simon and Schuster.

Sheehy, Gail. 1986. *Spirit of Survival.* New York: Bantam.

Shukovsky, Paul. 2003. "Local Man Is Indicted in Tourism Sex Case," *Seattle Post-Intelligencer,* 21 November, B2.

Sichan Siv. 2008. *Golden Bones: An Extraordinary Journey from Hell in Cambodia to a New Life in America.* New York: Harper Perennial.

Silka, Linda. 2007. "Transforming Experiences: When Host Communities Become Home Communities." In *Southeast Asian Refugees and Immigrants in the Mill City: Changing Families, Communities, Institutions—Thirty Years Afterward,* ed. Tuyet-Lan Pho, Jeffrey N Gerson, and Sylvia R Cowan, 192–204. Burlington: University of Vermont Press.

Silliman, Mark. 2006. "Master Sgt. Sarun Sar, Silver Star Recipient, Shares His Story with the West Pearl Harbor Rotary Club," Cambodian Community of Hawaii. Retrieved 1 April 2011 from http://www.hawaii.cambodia world-wide.com/ sarunsar.html.

Silove, Derrick, R Chang and V Manicavasgar. 1995. "Impact of Recounting Trauma Stories on the Emotional State of Cambodian Refugees," *Psychiatric Services* 46(12): 1287–88.

Simms, L, and Ang Chorn-Pond. 2002. "Between Tigers and Crocodiles: Interview with Arn Chorn-Pond," *Parabola* 27(4): 24–31.

Smith, Alexandra. 1989. "Eyes That Saw Horrors Now See Only Shadows," *Long Beach Journal,* September 8.

Smith, Frank. 1989. *Interpretive Accounts of the Khmer Rouge Years: Personal Experience in Cambodian Peasant World View.* Wisconsin Papers on Southeast Asia 18. Madison: Center for Southeast Asian Studies, University of Wisconsin-Madison.

Smith-Hefner, Nancy J. 1995. "The Culture of Entrepreneurship among Khmer Refugees." In *New Migrants in the Marketplace: Boston's Ethnic Entrepreneurs,* ed. Marilyn Halter, 141–58. Amherst: University of Massachusetts Press.

———. 1999. *Khmer American: Identity and Moral Education in a Diasporic Community.* Berkeley: University of California Press.

Sody Lay. 2001. "Remembering the Cambodian Tragedy," Khmer Institute. Retrieved 31 October 2011 from http://www.khmer institute.org/articles/art04z.html.

———. 2010. "Nature of Cambodian Gangs in America." In *Cambodian American Experiences: Histories, Communities, Cultures and Identities*, ed. Jonathan HX Lee, 115–23. Dubuque, IA: Kendall Hunt Publishing.

Someth May. 1986. *Cambodian Witness: The Autobiography of Someth May*. London: Faber and Faber.

Sopheap Ly. 2009. *No Dream Beyond My Reach: One Woman's Remarkable Journey from Cambodian Refugee to American MD*. Bloomington, IN: AuthorHouse, 2009.

Soth Polin. 1980. "Pol Pot's Diabolical Sweetness," *Index on Censorship* 9(5): 43–45.

Southeast Asia Resource Action Center. 2002. "US, Cambodian Governments Plan to Force Refugees back to Cambodia," Southeast Asia Resource Action Center, May 7. Retrieved 31 March 2011 from http://www.searac.org/prcamo05_02.html.

Humanities at Stanford. "Archive Preserves Ancient Cambodian Music," Stanford Humanities Center, 2 August. Retrieved 15 October 2016 from http://shc.stanford.edu/news/research/archive-preserves-ancient-cambodian-music. 2010.

Stein, Barry N. 1979. "Occupational Adjustment of Refugees: The Vietnamese in the United States," *International Migration Review* 13(4): 25–45.

———. 1981. "Understanding the Refugee Experience: Foundations of a Better-Resettlement System," *Journal of Refugee Resettlement* 1(4): 62–71.

Steinberg, Stephen. 1989. *The Ethnic Myth. Race, Ethnicity, and Class in America*. Boston: Beacon Press.

St Petersburg Times. 2003. "Obituaries," *St Petersburg Times*, 28 September, 11. Retrieved 18 September 2012 from http://www.sptimes.com/2003archive/09/28/Obits.shtml.

Straub, Becky, Cathy Melvin, and Miriam Labbok. 2008. "A Descriptive Study of Cambodian Refugee Infant Feeding Practices in the United States." *International Breastfeeding Journal* 3(2).

Szymusiak, Molyda. 1986. *The Stones Cry Out: A Cambodian Childhood, 1975–80*. New York: Farrar, Straus and Giroux.

Tajima, Emiko A, and Tracy W Harachi. 2010. "Parenting Beliefs and Physical Discipline Practices among Southeast Asian Immigrants: Parenting in the Context of Cultural Adaptation to the United States," *Journal of Cross-Cultural Psychology* 41(2): 212–35.

Tauch Chhuong. 1994. *Battambang during the Time of the Lord Governor*, trans. Hin Sinthan, Carol A Mortland, and Judy Ledgerwood. Phnom Penh: Cedoreck.

Teteak, Christopher. 1992. "Khmer Buddhist Temples in North America: Survival in a Different Society," MA thesis. Cornell University, Ithaca, NY.

Theanvy Kuoch. 2000. "Buddhism and Mental Health among Cambodian Refugees." In *Women's Buddhism: Buddhism's Women. Tradition, Revision, Renewal*, ed. Ellison Banks Findly, 425–32. Somerville, MA: Wisdom Publications.

———. 2015. "Health Crisis," *Cambodian Health Network*. Retrieved March 6, 2015 from http://www.cambodianhealth.org/healthcrisis.asp.

Theanvy, Kuoch, and M Scully. 1984. "Cambodians' Voices and Perceptions: A Collection of Materials, Experiences, and Cross-Cultural Understandings," unpublished.

Theanvy Kuoch et al. 1996. *Health Crisis in the Cambodian Community.* West Hartford, CT: Khmer Health Advocates.

Thierry, Solange. 1978. *Etude d'un corpus de contes cambodgiens traditionnels: Essai d'analyse thematique et morphologique.* Paris: H Champion.

Thompson, Larry Clinton. 2010. *Refugee Workers in the Indochina Exodus, 1975–1982.* Jefferson, NC: McFarland.

Thompson, Lynn, and Christine Clarridge. 2010. "West Seattle Survivors Relive Terror, Struggle to Understand," *Seattle Times,* 24 September.

Tollefson, James W. 1989. *Alien Winds: The Reeducation of America's Indochinese Refugees.* New York: Praeger.

Toness, Bianca Vazquez. 2010. "Invisible Communities, Part 3: Cambodian Gang Members Seek Redemption in Lowell," *WBUR News,* 12 May. Retrieved 18 March 2011 from http://www.wbur.org/2010/05/12/invisible-communities-iii.

Truong, Michael H. 2007. "Welfare Reform and Liberal Governance: Disciplining Cambodian-American Bodies," *International Journal of Social Welfare* 16(3): 258–68.

Tuyet-Lan Pho and Anne Mulvey. 2003. "Southeast Asian Women in Lowell: Family Relations, Gender Roles, and Community Concerns," *Frontiers: A Journal of Women's Studies* 24(91): 101–29.

Tyrity, Kathy. 1981. "United Nations Official: Refugees Are No Oddity," *Sarasota Herald-Tribune,* 26 October. Retrieved 27 July 2012 from http://news.google.com/newspapers?nid=1755&dat=19811026&id= U50cAAAA IBAJ&sjid=GGgE AAAAIBAJ&pg=6807,5676723.

Uehara, ES. 2001. "Understanding the Dynamics of Illness and Help-Seeking: Event-Structure Analysis and a Cambodian-American Narrative of 'Spirit Invasion,'" *Social Science & Medicine* 52(4): 519–36.

Um Khatharya. 1999. "Scars of War: Educational Issues and Challenges for Cambodian-American Students." In *Asian-American Education Prospects and Challenges,* ed. CC Park and MM-Y Chi, 89–104. Westport, CT: Bergin and Garvey.

UNHCR. 2014. "Flowing across Borders," United Nations High Commissioner for Refugees, the UN Refugee Agency. Retrieved 3 April 2013 from http://www.unhcr.org/pages/49c3646c125.html.

United States Catholic Conference. 1975. *Cultural and Historical Notes on the Cambodians.* Washington, DC: United States Catholic Conference.

United States Department of Agriculture. 1982. *Nutritional Status of Southeast Asian Americans.* Washington DC: US Department of Agriculture, Food and Nutrition Service.

Urban Dictionary. 2012a. "Cha ma." *Urban Dictionary.* Retrieved 3 May 2012 from http://www.urbandictionary.com/define.php? term= Cha%20 ma&defid=5207904.

———. 2012b. "Fobulous." *Urban Dictionary.* Retrieved 27 March 2012 from http://www.urbandictionary.com;define.php?term=fobulous.

U Sam Oeur. 1998. *Sacred Vows: Poetry by U. Sam Oeur,* trans. Ken McCullough. Minneapolis, MN: Coffee House Press.

US Committee for Refugees. 1982. *Cambodian Refugees in Thailand: The Limits of Asylum.* New York: American Council for Nationalities Service, US Committee for Refugees.

Vaddhana Kchao. 1989. "Khmer: The Lost Generation," *Changing East Asia* 1(1): 12–13.

Van Boemel, Gretchen B, and Patricia D Rozee. 1992. "Treatment for Psychosomatic Blindness among Cambodian Refugee Women," *Women & Therapy* 13(3): 239–66.

Vatey Seng. 2005. *The Price We Paid: A Life Experience in the Khmer Rouge Regime, Cambodia.* iUniverse, self-published.

Vek Huong Taing with Sharon Fischer. 1980. *Ordeal in Cambodia: One Family's Miraculous Survival—Escape from the Khmer Rouge.* San Bernardino, CA: Here's Life Publishers.

Vichet Chhuon and C Hudley. 2010. "Asian American Ethnic Options: How Cambodian Students Negotiate Ethnic Identities in a US Urban School," *Anthropology & Education Quarterly* 41(4): 341–59.

Vickery, Michael. 1989. "Cambodia (Kampuchea): History, Tragedy, and Uncertain Future," *Bulletin of Concerned Asian Scholars* 21(2–4): 35–58.

———. 1990a. "Cultural Survival in Cambodian Language and Literature," *Cambodia 1990, Cultural Survival Quarterly* 14(3): 49–52.

———. 1990b. "Refugee Politics: The Khmer Camp System in Thailand." In *The Cambodian Agony,* ed. David A. Ablin and Marlowe Hood, 293–331. Armonk, NY: ME Sharpe.

Virak Khiev. 1992. "My Turn," *Newsweek* 119(17): 8, 27.

Wagner, Bhavia C. 2008. *Soul Survivors: Stories of Women and Children in Cambodia.* Eugene, OR: Wild Iris.

Watanabe, Teresa. 2003. "Cambodians Fear Possible Deportation," *Los Angeles Times,* 21 February. Retrieved 15 February 2011 from http://articles.latimes.com/2003/feb/21/local /me-cambodian21.

Watters, Charles. 2001. "Emerging Paradigms in the Mental Health Care of Refugees," *Social Science & Medicine* 52(11): 1709–18.

Welaratna, Usha. 1993. *Beyond the Killing Fields: Voices of Nine Cambodian Survivors.* Palo Alto, CA: Stanford University Press.

Wheelock, Julie. 1990. "A Royal Dance Survives in Van Nuys," *Los Angeles Times,* 20 April. Retrieved 7 March 2012 from http://articles.latimes.com/1990-04-20/ entertainment/ca-1495_1_van-nuys.

Whitaker, Donald et al. 1973. *Area Handbook for the Khmer Republic (Cambodia).* Washington, DC: US Government Printing Office.

White, Peter T. 1982. "Kampuchea Wakens from a Nightmare," *National Geographic* 161(5): 590–622.

Wiley, Shaun, Krystal Perkins, and Kay Deaux. 2008. "Through the Looking Glass: Ethnic and Generational Patterns of Immigrant Identity," *International Journal of Intercultural Relations* 32(5): 385–98.

Wilkinson, Alex. 1994. "A Changed Vision of God," *New Yorker,* 24 January, 52–68.

Wiscombe, Janet. 1998. "The Mighty Pen of New Phnom Penh," *Los Angeles Times,* 26 April. Retrieved 9 October 2011 from http://articles.latimes.com/1998/apr/26/news/ls-43062.

Wisconsin State Journal. 2007. "Obituaries," *Wisconsin State Journal,* 18 June, A4.

Wood, Richard. 2002. *Call Sign Rustic: The Secret Air War over Cambodia, 1970–1973.* Washington, DC: Smithsonian Institution Press.

Wride, Nancy. 2004. "Long Beach Shootings Are Called Random," *Los Angeles Times,* 2 January. Retrieved 16 February 2011 from http://articles.latimes.com/2004/jan/02/local/me-cambodians.

Wright, Wayne E. 2003. "Khmer (Cambodian) Heritage Language Programs: Will the Khmer Language Survive in California?" *The Multilingual Education* 4(1): 28–31.

———. 2007. "Heritage Language Programs in the Era of English-Only and No Child Left Behind," *Heritage Language Journal* 5(1): 1–26.

———. 2010. "Khmer as a Heritage Language in the United States: Historical Sketch, Current Realities, and Future Prospects," *Heritage Language Journal* 7(1): 117–47.

Yang Sam. 1985. "The Cambodian Worldview: Buddhism, Family and Community." In *Cambodian Mental Health: A Day to Explore Issues and Alternative Approaches to Care,* ed. Cambodian Women's Project, 13–16. New York: American Friends Service Committee, conference proceedings, 24 May.

Yee, Barbara WK, and Nguyen Dinh Thu. 1987. "Correlates of Drug Use and Abuse among Indochinese Refugees: Mental Health Implications," *Journal of Psychoactive Drugs* 19(1): 77–83.

Yimsut, Ronnie. 2011. *Facing the Khmer Rouge: A Cambodian Journey.* New Brunswick, NJ: Rutgers University Press.

Index

www.ingramcontent.com/pod-product-compliance
Lightning Source LLC
Chambersburg PA
CBHW070912030426
42336CB00014BA/2376